PROFITABLE EXPORTING

A Complete Guide to Marketing Your Products Abroad

Second Edition

JOHN S. GORDON

John Wiley & Sons, Inc.

New York · Chichester · Brisbane · Toronto · Singapore

HF 1416
.5
.G67
1993 X

Library of Congress Cataloging-in-Publication Data:

Gordon, John S., 1944–
    Profitable exporting / by John S. Gordon. — 2nd ed.
        p.   cm.
    Includes index.
    ISBN 0-471-57514-3
    1. Export marketing—United States. I. Title.
HF1416.5.G67 1992
658.8′48—dc20   92-14983

Foreword

U.S. exports have increased dramatically during the past five years due to favorable monetary policies, expanding markets, and fewer government restrictions. Today is a far cry from the environment of the early 1980s when U.S. industries took a drubbing in international trade. We are now at the beginning of what some people call the decade of exports.

It certainly makes sense for U.S. companies to set their sights on foreign markets. After all, the United States represents only 5 percent of the world's population; it would be a folly to ignore the other 95 percent. And as other economies grow, they will be increasingly attractive markets for exports.

Happily, many companies are realizing this. But for others, the prospect of trying to sell something overseas seems daunting. Unfamiliar cultures, business methods, and the sheer problem of doing business half a world away will cause some to abandon the field. Government policies in particular—both our own and others—present their own challenge; hence the need for comprehensive knowledge of important government players and the regulations they enforce. John Gordon's *Profitable Exporting* is an excellent step in this direction.

At Boeing, we recognize the challenges as well as the benefits of exporting, for we have been involved with exporting since our inception. In fact, the very first Boeing airplane—a wood and wire seaplane—was sold to the government of New Zealand in 1918. Since then, our customer base has expanded to include over 400 operators in 120 nations throughout the world. Boeing jets have carried over 7 billion passengers between cities all over the globe.

William E. Boeing, the company's founder, established the foundation for this success on the basis of a simple credo: "To be everlastingly at it." Today this credo finds expression in continuous quality improvement. Its tools and methods affect the actions of everyone, from the chairman to the smallest supplier. At stake is Boeing's leadership in the commercial aircraft market and its role as the nation's preeminent exporter of manufactured products.

Our goal is not necessarily to be the first to bring a new product to market, but to be the best: best at understanding our customers, best at assessing the available technology, and best at incorporating that technology into timely, cost-effective products. This is the formula for market leadership and contin-ued success in today's globally competitive marketplace.

Boeing not only sells but also buys internationally. Boeing has a wide range of international business arrangements with aerospace firms, including sub-contracting, risk-sharing agreements, partnerships, and consortia. Boeing works with over 3,000 suppliers in the United States and 23 foreign countries. We seek to use the best ideas from around the world and integrate them into successful products.

International competition has never been keener. For the company with the right product, planning, and commitment, the rewards of exporting far exceed its challenges. Books such as this can help uncover the path to profitable exporting.

For the newcomer to exporting who must make his or her first foray through the bureaucratic tangle that is inevitable, at least initially, or the practiced global businessperson who needs to research entry strategies into new markets, *Profitable Exporting* will be an invaluable reference. Its step-by-step approach to the export process will lead a great many businesses to the establishment of a quality export plan, which all significant American busi-nesses must undertake, sooner rather than later, if our economy is to remain competitive in the global marketplace.

RAYMOND J. WALDMANN
Director—Government Affairs
Boeing Commercial Aircraft Corporation

Preface

Exporting was the growth industry of the 1980s and it will be the engine of growth for the 1990s. The free trade agreements in Europe and North America, the improved markets of Latin America, and the success of the newly industrialized countries in Asia, Latin America, and Europe provide expanding and fertile markets for U.S. goods and services.

Many large companies have been successful participants in exporting and international trade, while some have lacked the foresight, commitment, or perspective for success. Emerging firms across all industry sectors have learned that export marketing can open the door to markets of opportunity two and three times the size of the U.S. market. Small companies are being told that exporting is a key to success for the future.

This book is important for each of these corporate segments. Most of the skills needed for success in the export business cannot be learned in the classroom. Companies do not have the time and financing capacity to start from scratch and reeducate their staff in order to move into the export business. This book gives the reader an overview of the export business; an understanding of the issues, practices, and techniques; and an appreciation for the strategies necessary for success in this rapidly evolving world market.

The corporate executive will find this book a reference and guide, useful for a quick and comprehensive understanding of the export business. The business owner will find it provides the needed guidance for successful entry into, and management of, the export business. It is a road map for the new venture, a pathway for planning and implementation. Students, government officials, instructors, and trainers will find it a valuable instructional tool for the practical business of exporting; it complements the theories of the leading academic texts on international business and international marketing.

JOHN S. GORDON

v

Acknowledgments

Many professionals made valuable contributions to this book. My thanks to each one.

To Ms. Naomi Armstrong, Vice President, International Operations, U.S. Bank of Washington, for providing useful and integrated examples of export financing documents.

To Mr. Richard Barovick, Editor, *Washington Export Letter* and *Eximbank Letter,* for his observations on government programs supporting exports.

To Mr. Robert C. Broadfoot, Managing Director, Political & Commercial Risk Consultancy, Ltd., Hong Kong, for his insightful commentary on the Asia of the 1990s, and for the illustrations on pages 281–284, 308, and 309.

To Mrs. Leann David-Valentine, Government Affairs and Customs Specialist, Airborne Freight Corp., for her guidance on the export licensing process.

To Mr. Mike Giambattista, Vice President, Sales, RAIMA Corp., for his commentary on the market-entry process and his focus on the dominant items within your market-entry strategy.

To Mr. R. Steve Hatch, President, Washington State International Trade Fair, for his comments on the value and use of international trade fairs as a strategy for market research and the development of foreign representatives.

To Mr. Fred Jones, Vice President, Sales, Applied Microsystems Corp., for his commentary on service and the management of the customer service segment of your business.

To Mr. Joel Junker, Partner, International Practice, Graham & Dunn, for his commentary on the nature and extent of the barriers you will face in the export business.

To Mr. Robert Kapp, President, Washington Council on International Trade, for his comprehensive discussion of the issues of trade blocs.

To Mr. Ted Kennard, President, B. A. McKenzie & Co., for his useful background notes on the marine insurance business.

To Mr. Larry Kiser, Intermodal Marketing Specialist, Port of Seattle (retired), for his valuable insights on the logistics of exporting.

To Mr. John Peterson, Partner, Neville, Peterson, and Williams, for his commentary on the nature and impact of the North American Free Trade Agreement.

To Ms. Jaime Powlesland, Executive Director, NTC International, for her commentary on the issues faced by the traveling female business executive.

To Mr. Darren Schulman, Vice President, MTB Banking Corp., for his views on the importance and availability of export financing for today's companies.

To Mr. Melvyn Jay Simburg, Partner, Simburg, Haley, Sheppard & Purdy, P. S., for his valuable contributions on distributor agreements, contracts, and the legal issues of trade.

To Mr. L. Stroh, Managing Editor and Publisher, *The EXPORTER* magazine, for his overview of the export business and participation by emerging businesses.

To Mr. Peter A. D. Teare, Partner (London), Crowell & Moring, for his review of the issues involved in the new European Community and Europe 92.

To James Hellwig, Richard Henry, Karen Taylor, Sandy Owen, and W. M. Buck, at the US&FCS (Seattle), for their cheerful assistance.

To Mr. Neal Maillet, my editor at John Wiley & Sons, Inc., for his support and encouragement of the development of this second edition.

To Martha Gordon, Chairman of the Board, and spouse, for her commitment to this effort and her vigorous support of my international business activities.

To Mr. Jack R. Arnold, my mentor and friend, whose support and encouragement I will always treasure.

J. S. G.

Contents

PART ONE
ORGANIZE FOR EXPORT

1 The Export Business 3

Exporting Versus Domestic
  Business 5
Why Export? 6
The Issues 7
Export Readiness 8
Resources 9

**2 Organize for
Export Success** 10

The Issues 11
Critical Success Factors 12
How Foreign Buyers Perceive
  U.S. Exporters 16
Mistakes of New
  Exporters 17
Organization Is the Key to
  Success 19
Resources 20

**3 How to Find the Best
Overseas Market** 21

The National Trade Data
  Bank 22
The U.S. Department of
  Commerce 27
Other Research and Market
  Information Sources 28
Resources 32

4 Meet Your Market 34

Preparation 34
A Trip to Germany 36
Checklists for Foreign
  Travel 43
For the Female Business
  Traveler 46
Resources 48

PART TWO
MARKET DEVELOPMENT

**5 Direct Market Entry
Strategies** 53

Decision Factors 54
Strategies 54

Agent or Distributor? 56
The Selection Process 59
The Survey 60
Territorial Factors 66
Meeting the Representative 66

The Written Agreement 67
Contracts for the
   International Sale of
   Goods 76
Managing the
   Representative 77
Advertising Abroad 79
Summary 81
Resources 81

6 Indirect Exports   83

Indirect Export
   Alternatives 84
A Final Caution 92
Resources 93

7 Foreign Investment and
   Joint Ventures   94

Forms of Foreign
   Investment 94
Some Pre-Investment
   Questions 95
Terms of Your Investment 97
Licensing Agreements 98
Financial Assistance for
   Foreign Investments 101
Resources 103

8 Pricing for Profits   104

Your Cost Structure 104
Other Functional Areas and
   Pricing 109
The Export Costing
   Worksheet 110
Summary 115
Resources 115

9 Customer Service   117

Service 118
Service Delivery Options 119
Summary 122
Resources 122

10 Communications,
    Negotiations, Offers,
    and Complaints   124

Communications
   Abroad 125
Oral Communication 127
Offers and Counteroffers 127
The Pro Forma Invoice 130
Complaints 133
Ambiguous Terms 134
Summary 135
Resources 136

PART THREE
EXPORT FINANCE

11 Financing Techniques   139

Payment Alternatives 139
Types of Risks 141
Terms of Payment 143
Risks and Payment Terms 156
Finding a Bank 158
How to Get Export
   Financing 162
Resources 170

12 Financing in the
    Marketing Mix   173

The Role of
   Financing 173
Strategies for Sales
   Finance 175
Summary 183
Resources 183

13 Foreign Exchange   185

Evolution of Foreign
   Exchange Activity 186
The Global Economy and the
   Dollar 186
Control of Foreign
   Exchange 188
Two Types of Transactions 188
Banks and Brokers 193
Resources 195

14 Barter and
   Countertrade   197

Reasons for
   Countertrade 197
Types of Countertrade 198
Switch Traders 203
Terms of Countertrade 203
Summary 204
Resources 205

**PART FOUR
MOVEMENT OF THE GOODS**

15 Logistics   209

Modes of Transportation 210
Intermodal and Multimodal
   Shipments 221
Terms of Trade 221
Packing and Marking 223
Resources 225

16 Marine Insurance   227

Getting Started 228
Types of Policies 230
Endorsements 232
Other Clauses 233
Insurance Purchased by the
   Buyer 234
Special Coverage 235
Claims 235
Summary 239
Partial Glossary of Marine
   Insurance Terms 239

17 Export Documents   241

Shipper's Export
   Declaration 242
Commercial Invoice 244
Packing List 245
Draft 246
Bill of Lading 246
Insurance Certificate or
   Policy 247
Beneficiary's Certificate 247
Consular Invoice 247
Dock Receipt 249
Shipper's Letter of Instruction
   (SLI) 249
Standardization of
   Documents 254
Summary 255
Resources 255

**PART FIVE
GOVERNMENT REGULATIONS**

18 Licensing Your Exports   261

Export Controls 262
The Export License
   Process 264

Types of Export Licenses 266
Export License Management
   System 269
Resources 270

19 Barriers to Export   272

Tariffs 273
Nontariff Barriers 275

General Agreements on Tariffs
  and Trade (GATT) 276
Resources 277

PART SIX
GLOBAL TRADING BLOCS

20 The European Bloc   285

The Scope of the Single
  Market 286
Principal Areas of Integration
  in the Single Market 288
Major Issues for
  Exporters 289
Export Strategy
  Considerations 295
Summary 298
Resources 299

21 The Asian Bloc   301

The Japanese Sphere of
  Influence 303

The Scope of the Asian Bloc 304
Major Issues for Exporters 308
Export Strategy
  Considerations 311
Resources 312

22 The North American Bloc   314

The Scope of the North
  American Free Trade
  Agreement (NAFTA) 314
Major Issues for Exporters 319
Export Strategy
  Considerations 322
Summary 324
Resources 324

PART SEVEN
SUMMARY

23 Your Export Plan   331

Planning Issues 332
An Export Business Plan
  Outline 334

Summary 339
Resources 339

APPENDIXES

**A International Trade
  Administration/US&FCS
  District Offices 341**

**B US&FCS Overseas
  Commercial Sections 345**

**C Industry Specialists: U.S.
  Department of Commerce,
  International Trade
  Administration 351**

**D Country Specialists: U.S.
  Department of Commerce,
  International Trade
  Administration 364**

**E Schedule of Weights and
  Measures 368**

Glossary 370

Index 382

PART ONE
Organize for Export

In the 1980s, U.S. business stuck its collective toe in the international market-place—and the rest of the foot soon followed. Many companies have achieved remarkable success, while others have failed to achieve their ambitions. On a percentage basis, the United States now exports about the same level of its gross national product (GNP) as Japan. We're even with Germany as the world's leading exporter. About 20 percent of our gross economic activity is based on international trade and about 46 percent of that is export related. This is big business, and it's growing much faster than the U.S. economy.

Our leading corporations have dabbled in exporting for decades, with mixed results. Leaders include forward-thinking companies like Microsoft, Toro, Boeing, 3M, and Sun Microsystems and smaller companies like Fluoroware Systems, Emerald Technology, MARCO, and others. Do not base your export strategies on the failures of our aging industrial giants. The successes of today's leaders came from an understanding of the need to adapt to foreign markets. They have achieved current and long-term rewards.

Emerging companies can also adapt to foreign markets; the barriers and obstacles are manageable. One of the strongest and most formidable barriers faced by all companies—small, emerging, and large—is the vision and competence of management, which dictates the organization, budgets, and actions of the firm.

Part One, Chapters 1 through 4, identifies the critical path any firm must follow to successfully enter the export business.

The management issues that drive the decision to export include:

1. Executive-level commitment to the business of exporting.

2. The profit opportunities available by reaching out to a new market-place with over 650 million well-off industrial, commercial, and individual consumers (the European Community, European Free Trade Association, North America, Japan, developed Asia, and Oceania).

3. Adequacy of cash flows.
4. Debt capacity and leverage.
5. Cost of capital.
6. Support of your lenders.
7. Production capacity.
8. Capacity utilization.
9. Inventory management.
10. Distribution support and costs.
11. Repair, service, and warranty requirements.
12. Personnel management.

Exports can be a very effective counter to the swings in the domestic economy. Also, the volume that goes to exports can be the extra output beyond break-even that makes each year a "better" year instead of a "good" year. The development of an export market can mean more stability to staffing and planning, more efficiency to production runs, and decreased marginal costs of production. It can add volume, which creates marketing options. Export profits can also support increased capacity for research and development expenditures.

The effective organization of your company's resources is key to the beginning and continuing success of any export effort. Success is critical. Effective organization of your export resources will position the company for expansion into new markets and for market share growth within existing markets and regions. With this client, revenue, and market base, the company can quickly take on more direct activities such as branching, subsidiary operations, and joint ventures.

1 The Export Business

Exporting can be an important and profitable segment of your business. It is just that for over 125,000 companies in the United States, most of them small or emerging firms. There is plenty of room in the export marketplace. True, only 300 companies account for over 50 percent of U.S. exports, and over 85 percent of all exports are made by about 4,000 companies. Yet the remaining 3 percent still export over US$63 billion per year, leaving a fair amount for any emerging firm. Exports can double or triple your existing market in size and potential.

Leslie Stroh, publisher and managing editor of *The EXPORTER Magazine,* does a marvelous job of summarizing the key challenges and concerns facing the business new to exporting:

> Exporting can mean better profits than domestic sales, but new-to-export firms have to organize to get those profits. While exporting can be exceptionally profitable, sales success without organization is one of the quickest ways to go bankrupt.
>
> The learning curve for export procedures is steep: The more frequently you ship to the same customer the easier it becomes. Breaking into the business of exporting may mean hiring a consultant to keep all the different parts of the company focused on exporting.
>
> The process of exporting is not rocket science but it is very detailed; you cannot afford to be sloppy. You can hire others to handle the export process for you—outsourcing is a short-cut; it can also mean losing control of the process and losing control of the profits.
>
> Success in exporting can mean rapid growth of booked profits, but a decline in cash flow. Your payables keep the same schedule but your receivables can stretch out from 30 to 150 days. Control of these export receivables and the associated transaction costs is one of the critical issues in exporting. You may have to look for alternatives to bank financing in order to grow your export business. These alternatives, although expensive, do exist.
>
> Success isn't difficult if you set realistic goals. If you can find eight customers within the 19 countries of the European Community of the future (the EC plus EFTA, a market of over 380 million people) who buy from you six times a year, you will be exporting more frequently than 85 percent of all U.S. exporters.
>
> Look for customers who are structured to give you repeat business. Handling costs for the first shipment are high, and every customer in every country will

require you to establish a separate distribution channel. Commit to on-time delivery, in good markets or bad. Repeat customers are profitable customers.

Organize your business around a realistic order size. The average order and your gross margin have a lot to do with pricing and your ability to cover transaction costs. While your business may be different, 85 percent of U.S. exporters of manufactured goods get an average order of less than $25,000; almost 35 percent get an average order of less than $5,000.

There are plenty of potential customers out there, and there is plenty of demand for your product. Your domestic competitors are exporting. If you can compete with imports here, you can compete over there. Take care in signing representation contracts. In many countries you can't fire a salesperson, and they can recover damages even if they do nothing.

Setting a goal for exports as a percentage of sales is the first step in opening this new territory. Commitment, focus, and control of the process are the ingredients that create successful exporters.

Can you profit by exporting?

1. Is your product or service well received in your region?

2. Is your product or service competitive within its segment in both price and quality?

3. Are you willing to expand your perspectives?

If you answered yes to all three questions, you can export profitably.

There are a number of ways to enter foreign markets, but only one way to control your international business destiny; this is by thorough advance planning and a commitment to follow through. To do so:

1. The chief executive must be involved to a meaningful degree.

2. Sufficient production capacity (or delivery capacity if a service firm) must be available at all times so domestic and international requirements can be met promptly.

3. The company must have an "export mindset" that permeates the organization. This could be a committee of managers, an export department, or a management process that stresses the importance of export to the success of the firm. This "export mindset" establishes throughout the company the fact that export accounts are as important as domestic accounts; everybody should know it. Exports spread manufacturing, product, and market risks. Exports are more than just another dollar of sales.

In addition to exporting, another option to consider for entry into the international marketplace is investment. Your investment can be an equity investment such as a *wholly-owned operation* or a *joint venture.* The investment can be a nonequity type, by *license, franchise,* or other form of sale or rent of your intellectual property or product/service capabilities. For designers, contractors, and management firms, *project management* and *turnkey projects* are traditional examples of nonequity foreign activities.

EXPORTING VERSUS DOMESTIC BUSINESS

There are some significant differences between export operations and domestic operations. Many of these differences are fairly easily identified, centering in areas such as language, customs, and culture. Other differences are more obscure. These include differences in logistics practices, payment practices, legal systems, and in product marking, packaging, and promotion. There are more.

The objective of this book is to give the business owner or manager information and guidance on "what's next" in the business of exporting. This book will give you the understanding of the export business necessary to take your company into new markets successfully and profitably.

Does the following scenario sound familiar? Your company receives inquiries on your products from around the world. Your response has traditionally been, "We'll get to it in time." This has gone on long enough and you've decided to establish an export department. Perhaps your sales department hasn't been effective in serving the international needs of your domestic clients. It's time for a change. How?

Well, if you're like most companies, you call in Charlie (or Charlene) in production (from any well-run department). He knows the product and gets things done. Friday morning you tell him that next Monday he's in charge of international and you want it working quickly. What does Charlie do now? Where does he turn, how does he get his arms around the subject and learn the issues, risks, and solutions so he can be effective? This book will give Charlie (Charlene) the needed grounding in marketing, finance, logistics, government programs, regulations, and issues so that on Monday he can hit the office running.

There are many hurdles to entry into the export business. They are no more onerous than the hurdles to entry into any other business, but they're different and they're unknown. One hurdle many emerging firms face is based on perception. One situation stands out for me and probably for you: A government official, usually at the state level, tells you that you have to have "export potential," you "have to be ready to export."

He or she implies there's some secret rite of passage into this business. There isn't. We'll cover this question in depth.[1]

WHY EXPORT?

The United States has a wealth of productive talent and products galore, most of which can be exported. We are also a leading exporter of services such as technology, engineering, design, management, and information—fields in which the United States has been the recognized leader.

Exports have a major impact on the U.S. economy; they balance the swings in our domestic economy, stabilize inventories, spread manufacturing and other business risks, and enable businesses to create marginal efficiencies. Export volumes support stable and increasing employment in all active business segments. Formal and informal studies alike reveal fairly consistent reasons why individual companies enter the export business. Undergraduate and graduate texts list the same reasons. The reasons are:

1. There is excess production capacity, capacity not used to the optimum.

2. Unsolicited orders have been received.

3. Domestic market share has been lost, sales have dropped, and margins are down.

4. There may be greater profits overseas.

5. Export markets offer new markets for older technology.

6. Exports offer the opportunity to increase marginal efficiencies.

7. Exports let you grow with growing markets. Economic growth in the United States has been slower than in other developed markets around the world.

Export Relationships

Trust is a major issue in managing a successful export operation. It can take months and sometimes years to develop the trust and comfort between exporter and importer (or dealer, distributor, end user) that is necessary to conduct business on a basis similar to that within the United States.

There are differences in culture, language, perspectives and education, legal and economic systems, business practices, and expectations. Successful rela-

---

[1]Comments regarding manufacturers apply with equal force to distributors and sellers of services or exporters of "time" such as engineering, financial, marketing, advertising, or other consultative types of services. These comments also apply to those businesspeople who wish to engage in trading, the transaction-oriented business of buying various products of opportunity from unrelated suppliers, and selling them to various unrelated buyers.

tionships, of trust, must be developed by demonstrating unquestioned reliability, by performing exactly when promised, and by keeping the buyers fully informed on the status of their transaction. There must be complete understanding at all times between exporter (seller) and importer (buyer). Successful completion of each transaction with each importer strengthens this trust, and as the sought-after relationship begins to develop, the significant potential for long-term rewards can be fulfilled.

It's important to convey the characteristics of prestige and reliability. They are more critical abroad because your firm does not have a local history *there*. Your history must be conveyed by the way you communicate and the way you and your officers meet and present your company and yourselves.

Little things are important to this export effort. The look, feel, and quality of your stationery, letterhead, brochures, and product information convey more than the printed information. They convey who you are and what you stand for. Every time you contact a foreign company you are making a sales contact. Each communication with that potential buyer is an opportunity to sell your company, your product, and yourself. Your telexes, cables, faxes, and telephone calls leave an impression that endures beyond the words. First impressions are so important to your future success that every reasonable effort should be made to ensure that these impressions are positive.

You must also develop a strong and supportive relationship with the many offices, agencies, and resources that can help you. The number and type of these resources depend on your industry and the countries in which your buyers are located.

These resources include your bank; shipping agents representing ocean carriers; air, rail, and truck operators; marine insurance agents; freight forwarders; factors; export financiers; the Export-Import Bank of the United States (**Eximbank**), the U.S. & Foreign Commercial Service of the U.S. Department of Commerce (**US&FCS**), and others. Each will be discussed in detail in later chapters.

Exporting is a unique enterprise in that experts from all of these organizations are prepared to give professional advice and work hard on your behalf with little or no immediate compensation. Their compensation comes through your success. Cultivate these resources carefully, as carefully as you do the foreign buyer. Each can save you a great deal of time, money, and frustration. No other business has such a battery of experts readily available to assist you toward your success.

THE ISSUES

This book deals with the important management and marketing issues faced by any growing firm. Its objective is twofold: (1) to enable your company to increase its profitability by increasing markets and (2) to give you the knowledge to manage this activity successfully.

The *management* issues are:

- Preparedness.
- Commitment.
- Product quality and performance.
- Capacities of the firm.

The *marketing* issues are founded in the marketing mix:

- Selecting the markets with the greatest potential.
- Selecting, adapting, or developing products.
- Determining the appropriate pricing strategy.
- Developing a promotion plan.
- Deciding on the channels of distribution.
- Developing strategies to maintain and increase market share.

EXPORT READINESS

The U.S. Department of Commerce (**USDOC**) has developed a Computerized Export Qualifier Program (EQP) to help growing firms do some useful self-analysis. The EQP is administered by the U.S. & Foreign Commercial Service (US&FCS)[2] district offices and branches. All companies interested in exporting are encouraged to use it as a reference point. The US&FCS carries out the U.S. government's export promotion activities for goods and services. The U.S. Department of Agriculture Foreign Agricultural Service (FAS) does the same for the export of U.S. agricultural products.[3]

The EQP can help a firm assess critical internal characteristics. It works through a questionnaire. The exporter or potential exporter answers five sets of questions. The responses are fed into a US&FCS computer program, and the results are sent to the exporter within about two weeks.

These five sets of questions deal with:

1. *Business background.* These questions seek to identify your ability and capacity to take on new business opportunities.

---

[2]Formerly called the ITA, the name was changed to reflect its role, which is commercial service in the United States and abroad. The US&FCS is part of the International Trade Administration, a branch of the U.S. Department of Commerce.

[3]This now includes forest products.

2. *Market-specific strengths.* These questions address product characteristics as they relate to foreign markets. The questions assume you have done the appropriate research.

3. *Product strengths.* These questions are designed to indicate strengths or weaknesses that may encourage or hinder the product's success in foreign markets.

4. *Top management commitment.* Commitment by owners and senior managers is the single most important factor in the export success of any firm. With the appropriate level of commitment, the company will take the actions necessary to export profitably.

5. *Motivation for going international.* These questions focus on your understanding of why you want to export or increase exports as a percentage of gross sales. Understanding your motives is critical to the development of appropriate strategies for exporting.

The EQP is a guide, nothing more. It is not a test that delivers a pass/fail judgment. There is no right or wrong in the responses. It's a management tool and should be used like one. The analysis for the respondent firm is compared to that of companies that are successful exporters. This comparative information can be a useful tool for managing change or developing export goals and strategies. The information can save you time, money, and frustration.

RESOURCES

1. See Appendix A for your US&FCS district offices. Their Computerized Export Qualifier Program is available to all companies interested in exporting.

2. *The EXPORTER Magazine* provides a wealth of current and topical information on the business of exporting for new and experienced exporters alike. To subscribe, contact *The EXPORTER Magazine,* Trade Data Reports, Inc., 34 West 37th St., New York, NY 10018.

2 Organize for Export Success

The export process will have significant impacts throughout your company, regardless of its size. When you begin this process, a number of management actions will take place, in small and large companies alike, in order to create, nurture, and expand this new business activity.

Management commitment is the starting point. With this one factor, even companies that are organizational nightmares will succeed. Without this commitment, even companies with the most efficient, modern, and fluid structures will achieve only marginal success at best. Why? Unless management places export business on a par (or ahead of) domestic business, results will be nil.

When personnel are measured on a certain type of success, that is the performance one gets. Measure export success (increased sales, new markets, increased profits) and you will get export performance. Measure domestic sales penetration, growth of market share, cost-control manufacturing efficiencies, advertising impact, and so forth and you will get performance there.

Chapter 1 discussed a short questionnaire that is used by the US&FCS to gauge a firm's readiness to export. The results of this process will indicate areas within your company where more work is needed for your success. This additional attention could be with the product, the sales process, the price, management attitude and commitment, personnel, or other areas.

Chapter 3 will focus on understanding the potential for your products in foreign markets and identifying the markets that may offer the greatest opportunity. The recommended research and information-gathering process must take place within a framework that is geared for success in exporting; telling Charlie to "do some research on XYZ country" will not work. The research and development process can be complex, time consuming, and costly. You need to be prepared for this.

THE ISSUES

The organizational issues involved in exporting involve every facet of your company. Entry into the export business is a major undertaking, requiring no less commitment and energy than developing and introducing a new product line or taking your products into a major new distribution region of the United States.

Senior management must make the decision to begin the process. With that decision, a number of issues now confront management. Foremost among these issues is that of commitment (much different than a decision). You must also consider the capacity of your managers, employees, and facilities; your products and their fit into the export markets; the quality of your products and your ability to control quality over time; and your ability to service your products and support your reputation in new markets.

An organization must be developed to deal with both your internal needs and the external requirements of your new market. It is important that this process be thorough. If it is, this process of organizing for export will give your company and its personnel an *export mindset*. Employees will take an active interest to the project. This export mindset is an important factor in your approach to foreign markets; it is a key to a cohesive company approach to this new business.

To organize for export you should first draw on and utilize your existing organizational structure. You may feel uncomfortable with the idea of a new export function or export department in your company and may not know how to start one up. That's normal; industry groups, government agencies, and international trade consultants can assist in this organizational evaluation and assessment.

There are a number of basic management functions common to every company, although each company will carry these out in a different manner. These differences in organizational philosophy are not the issue. Management needs to deal with the functional requirements of the export process. You need to involve the following functional areas:

- Manufacturing and product development.
- Warehousing and inventory control.
- Traffic and distribution/transportation.
- Marketing and sales.
- Finance and risk management.
- Personnel and labor.

In a large company, there may be a manager for each of these areas or there may be a group of managers for each of these functions, while the owner/manager may perform all or almost all of these functions in a smaller, emerging company.

Each person responsible for one or more of these activities needs to be a part of the planning and decision-making process for your export business. Some may be involved more than others, but all functions must be involved to some degree. (For example, if engineering doesn't talk to marketing, now is the time to change, because you will sell a "different" product to a foreign buyer.)

Dealing with the internal needs—commitment, quality, long-term perspective, and environment—will enable the company to meet the new external needs: building trust, proving reliability, and enhancing your reputation. The maxim "You only have one chance to make a first impression" is at the heart of this discussion, and you can rarely make a good first impression without preparation.

CRITICAL SUCCESS FACTORS

There are a few consistent, critical success factors. The exporter must build trust on the part of the foreign buyer and foreign distributor. The exporter must be demonstrably reliable, with a long-term resolve and commitment. The exporter must deliver quality and unparalleled service.

If the exporter delivers in the areas of reliability, quality, and service, trust will follow. With trust, you can become the preferred supplier with the benefit that price may become somewhat secondary. You often will find that consistent product quality and service will be more important to the buyer than minor differentiations in price.

To deliver in these three areas, the exporter must have the commitment and involvement of the six major functional areas of the company listed previously. Following are some of the primary issues that must be dealt with in order to install and carry out an effective export operation.

Manufacturing and Product Development

Is your product right for the foreign market? Does it need modification? How does it need to be modified? These are some of the manufacturing and product development issues that must be addressed and evaluated:

1. Is conversion to metric measurements necessary?

2. Is conversion to different AC voltage necessary?

3. Is conversion from AC to DC power necessary? For which countries?

4. Is conversion to portable power necessary?

5. Is the size (of the product, the package) compatible with that accepted in the market?

6. Is the color acceptable?

7. Is there an appropriate number of pieces per package or unit of sale?

8. Are language, content, diagrams, and other marks acceptable?

9. Is the technology of the product appropriate to the market?

10. Can production for export be done within the firm's existing physical capacity or must capacity be added?

11. Should components be made in the buyer's country or a third country?

12. Will additional production workers be needed?

13. Can a Foreign Trade Zone (FTZ) be used for assembly for export?

14. Do you need to redesign for export to cut handling, shipping, or manufacturing costs?

Warehousing and Inventory Control

Your export markets may have seasonal characteristics similar to the patterns of your domestic market. However, these patterns may occur at different times of the year. Order patterns may differ from those in the United States.[1] Shipping may be convenient or cumbersome. Export sales may add to your sales volumes, which may change your facilities and handling requirements. Here are some of the issues that need to be dealt with:

1. Do you need added warehouse capacity for goods in process and raw materials and for goods awaiting shipment?

2. Are you going to use imported parts in the manufacture or assembly of your goods for export? With effective planning, duties on these imports can be eliminated or deferred.

3. Do you need to establish a warehousing facility in a FTZ? (See "Resources" at the end of this chapter.)

4. Do you need separate inventory-control systems to manage inventory produced for export?

5. What special handling is required for export goods?

---

[1] A caution on the use of the term "United States." When dealing with a foreign national and referring to your home country, use the term USA or United States of America. Other countries, such as Mexico, use the words "United States" in the complete name of their nation, e.g., Estados Unidos de Mexico.

Traffic and Distribution/Transportation

The process of moving the merchandise from your place of business to the location of the distributor or buyer[2] can be one of the ongoing challenges of exporting. This requires good information and continued follow through.

1. Who will handle preparation of the documents for the export shipment?

2. Are these persons trained? Qualified?

3. Can a freight forwarder train company personnel? Can a freight forwarder handle the required export documentation?

4. How do the goods move from your warehouse to the point of export? Is it more cost effective to use rail or truck? Are there cost/volume trade-offs?

5. Is an export license required? This is an important factor, as the penalties for failure to obtain an export license when one is required can be severe, up to and including permanent revocation of the privilege of exporting. (Chapter 18 covers the issue of export licenses.) Have your traffic department and an engineer or product manager who knows your manufacturing functions review the need for an export license *together*. Assign the export license function to one person or department in order to develop both in-house skills and accountability. If you assign the export license determination to a freight forwarder, *you remain liable for compliance*.

6. What is the most efficient size of shipment to make to the foreign buyer? Air freight is based on the greater of kilograms or volume shipped, with rate breakpoints and minimums. Ocean freight is based on the greater of cubic meters or weight shipped, with minimums, by type of cargo. This subject is covered in depth in Chapter 15.

7. Does the firm have experience in export packing? Can you pack to protect for all the handling risks inherent in an export movement?

Marketing and Sales

The traditional *marketing mix* impacts almost every facet of your preparation for and management of the export function. Marketing, the performance of business activities that direct the flow of a company's goods and services to consumers or users in another nation for a profit,[3] must be behind all prospect

---

[2]For ease of use throughout this book, I shall refer to your overseas client as the buyer or representative. This firm may be a distributor, sales organization, end user, OEM account, or other type of organization.

[3]Phillip Cateora, *International Marketing* (New York: Irwin, 1991).

and client contacts to ensure that the program you present to the buyer is consistent and well thought out. This includes product development, availability from the warehouse, and the speed and quality of service in moving the goods. Marketing considerations include:

1. Packaging for point of sale or use.

2. Labeling in the appropriate language(s). For example, in Québec, Canada, French language on the label must be of at least equal prominence with the English language used on the same label, whereas in the rest of Canada, the requirement is that French must be used on the label.

3. Colors in packaging, labeling, the product, and other applications. Some colors have cultural implications quite apart from one's experience and expectations.

4. Media use and arrangement. How do you advertise, if at all, and what must you provide to your buyer in support of media use in each country or region?

5. How to price the product for the market. How do you position the product? This is a consideration beyond the basic issue of gross margin. Your product quality and the service and support you provide may enable you to price the product at or above the local price or that of other competitor's products. However, a strong price without the best of service and support will give you a bad name in the market.

6. Buyer relations are usually left to the marketing and sales staff. In the international marketplace, others will need to be involved because there are significantly different considerations in export marketing management. Chapter 5 deals with the multiple issues you must address.

Finance and Risk Management

In addition to buyer relations, the finance function will have impact on a broad variety of topics including:

1. Manufacturing costs, capacity utilization, and additional capacity requirements, labor rates, and so on.

2. Inventory levels and how to finance additional inventory levels, inventory peaks, or extended carrying times.

3. Transportation costs as a component of export pricing.

4. The export sales arrangement and the demands that arrangement may place on cash flow.

5. Risk management of export inventory, of export accounts receivable, and of the goods in transit by any mode of transport.

6. Financing the buyer. Is buyer finance internal, with the risks of loss absorbed by the company? Is buyer finance external, with the risk of buyer nonpayment shared with a third party? Part Three addresses the issues of export finance and your options.

7. How will the costs of the export business and the financing required fit into your company's financing program? This is a key component of the export business plan. (See Chapter 23.)

8. Will your bank finance your export accounts receivable? If not, what are your options? (See Part Three.)

9. Will your bank lend to support the buildup of inventory or capacity for your export operations?

10. Who will look into the alternatives to exporting directly, and how will the financial impacts of those alternatives be evaluated?

Personnel and Labor

All employees must be actively aware of the export business and its importance to the firm. There may be different motivations and constraints in dealing with nonunion employees and unionized employees, but the ability of the firm to provide consistent quality and timely service is a requirement that touches all areas of the firm.

The U.S. exporter is operating at some distance from the foreign buyer, in a different time zone, and in a different language. He or she is confronted with a different set of expectations and cultural biases.

A foreign buyer 3,000 miles away cannot be dealt with in the same way as a U.S. buyer 3,000 miles distant. Because this is the case, each of your employees must be made aware of the importance of the export business to the company. Your employees, union and nonunion alike, should know that exports create and maintain jobs.

Exports for your company mean:

1. There will be longer production runs and lower costs per unit of production, which makes the company more profitable.

2. Broader markets add stability in the demand for your products, which means less seasonal variations and less seasonal layoffs.

3. There will be more potential for personal growth within the company.

HOW FOREIGN BUYERS PERCEIVE U.S. EXPORTERS

The Bureau of the Census reports that there are over 18 million companies in the United States, and that number is increasing at about 1 million per year.

The EXPORTER Magazine recently advised that less than 130,000 U.S. companies export.

Of these firms, few export on a consistent basis. In the history of U.S. business, many export markets have been used as:

1. Dumping grounds for excess production.
2. Safety valves when U.S. market demand slows down.
3. A home for obsolete goods or manufactures.

The U.S. companies that have been successful in their export sales are those that have taken their best products, modified them for the local (foreign) market, provided first-class service, and committed the time to the development of the market. Many of these successful companies include names we all know, such as Boeing, General Electric, Microsoft, Honeywell, Toro, Caterpillar, 3M. They set the example. However, it isn't necessary to be a household name to be a success.

Many foreign buyers generally view new entrants into the export business with some hesitancy. Some of their concerns are based on earlier experiences with U.S. exporters. Poor quality, inconsistent interest in the market, limited follow-up service, erratic pricing, and spotty dealer/distributor support are reasons why the average foreign buyer may not be overwhelmed at the opportunity to do business with you. It can be difficult to overcome the faults of your predecessors.

It is also true that, for the most part, businesspeople and products from the U.S. are generally well liked. It's difficult to account for this dichotomy; it's just a fact of business. The implications are, however, quite subtle and often trying; while you will be well received, your proposal for a business arrangement may be embraced more slowly. Understanding this reluctance will aid you in your dealings with the foreign buyer.

MISTAKES OF NEW EXPORTERS

The US&FCS has determined that new exporters tend to encounter similar problems and make similar mistakes. These can be grouped into 12 areas:

1. *Failure to obtain qualified export counseling* and to develop an overall international marketing plan before starting an export operation. A successful firm will first clearly define goals, objectives, and the problems to be addressed. This firm will then develop a definitive plan to accomplish an objective despite the problems involved. Many firms are not blessed with employees holding the necessary export expertise. These companies should not proceed without qualified outside guidance.

2. *Insufficient commitment by top management* to overcome the organizational and financial requirements of exporting. It may take more time and effort to establish foreign markets than domestic markets. Companies should take a long-range view of this process and carefully monitor international marketing efforts through the often slow early stages. A good foundation should deliver benefits that eventually outweigh the investment.

3. *Insufficient care in selecting overseas distributors* or representation. This selection is critical. The complications involved in overseas communications and transportation require international representatives to act with greater independence than their domestic counterparts. As a new and unknown entrant the exporter may need to rely on the foreign representative's reputation in the target market. The exporter should conduct an in-depth evaluation of the representative's facilities, personnel, and management methods.

4. *Chasing orders from around the world*, rather than establishing a program for orderly and profitable growth. Foreign representatives must be trained, assisted, and monitored in their performance. The exporter may need to assign a marketing executive to that region. New exporters should concentrate on one or two geographic areas in order to support that marketing executive. After successful penetration of this initial area, the exporter can then profitably expand into the next selected geographic area.

5. *Neglecting exports when the U.S. market booms.* Many companies turn to exporting when business in the United States falls off and put exports second (or dead last) when the U.S. economy turns. This on-off program is well understood by foreign firms. Most have little patience with this practice and will not tolerate it. Exporters who conduct their affairs in this manner face the challenge of constant development of new export markets.

6. *Failure to treat international distributors on an equal basis* with domestic counterparts. To promote success in foreign markets, those representatives need the same level of support and attention as that given to their domestic counterparts, such as ad campaigns, special discount offers, sales incentive programs, special credit programs, warranty offers, training, and more.

7. *Assuming that one product and strategy will work in all markets.* Each foreign market, and often regions within markets, has to be treated as individual and distinct in order to ensure the best opportunity for success.

8. *Failure to modify products to meet the regulations or cultural preferences of other countries.* Your foreign representative (or your buyer) must deal with local safety and product performance regulations, as well as import controls. These cannot be ignored. Products can be modified at the exporter's production facility, in a FTZ, or at the buyer's location. The greater the distance from the exporter, the greater the cost to modify and the greater the opportunity to do it wrong. Note that many product modifications may be nominal, with the concomitant benefit that the product is then identified as custom made for a specific market.

9. *Failure to use the language of the target market* in print, service, sales, and warranty messages. While the senior officers of your representative or buyer may speak and read English with great ease, one cannot assume the same facility by service, maintenance, installation, or other personnel. At a nominal cost, you can give the buyer or your representative's field personnel the ability to understand your message and achieve the benefits you seek to deliver.

10. *Failure to consider use of an export management company or export trading company.* An export management company can act as the export department for an emerging company or take on one or more specific markets in order to increase the implementation pace of an export plan. An export trading company can often get your product into a new market faster, at a lower front-end cost, than an in-house export program. This is a useful option for expansion into multiple markets or for experimentation with the export process.

11. *Failure to consider licensing or joint-venture agreements.* By their nature, many products are difficult, costly, or cumbersome to export. Others may encounter import barriers and market restrictions. Licensing and joint ventures offer flexible and powerful marketing alternatives for these products. Companies experiencing fast growth or those with limited personnel or financial resources can utilize these options to enter or expand markets. The trade-off is a dilution of direct and timely control.

12. *Failure to provide quality local service for the product.* A U.S. product without the necessary on-site support in the foreign market will earn a poor reputation and fail to grow.

ORGANIZATION IS THE KEY TO SUCCESS

Success in the export business is a direct result of the amount of energy and planning you put into your development of the business. You earn the results you work for. If your approach is well reasoned, well planned, and thorough, export markets will be excellent contributors to the overall health and profitability of your firm.

The internal organization for your export business does not require added staff and layers of management unless and until the volume of new business warrants the expenditure. Existing staff can take on quite a bit of the effort; the opportunity to participate in the opening of a new business will be an exciting challenge for your employees. We have all learned that people are at their best when they are challenged, when there is a meaningful goal to be achieved.

The functions that need to be addressed by small and large companies alike have been identified. Each functional area of your organization has a role in the export process. Allocate the export functions presented here based on in-house expertise and capacities. Set performance marks and timelines. Each function is important, although some stand out. Commitment has to be there. Financing is critical. Export licensing has to be addressed early on.

If you currently lack people or time, call on the resources and agencies mentioned in Chapter 1. These organizations want to help you succeed. Banks, carriers, forwarders, and other service providers prosper by your success.

RESOURCES

1. See Roger Axtell's, *Do's and Taboos Around the World* (New York: John Wiley & Sons, 1991) for the cultural implications of colors, gestures, communications, and more.

2. *The New York Journal of Commerce* reports weekly on companies that are recipients of the President's E Award for export excellence. These firms cover the United States, and range from the very small one- or two-person operation to some of the largest companies and organizations in the country.

3. A Foreign Trade Zone (FTZ) is a place, usually within a port, that is considered separate from the United States for duty purposes. An exporter can import parts, components, subassemblies, or pieces into the FTZ and then add or modify these items within the FTZ. Only upon leaving the FTZ and entering into the commerce of the United States does the imported good become dutiable. Imported automobiles are handled in this manner.

   Goods imported into the FTZ, modified, and subsequently exported are not subject to duty by the U.S. To learn more about the value of an FTZ for your business, contact The Foreign Trade Zone Board at the U.S. Department of Commerce, 14th and Pennsylvania Avenue N.W., Washington, DC 20230. John J. Da Ponte, Jr., is the director.

   New regulations covering the activities of Foreign Trade Zones were effective November 7, 1991. They were published in *56 Federal Register 50790-50808* on October 8, 1991.

3 How to Find the Best Overseas Market

Identification and evaluation of potential export markets is the first step in implementing your plan for profitable exporting. Exporters have proven that almost any product has an export market; most services also have opportunities in foreign markets.

U.S. companies export sand, cement, metal buttons, ball-point pen refills, single-family house plans, and audio tapes of English-language children's songs, to name just a very few of the low-technology products and services that do well overseas. Architectural, engineering, advertising, and communications services continue to grow from sales and services to foreign buyers. This chapter illustrates how you, the exporter, can identify the best foreign market for your product or service. The *best* market may be the one that is experiencing the greatest growth, has the most experience with your type of product, has the most developed base of application opportunities, or is the best fit of consumer variables.

There are tremendous information resources available to you for initial research, in-depth research, and specific identification of export potentials. There are two principal starting tracks to this research. They are presented here without order of preference.

First, *identify the criteria that best describe the characteristics of your buyers.* If, for example, you sell an industrial product such as an industrial lubricant, the target country might have one or more of the following characteristics:

1. It has a well-developed industrial base.
2. It has a functioning manufacturing industry.
3. It has a machine tool industry.
4. It has a per capita GNP at or above the level of Third World nations. (The World Bank defines a Low Income Economy as one with 1985 per capita GNP of US$400 or less.)

5. It is an exporter of manufactured goods.

6. It is an importer of manufactured goods.

7. It has other characteristics that indicate potential buyers of your lubricants.

There are on-line data bases that can utilize your parameters to select or qualify countries for further investigation. CompuServe, PCGlobe, World Almanac, and DIALOG are just four of the many that are available.

Second, *identify which countries currently import your product or similar products.* Do this in addition to, or instead of, the first research track. You will achieve the best results if you begin this research phase armed with some basic information.

1. Get the **SIC** code for your business. This is the Standard Industrial Classification, a U.S. production-based code. A SIC code directory is available at most larger libraries, at all US&FCS offices, and at college and university libraries that are U.S. government document depositories.

2. Get the **SITC** code for your products. This is the United Nations Standard International Trade Classification. Members of the United Nations annually report their international trade activity under this code system. You may purchase a SITC directory from the United Nations in New York. Most US&FCS offices should have a copy.

3. Get the Schedule B number for your product. This Schedule B number is a 10-digit number that identifies your product on a worldwide basis. Over 5,000 products are listed by Schedule B number. The Schedule B number is used for export reporting on the **Shipper's Export Declaration** (see Chapter 16). The Harmonized Tariff Schedule (HTS or **HS**) is a 12,000-plus import product identification system which gives a finer breakdown of products than Schedule B and is used for U.S. Customs duty-collection purposes.

With the Schedule B numbers for your product(s), you can tap into a broad range of information on the volume and direction of export activity in your product field. The SITC information will help when you look for information on export of your product type from other countries to your target markets. The SIC numbers will help you identify other U.S. firms that manufacture or distribute your product types.

THE NATIONAL TRADE DATA BANK

Before mid-1991, one of the principal sources of trade information was hardcopy government documents such as the FT 410 and microfiche records of trade data such as the EMS 546 (the Export Monthly 546 from the Bureau of the Census).

In early 1991, the U.S. Department of Commerce introduced the National Trade Data Bank (NTDB). This is a CD-ROM data base of international trade information from most principal agencies of the U.S. government, updated monthly. The NTDB contains over 100,000 different documents, all relating to the international trade activity of the United States. Companies and individuals can purchase one or more months of reports or subscribe to the NTDB and receive the monthly information updates on a CD-ROM disk for a nominal fee. The NTDB is accessible at all US&FCS offices in the United States, at all World Trade Centers, and at government document depository libraries. Figure 3.1 lists the agencies (and number of sources) that provide information to the NTDB. Figure 3.2 lists the source documents available from the Bureau of the Census, and Figure 3.3 lists the source documents available from the U.S. Department of Commerce.

The value of this information can be tremendous. A skilled user can obtain information on:

1. The history, culture, society, market, population, economic situation, and political climate of any country.

2. Current status of trade relations, overseas investment policy, and government export guarantee and insurance policies, by country.

3. Information on trade embargoes, restrictions, and disputes with customs, by country.

```
   SOURCE      TOPIC      PROGRAM      SUBJECT      ITEM      QUIT

    5   Board of Governors of the Federal Reserve System
    2   Central Intelligence Agency
    1   Export-Import Bank of the United States
    2   Office of U.S. Trade Representative
    1   Overseas Private Investment Corporation
    2   U.S. Department of State
    1   U.S. International Trade Commission
    1   University of Massachusetts, (MISER)
    1   USDA, Foreign Agricultural Service
   13   USDOC, Bureau of Economic Analysis
    7   USDOC, Bureau of the Census
   10   USDOC, International Trade Administration
    1   USDOC, National Institute of Standards and Technology
    2   USDOC, Office of Business Analysis
    1   USDOE, Energy Information Administration
    2   USDOL, Bureau of Labor Statistics


 F1=HELP  F2=INFO                               HOME   END   PgUp   PgDn
 • Position                       ⌐ • Select           ESC • Exit
```

Figure 3.1 Agencies Providing Information to the NTDB. The number next to the agency name indicates the number of different source documents available from that agency. This is a source screen of the NTDB.

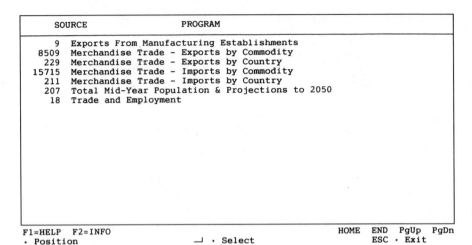

Figure 3.2 Source Documents Available from the Bureau of the Census. The number next to the document name indicates the number of files within that category.

4. Labor and employment information and product standards, by country.

5. Export and import statistics and patterns, by product, by country, with trends in US$ and unit volume, for seven years and the year to date (YTD) for the current and prior years.

6. Trade leads, and more.

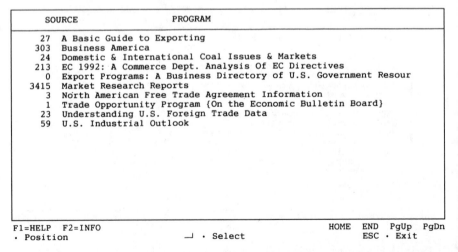

Figure 3.3 Source Documents Available from the Department of Commerce

Table 3.1 lists only a few of the over 12,000 products exported from the United States. This kind of information will tell you if there is a market for your products anywhere in the world.

The information in Table 3.1 was taken from the February 1992 NTDB. Each of these product categories has detail on the dollar amount and units exported to each country of the world, for each of seven reporting periods (1986–1990, plus YTD 1990 and 1991). This table demonstrates the extreme variety of products exported by U.S. companies. Some of these may be surprising, such as parts of baby carriages, buttons, or copper parts.

The NTDB CD-ROM contains two resource banks. The second is the Foreign Traders Index (FTI). With the FTI, the user can identify companies, in all or selected foreign markets, that have purchased from or expressed an interest in purchasing goods or services from U.S. suppliers, by product type (Schedule B number).

The information within the FTI includes:

1. The name of the company.

2. Address.

3. Telephone, cable, telex, or fax.

4. Managing officer, name and title.

5. Year established, number of employees, relative size (an indication only, as relative size is determined by the US&FCS staffer on site, based on that person's understanding of the size of firms in the marketplace).

6. The business of the firm, by SIC code, and business type.

The FTI, coupled with the NTDB, can provide a useful base of information on a target market and the prospects for your firm. The information will require intelligent analysis.

From Bureau of the Census sources, you can obtain information on the trend of export sales of your product over the past seven years, by country. The product is reported by Schedule B number. The export data are reported alphabetically by country, by US$ sales per year.

From the Department of Commerce sources, you can obtain market research information through the Market Research Reports files. This source contains over 3,400 reports on foreign markets for specific U.S. products. The full reports are available on the NTDB CD-ROM disk.

With the NTDB, your company can readily generate historical data on your target country and region and identify markets, trends, potential buyers, market research information, and other relevant detail on your product, its overseas markets, and the characteristics of the market.

Table 3.1
Sample of Range of Products Exported in 1991

Schedule B Number	Commodity Description	Exports 11 Mos. 1991 US$000
1404100000	Raw vegetable materials used in dyeing and tan . . .	314
2005200020	Potato chips, prepared or preserved nesoi	61,516
2530100000	Vermiculite, perlite and chlorites, unexpanded	5,353
2816300000	Barium ozides, hydroxides and peroxides	3,194
3002200000	Vaccines for human medicine	76,924
3215110020	Printing ink, black, flexographic	546
3701996030	Graphic art film except for color photo	22,581
3811110000	Antiknock preparations, based on lead compounds	213,526
3914000000	Ion exchangers, based on polymers of . . .	32,132
3926905500	Belting & belts, for machinery, cont text	3,920
4403910040	Oak, except red oak, wood, in the rough	52,381
5107100000	Yarn of combed wool, not for retail sale	1,128
6109100062	Women's and girls tank tops of cotton, knitted	844
6909191000	Ferrite core memories	10,148
7322110000	Radiators for central heating and parts, cast iron	700
7403110000	Refined copper cathodes and sections of cathodes	564,462
7616106000	Threaded fasteners of aluminum	5,784
8302200000	Castors, and parts thereof, of base metal	17,869
8471934540	Hard magnetic disk drive units	1,186,314
8525010000	Radio transceivers, citizens band (cb) type	12,265
8541407040	Chips, dicd and wafer for photosensitive trans.	40,145
8715000040	Parts of baby carriages	1,935
9015400000	Photogrammetrical surveying instruments & appl	6,791
9027308020	Spectroscopes using optical radiations, nonelec	856
9403200010	Metal furniture of a kind used in household	43,057
9507100080	Fishing rods parts and accessories	6,675
9606220000	Buttons, of base metal, not covered w/text. mat	5,084

United Nations data, available from U.N. sources, can provide a picture of the exports of your product, by all nations and to all nations. The SITC number is key to this portion of your research.

In some cases, data is available by unit sales in addition to dollar values. This can give you a rough idea of unit values.

THE U.S. DEPARTMENT OF COMMERCE

The U.S. Department of Commerce (USDOC) has industry specialists and country specialists in Washington, D.C. Industry specialists are listed in Appendix C. They are available to give you information on the current state of your product overseas, comment on marketing and sales strategies, inform you of trade shows and events, and give other counsel as you may request.

Country specialists are listed in Appendix D. These people, one or more per country, are available to give you information on your target country, current trade issues with the United States, customs and tariff information, insight on the business climate and culture, and more.

The export promotion functions of the USDOC are carried out by the U.S. & Foreign Commercial Service (US&FCS). This service has a number of other resources available to assist you in identifying both potential markets and potential buyers. Three important services are described.

The *Agent/Distributor Service* (ADS) is a fee-based, contact-identification service. You select a country, and the in-country US&FCS officers will provide you with a detailed listing of up to six qualified firms that have expressed interest in your business proposal. One successful exporter has utilized the ADS exclusively to identify representatives for his products. Others report little success. The conclusion: Success with this (or any program) depends on you, your product, its marketing mix (quality, price, promotion, distribution), and the markets you select.

The *New Comparison Shopping Service* is another fee-based service. It provides customized research to assist you in evaluating the overall marketability of your product in a selected market. The service is available in a limited number of countries. (Call your US&FCS office, found in Appendix A, for a list.)

The *Gold Key Service* is a package of services available at some US&FCS foreign offices. This package usually includes:

1. Arrangement of on-site appointments with qualified potential representatives.

2. Use of the US&FCS offices as an office away from home.

3. Translation, communications, and office services.

4. Orientation to the market and the culture.

Contact your local US&FCS office to pursue this service.

OTHER RESEARCH AND MARKET INFORMATION SOURCES

World Trade Centers. The World Trade Center Association has 207 (1991) members in 190 cities and 64 countries worldwide. There are 79 members in the United States. Initially developed as real estate projects, many centers provide research libraries; access to the NTDB; office, translation, and communication services; product display space; meeting rooms; and teleconference, videoconference, and other business facilities for local and visiting members. There is a WTC Network for the exchange of buy and sell offers, which can uncover business opportunities. Local management can assist and guide you when traveling in your target market.

World Trade Clubs or World Trade Associations. These international trade-oriented groups are active in most larger cities throughout the United States. They can be a source of current information on markets, business practices, banking, and other services available in the community. Some organizations have country-specific activities to encourage an exchange of ideas, practices, and experiences relating to specific markets. Members include companies and individuals engaged in export or import. Lawyers, accountants, and bankers are often a major portion of the membership.

Chambers of Commerce. Chambers of commerce often have libraries of information, a contact list, and a mailing list for export or import inquiries received from overseas. Some have international trade committees. Chambers of commerce in other countries are often the central focus of the business community in a city or region. Membership is expected (often mandatory), and the chamber is active in the regulation of business in its territory. These overseas chambers are used by their members to develop contacts in the United States and elsewhere.

American Chambers of Commerce Abroad (AmCham). American Chambers of Commerce Abroad function as meeting places for U.S. businesspeople and much more. Located in the principal city of each country, the AmCham is run by and for American business abroad. In your targeted country, the AmCham can be an excellent resource for information and guidance on indigenous business practices. American businesspeople can often share their experiences with you and offer guidance on the ground rules for profitable exporting to their host country.

Trade Associations/Industry Groups. Trade associations or industry groups have become more sophisticated in the past decade and now understand the importance of foreign markets for their members. Participation in your trade or industry association can give you access to association personnel charged to assist members in marketing their products abroad and access to trade libraries and other resources that may have been developed.

International Organizations. International organizations such as the U.S. Agency for International Development (USAID);[1] departments of the United Nations such as the United Nations Children's Fund (UNICEF), the World Health Organization (WHO), or the United Nations Conference on Trade and Development (UNCTAD); supranational financial institutions such as the World Bank and the International Monetary Fund; and other global or regional organizations can be valuable as an information resource, a contracting body, or both. Many of these organizations have newsletters, magazines, or other programs to promote participation in their objectives.

Associations and Societies. Most larger cities in the United States have social groups that focus on a particular country, such as the Japan American Society, the Canadian Society, and such. These groups are an excellent place to meet foreign nationals, foreign government officials traveling through, U.S.-based foreign consuls and commercial officers, and people who deal with that country on a personal or business level.

Your Industry. Your industry will have one or more leading companies that are active overseas. Research on these firms can provide you with useful information on markets, contacts, pricing, and marketing strategies. If these larger competitors are publicly traded companies, information can be obtained from the annual reports, 10-K and 10-Q reports, analyst reports, and other sources.

The Small Business Administration (SBA). The SBA has its own international trade section. One of its services is called the *Export Information System* (XIS), which provides exporters with the largest importing markets for their products, in descending order, along with a list of the countries that currently supply the product to those markets. SBA needs the SITC code for your product to conduct the computer search. The service is without charge.

I have found that companies in similar industries (not direct competitors) are quite willing to share information and discuss their success in exporting. There is a justifiable pride of accomplishment from those who have achieved their objective.

Figure 3.4, the International Trade Information Matrix, gives some additional sources of information on exporting. I would caution that these are

---

[1]See Part Three, Export Finance, for more information on USAID.

IF YOU ARE SEEKING INFORMATION OR ASSISTANCE REGARDING →

USE →

	Potential Markets	Market Research	Direct Sales Leads	Agents/Distributors	Licenses	Credit Analysis	Financial Assistance	Risk Insurance	Tax Incentives	Export Counseling	Export Regulations	Overseas Contracts	Marketing Strategies	Trade Complaints	Customs Advantages	Carnet
U.S. & Foreign Commercial Service	●	●	●		●					●	●		●	●		
District Export Councils (DEC)										●						
Trade Opportunities Program			●		●							●				
Agent/Distributor Service				●												
Overseas Business Reports	●	●														
Foreign Economic Trends	●	●														
Small Business Administration		●					●			●						
International Chambers of Commerce											●					●
Export Statistics Profiles	●	●														
Export Information System Data Reports	●	●														
Annual Worldwide Industry Reviews	●	●														
International Market Research	●	●														
Country Market Surveys	●	●														
Custom Statistical Service	●	●														
Product Market Profile	●	●														

Market Share Reports

Country Market Profiles

Country Trade Statistics

Background Notes

International Economic Indicators

World Traders Data Reports

Commercial News USA

Export-Import Bank

Export Mailing List Service

Commerce Trade Shows

Commerce Trade Missions

Export Development Offices

Catalog Exhibitions

Major Projects Program

Overseas Private Investment Corporation

Private Export Funding Corporation

Foreign Sales Corporation

Commerce Business Daily

Free Ports & Free Trade Zones

International Trade Consultants

Figure 3.4 International Trade Information Matrix

broad suggestions, and any particular organization may be of infinite or limited value to you and your project.

RESOURCES

1. The World Trade Center Association is at One World Trade Center, Suite 7701, New York, NY 10048. Tel: 212-313-4600; fax: 212-488-0064.

2. For USDOC Country officers, see Appendix D.

3. For USDOC Industry officers, see Appendix C.

4. The National Trade Data Bank, the CD-ROM data base, is available from the USDOC in single-disk or annual subscription. To order or learn more, call the NTDB helpline: 202-482-1986. Single-disk price is $35; annual subscription is $360 (as of September 1992).

5. The Small Business Administration has a couple of programs designed to assist U.S. exporters. Contact your local SBA office and ask for the international officer, or write to the SBA Office of International Trade, 1414 L St., NW, Room 501-A, Washington, DC 20416.

6. The U.S. Government Bookstore publishes *Books for Business Professionals,* which offers a number of publications that may be of interest. Contact your nearest U.S. Government Bookstore or write U.S. Superintendent of Documents, U.S. Government Printing Office, Washington, DC 20402.

7. The Trade Promotion Coordinating Committee is a U.S. government group formed in 1990 to coordinate export promotion efforts across government departments. It has developed a guide, *Export Programs: A Business Directory of U.S. Government Resources,* which lists federal-level organizations, services, addresses, telephone and fax numbers, and contacts. This booklet is available from the U.S. Department of Commerce, TPCC, 14th St. & Constitution Ave., NW, Washington, DC 20230.

8. *The Exporter's Encyclopedia,* published by Dunn & Bradstreet, offers detailed information for exporters, by country. There is an overview section and a section for each country that trades with the United States. This excellent resource is available for review at most US&FCS offices, most World Trade Centers, and at many foreign freight forwarders (see Chapter 15).

9. The Bureau of National Affairs publishes *The International Trade Reporter,* which also provides information on a country-by-country

basis. It can be used in conjunction with *The Exporter's Encyclopedia* for a more thorough review of a country.

10. *The Official Export Guide* is official only to the publisher, North American Publishing Company. This reference book contains some information similar to the preceding two publications. It also contains an abbreviated Schedule B directory and Export Administration Regulations. Most freight forwarders have a copy.

11. The SBA Export Information System (XIS) Data Reports are available through your local SBA office (government listings in the telephone book) or call 800-827-5722.

12. The US&FCS office closest to you can be an excellent resource for large and small companies alike. Because the US&FCS has been drastically underfunded by the Reagan and Bush administrations, service time must be directed to those firms with more likelihood of export success. Other smaller firms are directed to other resources in each community.

13. The Equal Opportunity Hotline, operated by the Small Business Foundation of America, reports that it can answer questions on foreign market research, export financing, licensing and insurance, documentation, and finding hands-on help. The telephone number is 800-243-7232.[2]

14. *The Export Hotline* is a fax-based information retrieval system. It has information on over 50 industries in over 60 countries. Access to the system is by fax line. Call 1-800-872-9767.

[2]Reported in *Inc.* magazine, December 1991.

4 Meet Your Market

Many U.S. businesspeople return from a sales trip to a foreign country with no business finalized and little apparent chance of closing sales in the future. Even though the executive had been assured that the company's products were acceptable in the country, that prices seemed competitive, that packaging was right for the market, and that shipment schedules were appropriate to the prospects' needs, no contracts were signed and no purchase orders were taken. Expert advisors had recommended the trip to personally call on buyers and book initial orders. No orders resulted. What went wrong? Preparation, most likely.

PREPARATION

Preparation is the key to success in business dealings in the United States, and preparation is more important when dealing with prospects and clients in another country. It's probable that those things that should have been done to ensure success had been left undone. Lack of understanding led to lack of preparation, which led to failure.

It is likely that the planning was faulty; information needed before visiting any foreign country was probably nonexistent. If the trip was given any planning time, it was probably done as one would plan a trip to New York, Chicago, Miami, or Los Angeles. A secretary or aide would make travel and hotel reservations and set up appointments. The executive would fly to the destination, call on the accounts, socialize if time permitted, and return with orders. Well and good for business in the United States. It would be wasted time, money, and energy for business dealings outside of the United States.

There are a number of reasons for international business travel. The initial trips are the most critical for long-term success and warrant the most attention. The executive travels:

1. To meet with potential representatives, agents, and distributors. (Chapter 5 identifies appropriate strategies.)

2. To follow up on initial meetings, confirm understandings, conduct sales training, and establish or review service operations.

3. To attend a relevant trade show in order to learn about competitors, identify potential buyers (end users, distributors, reps), and learn about the country.

4. To participate in a relevant trade show; to meet and sign representatives, agents, and distributors; to learn more about the competition, and to expand market penetration.

The initial trip overseas, to the market(s) identified by the research suggested in Chapter 3, is often exploratory and not necessarily to close sales. It is undertaken to meet with those companies your research has identified as most likely to best serve your needs in that market. It is undertaken to "get the lay of the land" and familiarize the executive with the environment of the marketplace and the feel of the country and its people.

This first-hand exposure to the culture and business climate is something one cannot obtain from a book, a tape, interviews, or training sessions. A great way to get this exposure and meet these researched companies is at an international trade fair. Steve Hatch,[1] president of the Washington State International Trade Fair, tells why:

Finding the "right" partner/distributor overseas is probably the most critical piece of the export puzzle. This partnership will establish or malign your sales and company image in the export markets.

There's great truth in the adage "The cost to elevate a mediocre distributor up to your company's standards (over time) can easily dwarf the expense you would have used to locate the best candidate as you began to export." By the time you discover that you need to change your distributor, a substantial sum has been invested. Still, many firms are flattered by their first export prospect, and agree to sign distributors quickly. A hasty selection can cost plenty!

So how can a small exporter find and compare the "best" distributor candidates at the start? One excellent way is through participation in a leading and established trade fair within the target market area. European trade fairs offer a stark contrast to trade show experiences in the U.S. In the EC, a local company may commonly *sell* up to 30 or 40% of its annual production during one trade show! There are well established, annual trade fairs in most major European cities, and qualified *buyers* (distributors/agents and representatives) consider attendance as mandatory. Also, the fairs themselves are becoming increasingly VERTICAL, which means that the products on display are limited to narrowly defined categories.

Vertical fairs in Europe and Asia are also valuable places to meet, evaluate, select and encourage high quality distributor partners for new US exporters. Every developed market has an abundance of trade fair choices. Give your company plenty of time to prepare—10 to 12 months before the show should do well.

Here are 10 ideas on how to get the most out of these events and how to attract the top candidates to your stand at the fair:

[1]Copyright © WSITF, Inc., Seattle. Reprinted with permission.

1. Assemble your top people to identify goals which you have for exporting.

2. Select a fair with a minimum of three years of successful history. If you are impressed, VISIT the show as a guest first.

3. Request demographic detail from the organizer which will provide you with the titles, buying influence, and numbers of buyers who will attend.

4. Obtain a copy of the U.S. Dept. of Commerce publication *Export Promotion Calendar* which lists "Commerce Department Certified" shows around the world. Consult your local library, local US&FCS office, or trade groups about two publications: *World Convention Dates* and *Exhibits Schedule*.

5. Always pre-invite candidates to visit your booth.

6. Prepare media packets. These are vital to success for any size company. Go prepared.

7. Staff your booth with top people. While not mandatory, it will be a significant benefit to have local language capabilities at hand.

8. Employ translated graphics and literature in your booth.

9. Never make promises during the show which you have no intention of keeping.

10. Don't rush home. Spend some time in the region to pay a visit to the top two or three distributor candidates at their place of business. They will appreciate it, and you will gain considerable prestige.

Success in exporting requires that the president down to the mail clerk understand the decision to enter and succeed in exporting. Begin planning early, and choose the right (vertical) show. These are the two most important keys to getting the most from an international show. Above all, never overlook the value of a leading trade fair to economically find your best distributor or middleman prospects abroad. Trade fairs are the perfect planned selling environment to find your best export partners.

A TRIP TO GERMANY

Planning for a trip to the foreign market must cover several topics and should begin as early as possible. A six-month planning horizon is not too long. To illustrate this, I will assume that you have done your research and have chosen Germany as your target country.[2]

You have reviewed your research findings with the trade specialist at the US&FCS district office near you (see Appendix A). If necessary, other research was done. Based on this complete and objective research, your company has identified Germany as the "best" initial target for your export marketing efforts. "Best" can mean one or more of the following:

1. The market holds the greatest potential demand.

2. The market has a history of purchases of your product type.

[2]Germany is used as an illustration only. You should follow the same steps for any country you target. A well-thought-out and thorough process is applicable to any market.

3. The market price structure offers the optimum profit opportunities.

4. The market is easiest to enter.

5. The market is fragmented, offering market share potential.

6. Your firm has a relevant history with this market.

The trade specialist can provide, or direct you to, answers to a number of questions about your trip to Germany: the best time to visit, a list of holidays, hours of business, usual terms of trade, agent's usual commissions, the channels of distribution for your product type, the best methods of transportation while in-country, and medical requirements. The trade specialist can also arrange access to and services by U.S. foreign service posts.

US&FCS officers abroad have only limited time to devote to any one firm, although special programs have been developed at a number of foreign posts. One of these programs is the Gold Key Service.

The **Gold Key Service** is custom tailored for a U.S. firm planning to visit a country. It includes assistance with hotel reservations (often at embassy rates), market orientation briefings, market research, introductions to potential partners, an interpreter for meetings, and assistance in developing a sound market strategy and an effective follow-up plan.[3] All US&FCS posts abroad offer a range of services that encompass many of the Gold Key features. Note that there may be nominal fees for some of the services.

Keep in mind that an important part of the trip-planning process concerns the identification and appointment of agents, representatives, and distributors. (Chapter 5 deals with these market entry strategies in detail.)

Before arranging any appointments in Germany, consider how jet lag will affect you. This is important. Any travel east on Sunday for an appointment on Monday is not a good idea. Frankfurt is 7 hours ahead of Chicago, and a direct flight is $8\frac{1}{2}$ hours. This $15\frac{1}{2}$ hours will have an impact. Jet lag will damage your performance, so allow for it. There are a number of publications available about how to deal with jet lag. Get a good one and follow its instructions.

Because of jet lag, your first day (even if a Monday or weekday) should consist of rest, sightseeing, and a check-in with the U.S. consulate. This check-in is important: In the event of a lost passport, accident, theft, or other calamity, you will be known to the consulate and afforded suitable treatment.

---

[3]Foreign service posts that offer Gold Key Service are Athens, Bangkok, Brussels, Buenos Aires, Casablanca, Guatemala City, Helsinki, Hong Kong, Jakarta, Johannesburg, Lisbon, London, Madrid, Mexico City, Nairobi, New Delhi, Oslo, Paris, Rome, San Jose, Seoul, Sydney, and Warsaw (as of 12-91).

If the time difference is eight hours or more, take the extra time to arrive on a Friday or the day before a holiday. This will ensure adequate time for rest. The significant time change ($15\frac{1}{2}$ hours) can disrupt your natural body rhythms, dull your thinking, impair your memory, and press your performance to a very low level. It's important that you be sharp and alert for your initial meetings.

Culture and Practices

One of your most important preparatory tasks is to learn as many of the target country's social customs as possible. Obtain books and periodicals on the social customs and cultural practices of Germany (and your relevant region) and study them thoroughly.

Lacking information on customary social and cultural practices, the executive may unknowingly show disrespect to or insult the client, prospect, or host and do irreparable harm to a budding business relationship. This has happened in the past and it will happen in the future. You can avoid it if you do your homework before the trip. Here are some useful points:

1. Always use titles (*doktor*, engineer, professor); use first names only after given permission to do so.

2. Be punctual—this is essential. Make or cancel appointments well in advance.

3. An invitation into a German home is a special privilege. Present flowers to the hostess (no red roses) upon greeting her.

4. In casual conversation, avoid reference to baseball, basketball, or American football and talk instead of the German countryside, hobbies, and European sports such as soccer.

5. For business travel to Germany, an American citizen must have a valid U.S. passport. Visas are not required.

6. Travelers who plan to bring articles into Germany for demonstration purposes should make arrangements with the German customs authorities prior to arrival. The *Carnet de Passage,* covered later in this chapter, will provide the necessary permissions.

7. Advance hotel reservations are advised, particularly for larger cities where international trade fairs are held. These include Dusseldorf, Hanover, Cologne, Frankfurt, Munich, and Berlin. These advance reservations are particularly important for travel during the major trade fair seasons of February–June and October–November.

8. German law is quite stringent in its requirements for ethical and acceptable business standards. Defamation of a competitor's name or

product, misrepresentation in advertising, and other infringements are prohibited.

9. American executives in Germany often have difficulty with Germany's Promotional Gifts Ordinance (*Zugabeverordnung*) which prohibits giveaways except calendars, consumer periodicals, or other promotional material of nominal value bearing the company's name. A promotional gift associated with a single transaction is distinguished from a business gift that is presented in order to maintain good business relations. Business gifts are generally considered in good taste if their value does not exceed DM100.

10. Expedited handling of correspondence is indispensable. Use airmail, postal routing codes, and fax.

11. German business dress and manner are more formal than usual American practice. Do not be put off by this cultural norm.

12. German is the language preferred by most firms even though most companies engaged in international trade are able to correspond in English and other languages. American firms must print promotional literature and product manuals in German as this is expected at the retail and end-user levels.

13. Time reference and notation outside the United States is usually on a 24-hour clock. In Germany, business hours are 0900–1200 (9 A.M. to noon) and 1430 to 1700 (2:30–5:00 P.M.) on weekdays, except Friday afternoons or during trade fairs.

14. There are legal holidays observed throughout Germany: New Year's Day, Good Friday, Easter Monday, Labor Day (May 1), Ascension Day (40 days after Easter), Pentecost or Whitmonday (Day of German Unity, October 3), Repentance Day (in November), Christmas Day, and December 26. Other legal and religious holidays are celebrated in various German cities and regions. Check with the US&FCS prior to scheduling your trip.

15. The metric system is the standard for weights and measures. Electric circuits carry 220 or 380 volt, 50-cycle alternating current.

In-country travel is convenient and reliable. Germany has excellent rail, motor, and air services throughout the nation.

The Deutsche mark (DM) is one of the world's leading currencies. It is freely convertible and its value fluctuates freely in relation to other world currencies. The inflation rate is low by world standards, averaging less than 3 percent for the period 1988–1990 and projected to be less than 5 percent for 1992–1994. Real economic growth is projected at approximately 3 percent for 1991 and beyond, after accounting for absorption of the former East Germany.

Customary sales terms are FOB (Free On Board), CFR (Cost and Freight), and CIF (Cost, Insurance, and Freight). These terms are discussed in depth in Chapter 15.

Other information of this type—on advertising, media use, marketing practices, and more—is readily available from a number of sources. In addition to those mentioned at the end of Chapter 3, you should obtain a copy of the most recent *Foreign Economic Trends and Their Implications for the United States* and the *Overseas Business Report* on your target country. They are available on the NTDB.

Money

Each foreign country has different controls on the availability of its currency. Contact your bank's international department or **foreign exchange** department for information on existing currency regulations. If your bank does not have an international department or foreign exchange department, ask your banking officer to contact the international department at its correspondent bank.[4]

When you arrive in Germany, you will need some local currency to get to your hotel, to tip for services, and for other various small purchases. Your bank, its correspondent, or a dealer in foreign exchange such as Thomas Cook Foreign Exchange (formerly Deak & Co.) can provide you with foreign currency in modest amounts. These "tip packs," if available, usually contain coin and currency of up to about US$50. The convenience overcomes the poor exchange rate.

If your bank or dealer does not have one of these packs, purchase paper currency sufficient to meet your needs on arrival. Exchange kiosks are available in airports on arrival, and exchange services are readily available at banks in Germany. American Express and other major credit cards may be used to pay for the majority of your purchases in Germany.

The Schedule

As soon as you have your tentative itinerary, ask your travel agent to book transportation and hotels. Review these arrangements with your US&FCS trade specialist to draw on his or her experience and perspective as to your scheduling. Leave ample time if you plan to visit more than one country. When your schedule is firm, send a copy to the US&FCS office in your target country. Request comments and suggestions in regard to your objectives.

---

[4]A "correspondent bank" is a larger bank that provides services to smaller banks. Services include loan participations, letter of credit issuance, export financing, clearings, and foreign exchange trading.

Veteran international travelers recommend allowing more (extra) time for each call you plan to make and more (extra) time in each city you visit. This extra time will reduce your self-imposed stress, relieve the pressure attendant to the required punctuality, and permit your calls to be more productive. Also set aside some time for recreation and relaxation; you will do a better job during working hours.

Your Company

Take complete data on your company, including its history, number of employees, production capabilities and capacities, financial condition or capabilities, banker's and other references, and any other relevant information about your firm's ability to perform. Remember, you are no longer in the United States. Your reputation in the United States or your hometown may be of little or no value to you in Germany or in any other foreign marketplace. Any quality distributor or representative will want to know your company and its reputation, just as you want that information on your counterparty.

Take company letterhead, envelopes, and more business cards than you could imagine using in a visit three times as lengthy. If feasible, have the local language translation printed on the reverse of your cards; some international airlines provide such a printing service, and your in-country hotel may arrange it on an overnight basis. The letterhead will allow official communications, an important ability when far from home.

If the language of the target country is English, take brochures. If it's German, weigh the cost of translating part of the information into German. The cost of one page of translation is nominal ($50 to $100 if nontechnical), and the impact on your German contacts will be powerful. It is a demonstration that you are serious about doing business in their country, on their terms.

If your products are such that you carry samples (recall our example of the firm that seeks to export lubricants), apply for an **ATA Carnet** or Carnet de Passage. This is a permit for temporary admission of your product under an international protocol.

Carnet de Passage

The Carnet de Passage is a document that allows you to take samples into any country subscribing to the ATA Carnet protocol. Most countries accept the carnet procedure. The admission of samples is duty free and there is no delay or hassle at the border. The carnet has a number of stubs or tickets. When you arrive in Germany, the Customs official will remove an entry ticket, stamp the carnet, and you may enter the country with your samples. Under the carnet arrangement, you must remove the samples within one year. If you do not do so, the host country will make a claim on the carnet for duty and penalties. The issuing office will then forfeit your bond or claim on the letter of credit received from your bank. When you leave the foreign country, you again present the carnet to the Customs official who will remove an exit ticket and stamp the carnet as proof that you have taken the samples out of the country.

The *Carnet de Passage* is issued by the United States Council for International Business (USCIB). Call or write for an application (see "Resources"), and the form will be sent to you. List the details of each sample and its value. A small fee is charged, and you must deposit a cash bond or letter of credit at 40 percent of the value of the samples with the USCIB.

U.S. Customs will inspect the samples and certify the carnet before your departure. The carnet is valid for 12 months from date of issue and may be used during that time in as many subscriber countries as you may wish to visit with your samples. (A list of subscribing countries is on the application form.)

On return to the United States, notify the USCIB. It will return your cash bond or letter of credit after checking the exit stamps on the carnet. Be sure a customs official in each foreign country removes an exit stub and stamps the carnet in the exit column.

If you follow these suggestions, your trip should be productive and enjoyable. Preparation is the key to this success, and research is the backbone of preparation. In their haste to nail down a deal, many companies have accelerated their foreign travel programs to meet with potential buyers or representatives. Many have come home empty-handed.

A calculated schedule for a trip, sufficient to do the critical research and preparation, will serve the U.S. company well and profitably in the long run. Knowledge of the culture and the business practices, a thorough packaging of company information and samples, and a relaxed company executive will put your company in the best possible light in the foreign environment.

Passport, Visa, and Driver's License

Don't overlook the obvious. Is your passport valid for your total trip? If not, make this a priority.

When ordering passport photos for a new passport or otherwise, have a half-dozen extra copies made. With two photos, your driver's license, and a small fee, you can obtain an international driver's license from the American Automobile Association. With this you can rent a car in your target country during the validity of the license. This is not necessary for Germany. The additional photos will be helpful if you plan to visit neighboring countries or have short-notice visa requirements.[5]

---

[5]The author was in Caracas, Venezuela, and had to make an unanticipated call in a neighboring Latin nation. A visa was required for entry, which required passport photos. The process of acquiring passport photos in an unfamiliar city, on short notice, can be chaotic. Luckily, he followed his own advice and had extras on hand.

CHECKLISTS FOR FOREIGN TRAVEL

The following checklists are appropriate for any country to which you may travel. Each point may affect the success of your trip.

Three Months before Departure

_____ 1. Have your travel agent book your travel arrangements. If the time change is four hours or more at destination, arrive either on a Friday or the day before a holiday to assure at least 48 hours of rest to compensate for jet lag.

_____ 2. Discuss your planned itinerary with the trade specialist at the US&FCS district office. Request that he or she send it to the commercial officer at the appropriate foreign service post for any changes or suggestions.

_____ 3. Have your travel agent book hotel reservations. The Gold Key Service or similar service from the US&FCS foreign post may assist with this.

_____ 4. Obtain a new passport or make sure that your existing passport will be valid for the duration of the trip. If not, renew it. Get extra passport photos.

_____ 5. If your target country requires a visa, apply to the consulate of that country in Washington D.C. Your travel agent may state that the agency can take care of this for you. *Caution:* The agency may not be aware of current regulations in a rapidly changing international environment. If you plan to travel from one country to another, make the necessary visa arrangements through the consulate of the foreign countries involved rather than through your travel agent.

_____ 6. Check with your physician. If you have a medical problem, get written information you can give to a doctor in the target country if your problem requires treatment. Have any necessary inoculations or vaccinations done at this time and have the appropriate certificates completed.

_____ 7. Study the history and social customs of the target country. Get books from the public or university library. Use the resources of the US&FCS district offices.

_____ 8. Apply for extra medical insurance, to be effective during your trip. Make sure that your medical insurance covers services provided outside the United States. Clarify what restrictions apply as to service providers, types of service, and limits.

_____ 9. If you are taking samples, apply to the U.S. Council for International Business for a *Carnet de Passage*.

Two Months before Departure

_____ 1. *Prices.* Determine your export pricing basis (see Chapter 8) and develop CIF and CFR prices from your plant to the principal ports in your target country. Freight costs will vary by the size of shipment (weight or measure), the product type, and the services provided by your forwarder. Insurance costs will vary by type of coverage. See Part Four, Movement of the Goods, for a complete discussion of these factors.

_____ 2. *Currency.* Contact your bank's foreign exchange department. Learn how any foreign exchange or currency controls affect your trip. Learn how much currency you can take in, including US$ traveler's checks. Ask about "tip packs" or similar pocket-money arrangements.

_____ 3. *Clothes.* Learn about the appropriate business attire for your target country and the season of your travel.

One Month before Departure

_____ 1. *International driver's license.* Take two passport photos and your valid driver's license to your local AAA office. An international driver's license can be issued for a nominal fee.

_____ 2. *Samples or display goods.* Obtain a *Carnet de Passage* (ATA Carnet) from the U.S. Council for International Business. Arrange for a U.S. Customs officer to be at your departure port at the time of your departure to certify the carnet, or have U.S. Customs check the goods and validate the Carnet prior to your departure.

What to Pack

_____ 1. Airline or transport tickets and hotel confirmations.

_____ 2. Business cards, company letterhead, and envelopes.

_____ 3. Small company and personal gifts.

_____ 4. Company brochures, catalog sheets, and company background information.

_____ 5. Health insurance policies or proofs of coverage.

_____ 6. Any required medication or health certificates.

_____ 7. Passport and visa(s) and extra passport photos.

_____ 8. *Carnet de Passage.*

_____ 9. International driver's license.

_____ 10. Traveler's checks and foreign currency(ies).

_____ 11. Three copies of your itinerary: one in your briefcase, one in your carry-on, and one in your other piece of luggage (if any). Be sure to leave a complete copy (with hotels, airlines, contact names, addresses, and telephone/fax numbers) at your office and at home.

On Arrival and In-Country

_____ 1. Take 24 to 48 hours to adjust, relax, and prepare.

_____ 2. Contact the U.S. Embassy or Consulate Commercial Section the first day and arrange a meeting for the next day.

_____ 3. Make notes after each contact; clear the slate for the following day's agenda. Each evening write thank-you notes to your prospects or contacts confirming your discussions.

_____ 4. Continue to remind yourself that you are in a different culture. Ethnocentrism and a self-reference criterion will create undue difficulties for you and your company. Appreciate and participate in the local social customs; accept local culture and business practices.

On Your Return to the United States

_____ 1. Take 24 to 48 hours to adjust. If your mindset or boss dictates that you must go into the office immediately, do so only to drop off your notes and business papers and to arrange meetings for the next work day. Then leave.

_____ 2. Send promised information to prospective buyers. Write to each contact confirming your interest, future contacts, and future prospects.

_____ 3. Write thank-you letters to both the trade officer at the foreign service post and the trade specialist at your local US&FCS office. Advise them of your progress and express your appreciation. This will foster improved assistance for your next trip.

_____ 4. On a regular basis, contact the trade specialist at your local US&FCS office and advise him or her of your progress with your target market(s) and prospects/clients. This regular positive contact can develop a strong and productive tie that will serve you well over time.

_____ 5. Be persistent with your foreign prospects. On a regular six- to eight-week schedule, contact all prospective foreign buyers. Send new or useful information and continue the sales process. If you have appointed an agent for a territory, send copies of all correspondence within that territory to your agent. Keep your people in the loop.

FOR THE FEMALE BUSINESS TRAVELER

The 1980s brought change in the treatment and acceptance of female business travelers. This improved degree of acceptance is increasing in the 1990s.

Equality is not the standard around the world, however, and a few cautions may be useful for the female business traveler. There are differences women need to be aware of in order to overcome certain impediments to success in the export business.

Ms. Jaime Powlesland, managing director of NTC International, Inc., Seattle, explains:

> The successful American businesswoman must find a way to balance firm professionalism with the appropriate level of femininity. Striking the proper balance can do more than simply help relations progress smoothly. A businesswoman knowledgeable about the technical aspects of the product or project as well as the corporate culture of the clients may actually be more successful than the American male in the same setting.
>
> Don't allow personal feelings about the "fairness" of the foreign socio-economic system embitter the business relationship. The female executive should, without compromising her integrity, be sensitive to her foreign counterparts' frame of reference, criteria and social mores, even if she doesn't agree with certain aspects of them.
>
> There is no doubt that women in international business face challenges that men don't encounter. With ample preparation and sensitivity to the relevant issues in each country, these can usually be overcome and everyone can focus on developing mutually profitable business relationships.

As a general guideline, women must at all times be businesslike and somewhat formal, even in informal situations. The businesswoman has to be extremely well prepared and professional at all times, perhaps better prepared than her male counterpart. At the same time the businesswoman will not be accepted as one of the boys.

In business meetings and business calls, use presentation materials such as slides, viewgraphs, audio-visuals, and other material. This will focus attention on the presentation and guide the discussion to your objective. It will move interest to the product and away from the presenter. One woman executive put it in these terms: "A woman can't cruise through a meeting the way a man may be able to." Successful females are well aware of this difficulty and have learned to deal with it in the United States.

Perceptions can be turned to a perverse advantage for the well-prepared businesswoman. In many cultures, men may "expect" weakness in a businesswoman's presentation and thereby pay more attention to the content of the presentation, perhaps looking for failure. With this focused attention, a powerful presentation can become even more effective.

The same expectations apply to the negotiating process. In the United States, female executives have proven to be strong negotiators in all fields. This strength has not been experienced in the male-dominated environments in many other nations. Women business travelers need to internalize these differences in belief and expectation and utilize them to their advantage.

Dress conservatively. Wear suits for business—no pants, no low necklines, no dresses. For informal occasions, be conservatively comfortable; again, no dresses or low necklines. For the evening, black is always appropriate; wear dresses or gowns with cap sleeves or long sleeves and a covered bodice or high neckline. Measured and conservative is the persona you should seek.

In a foreign city and alone, the businesswoman should ask the concierge about the areas of the city that are safe for a woman alone. There are two advantages: (1) You get good information on a strange city or its lesser known sites, and (2) a responsible person knows where you will be in the event of an unforseen difficulty.

The female executive needs to be certain that business is the only agenda at a business meeting. While this may continue to be an issue in the United States, it is more important in other countries where a woman in business is a new cultural role.

In Asia, businessmen look on women as subservient because that is the overriding cultural norm. In Europe, women in business are more accepted. Latin America is slow to change, with the Middle East perhaps the most difficult of all business environments for women. Women have an accepted business role in most of Eastern Europe and much of the People's Republic of China.

Asian cultures are the most divergent from U.S. culture. This issue is important because, as a region, Asia takes more than 50 percent of U.S. exports. This shift occurred in the mid-1980s. It will have long reaching effects on all of us. For women, adapting to the cultural differences with Asia will be somewhat more important and more challenging than adapting to business in Europe or Latin America. You will have to deal as a "woman businessman" for some time to come.

Do not let your gender get in the way of doing business in a foreign location. Hold your own and be professional. Be confident and assertive rather than aggressive. Treat your business associates with the respect due their positions. You will earn the respect, confidence, and consideration of your business associates that all business executives seek.

Each country and region of the world has customs and business practices that will affect the female business traveler. Learn of these by reading. Talk with your peers, contacts, and associates who have experience in your targeted part of the world. Call on the local US&FCS office and learn of any trade or business associations that focus on your target country. Meet with that group, and don't hesitate to ask about situations that concern you.

Many colleges, universities, and community colleges offer courses and training on the cultures, practices, and ethics of different countries and regions. Look into these. Your homework will pay off in productive business meetings and the development of useful business relationships with your foreign contacts.

RESOURCES

1. A number of publications offer guidance on the cultures of other nations. Among these is *Do's and Taboos Around the World* edited by Roger Axtell, published by John Wiley & Sons. Mr. Axtell offers valuable and entertaining insights into some of the many cross-cultural situations the business traveler may encounter.

2. The Atlantic Bridge (Atlantik Bruecke) publishes many useful documents on German trade customs and business etiquette, including "These Strange German Ways," "German Holidays and Folk Customs," and "Meeting German Business." The address is Atlantik Bruecke e.V., Herschredder 52, 2000 Hamburg 63, FRG.

3. Metric weights and measures can be found in Appendix G.

4. The American Chamber of Commerce in Germany has offices in Frankfurt, Frechen/Koenigsdorf, Obertshausen, Stuttgart, and Muenchen (Munich). Its U.S. representative is Mr. R. T. Thomas of Squire, Sanders & Dempsey, 1201 Pennsylvania Ave., NW, Washington, DC 20024 Tel: 202-626-6600.

5. For additional information on currency restrictions or controls, see the International Monetary Fund's *Annual Report on Exchange Arrangements and Exchange Restrictions,* available at larger public libraries and government document depositories. Address orders to International Monetary Fund Publication Services Unit, Washington, DC 20431. The price is $39.50.

6. NTC International is a subsidiary of KIRO, Inc., a multimedia corporation. NTC specializes in Japan-U.S. trade communications. The company provides U.S.- and Japanese-based translation services, cross-cultural training, and support in the negotiation process.

7. The Washington State International Trade Fair is a public/private venture to increase exports by training and taking northwest firms to international trade fairs, worldwide. Northwest firms interested in trade fair information or participation should contact Mr. R. Steve Hatch, President, Washington State International Trade Fair, 3501 First Interstate Center, Seattle, WA 98104. Tel: 206-682-6900.

8. The Trade Show Bureau is the leading national organization for trade show information, training, and participation services. Any company interested in learning how participation in an international trade show could benefit its export sales and marketing efforts should contact The Trade Show Bureau, 1660 Lincoln St., Suite 2080, Denver, CO 80264. Tel: 303-860-7626; fax: 303-860-7479.

9. Cross-cultural education and training may be available at local colleges, universities, and adult education or continuing education programs at community colleges.

10. The U.S. Council for International Business is at 1212 Avenue of the Americas, New York, NY 10036. Tel: 212-354-4480.

PART TWO
Market Development

Chapters 5 through 10 identify many of the challenges that must be addressed in the development of an export market. Each company is different; each will have a unique perspective and approach to the export business and the objectives of the firm. The following observations, by Mike Giambattista,[1] Vice President, International Sales, RAIMA Corporation, are important to all exporters of any product.

Most organizations enter export markets "passively." Domestic marketing activities such as trade shows, product press releases, trade or other media advertising invariably will attract overseas interest. Many companies often find overseas units of their domestic customers directly ordering for delivery abroad.

This "spillover"into international markets typically has not been anticipated, nor will the accompanying issues have been planned for. Even if anticipated, the international spillover causes the organization to quickly realize that there are essential differences in doing business abroad.

A legitimate response to overseas inquiries under a passive strategy is to offer the product or service *as is*. The organization in effect is selling what it already makes to new markets. Given the usual internal competition for the organization's scarce resources, a passive international strategy can be a low-risk alternative promising incremental revenues.

Organizations may plan an active strategy at the outset or it may evolve over time. Eventually, the export volume becomes significant, that is, if the international sales were lost, the organization would have to seek alternative revenues. Often the understanding that international revenues are significant coincides with management's realization that if the products were modified to meet overseas requirements, even greater market shares could be gained. The convergence of these two factors usually forces an "active" international strategy.

---

[1]Michael Giambattista has an extensive international business background: Marketing Director, HB Foods, Ireland, a division of Unilever; European Market Development Director, Omron Electric, Japan; President, Erskin Westayr Ltd, UK; President, Shakleys Corp. International B.V., Netherlands; and President, Match Inc., UK.

An active international strategy suggests that the organization either must design products to meet the needs for foreign markets or adapt what it makes to meet these needs. Within this general context, an active strategy in major selected industrial markets and a passive strategy for all other markets may be appropriate. Each planning period should evaluate and adapt the entry and follow-on strategies for each target market.

Once the general international market-entry strategy has been set, the organization next must decide upon the distribution method to be used. There are two broad choices: indirect or direct.

Indirect international distribution is the most commonly selected strategy for a variety of reasons that are well covered in this text. Indirect distribution has the advantages of relatively low capital requirements, reliance upon export specialists, and national marketing organizations. The chief disadvantage is less control of marketing by the producing organization.

Direct distribution implies ownership of the means utilized in international sales. Most organizations new to international business understandably are daunted by the tax, legal, organizational, and capital requirements associated with direct distribution. Nevertheless, most successful exporters find the need for a local presence in key overseas markets compelling in relatively short timeframes.

Regardless of the entry strategy and distribution channel selected, the exporter's success demands an awareness of and attention to the key issues covered in this text.

Of all of the issues, pricing is often the most difficult to master. Usually the first thing requested by a potential overseas prospect, price generally should be the final item discussed. Initial requests for pricing are usually to get an indication of the product's relative value *vis à vis* competition. An overseas distributor wants to know its acquisition price in order to assess potential profitability in the local market. However, until the prospective distributor's evaluation is complete, an indication of the current domestic price should suffice at the initial inquiry stage.

International pricing is and should be different from domestic pricing. An adage is applicable to the situation: "The middleman can be eliminated but not his functions." Shipping, insuring, customs clearance, local transportation, in-country marketing and sales, inventory, warranties, after-sales service, and so on are likely to be different from domestic practices. All too often exporters attempt to ignore the reality of who is taking what risks and who is responsible for what costs when setting export prices.

The local market conditions (including competition, import restrictions, distribution practices, and the marketing position chosen) will provide one framework to determine export pricing. The exporter's ex-works price, which should reflect the desired gross profit margin, provides a second. The exporter must then consider these two models and negotiate as appropriate to a "landed cost" for the importer. Every situation is a negotiation.

Since the circumstances for the same product in each overseas market will be different, it is usual to have different prices for each country. Exporters should be comfortable with this situation so long as it represents a fair and realistic assessment of the risk/return to all parties involved.

Suffice it to say, *in exporting, everything is negotiable.*

5 Direct Market Entry Strategies

Exporting is the primary strategy for introducing your product or service into a foreign market. With a successful track record in the United States, a company can use the tools presented in this book, and the abilities and skills it has developed through its U.S. business, to establish a successful export program into a number of markets.

When your export market position is solid and growing, your firm can consider other forms of market expansion. These could include joint-venture manufacturing operations with a company located in the region, licensing, franchising, or wholly-owned investments in operating subsidiaries.

The starting point is a strong export position, an excellent track record, and a reputation for performance over time. The timeframe for this accomplishment will differ by type of company. Heavy equipment manufacturers, builders, engineers, designers, and other firms with a long time horizon for their operations will have a longer timeframe than software firms, publishers, food products exporters, and sellers of seasonal products. There is no *correct* time to move to other forms of international operation, if ever. Exporting is a key activity for all of the leading U.S. international and multinational firms.

There are two modes of entry into export activity. This chapter deals with direct-market entry strategies. Chapter 6 deals with indirect market entry.

The principal characteristics of all direct market entry strategies are *control* and *risk management*. With a direct entry strategy, your firm is in control of your export selling price, promotion of the product, inventory levels, sales and receivables policies, and management of your sales force abroad. Your firm manages the risks inherent in the process. In addition to the risks associated with expanding sales into a lesser known territory (production scheduling, inventory management, etc.), they include product performance, service and repair, product liability, transportation, and payment.

DECISION FACTORS

The factors that influence the decision to pursue a direct-market entry strategy include:

Factors in Favor of Direct Market Entry

1. There is a potential for greater profit.
2. You have control over the authority given to third parties.
3. Your product will be actively promoted in the selected markets.
4. There is knowledge/measurement of performance by product segment or type and performance by sales and management personnel.

Factors against Direct Market Entry

1. It can place a tremendous strain on a company's resources.
2. It requires a significant commitment of money and time to the development and maintenance of the market.
3. Long lead times may be required.
4. It may be difficult to control your foreign representative (agent, distributor, etc.).

Your product type may determine the options you select within a direct-market entry strategy. For example, a manufacturer of consumer-pack canned food will utilize a different arrangement than a manufacturer of clothing or transportation equipment.

STRATEGIES

A direct-market entry strategy is accomplished utilizing one or more of the following arrangements.

Foreign Sales Representative

This individual or firm will represent your product, among others. The foreign sales representative will utilize your price schedules and function much the same as an independent sales rep in the United States. Use caution in the appointment: you are operating within a different legal system and your understandings based on experience and practice in the United States are not valid in any foreign market. You may not be able to control a sales territory or its exclusivity. Your product will be new to the rep and, therefore, will receive limited attention or effort until it generates sufficient commissions.

End-User Sales

If you sell heavy equipment, industrial goods, or other products with high contract prices and/or complex technical specifications, your most effective sales strategy may be direct sales to end users. Your own technical staff and sales personnel will be effective for you, complimented by a host-country or third-country national service arrangement. In purchasing your product, the end user is purchasing your commitment to continued performance, service, and attention. This package is your product. Aircraft, machine tools, engineering or management services, telecommunications, and hydro and other power systems are a few examples of products sold direct to end users.

State Buying Company

As the number of nonmarket economies decreases, the number of state buying companies will diminish. These organizations function as purchasing arms of a government. The People's Republic of China (only one example) carries out purchase activities through state companies. Purchases are made within a plan and budget, and the payment obligations are usually that of a central or regional government. Many state buying companies operate within the United States; however, they often do not publicize their state ownership or affiliation. To determine whether a nation operates in this manner, do the following:

1. Determine if the country has a controlled economy. Is it a nonmarket economy? Where are decisions made regarding your transactions?

2. Contact that country's consulate nearest your location and ask the commercial officer if his or her nation has a buying company for your industry in the United States and, if not, how you would contact the appropriate buying company.

3. Contact the country officer at the International Trade Administration in Washington, DC, and ask that officer about state buying companies.

Branch or Subsidiary Operations

This option was introduced at the beginning of the chapter. This is a high-risk, initial-entry strategy. The costs of opening a branch or creating a subsidiary in a foreign location are high. Seasoned professionals report that an effective branch or subsidiary program for a high-tech manufacturer (for example) can be launched for approximately $250,000 per year (as of 1991). Others report that executives have spent up to $1,000,000 to open a sales office in a foreign location.

One should question the competence of management with this type of disparity, particularly when the investment is in a new or untried market.[1] Management competence is the principal concern of the backers of any growing firm.

A record of successful exports into the target country is the foundation for a successful branch or subsidiary launch. Customers are in hand and revenues flow from existing activity in support of this new venture. The progression is reasonable and is in the best interests of the firm's stakeholders.

Agents or Distributors

Use of one or both of these options is the method of market entry for most exporting firms. This is the general and standard practice for even the most sophisticated and well-established U.S. exporters.

The selection of an agent or distributor must be thorough because you want to deal with a firm that will devote its interests and energies to your product, promote your interests, and succeed. (Throughout the book, I will refer interchangeably to either the *exporter* or the *vendor,* and your agent or distributor abroad may be called your *representative.*)

You may wish to have the leading representative of related products take on your products or product line. That's reasonable; however, you may find you are just another number in a catalog; you are not getting the attention and selling effort you had anticipated. You may also find yourself unable to change this relationship without some unforeseen, and often significant, "compensation" paid to the representative you wish to fire. You are especially vulnerable if your product is not well known. This lack of market presence could mean limited efforts by your representative because you may be perceived as offering limited profit opportunities as compared to better known products.

A smaller firm may be a better match because you are relatively more important to that smaller representative. You may offer new or expanded product and market opportunities to a newer firm or a firm seeking to expand either its product lines or territories. The variables here are the type of market coverage you need, the service and warranty support your products require (critical over time), and the financial capacity of your representative.

AGENT OR DISTRIBUTOR?

In order to make the choice between the services of an agent or a distributor for a target market, work through the following comparison process to

[1]This is one of many areas where the guidance of an experienced international trade consultant or advisor can be valuable.

determine which best suits your needs. The statements are general truths, subject to change by the operative laws and customs of each country. Your agreement may contain a combination of these characteristics and appear to be one form while bearing the name of the other.[2]

Distributor

1. It purchases goods from you and carries them as inventory.
2. Payment arrangements relate to delivery of the goods to the distributor.
3. The distributor controls the resale price.
4. The distributor takes title and control of the goods.
5. Risk of loss is attached to ownership and possession of the goods.
6. Antitrust laws make it difficult for exporters to restrain the distributor's sales outside the stated country or territory.
7. Trademark use is more restrictive than for an agent. The distributor may not use the trademark as part of its own trade name.
8. The distributor is more likely than an agency to staff and maintain a full-time marketing effort. The distributor is more likely to stock other product lines.
9. The distributor controls the in-country marketing methods.
10. The distributor is self-financed and may require less financial support from the exporter.
11. The distributor operates as an independent contractor.
12. The distributorship relationship is assignable and transferable.
13. Product warranty and service are provided by the distributor.
14. The distributor provides better insulation from liability for the exporter.
15. The distributor is a better insulator from local taxation.
16. In some jurisdictions, the distributorship is easier to terminate.

Agent

1. The agent does not inventory goods, or goods are carried as consignment inventory.

[2]Adapted from works by Melvin Jay Simburg, Partner, Simburg, Ketter, Sheppard, and Purdy, P.S., Seattle, WA. Copyright © 1985, 1987.

2. Payment is based on delivery to the ultimate buyer.

3. The exporter sets the retail price.

4. The exporter retains title and control of the goods.

5. The risk of loss, of the goods and of the payment, remains with the exporter.

6. Exclusive marketing territories may be more readily established.

7. An agent may operate under the trademark and trade name of the exporter.

8. An agency may or may not be exclusive, and the time devoted to a product may vary accordingly.

9. The exporter controls the marketing methods.

10. The exporter finances the agent's operations.

11. The agent may operate as an independent contractor or as an employee.

12. The agency is personal and may not be transferred or assigned.

13. The exporter arranges local warranty and service.

14. The exporter has potential vicarious liability to the end user.

15. The exporter has the potential for local taxation.

16. Some jurisdictions make termination difficult.

Other Considerations

In either the distributor or agent alternative, you cannot expect yours to be the only product handled, although yours should be the only one in your line. This is a primary factor in your selection of either a distributor or agent. It is also paramount in your choice among distributors or among agents. Complimentary product lines will help your sales; the representative will attract more potential buyers with a broader offering.

Financing is another area where differences can exist. An agent expects you to give terms to the buyer (a form of end-user financing), and a distributor may expect you to give him or her terms as part of your relationship. The impact on your cash flow is not appreciably different in either case. However, while the distributor may arrange buyer financing as part of his or her marketing package, that same distributor may also look to you to provide end-user financing in support of his or her sales activities. This can be an unforseen extension of your cash receipts cycle or an effective sales strategy (Chapter 12, Financing in the Marketing Mix).

THE SELECTION PROCESS

When you have determined whether you will use an agent or a distributor, you can begin the process of selecting the right one. You should have some well-focused and clearly defined criteria for making this selection decision. Because you have gone through the steps in Chapters 1 through 4, you have begun to acquire a data base of potential representatives.

You may have used the Agent-Distributor Service of the US&FCS (see Chapter 3). You may have attended one or more foreign trade shows and met potential representatives there (Chapter 4). Use other informed sources to identify prospective agents or distributors: other suppliers, exporters of complimentary products, industry experts, your industry association, international trade groups, your commercial bank, American Chambers of Commerce Abroad, the Foreign Traders Index of the National Trade Data Bank (FTI of the NTDB in governmentspeak), trade and commercial directories of target countries, international trade consultants, and potential end users or buyers. Manufacturers and exporters of complimentary products are an excellent resource. In many industries, there is a close and frequent interchange of noncompetitive information among participants. This is particularly true in the export business.

With this multiple sourcing for prospective representatives, you may see an overlap—companies mentioned more than once, favorably or not. You can begin to narrow the data to those well spoken of by your sources.

In the selection process, the potential representative will also want to know about you and the products you sell. This is a two-sided relationship. I recommend that you develop a package of information about your company and your products. This package should include some or all of the following:

1. A cover letter introducing your firm and your objectives.

2. Product brochures and catalog sheets.

3. Background on the company: ownership, management, market position, time in business, indication of capacity.

4. Background on the product and the manufacturing process (or services, processes, and credentials).

5. Other information you believe a potential business associate will wish to know.

6. A dealer/distributor questionnaire/survey.

Government and private-sector advisors usually instruct new-to-export or expanding firms to include complete price lists and *pro forma* quotations with this initial package of information. In some instances, this is effective. In other circumstances, it is counterproductive. A price list or a *pro forma* may indicate a lack of flexibility, a message that you are not willing to negotiate.

The price of your product to any potential dealer, distributor, agent, or end user is made up of a number of components, such as order size, packaging, mode of shipment, time of year, special marks or labels, terms of payment, discounts, competitive pricing in the target market, discount structures applicable in the target country, and more. These are addressed in Chapter 8, Pricing for Profits.

In the early negotiations with potential representatives, use care in the discussion of pricing. Flexibility and the willingness to negotiate are important variables in establishing a strong working relationship. A firm stand on pricing, however well intended, may portray a corporate attitude that the potential partner may find unacceptable on its face. A workable alternative is to indicate the retail or end-user pricing of the product in the U.S. marketplace. This will give your contact a useful perspective. He or she can slot your product into his or her known universe (marketplace and product line), and respond intelligently to your query.

THE SURVEY

As part of the investigative process, you will want the representative to tell you about his or her business and provide you with information that you can use for evaluation purposes. You will want to compare potential representatives with each other.

At the point where you and a potential representative get serious, you should begin a process for your dealings that *in itself* informs the representative that you are serious; have the potential representative complete an application, survey, or questionnaire (Figure 5.1). If the prospect will not complete this type of information request, you must do one of three things:

1. Ask yourself why and resolve it satisfactorily.

2. Ask the representative for an explanation, which must make sense, be complete, and satisfy all your questions. Possible reasons for the failure to answer could include competitive information, proprietary information, lack of a track record, or a blemished past. It's important to get complete and useful answers.

3. Move on to other potential representatives, those who are forthcoming and honest.

The completed survey will give you useful information for evaluating the prospect. Figure 5.1 is a questionnaire structured for a company in the electronics and communications industry. Response to the survey will equip

[Company Letterhead]
SURVEY AND REQUEST FOR INFORMATION
Please return completed questionnaire/application to:

_____

_____

GENERAL INFORMATION
Name and address of your company:

_____ Telephone: _____

Address: Telex: _____

_____ Answer back: _____

_____ Cable: _____

_____ Fax: _____

Country: _____

Company organization: Proprietorship _____ Corporation _____

Partnership _____ Limited Liability_____

Date organized _____

Principal officers or owners:

(1) Name: _____   (2) Name: _____

     Title: _____   Title: _____

     Home address: _____   Home address: _____

     _____   _____

     _____   _____

     Home phone: _____   Home phone: _____

Figure 5.1 A Dealer/Distributor Application Form. This sample uses the electronics/communications industry for illustrative purposes only. (Adapted from samples provided by Richard Powell, District Director [retired], US&FCS, San Diego, CA, and Vice President [retired], International Marketing, Cubic Corporation, San Diego, CA.)

(3) Name: _____   (4) Name: _____

     Title: _____   Title: _____

     Home address: _____   Home address: _____

     _____   _____

     _____   _____

     Home phone: _____   Home phone: _____

If you are a subsidiary, list name and address of your parent company: _____

_____

Describe your company's major business activity: _____

_____

_____

List all your company's branch offices: _____

_____

_____

(use additional sheets if necessary)

Please identify the individual(s) in your company responsible for sales, service, and administration:

Sales: _____

Service: _____

Administration: _____

FINANCIAL INFORMATION

Sales (US$) for last year: _____

Sales (US$) for current year: _____

Sales forecast (US$) for next year: _____

Your company's paid-in capital (US$): _____

Figure 5.1 Continued

Bank name and complete address: _____

_____

Business references, including name, address, and contact person:

(a) _____

(b) _____

(c) _____

Please attach current financial information and/or annual report.

MARKETING INFORMATION

Are you currently a representative, dealer, or distributor in

[communications equipment]? Yes _____ No _____

Describe type of equipment sold, including brand names: _____

_____

_____

_____

How long have you been in the [communications business]? _____ Years

Check below those government or private organizations with whom you have a good current liaison:

Army _____ Navy _____ Air Force _____

Commercial _____

Other _____

Are you currently an agent, distributor, or representative of any other company that manufactures products similar to ours?

Yes _____ No _____ If yes, please name the companies: _____

_____

Do you have any objection to our contacting any such principals?

Yes _____ No _____

What is your geographic sales area for the above listed products?

_____

_____

Figure 5.1 Continued

What are projected sales of these products for the next fiscal year (US$)?

_____

_____

Will you maintain a [stock or supply] of equipment in your country for demonstration? Yes _____ No _____

Please describe your product display facility and/or product demonstration procedures: _____

_____

_____

TECHNICAL INFORMATION
(be as specific as necessary in this section)

Do you have your *own* service facility and workshop for repairs and overhaul of [HF/SSB and other radio and electronic equipment]?

Yes _____ No _____ If your answer is no, do you contract with an outside service workshop? Yes _____ No _____

If yes, give the name and address of the workshop: _____

_____

Company: _____   Telephone: _____

Address: _____   Telex/Fax: _____

_____   Cable: _____

Person to contact: _____

If you do not have a service facility, are you willing to establish one for support of our products? Yes ____ No ____

If yes, when: _____

Complete the following if you now have a service facility:

TEST EQUIPMENT FOR SERVICING HF/SSB AND OTHER RADIO AND ELECTRONIC INSTALLATION AND SERVICING

ITEM	MODEL	SPECIFICATIONS
(a) RF Signal Generator	_____	Freq. Range _____

Figure 5.1 Continued

ITEM	MODEL	SPECIFICATIONS
(b) Oscilloscope	_____	Bandwith _____
(c) Frequency Counter	_____	Freq. Range _____
(d) Wattmeter	_____	Watts _____
(e) Dummy Load	_____	Watts _____
(f) VTVM	_____	_____
(g) RF Voltmeter	_____	_____
(h) Audio VTVM	_____	_____
(i) Workshop DC Power Supply	_____	___ to ___ VDC at _____
(j) Spectrum Analyzer	_____	_____
(k) Other	_____	
	_____	
	_____	

Please attach a list of your test equipment, if available.
[List the types, by model and specifications, of the equipment you would expect to see listed for the service capacities you seek. Be sure to leave space for and ask the respondent to list other equipment they may have. Use as much space as necessary.]

How long have you serviced or installed HF/SSB transceivers? _____ Years
How long have you serviced or installed *other* radio and electronic equipment? _____ Years

[Our company] promises to keep the contents of the questionnaire confidential. Please attach any comments or documents helpful to our evaluation. Thank you. Questionnaire completed by:

Name: _____

Title: _____

Signature: _____ Date: _____

Figure 5.1 Continued

you with necessary information to learn more about your prospective business partner. You may wish to ask for more, or less, information than this sample. Modify it to your needs. You may wish to focus on the respondent's marketing and distribution networks or other product lines represented, with less emphasis on service or repair capabilities. Ask what you need to know in order to make an informed and reasoned decision.

The focus of the questionnaire for an agent arrangement would differ in that an agent generates sales and does not hold inventory, does not provide service, and does not provide warranty support.

TERRITORIAL FACTORS

Before you make your final selection of a representative, communicate with the candidates and discuss the critical factors in your decision-making process. One of those critical factors will be the territory granted your new representative.

The representative firm will often request a market territory that may exceed its ability in terms of knowledge of the market and contacts, facilities, and personnel. This is a particular caution when entering Europe. The reduction of internal barriers does not overcome the invisible boundaries of cultures, geographic concentrations, languages, and history. Just as your U.S. representatives handling Texas and Pennsylvania differ, so too will your representation in northern and southern Germany.

Your selection must be made with great care. Speed at this point is perilous. Your chosen representative is your sole voice, your presence, in that country or territory. The market's perception of you, your company, and your product line is based solely on the skills and acumen of your representative. *The representative is your company* in these foreign markets.

Termination laws vary by country. This is another reason for taking extra care in your selection, so that changes will not have to be made. Seek the advice of the US&FCS commercial officer in the country, the International Chamber of Commerce, the American Chamber of Commerce in that country, and from others who export related product lines to that country. Then, if necessary, obtain advice from an attorney in the target country and from competent counsel in the United States. The laws, regulations, and practices of the target country will often control the nature of your relationships in that country; those laws, regulations, and practices are always different from those in the United States.

MEETING THE REPRESENTATIVE

Once you have a good feel for who will represent you in your target market, it is time to go and meet with your future partner. This may be your first, second, or later trip to the target country. You may have done exploratory work by attending trade shows, industry exhibits, or international conventions. One or more trips may have been taken to meet with and cull prospects. This current trip will give you a chance to see your potential representative in action, on his or her home turf, in the competitive arena. It will be a very useful experience. The costs you incur on this trip are well spent in the assurance that you have chosen the right representation or that you have protected yourself from selecting the wrong representative.

This trip is important from another standpoint: Your potential representative will use your trip as an opportunity to make a decision about you and your company. Each of you has a decision to make.

If you have interviewed more than one firm on this trip, homework is in order. On your return, review the qualifications and characteristics of the candidates. Use the objective information you have obtained and the subjective information from your meetings to make your selection. Because the agent/distributor agreement is a touchstone for the future growth of your export sales and your presence in that target country, do not cut corners. Negotiate an effective agreement and prepare to profit from a successful relationship.

THE WRITTEN AGREEMENT

A written agreement is a mandatory part of the arrangement you have with your representative. The duties and responsibilities of each party differ significantly. The agreement should set these out and cover some basic issues common to either an agency or distributor agreement. This agreement should be finalized early in the relationship.

The most successful agency or distributor agreements are those that are least used or referred to after signature. Unfortunately, certain problems of international business dealings, such as distance, time, language, culture, and the expectations of both the representative and the exporter will lead to problems in even the best of arrangements.

The Basic Agreement

The basic agreement should resolve the primary areas of concern. To avoid extreme problems, identify these issues early in your process, evaluate your options, select the best method of representation for your purposes, and strike the most workable agreement. Include these basics:

1. *Scope of the relationship.* Responsibilities of the vendor, the buyer/distributor, or the agent.
2. *Term of the relationship.* Length in time (or in unit volume or sales volume) and frequency of review periods.

3. *Language of the agreement.* Which language is binding?

4. *Territory.* Is the agreement exclusive or nonexclusive for the territory? A nonexclusive agreement in writing gives you the option to add a distributor or agent if performance is lacking, while your verbal commitment is a moral obligation to retain exclusivity as long as performance warrants. This is done frequently when the product is an industry leader or is otherwise well known.

5. *Marketing and sales aids.* Which party is responsible for these sales, marketing, and promotional materials? How will the costs be allocated?

6. *Training and quality control.* The exporter is responsible for training the agent or distributor, providing quality control programs, and keeping the representative current on the product, its applications, and its requirements.

7. *Fees and pricing.* The fee structure is set out for the agent. For the distributor, the costing of the products, market pricing range, discounts, and other factors are covered.

8. *Dispute resolution.* This is one of the more important issues. When you and your representative disagree, how will you proceed with the courts and legal systems? What role will arbitration play? There are international arbitration groups active worldwide. The International Chamber of Commerce, headquartered in Paris, is the major international arbiter of disputes. The American Arbitration Association in New York is the principal U.S.-based arbiter of disputes. If you decide on arbitration as the dispute-resolution procedure, agree on the place of arbitration and the process of selecting arbiters. There are a variety of selection arrangements.

9. *Warranty and claims.* What are the responsibilities of the parties to repair, replace, service, and upgrade products?

10. *Product liability.* Increasing in importance in foreign markets, this issue must be resolved early on. Resolution may be based on the laws and practices of the target country, which may constrict the exporter's options.

11. *Termination.* You and your representative must set down the events that justify termination prior to the end of the term of the agreement, or provisions for adequate notice if a fixed term is not established.

12. *Trademarks, patents, copyrights, and trade secrets.* The responsibilities of the agent or distributor in obtaining the right to use your property to sell must be determined. Caution! Acquisition of the right to a trademark in a country may transfer ownership of that trademark to

the acquirer in that country. Consult competent legal counsel on this issue.

13. *Record keeping.* The exporter and the buyer or agent should keep simultaneous records of their transactions and enjoy the right to review each other's.

14. *Legal jurisdiction.* This is the basic issue of the law of the agreement. It also pertains to dispute resolution. The United States is a common-law country. If the agreement comes under the jurisdiction of a codified-law country, a different and unanticipated outcome could result. Language of the agreement is not at issue in this circumstance.

Variable Factors

There are a number of variables to any agreement. The principal factors are set out for reference. Consider these and others appropriate to your situation early on in the negotiation process. Each can involve significant costs and risks.

1. *Territorial definition and exclusivity.* The issue of exclusivity, if any, should conform to the antitrust laws of the United States and the target country. There is significant case and treaty law in place that will enable the careful establishment of a meaningful and enforceable agreement.

2. *Resale price maintenance.* National legislation often prohibits (France and Japan) or significantly restricts (Germany and Italy) resale price maintenance. The Single Market Directives will dictate resale price maintenance practices throughout the European Community. At this writing, there is no legislation on European Community pricing practices other than two articles of the Treaty of Rome and a directive on "transparency of pricing" practices.

3. *Returns and rejects.* The cost and burden of handling and disposing of returned goods may be significantly greater in foreign markets because of transportation costs, special modifications made in order to sell into a particular market, and the risk of finding an alternative buyer for the product in that (or a nearby) market without some degree of rework. Responsibilities for handling these items should be clearly stated in the agreement.

4. *Advertising and promotion.* The responsibilities of each party in terms of the nature of the programs, the authority to develop and modify a program, translation of sales materials, and periodic review of the programs should be clearly stated.

5. *Delivery and payment.* The factors of distance, foreign exchange risks that currently exist and may exist in the future, and import or export restrictions require special attention in the agreement.

6. *Ownership of the distributorship.* The agreement may appropriately include clauses that protect the exporter against transfer of ownership of a distributorship to an unknown or undesirable third party. This is particularly important where a market is dependent on the reputation and quality of the distributor. If the market develops, the exporter may be interested in acquisition, joint venture, or another form of ownership. This should be addressed in the agreement rather than later.

7. *Compliance with applicable laws and regulations and protection of proprietary products.* Responsibility for compliance with indigenous laws and regulations should lie clearly with the representative. Patents, trademarks, and copyrights should be registered by the owner with the proper agencies. The use, control, and return of these property rights should be covered in the agreement.

Termination: The Legal Aspect

Since the mid-1940s, there has been a proliferation of laws dealing with the termination of agency and distributor agreements. The beneficiaries of these laws are the agents and distributors who are subject to termination. These laws can typically override the provisions of the agreement if there is a conflict. These laws can also cause financial burden for the vendor in terms of the compensation that must be paid.

Other countries do not impose unusual financial burdens on the exporter or otherwise penalize or preclude the termination of an agency or distributor agreement. These countries generally believe that the parties to that contract act freely in negotiating and achieving that contract. They also believe this freedom includes the right to identify the causes for a termination and that the damages are payable by the offending party. Most of the countries in this category operate under Anglo-Saxon common-law principles, although some civil-law countries in Latin America, Europe (remember the effects of EC 92), Africa, and Asia also support the right to contractual freedom on the issue of termination of agency/distributor contracts.

The International Trade Administration of the U.S. Department of Commerce conducted a survey of contract termination laws and reported the following common characteristics:

1. All of these laws tend to strengthen the representative's position under the contract, requiring the vendor to compensate the representative based on a schedule of rates for damages or losses caused by termination of the agreement without *just* cause. These protective laws define the

term *just cause* or its equivalent, and this definition takes precedence even in situations where the contract has been terminated according to the law or the terms of the contract. Such laws then list and describe the reasons and situations under which an agency agreement may be validly terminated.

2. Some laws declare that mandatory compensation, and perhaps other rights, be granted to the representative.

3. Some legislation establishes the law of the enacting state as the sole applicable law and prohibits the parties from electing the laws of another jurisdiction to govern the contract. In these situations, you cannot demand that the jurisdiction be the United States.

4. Some laws place agents on the same footing as employees. The agents then have the benefit of local labor laws governing dismissal and compensation for discharge without just cause. Again, these laws override the stipulations of the contract.

5. Some laws require that the representative be given notice of termination some time prior to the effective date. Required compensation may be in the form of accrual of commissions during the notice period, payment for goodwill generated by the representative during the life of the agreement, or compensation in the form of a pension.

6. Some laws allow the representative to contest a notice of termination by submitting the controversy to arbitration to determine whether the principal has just cause to terminate.

These six items give you a sampling of the complexities of dealing with a foreign representative under a contractual arrangement.

The most successful arrangements build on mutual respect, trust, and understanding. They require little or no reference to the agreement once it's signed. Early recognition of the most common problems—distance, culture, performance expectations, competition, and quality—will help the exporter and representative maintain a good and effective working relationship.

Summary Checklist for Agreements

The following checklist outlines the principal points for inclusion in a comprehensive agreement between a U.S. exporter and a foreign sales representative. Each situation may call for a different emphasis within the agreement. The exporter should consult with advisors knowledgeable in international contract law.

    I. Basic Information
        A. The date of the agreement

    B. Identifications of the parties to the agreement

    C. The purpose of the agreement

 II. Character or Nature of the Appointment

    A. Distributor or agent

    B. Independent contractor or employee

    C. Exclusive or non-exclusive for the territory

    D. Products covered by the agreement

    E. The right to represent additional products or complimentary or competing product lines

III. Territory

    A. The geographic scope of the territory

    B. Rights of the exporter

      1. Same territory, same product, other representative

      2. Same territory, other product, other representative

    C. Exclusivity of territory for sales by others from outside the territory

    D. The right or intention to expand into other territories

IV. Duties of the Exporter

    A. Refer sales inquiries to representative

    B. Furnish pricing, delivery, technical, and general product information, including specifications, brochures, and catalogs

    C. Keep representative apprised of new product/process developments that may enjoy foreign markets

    D. Maintain updates and modifications to agreement products

    E. Provide technical assistance, training, and guidance as to product, storage, handling, marketing, and installation

    F. Provide up-to-date costing and charge schedules for above

    G. Fill all orders promptly in accordance with agreement

    H. Right to make direct sales and credit representative

 V. Duties of the Sales Representative (Distributor or Agent)

    A. Use best efforts to sell and promote

    B. Achieve purchase/sale quota requirements

    C. Sales staffing required

    D. Service staffing required

    E. Product representation at trade fairs/shows

    F. Limitations on rights to warrant product or delivery

    G. Sales reporting and forecasts

    H. Maintenance of customer lists

    I. Restrictions as to customers within the territory

1. U.S. military or other installation

2. Sales outside the territory or for use or resale outside the territory [also see Chapter 18, Licensing Your Exports]

J. Inventory control

K. Quality control

L. Trademark use restrictions

M. Confidentiality and protection of intellectual or industrial property rights

N. Prior approval requirements for labeling, packaging, packing, and marking

VI. Pricing and Terms

   A. Price basis

      1. Most competitive net price or other basis

   B. Quotation periods and frequency of variance

   C. Payment by representative to exporter

   D. Payment by exporter to representative

   E. Samples and payment policies

   F. Terms and manner of payment [also see Chapter 11]

      1. Price and payment in U.S. dollars or other currency

      2. Payment due dates, discount schedules

      3. Letter of credit criteria

      4. Pricing and payment policies for customer of agents

VII. Delivery [see Part Four]

   A. Terms and location, i.e., CIF, FOB, EX-DOCK, etc.

   B. Transportation, insurance, shipping dates

   C. Delivery of partial shipments

   D. Reasons for delay or nondelivery

   E. Transfer of title

   F. Bearer of risk of loss, if not set out above

   G. Required notifications

VIII. Inspection

   A. Location

   B. Independent agencies for the inspection of goods or inventory

   C. Notification period regarding defective merchandise

   D. Return or repair/storage policies

   E. Repair, credit, or replacement

IX. Warranty

   A. Warranty of exporter to representative

B. Warranty of representative to customer

C. Responsibilities for provision of warranty service

D. Variations in warranty by type of sale

E. Sharing of warranty expense

F. Manufacturer's indemnification and hold-harmless of representative

X. Industrial and Intellectual Property Rights

    A. Acknowledgment of exporter's ownership of all rights in trademarks, tradenames, patents, copyrights, trade secrets, and related documentation and literature

    B. Responsibility for obtaining foreign patents, trademarks, and copyrights

    C. Scope of permission for representative's use

    D. Maintenance procedure for confidentiality and protection of intellectual property rights

    E. Responsibility for reporting, prosecuting, or otherwise preventing infringement or unauthorized disclosure or use, and cost thereof

XI. Noncompetition

    A. Competing or similar products inside or outside territory

    B. Geographic scope of restrictions after termination

    C. Time period of noncompete restrictions after termination

    D. Restrictions on disclosure of industrial or intellectual property rights and other forms of confidential and proprietary information

XII. Accounting

    A. Periodic accounting

    B. Substantive content

    C. Documents to be furnished

    D. Inspection and independent auditing

XIII. Allocation of Duties

    A. Rights and responsibilities as to advertising

    B. Rights and responsibilities as to remarketing

    C. Rights and restrictions on assignment

    D. Responsibilities as to financing of sales and collection of receivables

XIV. Government Approvals [See Chapter 18, Licensing Your Exports]

    A. U.S. export control compliance and licenses are responsibility of exporter

        1. Agreement contingent upon approvals

    B. Representative to comply with all restrictions of whatever type and nature

    C. Representative to obtain all necessary import permits and licenses, and comply therewith

    D. Representative to obtain and comply with all necessary licenses and permits to market in the territory

E. Representative to pay all duties, excise, income, sales, and other taxes imposed within the territory, and hold exporter harmless therefrom

F. Exporter to pay all duties, excise, income, sales, and other taxes imposed by jurisdictions within the United States and hold the representative harmless therefrom

XV. Term and Termination

A. Term (months, years) of the agreement

B. Renewals (not automatic)

C. Notice periods

D. Termination upon failure to agree

1. Quotas

2. Prices

3. Products included or excluded

4. Other bases

E. Termination for cause

1. Failure to meet quota

2. Cure period for failure to meet quota

3. Cessation of business by either party

4. Failure to secure/renew required licenses and permits

5. Changes in tax laws or currency control causing a material adverse change and undue burden on one or both of the parties

6. Violations of term(s) of this agreement and failure to cure

F. Procedure on termination

1. Payment of all sums when due

2. Return of all proprietary and confidential information

3. Return of all product literature, brochures, price lists, sales tools, and other aids

4. Discontinue use of marks and indications of affiliation

5. Exporter option to reacquire inventories; return of all consigned merchandise

6. Listing of all outstanding quotes and orders to exporter; credit on these outstandings to the representative

XVI. Foreign Corrupt Practices Act

A. Representative acknowledges act and its provisions and agrees to comply

B. Violation is cause for termination without cure

C. Exporter held harmless from loss or damages arising from representative's violations of the act

XVII. Dispute Resolution

A. Friendly negotiations

B. Arbitration by a designated arbitral association

      C. Arbitration under specified rules of arbitration

      D. Location of arbitration or court proceedings

      E. Enforcement of awards and jurisdiction thereof

      F. Recovery of costs and expenses by prevailing party

      G. Locus of governing law

XVIII. Limitation on Damages

      A. No liability for delay beyond reasonable control

      B. No incidental or consequential damages

      C. Responsibilities of each party for own operating expenses

XIX. Integration Clause

This agreement contains the entire understanding between the parties and replaces and supercedes all prior or contemporaneous written or oral statements and understandings; there are no other agreements, representations, or warranties not set forth herein.

XX. Notices and Signatures

      A. Manner of communication and timing

      B. Names and addresses to receive notices

      C. Authorized signatures.[3]

CONTRACTS FOR THE INTERNATIONAL SALE OF GOODS[4]

On January 1, 1988, the United Nations Convention on Contracts for the International Sale of Goods (CISG) became effective. Contracting States, signatories to the CISG, apply the CISG to their international trade transactions. The CISG is parallel in many respects to the Uniform Commercial Code; however, there are important divergences. As of this writing, there are 32 signatory countries (plus the former USSR).

The CISG applies to sales of goods between a business in the United States and a business in a signatory country. In addition, the CISG applies in many transactions in which one of the parties is not located in a Contracting State, but the "choice-of-law" clause or "conflicts-of-law" rules require the contract to be governed by the law of a Contracting State.

Unless elected by a choice-of-law clause, the CISG does not apply to U.S. domestic transactions or to U.S. business transactions with nonsignatory countries. Sales to consumers of consumer products, sales of securities, sales

[3]Entire checklist copyright © 1985, 1987 Melvyn Jay Simburg of Simburg, Ketter, Haley, Sheppard & Purdy, P.S., Seattle, WA.

[4]From information under copyright provided by Melvyn Jay Simburg, Partner, Simburg, Ketter, Sheppard & Purdy, P.S., Seattle, WA. Copyright © 1985, 1987.

of vessels, and sales by auction are excluded from coverage of the CISG. The CISG also may be specifically excluded by contract language.

The CISG is an accepted form of international sales contract supported by agreements among the signatory nations. Your legal counsel or law department can assist you with the application of the CISG to your agent/distributor situation.

MANAGING THE REPRESENTATIVE

You have selected the company you believe to be the right agent or distributor to represent you in the target country. You have negotiated and executed a sound workable agreement. Well done!

You have completed the first stage of your responsibilities to the relationship. Now is the time to followup; this is where many manufacturers and exporters fail. If you want success, you must provide active support of the representative's efforts on your behalf. Supply him or her with all of the sales aids you have, translated as agreed. Answer each letter, telex, fax, or telephone message when it is received. Acknowledge each order immediately and state in your response the date you expect to ship. (One successful exporter has a *maximum* two-hour turnaround on any international queries.)

Above all, whether weekly, semimonthly, or on a prearranged schedule, send a copy of each invoice for shipments made against his orders or instructions. This has a double impact. First, it assures your representative that you are giving good, perhaps priority, service and it keeps interest and enthusiasm high. Second, the representative can notify purchasers of definite arrival times. Service to customers builds loyalty and repeat business.

On a regular and prearranged basis, send your representative a check, bank draft, or bank wire to pay any commissions or fees owing, along with a copy of every invoice for goods shipped to the representative's territory (as noted above, plus any direct shipments you have made into the territory).

If you are selling through a distributor, you will not be making commission payments. However, the shipment information is critical to your relationship in each market. Send the activity summary to assure the distributor that you are aware of both the contribution the distributor is making to the company and the contribution the company is making to the distributor.

You may receive orders directly from firms in the territory. These buyers may have learned of your product from the representative or from other sources such as trade journals or your competition. Be sure that (1) the goods are shipped and a copy of the invoice and the correct commission for the order is sent directly to the representative, or (2) the goods are shipped in accordance with your distributor's standard procedures such that the distributor can bill the buyer directly.

If you have never before had business from the buyer, contact your representative, give full details of the order, and ask whether the goods are to be shipped. This is important. Your representative may have chosen the best buyer in one market area and given an exclusive on your products. The order you received could be from a competitor going around your representative. Shipment without notification and approval from your representative could damage the representative's efforts in the territory. This would also put your relationship with the representative at risk. Don't let enthusiasm get in the way of good business practice.

A good representative gives its customers quality service, which is based in large part on information that enables it to manage the business and customer relations. If your representative knows, from your order-response system, where and when all shipments to the territory are moving, the size of the shipments, and planned shipment dates, internal shipments can be planned to ensure that all clients have sufficient product (yours) to keep their production line working. This leads to more loyalty and more profitable orders.

In the same vein, follow your representative's shipping instructions even if they make no sense to your sales or shipping departments. For example, the representative, a buyer of high-priced consumer electronics in the U.S. Virgin Islands, consistently demands that his purchases be shipped by U.S. mail. His supplier, the exporter, ships by air express thinking he has done the buyer a service. Not so! The buyer is upset because he is in a U.S. territory and the U.S. Postal Service provides domestic-rate service. This more than offsets the small increase in time taken to receive the goods.

The buyer, the representative, knew exactly what he wanted; the exporter erred to the detriment of the relationship. It's important to make every reasonable effort to perform in accordance with your buyer's instructions.[5]

Your foreign representative is equal in importance to your most important representatives in the United States. Your representative is *you* in that territory. Make every effort to keep your representative plugged into the information flow on changes to products, pricing, sales strategies, point-of-sale and point-of-purchase materials, advertising, and promotional programs. Ship export orders by the first possible transport, and keep your representative fully informed on the status of each order.

If your agent or distributor is not producing satisfactory results, investigate first, then deal with it. With accurate information, you can take timely and effective steps to correct a negative situation. Perhaps the fault lies within your office. Investigate this prior to contacting your representative.

---

[5]A particular exception: The U.S. government has two sets of Anti-Boycott legislation, each of which imposes punitive damages on those firms that violate these laws. Please refer to Chapter 11, Financing Techniques, for additional information.

If your officers and employees are not at fault, have not failed to provide the highest quality service and support, then contact the representative. Start with an encouraging letter, as there may be extenuating circumstances. Be positive and work with the representative to resolve any problems that are brought up—with the product, the promotional materials and support, or with the representatives operation. Cancel the contract or relationship only as a last resort.

Arrange for and conduct regular training programs in the representative's location and at your company offices. This will ensure that a trained sales and service organization is representing your product. It will also build loyalty on the part of the representative. If you are in a highly technical field, these programs should be extensive and frequent. Your representative is an important part of your organization and deserves every reasonable opportunity to succeed.

If sales, service, or other performance goals are met or exceeded, recognize this achievement just as you would with your domestic distribution organization. Trips to the company for additional or special training and orientation are appropriate.

When you travel to the representative's country, plan to include the representative's spouse in any social events, if appropriate to do so *in the culture of that country*. Small gifts for their children will be a long-remembered courtesy.

Join your representative on sales calls to meet with principal clients and prospects. This company support will strengthen your representative's stature in the local market, which will benefit your company. Consider joint participation in the appropriate regional, national, or international trade fairs. Work the booth and show in conjunction with your representative.

Small courtesies are long remembered. On sales calls or contacts, take notes and follow up promptly, with copies to your representative. After social events, be sure to telephone your host the next day and express your appreciation. Then write thank-you notes either before you leave the country or immediately after your return to your office. Few executives do these simple things that can add great value to international relationships.

ADVERTISING ABROAD

Advertising abroad introduces a number of new issues with which you must deal. Among them are legal and tax considerations, language limitations, cultural diversity, media limitations, and production and cost limitations.

In most countries, numerous channels can be used for advertising. As a rule, the less developed the country, the less sophisticated the media and its application. The many open avenues include newspapers, magazines, radio, television, cinema, sound trucks, town criers, billboards, in-store displays, coupons and free samples, direct mail, and trade fairs.

Often, a market survey or market research is needed to determine which option(s) will be most effective. Use of an experienced global advertising agency or a competent in-country firm may eliminate the need for the survey, if the firm has experience with your industry in your target country (not always the case).

If your target country has a low literacy rate, printed material will have limited impact. If it's also a low-income country, radio or television promotion may not be feasible. This will drive you to the use of sound trucks, town criers, or any number of variations including the use of cinema. The point is that the economic and cultural characteristics of the marketplace will determine the appropriate advertising and promotional options.

Strategies will differ by product type:

1. Industrial or commercial goods will be promoted more effectively through personal sales techniques, industry or business sector publications, or other targeted media, much the same as you would for the U.S. marketplace.

2. Consumer goods require strategies that allow your message to meet your targeted consumer. These strategies will vary by country and possibly by region within countries.

In the United States, there is no difficulty placing an ad in any media. The situation is different elsewhere. Production difficulties (reported to occur in Japan) or long lead times (German television advertising) may result in the rejection of your ad or the possibility that it would run at an inappropriate time.

Many countries tax advertising. Others restrict the amount you may spend. Some countries ban the use of words we would find usual and acceptable (e.g., "deodorant" in Italy).

Use care when hiring translation services for your advertising, packaging, or other communication with buyers and users of your products. Former nationals of a country, who have lived for some time in the United States, may be unfamiliar with current idiomatic expressions from home. Contact your peers, the US&FCS office in your region, or your state's trade development office to obtain the names of reliable translation services.

The use of a shared-cost advertising program has the theoretical benefit of mutually desired objectives and reduced costs. However, users have often been disappointed because it is difficult for one party to verify that the other has contributed the agreed share of advertising costs. This type of program seldom contributes to the representative's loyalty to the exporter.

Color is critical in international advertising, just as in the United States. Any color (such as red, white, black, blue) may have specific meanings within the culture of the target country. For example, red may mean any of hot, exciting, sexy, or powerful to an American and at the same time hold religious or ceremonial connotations within the culture of another country.

Research and knowledge of the culture, economy, and practices of the target market are the steppingstones to a successful advertising program.

SUMMARY

A relationship with a foreign company to market, sell, service, or represent your product is a major step forward in your export process. Successful relationships require a firm and long-term commitment. The strength of the relationship depends on how much you put into making it work.

The quality of your representation, whether by an agent or a distributor, is linked to the attention and support you provide. Too distant for day-to-day contact and your direct oversight, the representative must warrant your trust and continued attention.

Goodwill and good intentions must attend the execution of the representation agreement. Your reputation in the target country depends on your representation there. The success of your representative depends on the quality and continuity of the lines represented and the support received from the principals (you). Mutual commitment to a successful venture will bring profits to each of you.

RESOURCES

1. *Arbitration.* The International Chamber of Commerce, Paris, provides arbitration services. Contact the ICC Paris through its New York affiliate office. Tel: 212-354-4480. In the United States, contact the American Arbitration Association at 140 W. 51st Street, New York, NY 10020-1203. Tel: 212-484-4000.

2. *Exclusivity of representation.* Determine the standards for your industry and for the target country. Contact your trade association, companies in complementary industries, the American Chamber of Commerce in the target country, the ITA Country Officer, or the US&FCS office in that country to determine if exclusive territories are granted, the nature of the exclusivity, and enforceability and termination conditions.

3. *Representation (agency or distributor) agreements in the European Community.* Contact the Office of European Community Affairs, Single Market Initiative Information Service, U.S. Department of Commerce, International Trade Administration, Washington, DC 20230. Tel: 202-482-5276. This office can provide you with a *Comprehensive Listing of Directives* ($5.00) and a basic information packet and can answer other questions you may have.

4. *CISG.* Current information about the status of the convention may be obtained from the Treaty Section of the Office of Legal Affairs, United Nations, New York, NY 10017. Tel: 212-963-5047/5048.

5. *Advertising.* Chapter 14, Global Marketing Management, in the text *International Marketing* (7th ed.), by P. R. Cateora (New York: R. D. Irwin, 1990), provides an introductory summary of the issues and considerations of an international advertising program. The text, or similar introductory texts in international marketing, is available at college and university bookstores across the United States.

6. *Ogilvy on Advertising* by David Ogilvy (New York: Vintage Books for Random House, 1985) gives managers a frank perspective on advertising and how it can be used in any market.

6 Indirect Exports

Some business owners, managers, and executives do not have the desire or temperament to export. Many companies do not have the financial or operating capacity to take on and become active in the export marketing of their products. They do not wish to devote the time, energy, and interest to a business that is far away, is usually in another language, uses documents that may be unfamiliar, and possibly requires the assumption of risks that cannot be quantified by experience or instinct.

Indirect exporting means introducing your products (goods *or* services) into foreign markets through a third party. Some assume that indirect exports encompass everything other than foreign sales through your own foreign branch or subsidiary. As an owner, manager, or executive responsible for the international segment of the corporation, you differentiate indirect exports by the nature of the transaction and assumption of the financial risks.

An indirect exporter sells to a company in the United States, gets paid in the United States, delivers goods in the United States, operates under the U.S. legal system, and negotiates and deals in American English.

Exporting on an indirect basis is a valid market-entry option. It is a way to optimize limited resources, acquire the use of the resources of others, and retain the level of control you believe appropriate. Most of our leading industrial and commercial firms utilize indirect export strategies to reach small or difficult markets, move parts and supplies, or for other purposes. Here are two examples:

1. A leading aerospace manufacturer utilizes the services of a trading company to sell components and other goods to small foreign markets. This is an effective use of the manufacturer's resources and the trader's contacts.

2. A small bottler of gourmet food products utilizes an export trading company to export its products worldwide. The bottler attends international trade promotions; the balance of the activity rests with the export trading company. Both parties are pleased.

INDIRECT EXPORT ALTERNATIVES

There are many ways to develop a profitable indirect export program. Each of the forms listed has benefits and costs. Your principal alternatives are:

1. Trading company.
2. Export management company.
3. Export merchant.
4. Country-controlled buying agent.
5. Commission buying agent.
6. Piggybacking.

The Trading Company

Most sectors of U.S. commercial and industrial activity have felt the impact of the Japanese trading companies. These are often major companies—with worldwide organizations, hundreds of departments, and more telephone and telex machines than a major city—moving goods around the world.

The phenomenon is not unique to Japan. Korea, Taiwan, China, Hong Kong, Germany, the Netherlands, Sweden, England, the larger Latin American nations, and many others have trading companies of significant size.

Trading companies grew from both a well-focused demand for a good or goods and a unique capacity to fill that demand. The Hudson's Bay Company is a famous North American example of a trading company that served a focused demand (beaver pelt for fur hats) and had the unique capacity (control over the greater part of the North American continent and its beaver resource) to fulfill that demand. The Bay is one of the leading department stores in Canada, a direct descendent of The Hudson's Bay Company. The present day East India Company dates from 1694 and was formed to trade between Europe and China. Trading companies in controlled economies (also called nonmarket economies, such as the People's Republic of China) are state-run organizations that generally focus on a particular industry or resource segment.

Smaller product or industry-specific trading companies also exist. They focus on a single market or on a more specific line of products. In addition, these smaller trading companies may focus on the requirements of a specific group of retailers or wholesalers, and in this way do a better job of serving that industrial or retail market segment.

European trading companies are an outgrowth of the colonizing activities of European nations from the fifteenth century. These ventures resulted in companies carrying trade goods between markets under protection of the governments. Dominance in a market or product line evolved from that position. These companies continue to exist, and while many are under another name, they continue to be strong trading companies in their respective fields.

Historically, trading companies have been a minor focus of U.S. business activity, however major trading companies have evolved in the agriculture and petroleum industries. Major agricultural commodity traders have evolved to deal with our abundance of agricultural resources and the need or opportunity to exploit them. The giants in this sector are companies like Cargill, Continental Grain, Bunge, and ADM. Some have grown beyond their roots and are active traders in other nonagricultural commodities such as cement, steel, and alumina. The young oil companies evolved into major international traders with their activities focused on petroleum products and derivatives.

Export trading has not been a major sector of business activity in the United States. Remember, the United States began as one of the colonies goods were shipped *from* by those earlier trading companies. Exporting has never been a major activity of the leading U.S. firms, not a part of the nation's commercial life. The U.S. market has been huge, healthy, and has held immense growth opportunities. While there has always been a place for the small company that bought and exported for its own account, the larger exporting companies have found that more general trading activities complement export activity in their principal product lines. As industries have grown and matured, firms have turned to trading for increased profits. The auto and airframe manufacturers are examples of companies that have utilized their worldwide connections to generate profitable ancillary business. Similarly, General Electric, Westinghouse, and Control Data are diversified corporations that offer their international marketing and financial expertise to others. This activity enhances the value of their internal structures and capabilities and brings profits to the bottom line.

Once you have determined that your good is exportable, one of your first options and considerations is the use of a trading company as the vehicle to export for you.

Choosing a Trading Company

The major trading companies, both U.S. and foreign owned, may focus on either a market or a product line. Some will be so large as to have the capacity to handle your goods, irrespective of their nature. When dealing with a larger trading company, you will generally have to fit their mold. This means you must produce to meet the volume they determine will make the relationship profitable. You must have a product that commands the level of markup they require for their markets.

These volume and price criteria are important because they can be limiting factors in your relationship with a major trading company. Your product may not have the foreign market acceptance or potential to justify the interest of a large company. That larger trading company will be unwilling to commit overhead to the necessary market-development effort.

If your product does not appeal to the large trading house, there are many other options. Medium-sized trading companies may focus on a market that is a good fit for your product. They may specialize in your line of goods or your product may complement their existing line and fit in with its program. These smaller companies, more flexible because of their size, will be able to devote relatively more time to relatively lesser volume than the major trading companies. There is a potential tradeoff: the trader may require a further reduced price structure sufficient to compensate for the unknown or limited potential of your product.

Smaller trading companies tend to consist of 1 to 10 people with expertise either in one area of the world or in a narrow product line. The advantages of working with this smaller company are its need for your business, the fact that it is likely to be very well focused on a product line or market, and the attention you will get from one of the very senior people in the firm.

Your arrangement with a trading company will be much like the one you have with one of your major domestic distributors:

1. You sell to the trading company on preferential terms.
2. You give them the rights (exclusively or limited to varying degrees) to a territory, which could be anything from a part of a country (i.e., Bavaria in the Federal Republic of Germany) to all countries of the world outside of the United States.
3. You agree to provide the trading company with a certain level of support in the following areas:
   a. Inventory
   b. Turnaround time
   c. Advertising
   d. Packaging
   e. Pricing (see Chapter 8)
   f. Financing (see Part Three)

The trading company agrees to achieve a certain level of sales of your product in a certain period of time.

A relationship with a trading company can be very effective for a U.S. company that desires the benefits of an established export program but is reluctant to export for its own account.

The Export Trading Company Act of 1982

The Export Trading Company Act of 1982 was an attempt by Congress to increase the international competitiveness of U.S. firms. It made a number of significant changes in the way U.S. firms can do international business. There are four titles to the act, of which three are most important.

Title II—Bank Export Services made changes in banking law so that commercial bank holding companies could form subsidiary **export trading companies** (ETCs). These ETCs may take title to goods; contract for certain export-related services such as insurance, transportation, and freight brokerage; and participate in the profit or loss of commercial transactions much like any other enterprise. Banks, in the normal course of business, are prohibited by law from taking title to goods unless as a result of a business failure or loan default.

Few U.S. banks have taken up the opportunity this law provides. While a number of major banks have formed export trading companies under the act, most have been closed or become permanently inactive (First Chicago, Bank of America, and others). Closures were due to financial problems in other areas of the corporation, inept management of international trade activities, narrow margins, the nature of trading risks, and lack of commitment on the part of executive management.

Banks that are in the ETC business today have refined their focus, identified what they are good at or can be good at, and developed niches in those areas. They provide a financing and document-handling service. They are very transaction oriented (i.e., they want to see profit on each deal). In effect, the ETC Act provided bank holding companies with high margin loan opportunity that a few banks have recognized and successfully implemented.

Even with this limited scope, bank ETCs can be an added resource for you. They have extensive financing resources, and financing is one of the leading hurdles in the export business. They generally do not have the knowledge or perspective to take a long-term-development view toward an export market or export operation. Their interest may be greatest in single-sale situations in amounts over $500,000, or with repetitive sales to a single buyer that generate over $1,000,000 per year in transaction volume.

The bank ETC option may be of greatest interest to the company that has stretched its credit to the limit, has export volume the bank will not finance, or has export sales opportunities the business owner is reluctant to otherwise take on. For example, the bank ETC will, under contract with you, purchase the product from your suppliers or support your production process, pay on domestic commercial terms for your account, and resell the product to your foreign buyer at a profit. The export risk falls to the trading company rather than to you or the bank. The cost of these services (principally financing) can range upwards of 50 percent of the gross margin on an export transaction.

Title III—Export Certificate of Review is the most compelling feature of the Export Trading Company Act. The United States has actively enforced the Sherman Antitrust Act and other laws that prohibit or make illegal the combination of unrelated entities wherein the potential exists for the restraint of trade or the control of markets. Under Title III, this collusion is specifically permitted if the activity is certified by the Secretary of Commerce to be in the interests of promoting exports and does not have a deleterious effect on the domestic market. Prior to the act, only activities carried out under the Webb-Pomerene Act could enjoy any form of antitrust exemption. Companies in the same industry can, in order to compete in foreign markets, join together to allocate markets, fix prices, and allocate production.

The Application for Certificate of Review is straightforward in its requirements. At this writing, the Office of Export Trading Company Affairs advised that 129 Export Certificates of Review have been issued. No bank has applied for this certification. This suggests that banks take a passive role in promotion and expansion of exports of internationally traded goods.

Once certified, the companies engaging in the certified export activity are protected from antitrust action if the export activity is of the type covered by the certification. Certificates have been issued for small and large manufacturers, export intermediaries, shippers' associations, trade associations, service firms, and agricultural producers and processors. Sears, Roebuck & Co., in association with a major commercial finance house, received certification and formed an ETC under the act. After a brief and expensive organizational period, Sears withdrew from the ETC arena. One cannot translate Sears' ETC experience to other companies. However, a well-run company (or group of companies) with sufficient assets, a tight focus and objective, and competent management can succeed as an ETC under the act.

The advantage of the certification process is that exporting companies now have the opportunity to do the following:

1. Combine to control markets.

2. Establish export prices and price maintenance.

3. Share market-development costs.

4. Spread financing costs and credit risks.

5. Reduce transportation costs.

6. Manage technology licensing.

7. Reduce warehousing costs or insurance costs.

There are many other reasons for a company to participate in a certified ETC. Your export strategies could include the creation of an ETC under the corporate form of a Foreign Sales Corporation (see Chapter 8).

Your product may be one that would benefit from sale to and through one of these ETCs. You might benefit from its market-development efforts and expenditures, or your product might be effectively introduced into a number of foreign markets while you continue to make your domestic sales.

Title IV—Foreign Trade Antitrust Improvements makes specific amendments to the Sherman Antitrust Act and the Federal Trade Commission Act, reflected by the activities permitted under Title III.

The Export Management Company

Another method of indirect exporting is the use of an export management company (EMC). In the past, these firms were called combination export managers or CEMs. An EMC can perform a broad range of functions. The contractual arrangements you make with an EMC will spell out responsibilities for credit, collection of export receivables, and risk of loss on sales, in addition to many other factors.

An EMC generally acts as an export department for a number of manufacturers of related and noncompeting products. The EMC often will bring special expertise in a product line or in a market area.

Generally, an export management company will provide a broad range of services on your behalf and will receive payment by a commission on the sales that result from its efforts. There could be a salary or combination salary/commission arrangement. This can vary and will depend on the needs and interests of both the producer and the EMC. The EMC is, in effect, your export sales agent.

An EMC is an important relationship for:

1. The manufacturer who is reluctant to, or cannot afford to, enter into the export business directly.

2. The smaller firm that does not have the time or personnel and still desires the benefits of marketing its product overseas.

3. The firm that wishes to concentrate on major or specific markets and will let others take on smaller or other markets.

With expertise in a product line or a geographic market, your EMC will undertake market-development activity for your product line. It will perform a number of functions, which may include:

1. Contracting with overseas agents or distributors on your behalf.

2. Arranging for on-site product promotion and after-sale service.

3. Demonstrating products in markets.

4. Licensing as necessary to enter markets closed to imports from the United States.

5. Providing credit assistance.

Other functions can be defined by the contract between you and the EMC.

In most arrangements, the EMC may require or request advance payments from you to undertake the market-development work. If you encounter this situation, take some logical steps before you pay. Require a list of the EMC's other clients for reference purposes. Call them and verify that the EMC can do the job, that there is a reasonable chance of success, and that your dollars will be well spent.

Be sure you understand the nature of the agreement you have with the EMC. Be as specific as is reasonable under the circumstances. Just as in your domestic business, every point on the "standard" contract is negotiable. If the EMC is the best in the field in the United States, you will have limited room to negotiate. If the EMC is a start-up with few or no clients, you have the upper hand in the negotiations.

Remember the purpose of your relationship with the EMC in this give and take. It can help you expand your markets at nominal costs and bring a broad range of benefits to your business overall.

Take care in establishing the terms of sale arrangements with the EMC. If you are selling to the EMC and it is paying you independent of the receipt of payment from the foreign buyer, you, in fact, have a relationship with a distributor located in the United States. Your risk and control are much the same as you enjoy with any other domestic distributor. However, if you must wait for payment from the foreign buyer and are at risk for your funds until the foreign buyer pays, you have an agency relationship with the EMC and are a direct creditor to the foreign buyer. If that's the case, go to both Chapter 5 and Part Three; you have a situation in which the EMC is a contract sales organization, paid on a commission basis. That can be a good and productive relationship, as long you understand it going in. You also should have provisions in your contract with the EMC whereby you control the sales terms on *all* sales that are not cash in advance. This will protect you, let you decide on the level of payment risk you wish to assume, and keep the EMC focused on its objective: sales to the best buyers in the market. Understand this increased level of risk and manage the activity to control it.

The Export Merchant

The export merchant, a term in limited use today, is a well-established and well-financed corporation. It buys and sells for its own account, distributing product through an overseas marketing organization that may include distributors, branches, warehouses, and other facilities.

The export merchant relieves the manufacturer of all export responsibilities. Like the trading companies, the export merchant takes delivery of the goods in the United States and takes care of such details as warehousing, export packing, shipping, documentation, and collection. The export merchant differs from the trading company in that the merchant remarks or relabels the products as its own. In doing so, the merchant stands in front of the manufacturer in both the service and warranty processes.

The export merchant will insist on quality, reliability, and a very fine price. In return, the export merchant may provide an excellent avenue for increased production and sales. Association with an export merchant is not suitable if you want to build name and brand recognition for your products in foreign markets.

Country-Controlled Buying Agent

While most prevalent for nonmarket economies, and in limited use, country-controlled buying agents operate within the United States on behalf of many nations. A country-controlled buying agent purchases goods within the United States for export to its country. For many years, the Soviet Union, and now Russia, has had buying organizations in New York City. The People's Republic of China has similar arrangements in many cities across the United States.

Producers and suppliers are directed to these organizations when attempting to sell specific products to a country. The manufacturer sells to a government through the buying agent, delivers the goods in the United States, and receives payment in the United States. The risks and procedures associated with exporting are absent. The primary issue for the manufacturer is that of export controls. Does the product being sold to that buying agent fall under the export prohibitions of the United States, as set out in the Export Administration Regulations? (See Chapter 18.) If your product does require a Validated Export License for shipment to the buyer's country, you are required to inform the buyer of that fact. Failure to do so can open your firm to unwanted contact with the Bureau of Export Administration.

Commission Buying Agents

The commission buying agent represents a foreign buyer or group of buyers in an industry sector. It is paid a commission by the foreign firm for the buying services provided. Beyond the purchase, these services may include storage, shipment, insurance, and documentation. Difficult to identify, these commission buying agents will seek out suppliers that meet their principals' requirements. This type of organization faces considerable competition from trading companies, export merchants, and the expanded activities of foreign representatives of U.S. firms.

Piggybacking

This inelegant term is an excellent descriptor for a very effective method of exporting components, supplies, or complimentary products. Suppliers piggyback on the export activity of firms in related industries. Many larger companies have well-established export departments. Most have the capacity to take on extra volume with ease and are often eager to do so because it broadens their market presence. If your product is used in another finished good, in the completion of an installation or facility, or complements another product line,[1] you have a ready-made audience for the export of your product. For example, a manufacturer of portable power systems is an active exporter. Many of its systems utilize "sleds"—permanently affixed equipment to move the systems—and power transmission cables, among other items. The power system manufacturer does not manufacture the sleds or cables. A sled or cable manufacturer can piggyback on the system seller and achieve low-cost export sales.

In order for you to establish this type of arrangement, you may need to show the exporting company the benefits of the piggyback relationship. Your negotiating points are the quality of your product, the "fit" of your product to its application, a very advantageous price, the benefit of having broadened the exporter's offerings, and an improved "product package" for the buyer. It also can relieve the exporter from the issues of inventory, quality control, and product warranty.

The exporter provides a ready conduit for your product. The exporter buys from you at a reduced or preferential price, possibly with extended payment terms. (You have no domestic sales overhead, see Chapter 8, Pricing for Profits.) Your products expand and support the exporter's product line and make the buying decision easier for the client. As always, the best relationships tend to be "win-win."

A FINAL CAUTION

When making the decision to export indirectly, you must consider not only the positive aspects such as the cost-saving potential, the growth of sales, the increase of production runs, the decrease in marginal costs, and the more efficient use of your facilities and personnel, you must also weigh and consider the potential downside to this type of arrangement.

When you sell indirectly you will relinquish control over sales personnel and the manner in which they represent your products. In addition, service and warranty provisions may be out of your control. If these functions are not handled properly, your company may quickly get a poor name in the foreign market. If indirect exports are an interim step in your growth as a company

---

[1] For example, the p-SERVER™, a plotter-server for printers manufactured by Far Mountain Corporation, Issaquah, WA, complements the line of a distributor of CAD-CAM and engineering plotters and computer programs. One enhances the performance of the other.

and as an exporter, and your product requires service or customer-oriented care, be cautious in your selection of intermediaries.

As in any other important business decision, take the time to weigh all of the relevant factors. If uncertain of the situation, contact your peers and counsel with them. Talk with the US&FCS or with respected leaders in the international trade community. Members of your **District Export Council** **(DEC)** are an excellent and knowledgeable resource.

RESOURCES

1. An Application for Export Certificate of Review can be obtained from the Office of Export Trading Company Affairs, International Trade Administration, Room 5618, U.S. Department of Commerce, Washington, DC 20230. Tel: 202-482-5131. Contact your trade association to see if it is certified; many have done this for the benefit of their membership.

2. The Export Trading Company Act of 1982, Public Law 97-290, is available from the above office, from the Superintendent of Documents at the nearest branch of the U.S. Government Printing Office, through your closest US&FCS office, or from your senator or representative.

3. A useful guide on the scope of activities of the export management company, published by the International Trade Administration, is titled *The Export Management Company*. Also, the July, 1992, edition of *Business America* has a thorough article on EMCs.

4. The issues identified in the agent- or distributor-selection process reviewed in Chapter 5 provide additional information for consideration in an indirect export strategy.

5. The Bureau of Export Administration (BXA), Washington, DC 20230. Tel: 202-482-5301. The BXA is part of the U.S. Department of Commerce.

6. District Export Councils are comprised of businesspeople appointed by the U.S. Secretary of Commerce to counsel and encourage the development of increased exports within their states. There are 51 DECs in the United States. Contact your US&FCS district office for more information on DEC programs in your state. The author is a member of the Washington DEC.

7 Foreign Investment and Joint Ventures

Most markets of the world are open to exports from the United States. However, growing companies may find that a direct investment is the only suitable option available for entry into some foreign markets. Or, they may find that direct investment is a logical progression beyond, and complement to, their export activity.

As export alternatives, there are two principal reasons to make a foreign investment or enter joint-venture operations:

1. The target country has established barriers to the import of your product, and the target country appears to be an excellent market for your product. These barriers could be tariffs, quotas, an outright ban, or practices (see Chapter 19).

2. Your market entry into any target country is best achieved by a direct investment in that country. Even a moderately industrialized country can be an excellent production base for localized sales and regional distribution.

There are three principal reasons to make a foreign investment or enter a joint venture as a complement to your export activity: The market is of sufficient size, your presence is well established, and you wish to achieve a higher level of control and potentially more profits from sales into that market. This is a logical progression in the growth of a successful company.

Foreign investment or joint-venture operations are not a mandatory step in the internationalization process. They work for some companies and are inappropriate for others.

FORMS OF FOREIGN INVESTMENT

An indirect foreign investment is a portfolio investment such as you would make in the shares of a U.S. company, with the risks attendant to the offshore nature of the holdings.

With a direct foreign investment, the investor achieves some degree of control over the activities of the acquired activity. Following is a list of five types of direct foreign investment:

1. *Wholly-owned investment.* This gives the investor the greatest degree of control and the greatest exposure to risk. This investment could be a manufacturing operation or other type of subsidiary, a sales office, a branch, or another operation that conducts your business in the target market.

2. *Minority-owned investment.* This gives the investor the benefits of on-site involvement, some degree of control, participation in the benefits of ownership, and some insulation from the economic, political, and social attitudes toward Americans that may prevail in another country.

3. *Joint-venture (JV) investment.* The joint-venture arrangement is customary when firms with complementary skills, structures, or products join together to achieve a mutually desired goal. The JV could be with a host-country national, in which the U.S. firm would achieve the benefits noted in item 2 above. Or it could be a JV with a third-country firm, where you join to pursue a market foreign to each of you. The responsibilities, accountabilities, and risks in a joint venture are quite structured and formal as compared to a majority or minority investment situation. By agreement, management is shared. This can be difficult for managers accustomed to the exercise of independent authority.

4. *License.* This arrangement enables the U.S. firm to transfer technology or other knowledge products to a firm in the target country. The licensee will then utilize this knowledge to manufacture, produce, assemble, or otherwise make a product that will be sold in the host market. The licensor (the exporter of technology) will be compensated under a license agreement. The licensor has invested (put at risk) the product of the license.

5. *Franchise.* Similar to franchising in the United States, the franchisor transfers a business practice to the franchisee in return for a fee and an income stream. The franchisor has invested (put at risk) the value of the business practice subject to the franchise. Other than investment in a creation of an offshore/in-country franchise management organization, this option is the only internationalization strategy available to a franchisor.

SOME PRE-INVESTMENT QUESTIONS

Market research is necessary prior to investment in a foreign country. You must determine the following:

1. Do you know the level of potential demand for the product? If demand does exist, what alterations in style, size, packaging, and promotion must be made to conform to the culture and practice in that country?

2. Can you control your interests? Study the laws and regulations of the target country regarding foreign investment from the United States. Some countries do not allow foreign firms to establish within their borders; others allow foreign firms to hold only a minority interest (perhaps with a majority of home-country appointees on the board), while others allow foreign firms to hold a majority interest or outright ownership.

Change is rapid in the 1990s, particularly with the rules of foreign investment. India has changed its investment laws to permit majority ownership by foreigners of Indian manufacturing operations. (Union Carbide in Bhopal was burdened with minority ownership and lack of control over many of the critical aspects of its chemical operations in India.) This change by India is important as it improves access to and opportunity in an important market.

Mexico has amended its foreign investment laws and now permits majority and sole ownership of Mexican companies by foreign firms. Certain industries are protected, such as the petroleum industry.[1]

Many of the countries of Eastern Europe see direct investment as the key to economic success. They have established laws and procedures to attract foreign investment. Programs to encourage foreign direct investment are critical to the development of many countries.[2]

3. Can you repatriate capital and income? Can dividends, profits, and capital be readily taken out of the target country for return to the United States? Are there controls? What is the nature of existing controls on the money supply? Does the country have a history of blocking funds of foreign investors? Will the host government guarantee currency conversion and repatriation via simple application?

4. Are the raw materials or other manufacturing inputs (e.g., semiconductors from Japan for manufacture in France) available in the host country? Are there import barriers or restraints? What are the costs of these imports, including duties?

5. Is a suitable workforce available? Is it educated or trained? Will the host government train the workers at its cost? What are the wage and work laws? What are the work practices, the power of unions or other labor organizations? How many holidays must be observed? What is the usual leave/sick-day/vacation policy in the target country?

6. What is the cost and availability of power? Of water? Is the power supply of the same voltage and amperage as in the United States? If different, what is the cost of the necessary conversions or equipment replacements?

---

[1]This is an important issue in the North America Free Trade Agreement negotiations. U.S. and Canadian companies want the opportunity to drill for and acquire oil within Mexico.

[2]U.S. Department of Commerce, "World Bank: Progress in Developing World Requires Market-Government Interaction." *Business America*, July 15, 1991.

7. What is the taxing structure? What taxes must be paid: land, business, use, income, franchise, employee, other? What tax incentives are offered by the host country to encourage your investment in the country?

8. What incentives (including tax, above) are offered by the host country: waivers of rents, low- or no-interest loans, grants, training programs, health programs, infrastructure (roads, etc.) development, other?

9. What disincentives exist: labor laws or employment requirements (number, mix, etc.), export requirements, import substitution requirements, performance penalties, permit processes, legal complexities and uncertainties, other?

When all of these factors are known, you can identify costs of production and unit costs with reasonable certainty. Compare these costs to the costs of production in the United States or other potential host countries or regions. If your investment objective is to situate within a trade bloc (Part Six) to benefit from its structure, compare opportunities within the countries of the bloc. For example, an international strategy that includes investment in the EC requires that you research at least 19 countries (the 12 EC members and the 7 EFTA associates to the EC).

TERMS OF YOUR INVESTMENT

If you have determined that you will operate in the target country as a minority owner, there are a number of issues to be addressed in your agreement with the majority owner(s). The host country nationals may bring many benefits to the venture such as market knowledge, market acceptance, access to government officials, knowledge and the ability to "work" the local systems, an existing distribution system or channels, and perhaps experience with your products. These attributes enhance your capabilities and optimize the opportunities for profits.

Your agreement should specify the nature of the relationship and the responsibilities of each party. Your agreement should also address:

1. The distribution or reinvestment of cash flows and profits.

2. Levels of subscribed capital and its call provisions.

3. Responsibility for negotiations with the host governments, at the national, state or regional, and local levels. Your partner should know the procedures to apply for concessions regarding property taxes (real and personal), water and power rates and availability, guarantees of repatriation of profits or other incomes, and other investment incentives.

4. Responsibilities for compliance with applicable laws and regulations of the host country.

5. The applicability of and compliance with U.S. laws.[3]

6. Export incentives and free-trade zone benefits.

Negotiation of the agreement may be your responsibility; in most countries, the use of attorneys is a last resort rather than a "first step" as in the United States. Use competent counsel for the drafting and completion of the investment agreement, rather than for the negotiation; the use of an attorney may not be customary to your counterparty and could be insulting. Also seek advice from other professionals such as your CPA, your international banker, and your international business consultant. These advisors can identify and eliminate many of the issues and problems you may encounter in this type of expansion.

LICENSING AGREEMENTS

If your company has a unique technology with applications in foreign markets, licensing your product for manufacture and sale in foreign markets may be an appropriate international trade strategy. A well-drawn agreement is vital. This can be a profitable arrangement if handled properly. Use great care and exercise caution in these arrangements because many governments do not offer or enforce patent and other intellectual property protections to the degree experienced in the United States.

A licensing agreement, and the disclosures leading to that agreement with the foreign party, are "exports" under U.S. law and must comply with all licensing requirements of the U.S. Export Administration Act. All disclosures of technical data, software, and information used for development, production, or use of a product must be licensed (15 CFR 779.1[b]). Disclosures that require a prior license can take place by telephone call, factory tour, or presentation of documents at a negotiating session, as well as by mail, electronic transmission, or other form of delivery.[4]

No model agreement is applicable because regulations regarding foreign investments can vary widely by country. Under a license agreement, the usual practice is for a flat sum to be paid to the licensor in advance, compensating for the conveyance of technical information to the licensee. The amount is negotiable. (Remember, *everything* is negotiable.)

---

[3]The U.S. government enforces a doctrine of extraterritoriality. The result is the application of U.S. laws and regulations to the activities of U.S. firms abroad.

[4]Melvyn Jay Simburg, "Tips for Drafting International Business Agreements," July 1, 1989. Mr. Simburg manages the international practice of the firm Simburg, Ketter, Sheppard & Purdy, P.S., Seattle, WA.

To support this front-end fee, the licensor must substantiate the value of the technology (the property) and demonstrate its current and long-term potential. Lack of history, coupled with a lack of realistic projections, does not give the potential licensee a basis for valuing the property.

When agreed, the front-end fee may be paid in one lump sum or in installments, with or without interest. Use caution with an installment arrangement; U.S. and foreign tax laws and the host country's current and future prospects for convertibility of its currency may affect the value of your anticipated receipts.

A second revenue issue is the stream of royalty revenues that will result from the unit sales of your patented or trademarked product(s). Like the fixed fee, the rate of royalty is negotiable. The royalty continues for the life of the licencing agreement, subject to applicable laws and practices of the licensee's country. The agreement may call for a royalty that varies based on the level of sales, such that the licensee is encouraged to increase and maintain high levels of sales.

The following checklist can be modified to be useful for protecting intellectual property in almost every type of international agreement:

_____ 1. Acknowledge the manufacturer's ownership of all rights in all trademarks, trade names, patents, copyrights, trade secrets, and related documentation and literature.

_____ 2. Determine responsibility for obtaining registrations of foreign patents, trademarks, copyrights, and designs.

_____ 3. Determine the scope of permission to use by licensee, including substantive use, geographic scope, and period of time.

_____ 4. Determine procedures for use and ownership of improvements and additions to the intellectual property.

_____ 5. Determine the steps required to maintain confidentiality and protection of intellectual property rights.

_____ 6. Determine responsibility for reporting, prosecuting, and bearing expenses to prevent infringement and unauthorized disclosure or use.

_____ 7. Determine limitations on the right to make representations or warranties regarding the product or intellectual property.

_____ 8. Determine whether customer lists are to be disclosed and users registered together with the type of information to be included with such registration.

_____ 9. Require compliance with U.S. export laws, including restrictions on sale to certain customers and restrictions on re-export.

_____ 10. Determine compliance and monitoring requirements, including quality control specifications, form and frequency of reports, and auditing.

_____ 11. If appropriate, obtain required prior approval of the manufacturer for labeling, packaging, packing, and marking.[5]

For a patent license that includes marketing, reproduction of the product, and provision of a service center, the following checklist should prove useful:

_____ 1. Grant the license.

_____ 2. Appointment of licensee as service center.

_____ 3. Manufacturer's support.

_____ 4. Customer and service information.

_____ 5. Training including scope, location, number of trainees covered, charges, meals, housing, and transportation.

_____ 6. Facilities required of the licensee, including the number and location of service centers as well as the capabilities of the plant.

_____ 7. Staffing requirements.

_____ 8. Spare parts requirements.

_____ 9. Other parts or components not included in the initial inventory or to be obtained from other sources.

_____ 10. Protection of intellectual property rights.

_____ 11. Quality control.

_____ 12. Future developments.

_____ 13. Warranty, including disclaimers for warranty and liability, restrictions on representations and warranties by the licensee, and provision of warranty service.

_____ 14. Procedures for service, handling, shipping, and standards of performance.

_____ 15. Record keeping.

_____ 16. Reporting requirements.

_____ 17. Currency.

_____ 18. Royalties and payments.

_____ 19. Taxes.

[5]Ibid.

_____ 20. Term and termination.

_____ 21. Dispute resolution.

_____ 22. Other standard clauses appropriate to your activity.[6]

Licensing can be an excellent arrangement for expansion into a foreign market. The advantages, in the form of low-cost entry, reasonable control, added sales and royalty income, and expansion of your name and presence into and across a region, are significant.

FINANCIAL ASSISTANCE FOR FOREIGN INVESTMENTS

A number of U.S. and international organizations have been formed to support and encourage foreign investment. Some of these organizations provide debt financing and some provide investment guarantees. For the potential investor, participation in an investment supported by a U.S. or international organization has some strong strategic considerations:

1. Your investment requirement may be smaller because of participation by the international organization.

2. The political risk of your equity participation is reduced because the host country is also responsible to another nation (the United States) or a multinational institution and will usually protect that source of funds.

3. Your investment returns may be guaranteed.

4. You may be introduced to potential international partners to which you would otherwise have no exposure.

5. You will gain an international reputation that can serve you well in future situations.

Should your firm deal with one or more of the following organizations, perform to your highest standards at all times. These organizations have a long reach and a longer memory.

Overseas Private Investment Corporation (OPIC)

OPIC was established by the U.S. government to encourage investments in developing countries. OPIC provides insurance, financing, and guarantees.

OPIC insurance covers investors against the political risks of expropriation, inconvertibility of funds, and loss from war, revolution, civil strife, or insurrection.

[6]Ibid.

The OPIC Direct Investment Loan Fund participates in overseas investment projects for smaller firms by lending up to US$6 million per project.

The OPIC loan guarantee program is available for projects with significant U.S. involvement. These guarantees range up to $50 million.

Acceptable investments for OPIC insurance, loans, or guarantees include infrastructure development, manufacturing or production operations, and financial intermediaries, among others.

Trade and Development Program (TDP)

The TDP program of the U.S. government finances project-planning activities in countries that are potential export markets for U.S. firms. The Public Sector Program assists U.S. firms in winning feasibility contracts for major projects in developing countries. The Investor Assistance Program provides financial assistance to U.S. investors who take equity in business ventures in developing countries. These projects must generate exports from the United States.

The World Bank

The World Bank, also known as the International Bank for Reconstruction and Development (IBRD), is owned by its member countries (152 and rising). Its objective is to stimulate outside investments in developing nations.

The World Bank supports infrastructure projects. Two affiliate organizations, the International Development Association (IDA) and the International Finance Corporation (IFC), have complementary charters.

The IDA makes loans to the poorest countries for projects that have a reasonable chance to be successful. The IFC makes direct investments to promote private enterprise in developing countries.

The World Bank sponsors and funds in excess of $15 billion annually in projects around the world. Each project is an opportunity for a U.S. firm to participate, export, or invest. See the "Resources" section for contact information.

United Nations Development Program

The UNDP coordinates development programs through over 100 offices around the world. It also supports a number of other United Nations funds that focus on development.

Regional Development Banks

There are a number of regional development banks. Emphasis is on development of infrastructure, agriculture, or industrial projects within the region served. Three of the better known of these regional development banks are:

1. The InterAmerican Development Bank (IDB) focuses on countries in the Western Hemisphere.
2. The Asian Development Bank (ADB) addresses development in Southeast Asia.
3. The Caribbean Development Bank (CDB) deals with development in the Caribbean.

The African Development Bank (AfDB) is relatively new and attempts to fund and support development of infrastructure and industry in that region. A new development finance organization, the European Bank for Reconstruction and Development, has been formed and funded by EC member states to address the infrastructure needs of Eastern European nations.

Information on these organizations and others can be acquired through the World Bank and the United Nations.

RESOURCES

1. Useful additional reading on licensing includes: Shaul Ezer, *The International Transfer of Technology: International Exporting Agreements* (New York: Mathew Bender, 1989); Marks, et al., *Selling High Technology Products in the World Market: Legal Aspects* (San Diego: Harcourt Brace Jovanovich, Inc., Law & Business Books, 1984).

2. Contact OPIC at Overseas Private Investment Corporation, 1615 M St., NW, Washington, DC 20527. Tel: 800-424-6742 or 202-457-7010.

3. Contact the TDP at The Trade and Development Program, 309-SA-16, Washington, DC 20523. Tel: 703-875-4357.

4. Contact the World Bank at 1818 H St., NW, Washington, DC 20433. Tel: 202-477-1234.

5. Contact the United Nations Development Fund at UNDP, New York, NY 10017. Tel: 212-963-1234.

6. The UN publication *Development Forum* is an excellent resource for timely information on development projects supported by all offices of the United Nations. Write to Development Business, United Nations, P.O. Box 5850 Grand Central Station, New York, NY 10163-5850.

7. The Bureau of Export Administration develops and administers the export regulations of the United States. To obtain a copy of the Export Administration Regulations (US$87), write to Superintendent of Documents, P.O. Box 371954, Pittsburgh, PA 15250-7954. Tel: 202-512-2233 (credit cards only).

8 Pricing for Profits

Establishing an export price for your products or services may be one of the greatest challenges you will face when entering or expanding your export activity. A number of factors affect the creation of that export price, including:

1. Your production-cost structure and your margin objectives.
2. The price of competing goods in the target market.
3. The requirements of the other functional areas of your firm.
4. The cost of the export process.

YOUR COST STRUCTURE

Your production-cost structure includes all of the costs you currently factor into the production of the goods you offer for sale. You have factored in your cost of capital, costs of raw material and other product inputs, and costs of labor. The cost-of-goods-sold (COGS) figure is relatively firm, driven down principally by marginal efficiencies in production and sourcing. Sales costs, general and administrative costs, other corporate overhead, and taxes complete the basics of your cost structure.

Your domestic selling price builds on these production, operating, and overhead costs. Additional factors that impact your domestic pricing decision are assumptions as to market size and growth, expected sales volume, and the share of the market you will acquire. Your required operating and profit margins are also factored into your selling price.

Costing Alternatives

There are at least four cost-based alternatives one may use in establishing an export pricing structure. The fifth alternative is to price based on the competition in the marketplace. That is covered in the next section. Each costing option must bear the addition of specific export transaction costs.

104

The company can use (1) a standard ex factory cost (SEF), (2) a standard ex factory with no allocated marketing costs (SEFNAM), (3) marginal costing (MC), and (4) pricing from the market backwards or retrograde pricing (RP).

1. The standard ex factory (SEF) cost basis for export pricing includes your domestic sales, administrative, and overhead burdens in the price of each unit of export sales. This pricing basis may be inappropriate because it can price your product out of the market; you have already allocated sales, administrative, and overhead costs to your domestic production volumes.

2. The standard ex factory costs with no allocated marketing costs (SEFNAM) is a costing basis that recognizes that you have incurred no direct selling or promotion costs in the conduct of your export business. Those costs are being incurred by your foreign agent, representative, or distributor. Recognize that this pricing basis continues to include your domestic administrative and overhead allocations. These factors may increase your costs so that your product is uncompetitive in your target markets.

3. Marginal costing (MC) is an export costing basis that recognizes that incremental export sales do not require additional allocations of sales, administrative, or overhead factors. As you profit from your export activity and volume increases, you may have to add productive capacity or administrative personnel to deal with the paperwork and accounting. Only then is it appropriate to factor those costs into the per unit cost basis for your export sales.

An example of the differences in these three costing structures will be useful.

Category	SEF	SEFNAM	MC
COGS	$2,100	$2,100	$2,100
Allocated costs	420		
Allocated, less sales		210	
Ex factory cost	2,520	2,310	2,100
Price with 25% margin	$3,150	$2,888	$2,625

This demonstrates that there may be significant differences in the basis for your export pricing. The variations are a function of your flexibility and the recognition that many of your domestic costs are not applicable to the export environment.

Each market will differ, and some may offer you the opportunity to fully allocate all costs and prices under the SEF example above. However, you may be forced to offer pricing under the MC example in order to enter, expand, or maintain market share in your export markets.

4. Target pricing (TP) is a strategy based on pricing to the market. With the appropriate research (Chapter 3), you can identify the market price for your product category in the targeted distribution channel and market segment. With this information, you can back into a cost structure and determine your ability and interest in competing in that targeted marketplace.

a. Start with your target price in the marketplace.

b. Subtract the local markup(s) required by the dealer or distributor, or both. These will differ from the U.S. structure. This is an important variable as many markets have complex and deep distribution channels with many middlemen.

c. Subtract duties, fees, port, inland freight, and handling charges at the port of import.

d. Subtract export transaction costs (see below) you incur to export the goods, including banking charges, forwarder fees, handling charges, and other costs borne at the exporter's location.

e. Subtract MC, the marginal costs of production of the goods or COGS.

f. Subtract overhead costs you may wish to allocate.

g. The result is the potential profit or margin available to you given the prevailing pricing in the market.

This back-in view of pricing can give you a valuable insight into the structure of your costs in an export transaction. You and your competitors may differ on the following items (letters refer to preceding list):

b. Dealer or distributor margins or markups and agent's commissions, if any.

c. Duties based on the country of origin of the goods.

d. Export process costs, particularly freight, handling fees, and banking charges.

e. Marginal costs of production. Third-country suppliers or assemblers may be needed to drive costs down.

f. Overhead costs.

g. Profit or margin. Your international competition may have a lower target, given its costs of capital, ownership, or standards for an appropriate return in its own marketplace.

The Price of Competing Goods

Any export market you target for new or expanded activity will also have been targeted by exporters from the United States and other countries. The competition will come from in-country suppliers, other developed countries, and from suppliers in less developed countries (LDCs) or newly industrialized countries (NICs).

The price of the competing goods in the target market will have a range based on perceived quality of the goods, promotion, and the quality and efficacy of the distribution channels, given the source of the competing goods.

The exporter must conduct some form of market research to determine this range of prices. This research could be done, as suggested in Part One, by a market research firm or by the exporter's own personnel conducting on-site studies. Other than internationally traded commodity goods, prices will vary by source of the goods, location of sale or point of delivery, type of vendor, size of market, and the extent of competition in that market.

A solid understanding of the pricing offered by your competitors is critical. If your product can be offered through a variety of outlets or has a range of applications, you may be competing with different products in each market segment. These different products may be from various suppliers. If this is the case, you may compete on price in one segment, on quality in another, on delivery or service in another, and so on. Well-structured research is very important.

Foreign Sales Corporations

One important tactical option can be utilized to improve the pricing of your exports or to capture increased export profits. Creation and operation through a foreign sales corporation (FSC) can give you these benefits, at a nominal cost.

The FSC is the one financial incentive for exporters under the tax laws of the United States. The FSC legislation succeeded other laws that did not conform to the General Agreement on Tariffs and Trade (GATT).

The FSC offers an income tax savings on export sales revenues. Because a significant portion of the income of a FSC is exempt from U.S. income tax, exporters may be able to price products more competitively without reducing profits.

The FSC is a paper company. Tax benefits from use of a FSC are not available until the FSC is actually up and running. Benefits are not retroactive. The timely establishment of the FSC is important.

1. It must be organized under the laws of a "qualified" foreign country or U.S. possession. (Guam and the U.S. Virgin Islands are popular locations.)

2. At least one director must reside outside the United States.

3. A set of permanent books of account must be maintained at an office outside the United States.

Typically, these requirements are satisfied through contract with a local management company[1] or law firm, which routinely appoints the necessary non-

---

[1]There are a number of FSC management companies in the United States. Most good-sized accounting or law firms will undertake this type of project for an exporter client.

resident director and attends to the various other formalities in return for a fixed annual fee.

There are three structures available. Selection will be based on your export volume and your desire to set up an additional financial management structure within your firm.

1. The FSC (the standard) is available to all firms. It is a preferred option for larger firms, those with export sales in excess of $5,000,000.

2. A Shared FSC can be utilized by up to 25 firms that come together to enjoy FSC benefits with shared overhead costs.

3. A Small FSC is available by election; it allows FSC benefits on export sales of up to $5,000,000.

The FSC is a separate entity taxable by the United States, even though it is a foreign corporation. It files an annual tax return (Form 1120-FSC) and is required to make estimated tax payments. If properly structured, a significant portion of the FSC income is exempt from U.S. income tax. The full benefit of a FSC can be realized by locating the corporation in a jurisdiction where no local income tax is imposed.

The Value of a Foreign Sales Corporation.   All income of the FSC attributable to export trading activities may be distributed to the parent company free of tax:

1. Distributions out of exempt earnings of the FSC are tax free to the related parent company.

2. Distributions out of nonexempt "trading" income are eligible for a 100 percent dividends-received deduction.

Interest income and other nontrading income are fully taxable to the FSC, and distributions out of this type of income are taxed again to the parent company after a 70 percent dividends-received deduction. The government has established a formula for this calculation. FSC foreign trade income is determined as either:

1. 1.83 percent of gross sales of the FSC, or

2. 23 percent of the combined net taxable income of the FSC and the parent company, attributable to foreign sales by the FSC. Of this income, 15/23ds is tax exempt; the remainder is taxed to the FSC.

The pricing approach used (1.83 percent of gross or 23 percent of combined net) will generally depend on the net margin on export sales. The break point is about 8 percent. An example will be useful:

Export Sales	$50,000,000
Pretax income (the IRS assumes 8%)	4,000,000
FSC income	
1.83% of FSC sales, or	915,000
23% of combined net income	920,000
Tax exempt (15/23)	600,000
Tax benefit (34%)	204,000

This type of benefit, a reduction in taxes of $204,000 or .4 percent of gross export revenues, can offer some limited pricing flexibility.

The annual maintenance cost of an independent FSC can be as much as $15,000 (as of 1992). Fees may be higher where transactions are more complex. The annual maintenance cost for a Shared FSC is similar to the costs of participation in a regular FSC. Each participant must have a separate record-keeping and accounting system in place, so there is little group cost savings. Annual maintenance fees for a Shared FSC are based on each participant's gross foreign sales. The annual maintenance cost of a solely owned, Small FSC can be about $2,000. This means that break-even for a Small FSC is approximately $25,000 in export profits. Over 30,000 companies have formed FSCs and enjoy some level of tax benefit.

The Shared FSC is a legislative solution to a government-imposed problem; it does not work as planned. Reports indicate that the members of a Shared FSC usually incur costs at least equal to those that would apply had they formed their own FSC. The complexity of the management issues has created interesting income opportunities for consultants and CPAs, usually the U.S. managers of Shared FSCs. This Shared FSC option warrants careful analysis and consideration.

The Small FSC is a practical option for the smaller exporter with export revenues of up to $5,000,000 per year. Setup and administrative costs can be significantly reduced. Paperwork, administration, and reporting requirements are simplified. One FSC strategy would be to spin off divisions that export into separate FSCs to capture the tax savings.

The FSC option should be investigated by the senior executives of the firm or the managers of the finance functions. This is suggested in the following section.

OTHER FUNCTIONAL AREAS AND PRICING

Export activity does not take place in a vacuum. As recommended in Chapter 2, each functional area of the company should be involved in the export process. This *whole-systems* approach will ensure that each affected area of the firm has an understanding of your export objectives and an opportunity to contribute to the success of the export effort.

These functional areas will have their own perspective on the export pricing process.

1. Finance will be concerned that exports are profitable and generate a positive and predictable cash flow.

2. Legal will be concerned about potential antitrust issues should exports be priced differently to different customers (see "Export Trading Companies" in Chapter 6), control over intellectual property rights, and the jurisdiction and resolution of contracts.

3. Production will want export prices that generate increased demand, thereby increasing production runs and marginal efficiencies.

4. Domestic marketing will be concerned that export prices are set at a level such that those goods will not reenter the domestic market and compete with domestic sales activities.[2]

THE EXPORT COSTING WORKSHEET

Each export transaction incurs costs. At least one of these costs, freight, can be substantial. All of these export transaction costs taken together add significantly to the export price of your goods. If these costs are not managed effectively, they can price you out of an attractive export market.

Figure 8.1 is a sample export costing worksheet. This type of form or information capture process should be used for each of your buyers and each transaction. The information developed for one sale may be the basis for export pricing, shipping arrangements, and more routine activities that must be cost effective on future sales to the same buyer.

This worksheet ensures that no item of cost is overlooked and that a permanent record of the best route and carrier is maintained. It is also a record of the basis for quotations you may have tendered.

Two additional factors must be considered when developing information for your export pricing and this worksheet:

1. If any parts or components of your exported product were imported, you can apply for a refund, or *drawback*, from U.S. Customs for 99 percent of the duty that was paid on import of the goods.

2. If your export product has a high component of imported parts, use of a Foreign Trade Zone or Free Trade Zone can reduce your cash out-

---

[2]Adapted from D. A. Ball & W. H. McCulloch, *International Business,* 4th ed. (New York: Irwin, 1990), p. 488.

Filing Information:

Our Reference _____ Customer Reference _____ Country _____

Customer Information:

Name _____ Fax No. _____

Address _____ Telex No. _____

_____ Telephone No. _____

Product Information (appropriate to your business and products):

Product _____ Dimensions _____ x _____ x _____

No. of Units _____ Cubic Measure _____ (in.^{3}/cm^3/ft^3/m^3)

Net Weight per Unit _____ Total Measure _____ (in.^{3}/cm^3/ft^3/m^3)

Gross Weight _____ Schedule B/HTS Number _____

Product Charges:

Cost Per Unit _____ x _____ Units   =   Total   _____

Sales Commissions (name of sales rep or agent) _____   _____

Special Labels/Marks/Promos (source) _____   _____

Ex Factory (cost or price of the product at this point)   _____

Fees—Packing, Marking, Inland Freight:

Labeling/Marking (done by) _____   _____

Export Packing (done by) _____   _____

Strapping/Pallets (provided/done by) _____   _____

Freight Forwarder (Name/Tel) _____   _____

Other Charges—List _____   _____

Inland Freight to (name destination) _____   _____

Subtotal, at (name the point) _____   _____

Port Charges and Documents:

Unloading (heavy lift/bags/conveyor) _____   _____

Figure 8.1 Export Costing Worksheet

Terminal Charges (basis) _____   _____

Consular Documents (messenger used) _____   _____

Certificate of Origin (messenger used) _____   _____

Dock Receipt/Mates Receipt (who arranged) _____   _____

Other Documents or Charges (list) _____   _____

Export License—General Type ___ Validated No. _____   _____

FAS or FOB Vessel (name the port or location) _____   _____

Freight (named destination _____) :

Based on (check each that applies) Weight _____ Measure _____

Ocean ___ Air ___ On Deck ___ Under Deck ___ Reefer ___

Rate ___ per ___ Minimum Weight ___ Volume ___   Total   _____

Insurance:

Coverage Required by Seller ___ Buyer ___ Copy to Bank ___

Type _____ Coverage _____ Rate/$100 _____   Total   _____

FOB ___ , CFR ___ , CIF ___ , Port or Point of Destination ___   _____

Payment, i.e., Draft: Sight _ /Time _ L/C: Sight __ /Time _ , COD _ , Cash _

Other Notes Regarding This Buyer _____

Figure 8.1 Continued

flows. By processing your imports in an FTZ, you defer the payment of duties on the imported good until that good enters the commerce of the United States. If the good is exported out of the FTZ, you do not have to pay import duties and go through the drawback procedure. The use of an FTZ can, therefore, improve cash flow and improve internal operating efficiencies.

The "Filing" and "Customer" information entries are for your record-keeping purposes. You may wish to keep three files or reference systems for each transaction.

1. *Our Reference* refers to your internal system so you can trace this transaction now and in the future. It is a basic piece of an audit trail.

2. *Customer Reference* is a necessary record as your buyer or representative will use this number on all incoming correspondence, tracing, and so forth.

3. The *Country Filing* entry is important because this record of experience by country will give you ready information on your success in a market, the payment patterns for a market, and the product and order patterns if you have more than one representative there. Other basic information can also be derived based on your need for data. This information will be important if one of your executives travels there or meets with your country representatives. It is a history by country. It complements other data in your country files.

4. The *Product Information* section should be retained, by customer. Some of your clients may purchase only a portion of a line or more products. Modify the form to your requirements.

Records as to weights, dimensions, and Schedule B or HTS numbers are convenient to keep as they will save time on subsequent sales.

In the development of an export costing record, you may wish to calculate costs on a *per unit* or a *per ton* basis. The per unit basis is useful for pricing products sold by individual unit, set, or piece. The per ton basis is more appropriate to commodity products (steel scrap, grains, logs and lumber, etc.) where the purchaser's usual and customary market is quoted on a per ton basis.

5. *Product Charges* include the costs of the product, as noted under the pricing discussion at the beginning of the chapter. These product charges may be revised to account for other costs specifically related to exporting, such as advertising to a market, capital costs tied to the market (e.g., development costs), or other such items. You may wish to recover them on each unit of sales, given on your projections of unit sales by market or product.

This may be a difficult allocation process. It is useful to quantify, in cost per unit of sales terms, the resources you have allocated to the development of a market. These are market-related costs rather than product-related costs. Allocation should be on a market basis.

If, for example, costs of US$10,000 were incurred to develop a representative relationship in Country A, and $15,000 in costs were incurred to develop a representative in Country B, allocate these costs based on the country rather than the product. This will place your performance expectations on the appropriate representatives. (Country B should sell more units or sell them at a higher price.) Alternatively, you may wish to consider these export market development costs part of corporate overhead, which is then allocable over all units sold.

6. The *Fees* section identifies those costs paid to others to assist you in the export process. At some point, you may wish to assume these activities and internalize these costs.

Freight forwarders can provide your company with timely and effective services for the movement of your goods. Their services and costs are covered in Chapter 17, Export Documents.

Inland freight can be managed to achieve significant cost savings. Tariff (freight rate) structures vary by type of carrier, type of product being moved, and the size of your shipment. Freight rates, inland and international, are based on the higher of weight of the good or measure of the shipment. Rates are quoted by a "ton" of weight or a "ton" of measure. These terms are explained in more depth in Chapter 15, Logistics.[3]

7. *Port Charges and Documents* covers a series of costs particular to the port you use and the destination of the goods. This reaffirms the importance of this worksheet process for future shipments; this record can provide a leap in the learning curve and significant savings of staff time for the second and later shipments.

U.S. ports charge for special handling and the use of special equipment. Terminal and wharfage charges are fees assessed to recover the cost of maintaining port facilities.

Consular documents, certificates, receipts, and other documents may require fees and costs (Chapter 17). There is no fee for an export license; however, you may incur costs in order to obtain the required licenses for your export (see Chapter 18, Licensing Your Exports).

8. *Freight* refers to international freight. Shipments to Canada, Mexico, and parts of Central America may be made by truck or rail, while shipments to other destinations will be made by air or ocean carrier. Costs will vary by weight, volume, type of carrier, storage, and any special handling requirements (Chapter 15, Logistics). Note that goods stored on deck will be treated differently for insurance purposes as the risk of damage or loss increases by storage on deck. Refrigerated (reefer) containers or ships also require special treatment for insurance purposes, to cover for failure of the refrigeration equipment. Carriers do not provide adequate insurance.

9. *Insurance* will be addressed in Chapter 16, Marine Insurance. Important for this worksheet process is your notation of which party will provide the insurance. If you have negotiated terms of sale in which the buyer is to provide the marine insurance, make sure that you receive payment either in advance of shipment, on FOB or FAS terms, or on a letter of credit. Your risk increases when the buyer is to provide the insurance; the buyer may choose to

---

[3]Note that a "ton" of weight can be 2,000 pounds (short ton), 2,204 pounds (metric ton), or 2,200 pounds (long ton). One "ton" of measure can be either 40 cubic feet or 35 cubic meters. It is important to know the basis of your freight charges.

save the very nominal cost of marine insurance and elect to go "uncovered." In this situation, if the terms of payment are tied to the receipt of the goods in the buyer's country, and the goods fail to arrive due to perils at sea, the buyer may opt to not pay and suffer only the consequent damages of a lawsuit (in which jurisdiction?) and the potential loss of access to your product line. Contingent insurance is available to protect against this type of exposure.

10. *Ex Factory, FAS, FOB, CFR,* and *CIF* are terms of shipment. These terms are explained in Chapter 15, Logistics. Each term in common usage allocates responsibilities between the seller and the buyer. Each term also specifies when title to the goods passes. A firm understanding of these IN-COTERMS is paramount. Refer to Chapter 15.

SUMMARY

A number of factors influence the pricing of a product for sale into an export market. A key step in this pricing process is to either (1) determine the market price for your type of product in the target country or (2) identify the export selling prices of your U.S. competitors.

Your best answers will be approximate indications only. If you customize your product for the user, market and competitor information will be more obscure. Custom production will drive up the cost of each sale, whether made by your sales personnel or your country representative.

Export processing costs can be a major factor in your export selling price. Careful investigation of shipping options and service providers will enable you to control these costs to achieve the best balance between service and price. Each exporter will encounter a different series of costs. The export costing worksheet sets out the principal types.

Your buyer or representative may require that added costs be incurred in the export sales transaction. One of these costs could be for *inspection of the goods.* This cost should appropriately be borne by the importer or buyer as it is done at the buyer's request. Treat it separately in your quotation.

RESOURCES

1. Robert Morris and Associates (RMA), Philadelphia, PA, is a credit and financial analysis firm supporting the creditor community. The firm issues Annual Statement Studies in which most industry segments in the United States are analyzed based on information provided to RMA by commercial bankers and other commercial lenders. Your company, referenced by SIC code, is in the RMA. Your lender uses the RMA to

compare you to your industry when analyzing your financial performance. Most libraries or business schools have these reports.

2. Make your drawback proposal to the Regional Commissioner of Customs or the Drawback and Bonds Branch, Customs Headquarters. Information on drawback programs and procedures is available from Department of the Treasury, U.S. Customs Service, Washington, DC 20229. There are Regional Commissioners of Customs in Boston, Chicago, Houston, Los Angeles, Miami, New Orleans, and New York City. Drawback can significantly reduce the cost of inputs to exported products, thereby giving you the option of reducing your price.

3. The US&FCS district office, your state's international trade division, or the closest ocean port or airport can help you contact the appropriate FTZ for your purposes.

4. In addition to your lawyer and CPA, a well-informed resource on foreign sales corporations is Robert Thornton, a retired international partner of a leading CPA firm. You may reach him at Export FSC International Ltd., 11200 Montgomery Blvd., NE, #8, Albuquerque, NM 87111. Tel: 1-800-243-1372.

9 Customer Service

Service and communications are very important components of the "product" presented to any foreign market. Distance from the point of sale and cost to service from the United States only serve to highlight this point. To the buyer or representative, service capability may be a key feature of the sales process. Communication with your representative is important at all times. The quality of your communications is a key to the relationship you have with that representative. Fred S. Jones, Vice President of Sales for Applied Microsystems Corporation, writes:

> Over the past 20 years I have found several key ingredients for successful customer service in the international marketplace. These are: a proven product, a service policy and procedures, effective communications, and one person responsible for making it all work. Let's look at each of these items.
>
> **Proven product.** This is the most important ingredient. Having a product that works, that has market demand, with knowledge of how to support it, are essential before going overseas. The cost in time, resources, and reputation from the introduction of a bad product are often insurmountable. Even with a proven product, you need to assess local service requirements on a market-by-market basis. What is acceptable in one market may not work in another.
>
> International markets demand a high quality product; one that is reliable, performs as advertised, and has support. Therefore, success of imported products often depends on the level of customer service provided. Mercedes Benz is a great example.
>
> **Service policy and service procedure.** The next key ingredient is the type of customer service you provide and how you provide it. You should start with the local market requirements for warranty, liability, and duration and use these as a basis for your policy. Since most international markets are leaning toward customer satisfaction, you need to offer at least the same level of service as local competitors and a higher level if your product is not unique.
>
> Consider options such as free replacement or money-back guarantees. If the customer knows you stand behind your product he will be more willing to buy an

---

Portions of this discussion were adapted from John S. Gordon, "After Sales Service," *A Basic Guide to Exporting* (Washington, DC: U.S. Department of Commerce, International Trade Administration, 1991).

import. Other factors to consider: Will you offer support contracts or agreements? Do customers expect basic training or installation at no extra charge? Customers require a lot of hand-holding, especially in Europe and Japan. If it makes business sense, do it.

Communications. It is best to have your communications process established before you have to provide customer service. Since distributors and customers will have the same questions, problems, and support requirements, the sales department is often responsible for communications.

Your communications procedure should focus on timeliness and accuracy of response. In today's world, there is no excuse for a tardy response. Always respond immediately, no matter how trivial the question; even if just to acknowledge receipt and state when more information will be available. Very often an order may be waiting for some minor clarification. He who responds first is often the winner.

Summary. International success is very dependent on how well you provide customer service. One way to ensure this is to make a company commitment to providing service; put someone in charge, assign responsibilities, and make sure that people are accountable for follow up. In my many years of doing business in Japan, much of my success has been from taking a page titled "over-support" out of their book. I feel that my company has gotten it right when our Japanese customers perceive us as providing better service than our Japanese competitors!

SERVICE

Service has many definitions. It is the prompt delivery of the product. It is courteous sales personnel. It is a localized user's manual or service manual. It is ready access to a service facility. It is knowledgeable, cost-effective maintenance, repair, or replacement. It is location. It is dealer support.

Service varies by the product type, the quality of the product, the price of the product, and the distribution channel employed. If your products require no service, such as food products, some consumer goods, or commercial disposables, the issue is resolved when you identify the distribution channels, quality criteria, and return policies.

The characteristics of consumer durables and some consumables demand that service be available. Service is a product feature expected by the consumer.

All foreign markets are sophisticated. Foreign buyers of industrial goods place service at the forefront of the criteria they evaluate when making a purchasing decision. This fact must be clearly understood; the businesspeople you deal with in the most undeveloped country will be well educated and have sound business skills. It is for this and other good reasons that these people are successful in their respective markets.

Each market has expectations for its suppliers/vendors. Each U.S. exporter, whether manufacturer, distributor, or other, must ensure that its service performance is comparable to that of the predominant competitors active in the market. This level of performance is an important determinant in ensuring a competitive position, given the other factors of product quality, price, promotion, and delivery.

No Service

Your strategy and market-entry decision may dictate that you do not provide after-sale service. You may determine that your export objective is the single or multiple opportunistic entry into export markets. While this may work in the short run, secondary and later product offerings will be less successful. Buyers will recall your failure to provide expected levels of service. Your market development and sales expenditures may result in one-time sales. Your expenses are not spread over longer production runs, ongoing sales programs, and multiple sales to developed buyers.

SERVICE DELIVERY OPTIONS

Service is an important factor in the initial export sale and ongoing success of your products in foreign markets. You have many options for the delivery of service to your foreign buyers.

The lowest cost option, also the most inconvenient to your buyer (a retail, wholesale, commercial, or industrial consumer of your products) is for the product to be returned to your manufacturing or distribution facility in the United States for service or repair. The buyer will incur a very high cost, lose the utility of the product for an extended period of time, and you or the buyer will incur the return export costs of these same goods. You will need to re-license the goods for export (Chapter 18). There are practical, cost-effective alternatives to this option.

If your selected distribution channel is a joint venture (JV) or other partner arrangement, that partner may have a service or repair capability in the market(s) you seek to penetrate. Your negotiations and agreements with that JV partner should include provisions for repairs, maintenance, and warranty service. The cost of providing this service should be negotiated into the agreement.

For exporters of consumer goods sold at retail outlets, the best service option is to utilize local service facilities. This will require front-end expenses to identify service vendors and train local service outlets.

A Canadian company (now owned by a Dutch conglomerate) provides an excellent example for U.S. firms. This company, a leading manufacturer of personal-care items, uses U.S. distributors and sales reps to generate purchases by large and small retailers across the United States. The products are purchased at retail by individual consumers.

The Canadian exporter has identified and contracted with local consumer electronic repair facilities in leading cities in the United States. Each product sold at retail includes a warranty and service certificate listing "authorized" warranty and service centers in the United States. The local service firm contracts to provide service or replacement for the product line. The manufacturer can project anticipated warranty, replacement, and service costs based on experience within its existing markets. Each service facility can be audited annually (or more frequently) to ensure suitable performance.

There are administrative, training, and supervisory overhead costs associated with this warranty and service program. However, consumers believe the manufacturer is a local company and, therefore, it competes on equal footing with U.S. manufacturers. This is a good lesson for U.S. exporters. This is a way to localize your products in each market served.

Sales of your product into commercial or industrial markets may demand a different approach. Your selection of a representative to serve a region (Southeast Asia), a nation (Chile), or a market (the Dutch-speaking region of the EC) should be based on that distributor's ability and willingness to service your products, as well as factors identified in earlier chapters, such as the ability to cover the territory, understand the product, pay for the product in a timely manner, and inventory the product in suitable quantities.

In order to determine your potential representative's ability to service your products, you must ask questions about existing service facilities; the types, models, and age of existing service equipment; training practices for service personnel; and the firm's experience in servicing goods or equipment similar to yours.

If you manufacture products that are sold directly to end users, service and timely performance are key purchasing issues. Service drives your profitability. The nature of your product may require that you deliver on-site service to the buyer within some very specific time parameters. You may be required to maintain a parts store at or near the buyer's location. You may be required to train the buyer's personnel so they can service your equipment.

A marketing note: Add a service-training package to your product offering; train the users, increase their comfort with the product and your organization, and they will tend to purchase future requirements from your firm.

The Contract

Your sales contract should anticipate a reasonable level of on-site service and the costs involved. The contract price should include this reasonable level of service. Use existing performance and service history as a basis for estimating service and warranty requirements on your export sales, and cost your sale accordingly. This is a customary and accepted practice of small and large exporters alike.

At some level of export activity, it will become cost effective for your company to establish its own branch or subsidiary operation in the foreign market(s). This branch or subsidiary may be a one-person operation or a facility staffed with sales, administration, service, and other personnel. Most personnel should be nationals of the host country or third-country nationals.

While this is the high-cost option, it enables you to ensure sales and service quality. You must continue to train your personnel in sales, products, and service. This option increases your control (always an issue in sales and marketing management). This operation could be centrally located to serve a region that includes multiple markets, for example, Singapore for Southeast Asia, Panama for Latin America, and Belgium for the EC.

Manufacturers of similar or related products may find it cost effective to consolidate service, training, and support in each export market. Service can be delivered by U.S.-based personnel, a foreign facility under contract, or a jointly owned foreign-based service facility. This option will raise a number of competitive and anticompetitive issues.

This joint sales and service activity may be interpreted under U.S. laws to be in restraint of trade or otherwise market controlling or monopolistic. You should obtain competent legal guidance when developing this joint operating arrangement. A service company formed under the Export Trading Company Act of 1982 could carry out this joint service arrangement. Operating within the terms of the act may offer protection from U.S. antitrust laws. It is therefore imperative that your agreement with your representative be specific as to the form of the service facility, the number of people on the staff, inspection provisions, training programs, and payment of costs associated with the maintenance of a suitable facility.

The depth or breadth of your warranty in a country or region may be tied to the service facility you have in that market. You must be certain that you promise only what you can deliver. You must also ensure that your warranty offerings comply with the laws of the country of operation.

Another part of your agreement may detail the training you provide to your foreign representative. This can include frequency of training, who must be trained, where the training is provided, and which party absorbs travel and per diem costs.

New Sales Opportunities and Improved Customer Relations

Your foreign service facility may be the major contact point between your firm and the buyer. If this is the case, your reputation is created and maintained by this service facility. The service experience must be positive, reinforcing sales and the service encounter.

The service call can be an excellent sales opportunity. In your U.S. market-development efforts, your service personnel are trained to look for new sales opportunities and report them to your sales staff; do the same overseas. You must look to expand the capabilities of your overseas service personnel or service manager; train them in the benefits of your products, the performance options available within your line, and the flexibility of your programs (price, delivery, payment, etc.). This will strengthen your representative's capacity within a market, improve his or her sales opportunities, and thus improve your profitability.

More than one leading U.S. industrial products exporter sells its products as a "tool to do the job" rather than as "a truck," an "earth mover," a "cutting machine," or "software." This is an important product distinction. Your service capability enables your customer to complete his or her job more efficiently with your "tool." Training service managers and service personnel in this type of thinking will vitalize your service facilities and generate new sales opportunities.

Foreign service personnel can assist the customer in making life-cycle decisions regarding the efficient operation of your equipment, how to update it for more and longer cost-effective operation, and when to replace it as the task expands or changes. Each service contact is an opportunity to educate the customer and expand your product sales opportunities. You must train your foreign-based service personnel in this aspect of their job.

SUMMARY

Each foreign market offers a unique opportunity for the U.S. exporter. Care and attention to the development of in-country sales and distribution capabilities are paramount. Delivery of after-sales service is critical to the near- and long-term success of your efforts in any market.

RESOURCES

1. A humorous perspective on translation issues is offered by Roger E. Axtell, *The Do's and Taboos of International Trade* (New York: John Wiley & Sons, 1991).

2. Major vendors of international telecommunications services in the United States are USSprint, AT&T, and MCI. Many other companies across the country, such as Gateway USA,[sm] offer international telecommunications service programs. Contact your long distance service, refer to the yellow pages, or contact your peers or your trade association for their recommendations.

3. Fred Jones, Vice President of Sales at Applied Microsystems Corporation, is responsible for U.S. and international sales for this Redmond, WA, based leading manufacturer of computer emulator and debugging hardware and software. He has an extensive background in the establishment and management of international sales and service operations for major global corporations and emerging-growth companies.

10 Communications, Negotiations, Offers, and Complaints

Communications is important in any type of business, but it is vital in exporting. Buyers are always at a distance, often thousands of miles away, and English is usually the second language.

Many authorities advise U.S. exporters to use the language of the buyer in *all* situations. This may not be possible or cost effective. Unless you have a staff member fluent in the current idiom and usage of a particular language, this approach can be quite costly for you. It is a valuable courtesy to communicate in the language of your prospect or representative; however, your opportunity for error is quite high. Good translations are available, at a cost. Lower cost academic or student translations can often be incorrect or lack accuracy regarding important performance features and service, sales, price, or delivery options. These errors can be harmful to you and your future success in a market. Use great care when selecting a translation service.

Every term and condition of your export and service arrangements must be very clear to both parties at all times. There must be a meeting of the minds in every respect. Misunderstandings lead to disputes and, in a dispute, the exporter always loses. At best, the second sale will not occur.

As export transaction volume grows, it may be useful to have translation capacity in house. This is a cost issue for each firm. Does the translator bring other tangible values to the firm? (How do you keep this person gainfully productive for the balance of each week?)

Initial communication in English is acceptable; it is the language of business in most countries. Your contacts may respond in their language, suggesting they prefer their native language to English. (This is not the norm.) At that point, you have the option to translate or forego the (as yet unknown) opportunity. There is no hard and fast rule; each situation and relationship varies.

Contracts, sales promotion, and market development materials are a different matter. As noted in Chapter 5, the contract arrangement may be in English or another language, or both (Canadian government documents are a good example of this bilingual document practice). Further, each party must agree to a language for the relationship, just as they agree to the jurisdiction of the agreement, the arbitration venue, and other important issues.

Promotional literature, product brochures, and catalog pages should be translated into the language of the target market. By the nature of its use, this translation should be perfect. Business guides and textbooks are filled with both funny and horrific stories of large and sophisticated firms making obvious and unthinking errors when translating their product or promotional information.

In creating brochures and promotional literature for foreign markets, your existing artwork can often be used to good effect. The translated text information can be typeset and new material printed in short order. Cost for this process, without a new product photo session and associated extras, will be nominal. Test the artwork with people of the target market culture before you print.

COMMUNICATIONS ABROAD

Each communication with a foreign firm is a sales opportunity. Written communications take various forms: letter, fax, telex, or cable. Two of these mediums allow you to demonstrate your professionalism and the quality of your firm.

You would not let a salesperson make a domestic or foreign call in an ill-fitting suit or use dated, old, or inappropriate materials. Treat your written communications with the same concern. The initial contact letter is your first and best (and perhaps last) opportunity to make a good impression. It is well worth the expense to have special stationery for your international operations. This export stationery should be air-mail-weight paper (difficult to find), convey the perception of a solid organization, and provide the recipient with other useful information.

This letterhead should include:

1. The company logo.
2. The company street and mailing address, with the USA notation after the zip code.

3. The name and title of the sender. If appropriate, add wording to identify the sender as a representative of the export or international department/division.

4. The correct telephone and fax numbers. If you use telex or cable include those addresses.

5. The name and location of your bank.

The mailing envelopes, also air mail weight, should have your logo and your return address with USA after the zip code.

This type of communication will convey useful information and a clear impression that yours is a professional organization. It's important to maintain this level of presentation throughout your relationship.

Fax communications should receive the same degree of attention. If you use a fax cover sheet, be sure it is complete and informative. Do not clutter it with unnecessary information. This cover sheet should be only as long as is needed to carry the covering message, because international telephone charges apply by the minute or fractions of minutes. The longer the cover sheet, the higher your nonproductive telecommunication costs. A five-inch cover sheet (one-half page) works quite well.

Alternatively, have some inexpensive fax letterhead made up and use it. The letterhead contains the cover sheet information and the balance of the page is available for your message. This is even more cost effective. It is standard practice by firms in other countries.

Other forms of written communication are available, although there is decreased usage with the improvement in fax transmission speeds, equipment price, and transmission quality. Cable and telex are long-accepted forms of international communication. They have, for the most part, been replaced by more advanced communications services.

If you wish to have a third party provide services beyond the capabilities of advanced fax systems, contact at least two telecommunications service vendors, explain what you want to accomplish, and compare proposals. Factors that should affect your decision include basic cost of the package, minimum usage levels, equipment costs, transmissions speeds, billing basis, and number and spread of end-points served (can they get to your target country or city). As your export activity increases, you will need to become familiar with EDI (Electronic Data Interchange), an electronic messaging service used by major exporters, importers, freight forwarders, transportation companies, and others. EDI is also used by leading U.S. manufacturers and suppliers as a fast, accurate system of communicating product, shipment, sales, and payment information to their counterparties. Contact information on EDI is available from your port or freight forwarder.

ORAL COMMUNICATION

Each oral communication, particularly over the telephone at a distance, is both a sales opportunity and a relationship-reinforcement opportunity. Recognize that telephone rates from the United States to any non-U.S. destination are less expensive than long distance rates available in other countries (except Hong Kong). If it's your call, it's your budget; use the time wisely. Have a list of the items you wish to cover: negotiating points if any negotiating is to take place during the call, sales and service figures, new product notes, and other information that will add value to the relationship.

With incoming calls, let the caller set the agenda. Respect the fact that he or she may be concerned with the cost of the conversation along with the content. Socialize if the caller initiates it.

OFFERS AND COUNTEROFFERS

Your initial contact letter(s) may generate purchase inquiries. These inquiries may come in by fax, telephone, or mail. Respond promptly. Each is a sales opportunity, each is an opportunity to foster a potentially important representative relationship in the inquirer's country.

The inquirers will have some basic information about your company and your products. They may request samples, and they may request pricing for a sample or stocking order under any variety of shipping terms. Respond promptly. The corporate policy of at least one leading manufacturer (computer interface products) is a comprehensive reply within two hours of receipt of the query. For complex quotes, this initial reply may be an acknowledgment and a commitment to a complete response by a specific date and time.

If the response or query is by mail and does not appear to be as time sensitive, a mail response may be appropriate. Note the date stamp on the envelope and compare it to the date of receipt of the letter. It will take at least that many days for your reply to get back to the inquirer.

The Offer

The most important area of communications is making offers for the sale of goods—offers that result in sales. If your offer is accepted, you have a contract and you are legally bound to perform by shipping the goods exactly as stated in your offer. Therefore, it is important that you take extra care with every facet of the offer. Be sure that you can perform under the terms and conditions you have quoted. An offer can be in the form of a pro forma invoice, a fax, a letter, a cable, a telex, or a verbal communication.

Draft your offer, then review it. Review the clarity and precision of each of the following points:

1. Give a detailed description of each item you are offering.

2. How are the products packed?

3. What quantity are you offering? How many or how much?

4. What is the quality of the product? How is the quality ensured or guaranteed? Will a certificate from a third party be required? Is inspection or certification by a registered agency or a government department required?

5. How and when can you ship? By ocean vessel, plane, train, truck, express mail, or courier? When? Be sure your quoted mode is available at your quoted time; for example, do not quote an ocean shipment from your port to Santiago during March if a vessel serving both your port and Santiago does not call on your port in March.

6. What is your price? Are you quoting per unit, per shipment, with discounts for volume orders? What is the currency of your sale (Chapter 13)?

7. What are the terms of sale; where does the sale take place? FAS, CIP, CIF, CFR, or other terms (Chapter 12)?

8. What are the terms of payment? Open account, cash in advance, letter of credit, collection, or other (Chapter 11)? Which party will insure the goods?

9. Is this a sale of a job lot with a limited or uncertain future supply? If so, note this in your offer. Your buyers are sophisticated people; do not mislead them. Add the wording "subject to prior sale" if you have a number of offers out; or add the words "subject to supply" if there is an availability question.

10. State a timeframe during which your offer is available. Two phrases are in common use in the export business. The phrase "immediate acceptance necessary" means that the buyer must accept within 24 hours of receipt of your offer. "Prompt acceptance" usually means that a response within one week is required. To eliminate any confusion or uncertainty, state the date by which a response is required or state the last date for which your offer is available, e.g., 1700 U.S. West Coast Time on 22 April 19XX.

11. Can you make shipments regularly? How much can you ship on a regular basis? Do you have adequate capacity to dedicate or allocate to export markets and thereby ensure your buyer of continuous supplies?

The Counteroffer

Most offers are either accepted or rejected rather than ignored. On occasion, you may receive a counteroffer to your offer. Assume that you offered your goods to the buyer in Lyon at US$28.00 per unit, 100-unit minimum order, CIF Lyon, shipment 15 May 19XX. You receive this reply: "Will purchase 300 units CIF Lyon via sight letter of credit at US$25.50 per unit."

You are bound by your offer on the terms and conditions of your offer. Had the terms and conditions been accepted, you would have had a sale. However, your buyer did not accept your offer. The buyer made a counteroffer at US$25.50 per unit. This counteroffer cancels your offer; you are relieved of your obligation to deliver.

The buyer has now made you an offer by way of a counter. You can accept it, decline it, or make a counteroffer. You may reject this outright; however, you may want to give it some thought. This counteroffer is for triple the number of units, at a 8.93 percent discount. Did your original quote at US$28.00 include freight and handling costs? Will the freight and handling costs be US$2.50 per unit on the added 200 units? Probably not. Even if these costs did increase, what is the value of that additional 200 units to your production operations? Does an order of this magnitude warrant a discount of 8.93 percent?

Also consider the effects of your acceptance of this discounted order. You have then set a new price level for future orders from this same buyer. The US$28.00 per unit is gone. Negotiate! Consider a counteroffer at US$27.00. (American businesspeople are known worldwide as relatively poor negotiators, more interested in a quick sale than in the process of the sale. Many foreign buyers are willing to pay more than they offer. The offer is part of the cultural process of negotiation. Learn to participate in the process; it can be enjoyable and profitable.)

Acceptance

Acceptance of an offer can occur two ways:

1. The buyer communicates acceptance.

2. The buyer follows the terms of the offer. Your offer conditioned on a letter of credit could result in a letter of credit issued in your favor, for the amount and on the terms of the offer. This is acceptance of your offer.

Acknowledge this acceptance promptly. Use an *acknowledgment of order* form. It could read something like this:

This acknowledges with thanks your order number [   ] received [   ]. We expect to ship by [fill in the mode applicable] on or about [anticipated date of shipment] from [port, airport, or city]. Terms of sale are [as in your offer]. Thank you for the opportunity to be of service.

Silence does not make a contract. Do not advise the potential buyer that you "will ship 300 units at US$27.00 per unit CIF Lyon unless we hear from you by 1 May 19XX." You do not have a contract and the buyer is under no obligation to you. Acceptance of your counteroffer did not occur.

THE PRO FORMA INVOICE

A pro forma invoice is a quotation in the form of a written letter, memo, fax, cable, or telex. Until it is accepted by the buyer, it cannot be considered to constitute an agreement to sell. A pro forma invoice is a structured response to an order inquiry. It is the seller's half of the contract. A pro forma invoice is generally required in the following circumstances:

1. The seller specifies that payment for the transaction is to be by an irrevocable letter of credit. The buyer will use this to substantiate his need for a letter of credit to (a) his banker and (b) his government.
2. The buyer's country requires that an import license be issued for each import and must approve the pro forma invoice before making foreign exchange available for payment by the importer.

While not required for the conduct of international sales activities, the use of a standardized pro forma invoice is beneficial to communications between the parties to a sale.

Figure 10.1 shows a sample of a pro forma invoice. The pro forma invoice must contain the following information:

1. The seller's name and company address. If the corporate address is different from the point of manufacture or shipment, both should be noted. The buyer needs to know this.
2. The buyer's name and company address. If the shipment destination differs from the buyer's corporate address, both should be noted. The seller needs to know this.
3. The intermediate consignee/notify party. With prior agreement, the product may be directed to an intermediate party for customs clearing or handling purposes. The notify party would be the customshouse broker. With air shipments, the ultimate consignee on an air waybill receives effective title and ownership of the goods when the aircraft lands at its destination. Consignment to a bank or reputable third

NORTHWEST EXPORTERS, LTD.
8080 Parkway Blvd., Suite 500
Seattle, WA 98005-0505
Tel: 206-555-0500 Fax: 206-555-0005
Pro Forma Invoice

Buyer:	Pro Forma Date:	December 18, 19XX
KTS Corporation	Pro Forma Number:	K-320-9x
1638-3, Seocho-dong	Customer reference:	PO No. 23487
Gangnam-ku		
Seoul, 135 KOREA	Marks:	n/a
	Gross Weight:	16,500 kg

Quantity	Description	Unit Price	Amount
1 container	Used engine parts per P.O. 23487	n/a	US$29,784.50
	Ocean freight		1,250.00
	Forwarder and other charges		273.00
	Marine Insurance at 110% of invoice value		138.00
Total this quotation			US$31,445.50

Shipment from:	US Port
Shipment to:	Busan, Korea
Terms of shipment:	CIF, Busan, Korea
Terms of payment:	Letter of Credit

Special Instructions:

1. Terms of Payment: Irrevocable documentary letter of credit with 60-day sight drafts
2. Letter of credit to be advised through our bankers: U.S. Bank of Washington, Seattle, Washington
3. This quotation valid until January 5, 19XX
4. Shipment must occur on or before April 15, 19XX
5. Shipment will be made upon receipt and acceptance of your letter of credit

These commodities are licensed by the U.S. government for ultimate destination _____

_____
Authorized signature

Figure 10.1 Pro Forma Invoice

party tends to prevent release of the goods prior to payment or settlement by the buyer.

4. The type of transportation. The importer must agree to the method of shipment and advise whether partial shipments, transshipments, or other combined forms of shipment are to be made.

5. The seller's port of export must be specified.

6. The buyer's port of import must be specified.

7. Terms of sale must be specified. It will be useful to attach a page of "instructions for the issuance of a letter of credit" to inform the buyer of the standard letter-of-credit terms you require. This form is set out in Chapter 11.

8. Description of the goods. Provide an accurate and complete description of the goods, with the standard weights and physical measurements (metric is required) of each piece, unit, or package. Include net and gross weights. All shipping and packing marks should be identified. (To reduce theft or pilferage, packing boxes should not be marked with their contents or the brand name of the supplier.)

9. The individual value of each item should be set out. The cost of the goods should be separated out from the cost of the movement of the goods. State transportation charges, forwarder charges and fees, ocean freight, insurance, and other charges separately on your pro forma. Import duties are assessed on the value of the goods. You help your buyer if you help him or her reduce duty costs. These items should correspond to prior negotiations and agreements.

10. The timeframe for the validity of the pro forma should be stated. Do not leave the validity of your pro forma (your quotation) open ended. This could result in an unintended contract, at a date when your costs have changed. State your deadlines in specific terms such as dates (and hours if applicable). This will avoid misunderstandings.

11. The anticipated date of shipment should be the date on which the ship is available for loading or is scheduled to sail from your port of export, plus a hedge factor of at least a few days. Be sure to allow for your production time. This date of shipment should be subsequent to receipt of acceptance of the pro forma and receipt of the letter of credit, if any. *Note:* If you miss the latest shipping date stated on a letter of credit, you lose the protection of the letter of credit.

A pro forma can be prepared on the company letterhead or on a standard long-form commercial invoice form. If the latter is used, identify the form as a pro forma invoice.

COMPLAINTS

No matter how careful you are with each shipment, you will eventually receive a complaint. In the buyer's opinion, each complaint is well founded. You may or may not agree. How you resolve complaints will determine both the level of trust you develop with your buyer or representative and the degree of success you will enjoy in your targeted markets. Handle each complaint promptly. Be courteous and businesslike. Keep your word and live up to your representative's perceptions.

In a few trades, complaints are a result of the nature of the business. For example, the fish trade has its own set of performance criteria, and complaints are an accepted part of the business. Food products for humans and animals are trades subject to a high level of contention. Food products must pass inspectors, and a high percentage of food products can be rejected.[1] Buyers dictate the inspection agency acceptable to them. In addition to U.S. government inspection agencies, foreign buyers may want inspections by city, state, or other recognized inspection services in the United States. Your buyer may want inspection at the destination port. (Use caution, it's an expensive return trip for the goods.)

How can a company know if a complaint is justified? With food products, the issue is clear. The product will be inspected and rejected by food or health inspectors. Rejection warrants a full and timely refund to the buyer. For nonfood products, the answers may be less clear. The complaint and its resolution have an impact on the exporter's reputation. Some issues to consider are:

1. How long have you had business dealings with the complainant?

2. Is this buyer's business worth retaining?

3. Can this buyer influence others in his or her territory?

4. What is the cost to resolve the complaint? Can this cost be shared or negotiated?

If your relationship has been a good one for some time, the complaint may be justified. If it's a new or rocky relationship, noting the above list, you may wish to exercise more care in evaluating the complaint.

The first rule to follow with *all* complaints, even if you believe a complaint to be fictitious, is to express regret and concern. Then initiate the conversation to settle the complaint. The second rule is to notify your insurance carrier. You may have insurance to cover the situation at issue. And keep your insurer

---

[1]The USFDA inspects a broad range of products.

informed. Be sure your actions to resolve the complaint do not eliminate the loss, damage, or peril coverage you have purchased.

If the complaint is from a buyer with whom you have a longstanding relationship and is for damage, loss, or poor quality for a portion of the shipment and a settlement has not been requested, ask what the complainant considers to be fair. Because of the nature of this longstanding relationship, it may be appropriate to settle the claim without question; take the steps necessary to do so. Tell the complainant that "as you know the condition of the goods [whatever fits the nature of the claim], we will settle [pay, replace, etc.] immediately when we receive the full particulars." In an important and trusting relationship, do not be petty in the settlement of nominal complaints; the risk of damage to the relationship is too great.

If the complaint is from a buyer with whom you have a newer relationship, it is still serious. Start the communication with, "We are sorry that . . . [the nature of the complaint]." If practical, retain a recognized inspection agency to conduct an examination of the goods, products, or events that are the subject of the complaint. There is a cost for this type of inspection that must be weighed against the value of the claim or its settlement.

Do not reject a complaint before you consider the loss of goodwill of the complainant, even if you feel the complaint is frivolous. Don't hide behind inspectors and certificates; inspectors can and do make mistakes. Consider the face-saving gesture of a nominal settlement so both parties can win.

If you decide to reject a complaint with no compensation, be gracious by stating, "We are sorry that [state the complaint], but . . . ." Then state the reasons why you have not accepted any liability for the loss. In closing add, "If you have further evidence of [damage, loss, quality, etc.], we certainly will take it under consideration and make an adjustment if it is then possible."

Each contact with a buyer, representative, or prospect is an opportunity to build goodwill and increase sales. If you handle complaints promptly, consistently, and fairly, this will add to the strength of your reputation.

AMBIGUOUS TERMS

Different cultures, languages, practices, and expectations create many opportunities for confusion and misunderstanding. In each international communication, it is important to be clear and specific. Use standard terminology customary to the trade—terms that can be readily understood or interpreted by both parties. Three excellent examples demonstrate the possibilities for misunderstanding:

1. *Shipping or sales terms.* The standard for the interpretation of shipping terms in international trade is the INCOTERMS. The INCOTERMS are quite

specific about the meaning of such terms as CIF, CFR, FOB, and 10 others. INCOTERMS are also specific about the transfer of title and responsibility for goods, transport, and services. Failure to understand the implications of a shipping term can confuse your counterparty and result in the loss of the goods.

2. *The dollar.* There are 15 different "dollars" in use around the world.[2] Each has a value different from the U.S. dollar (also called USD or US$). Take care and always use the identifier USD or US$ when making a quotation or referencing a price in our currency. If your reference is another "dollar" currency (e.g., Canada or Hong Kong), clarify the usage (e.g., C$ or HK$).

3. *Ton.* This term has two sets of meanings, each with variations. A "ton" of weight is 2,000 pounds (short ton), 2,240 pounds (long ton), or 2,204 pounds (metric ton). A "ton" of measure is 35.3 cubic feet (metric) or 40 cubic feet (long ton). Be clear on the type and usage of your "tons."

Other opportunities for confusion arise from trade in particular types of goods. Usage and terminology are different from country to country. Make the nominal effort required to ensure that you are providing your counterparty with meaningful information.

SUMMARY

Effective communications will launch your export efforts and, more than any other single factor, dictate the extent of your success in foreign markets. Communications is a two-way process and it is incumbent on the exporter to listen, to hear, and to understand what the prospect or customer is communicating.

Make the commitment to translate key company and product information into the language of your strongest target markets. This will demonstrate your dedication to the marketplace and ensure at least a reading of your introductory material.

Structure your internal communications procedures so that any foreign buyer can effectively reach you 24 hours a day. Have a separate line for your fax machine. Have a 24-hour voice mail system with distinct and simple prompts.

Learn to negotiate. If you are currently an effective negotiator, take the next step and learn the nuances of the negotiating styles of your target countries.

Be flexible in your dealings with foreign prospects and clients. A well-handled complaint is truthfully a sales opportunity in disguise; solutions to

---

[2]Information provided by Ms. Gretchen Steele, Foreign Exchange Department, U.S. Bank of Washington.

problems can improve relationships and lead to new product or service markets.

RESOURCES

1. A directory of and instructions on the use of INCOTERMS can be purchased from ICC Publishing Corporation, 156 Fifth Avenue, New York, NY 10010. Tel: 212-206-1150.

2. The U.S. Food and Drug Administration has inspection offices in a number of locations across the United States. Look in the government listings section of your telephone book under the title "Health and Human Services, Department of." If this is not listed, contact your closest US&FCS office for the needed information.

3. 3M Corporation distributes at least two Post-It™ fax headers that save time, space, and telecommunications line costs.

4. Contract law in the United States is well defined by the Uniform Commercial Code and interpretations. Each export sales arrangement should clearly set out the applicable laws governing the contract. Competent legal counsel should be consulted when drafting any such contract. Each district office of the US&FCS, the local World Trade Club, or the closest World Trade Center can provide a list of attorneys that specialize in international sales contract matters. Refer also to the U.N. Convention on Contracts for the International Sale of Goods (CISG).

5. Study the culture of your target markets to develop appropriate negotiating skills. Many cost-effective cultural training programs are available on a regular basis. Contact the closest community college or the district office of the US&FCS for information on programs that may be offered in your area.

6. A limited number of commercial printers in major cities have stocks of international pro forma and commercial invoice forms. If you elect to use your own form or letterhead, add the line "These products are licensed by the U.S. government for export to the ultimate destination _____ or a destination control statement required by the
        (country)
   BXA."

PART THREE
Export Finance

Part Three introduces and reviews trade finance mechanisms, covers the issues you will confront in a barter or countertrade transaction, examines foreign exchange and its role, and suggests how financing can be used as a sales and marketing tool.

Tradition suggests that trade finance means the exporter receives a letter of credit, ships the goods, and gets paid. Many ill-informed advisors will tell you that is the *only* way to export. This is wrong. The world of international trade is changing rapidly and successful exporters must adapt.

Buyers in most developed countries expect and often can command terms more liberal than letters of credit. Buyers in many developing countries are able to negotiate payment terms as part of their purchase arrangements.

The exporter does not have to take on excessive or extraordinary risks to meet this type of competition. However, the exporter does have to be creative and call on the best its banks and financiers have to offer.

Most of the risks inherent in the export business can be managed, mitigated, or eliminated by passing them on to a third party. That third party is often a bank, insurance company, or other financial intermediary. Part Three deals with the financial risks that attend the export business and provides guidance on how to minimize or eliminate these risks.

Recent studies confirm that letters of credit are being used less frequently in international trade. They are certainly in use for trade with most less developed or economically challenged countries. However, these countries do not account for the majority of world trade. The United States, the European Community, and Japan alone account for over 60 percent of total world trade. The balance is parceled out among developed and less developed nations alike.

Your major markets of opportunity in the future will be dominated by the countries of the trading "blocs" suggested in Chapters 20, 21, and 22. Buyers in these countries, sought after just as quality buyers in the United States are sought by exporters from other nations, will negotiate seriously for advantageous payment terms.

Your success in foreign markets will be determined by the "packaging" of your products. One important feature of that packaging is the financing program you offer. Part Three will assist you in the development and management of suitable financing alternatives for your new clients in new and challenging markets.

11 Financing Techniques

The payment terms you offer the buyer in your export sale transaction are a major factor in your long-term success. You must know the standard payment terms for your product in the buyer's market, and you must be prepared to deal with the question of the financing you will offer to the buyer. This means you and your banker must talk—before the sale, before your trip. This meeting with your banker will allay the uncertainties you may have about the terms you can offer and subsequently finance. Don't find yourself in the position of selling on terms you are later unable to support.

PAYMENT ALTERNATIVES

Each export transaction or export relationship will require that the exporter establish payment terms. These terms may differ greatly from buyer to buyer, or terms may be similar for different buyers within a region. Customary payment terms for noncapital goods transactions or other short-term payment programs include:

1. Cash with order.
2. Confirmed irrevocable letter of credit (confirmed L/C).
3. Irrevocable letter of credit (L/C).
4. Revocable L/C.[1]
5. Sight draft, documents against payment (D/P).
6. Time draft, documents against acceptance (D/A).

---

[1]A revocable letter of credit is not in customary use. It is a high-risk transaction for the exporter. If you wish to learn about revocable letters of credit, contact your international banker or your international trade consultant.

7. Open account.

8. Consignment.

Factors That Determine the Terms of Payment

Before the exporter grants any of terms 2 through 8 above to the prospective buyer, he or she must evaluate the *conditions* of the sale. These conditions are:

1. The buyer's credit standing.

2. The amount of the sale or transaction.

3. The availability of foreign exchange in the buyer's country.

4. The exchange controls that exist in the buyer's country.

5. Political conditions in the buyer's country.

6. Risks associated with the type of merchandise to be shipped.

7. Customs in the trade; what is the usual practice.

8. Market conditions: a buyer's or a seller's market.

9. Payment terms offered by competitors.

Ask your buyer for a copy of his or her financial statements for the last three years. If received, review them as you would the financial reports of any potential debtor/client. If you have difficulty with the foreign currency accounting or accounting procedures, contact your banker, your accounting professional, or an international business consultant for guidance.

The nine conditions listed above will determine, in large part, the type of payment terms you will have to grant, negotiate, or agree to with any buyer or distributor. If you have tremendous leverage (or simply do not want the business) you can stick with the cash with order option. To open a market, build a presence, or strengthen a budding relationship, it may be necessary to give the buyer some support by way of extended payment terms.[2] Those terms, noted above, are set out in Table 11.1.

Each payment term you consider has four attendant risks: credit risk, exchange risk, transfer risk, and political risk. These risks are described briefly in Table 11.2. Table 11.3 sets out the interrelationship of the payment terms (Table 11.1) and the risks (Table 11.2).

---

[2]Chapter 12, Financing in the Marketing Mix, deals with the role of payment terms and financing in the buyer's decision process.

Table 11.1
Principal Terms of Sale in an Export Transaction

Cash with order	Self-explanatory
Confirmed irrevocable L/C	A letter of credit issued by the importer's bank and confirmed by a bank usually in the exporter's country. The obligation of the second bank is added to the obligation of the issuing bank to honor drafts presented in accordance with the terms of the credit.
Unconfirmed irrevocable L/C	A letter of credit issued by the importer's bank.
Revocable L/C	A letter of credit that may be withdrawn from the beneficiary at any time without prior notice to the exporter. It does not carry a bank's obligation to pay.
Sight draft	A draft so drawn as to be payable on presentation to the drawee.
Time draft	A draft maturing at a certain fixed time after presentation or acceptance.
Open account	No draft drawn. Transaction payable when specified on invoice.
Consignment	A shipment that is held by the importer until the merchandise has been sold, at which time payment is made to the exporter.

TYPES OF RISKS

When you negotiate the payment terms, your deliberations must be guided by the risks associated with both the buyer and the buyer's country.

Credit risk is the risk that the buyer will not pay, or fail to pay, on the agreed terms. Coupled with exchange, transfer, and political risks, you will make your terms-of-payment decision based on your analysis of the creditworthiness of a particular buyer. Evaluate the buyer's credit on the same basis as you would a U.S. company. Use the same basic types of data tempered by the differences that culture may proscribe. Trade groups, your international trade consultant, and the country officers at the International Trade Administration (ITA) can assist you in this evaluation.

Exchange risk does not exist if the sale is in U.S. dollars (although there may be a transfer risk). If the sale is in the buyer's currency, that currency may devalue or depreciate in terms of U.S. dollars before you receive and convert the currency into U.S. dollars. Contact your bank's international department to determine what type of exchange risk may exist. A good foreign exchange trader can give you a feel for the risks associated with a particular foreign currency over time. (See Chapter 13, Foreign Exchange.)

Table 11.2
Principal Risks

Credit risk	The buyer may not pay, or may fail to pay, under agreed terms.
Exchange risk	The buyer's currency may devalue/depreciate in terms of the seller's currency before the seller's currency is delivered for payment.
Transfer risk	Payment may not be made due to buyer's inability to obtain U.S. dollars and transfer to the seller. A risk after shipment is the imposition of a law or regulation prohibiting the transfer of U.S. dollars.
Political risk	These exist basically as risks after shipment: • Cancellation of import licenses/authorities • The imposition of a law or regulation preventing import by the buyer • War, rebellion, or revolution in buyer's country • Expropriation or confiscation of buyer's business • Increase in transport or other charges due to political causes that may not be recoverable from buyer

Transfer risk is the risk that payment will not be made due to the buyer's inability to obtain U.S. dollars and transfer them to the seller. Again, the foreign exchange department of your bank can assist you with this question. The *Yearbook of the International Monetary Fund* lists foreign exchange restrictions for countries that are signatories to the IMF. It is updated yearly. Your library, your bank's international department, or the business library of the leading college or university in your area will have a copy. Also, the country officer at the ITA in Washington, DC, can advise you on the existing foreign exchange controls in a particular country. If your buyer cannot get US$ to pay you, and if there is no market for that buyer's currency outside of the buyer's country, you should reconsider your sale to that buyer. Payment may need to be made in goods. This is a practical though difficult and expensive process (see Chapter 14, Barter and Countertrade).

Political risks are usually post-shipment risks. They result from a foreign political action. Examples of political risks are listed in Table 11.2. In addition, the U.S. government has on occasion created political risks. Embargoes on the export of grains, military goods, and transportation equipment are a few recent instances of U.S. action causing an unanticipated and uninsured loss for U.S. producers and manufacturers.

Some of these political risks can be covered by insurance. Some of them can be eliminated by the terms of sale, delivery of the goods, and receipt of payment in the United States. For marketing and competitive reasons, your options may be limited.

Table 11.3
Risks Associated with Various Terms of Payment

Basic Terms of Payment	Credit Risk 1–8	US$ Billing Exchange Risk 1	Foreign Currency Billing Exchange Risk 1–5+	Transfer Risk 1–2	Political Risk 1–3
Cash with order	1	1	1	1	1
Confirmed irrevocable L/C	2	1	2	1	1
Unconfirmed irrevocable L/C	3	1	3	2	2
Revocable L/C	4	1	3	2	2
Sight draft—collection	5	1	4	2	3
Time draft—collection	6	1	5	2	3
Open account	7	1	5+	2	3
Consignment	8	1	5+	2	3

Risk Scale: 1 = least risk

TERMS OF PAYMENT

There are advantages and disadvantages to each of the terms of payment.

Cash with order is the natural and ultimate objective of any exporter. It is also the least attractive to any importer. It is rarely used by parties that do not share common ownership. An exporter may encourage its use by giving significant discounts for cash. Cash in advance is sometimes used by related companies, between branch offices in different countries, or between the head office and branches in other countries, as this process reduces corporate exposure to foreign exchange problems and transaction costs. Companies that have dealt with each other for some time may also go to a cash with order basis for small orders; however, cash with order is the exception rather than the rule.

A **letter of credit** affords the next greatest degree of protection and is the primary mechanism for the payment of goods in international trade. There are a number of variations to a letter of credit. An importer/buyer establishes a letter of credit (L/C) by application to his or her bank. The buyer must have a line of credit, collateral, or cash sufficient to support this extension of credit by the bank; this is not your concern. To the exporter, the letter of credit is a promise by the buyer's bank to pay the exporter a specific amount when certain documents are presented to the bank.

There is a banking industry standard for handling letters of credit. It is UCP 400 (Uniform Customs and Practice for Documentary Credits, ICC Publication 400), which describes a letter of credit as any arrangement, however named or described, whereby a bank (the issuing bank) acting at the request and on the instructions of a customer (the applicant for the credit), *i.* is to make a payment to or to the order of a third party (the beneficiary), or is to pay or accept bills of exchange (drafts) drawn by the beneficiary, or *ii.* authorizes another bank to effect such payment, or to pay, accept or negotiate such bills of exchange (drafts), against stipulated documents, provided that the terms and conditions of the credit are complied with.

Banks that conform to the UCP agree to be bound by its conditions and to have disagreements settled by international arbitration. Any letter of credit you receive should refer in the positive to UCP 400. If it does not, call your banker. The People's Republic of China is the principal country that is not a signatory to UCP 400. The UPC 400 will be updated in 1993.

Letters of credit deal in documents, not in goods. Each letter of credit you receive will call for the presentation of certain documents for payment by the paying bank. These terms and conditions of the credit must be met exactly. There is a story about the exporter who did not misspell a word in one of his submitted documents, and his documents were rejected by the opening bank which did misspell that word in its L/C. That is an extreme case, but it is possible. Great care must be taken to see that you do what the L/C requires.

An **irrevocable letter of credit** cannot be canceled or changed without the agreement of all parties to the L/C. This is a protection to the seller, who then can act with the understanding that the terms of sale such as shipping date, amount of goods, price or value per unit, total value, port of export, port of import, description of goods, or other relevant details cannot be changed without his or her consent.

With a **confirmed irrevocable letter of credit,** a second bank, located in the United States or other location acceptable to the exporter, steps between the issuing bank and the exporter with the undertaking to pay (the *confirmation*), so the exporter can ignore the creditworthiness of the buyer's bank and the political risk associated with the buyer's country. This is particularly important to the exporter selling to a buyer in a country in which banks or the government are under financial pressure.[3] Traditionally, U.S. banks have been prepared to understand and weigh this risk. Their confirmation commission is payment for the service. In the 1990s, many U.S. banks—money center, regional, and local—have been reluctant to assume even short-term foreign risks. Exporters will need to consider the confirmation services of leading international banks, most of which have offices in the United States.

---

[3]Letters of credit from indigenous banks in many less developed countries, eastern Europe, the new independent nations of the former Soviet Union, and some other countries should be viewed with care. The negotiation section of your bank's letter of credit department can advise you on payment risks from a particular country.

With an **irrevocable letter of credit** that is not confirmed, the exporter has the obligation of the issuing bank (the buyer's bank alone) for payment against the documents.

A **revocable letter of credit** can be canceled at any time by the buyer without prior notice to the exporter. Use extreme caution when your buyer suggests a revocable letter of credit.

Understanding the Letter of Credit

When you receive a letter of credit covering the purchase of your goods, read it carefully and be sure you understand and agree with every one of the terms and conditions of the credit. The letter of credit is the document that embodies all of the terms of your sale agreement with your buyer: the goods, shipment, documents, price, and payment. Figure 11.1 directs your client to issue the letter of credit you want to receive.

Figure 11.2 is a sample of an irrevocable documentary letter of credit in the format received from the issuing bank. The "letter" is most often a telex or SWIFT message.[4] Figure 11.3 is the advice you will receive informing you of the letter of credit. Each is an important document. The advice provides you with direction and contact information. The letter of credit is the payment mechanism. If the letter of credit does not conform to your understanding of your sales arrangement, advise your buyer immediately, inform him or her of the changes you need, and request an amendment. You must accept the amendment(s) before they are applicable to the letter of credit.

After your review of the letter of credit, be sure to advise all concerned departments of your company as to the terms of the L/C. The letter of credit should go directly to your export department, which should inform:

1. Finance and administration.
2. Marketing.
3. Manufacturing and scheduling.
4. Shipping and traffic.
5. Your freight forwarder.

Be sure to give written instructions to each, preferably with a copy of the letter of credit. Now is the time to be sure all parties fully understand their roles and what is expected of them.

---

[4]SWIFT is the Society for Worldwide Interbank Financial Transactions, an interbank secure messaging system first put in place in the late 1970s.

INSTRUCTIONS TO OUR BUYER FOR THE ISSUANCE OF A LETTER OF CREDIT

Date   :   December 18, 19XX
Your Order :   P.O. No. 23487
Our Reference: Pro Forma No. K-320-9x

Please issue your letter of credit for the above order in accordance with these instructions:

Beneficiary: Northwest Exporters, Ltd.
                  8080 Parkway Blvd., Suite 400
                  Seattle, WA 98005-0505

Amount: US$31,445.50, CIF Busan, Korea

Advising Bank: This letter of credit must be advised through U.S. Bank of Washington, International Banking Division, P.O. Box 720, Seattle, WA USA 98111-0120
                  Fax No.: 206-344-5374
                  Telex No.: 3794092 USW UB
                  SWIFT Address: USBWUS66

Negotiation: U.S. Bank of Washington, Seattle, Washington, USA, must be designated negotiating bank, with authority to reimburse itself for drawings by telegraphic claim on the opening bank.

Documents: This letter of credit is to be available on presentation of the following documents:

                  Draft drawn on U.S. Bank of Washington
                  Commercial invoice in triplicate
                  Packing list in triplicate
                  Full set of clean on-board ocean bills of lading
                  Insurance policy or certificate, all risk, at 110% of invoice value

Transfer: This letter of credit is to be transferrable.

Shipments: Latest shipping date: April 15, 19XX

Expiry Date: Documents are to be presented within 14 days of shipment.

Notify Party: Buyer to notify beneficiary by fax of L/C number on date of issuance of L/C by buyer's bank.

On receipt and acceptance of your letter of credit, we will advise you of the anticipated shipping date and name of carrier.

Figure 11.1 Instructions to the Buyer for the Issuance of a Letter of Credit

```
                      IMPORT EXPORT BANK
                  HEAD OFFICE INTERNATIONAL
                       SEOUL, KOREA

          =========================================
          IRREVOCABLE DOCUMENTARY LETTER OF CREDIT
          =========================================

JANUARY 21, 1992

------------------------------------------------------------------
TO:                             |  ACCOUNTEE:
U.S. BANK OF WASHINGTON, N.A.   |  KTS CORPORATION
INTERNATIONAL DIVISION          |  SEOUL, KOREA
1414 4TH AVENUE, 5TH FLR.       |
SEATTLE, WA 98101               |
------------------------------------------------------------------
BENEFICIARY:                    |  LETTER OF CREDIT NUMBER:
NORTHWEST EXPORTERS             |  M187609SE0002
8080 PARKWAY BOULEVARD          |
SUITE 400                       |  EXPIRY DATE: APRIL 30, 1992
SEATTLE, WASHINGTON 98005       |  IN THE BENEFICIARY'S COUNTRY
------------------------------------------------------------------
AMOUNT:
UP TO AN AGGREGATE AMOUNT OF U.S. DOLLARS 31,445.50 ( THIRTY ONE
THOUSAND FOUR HUNDRED FORTY FIVE 50/100 U.S. DOLLARS )
------------------------------------------------------------------
WE HEREBY ISSUE THIS IRREVOCABLE DOCUMENTARY CREDIT AVAILABLE BY
BENEFICIARY'S DRAFT(S) FOR 100% OF INVOICE VALUE AT 60 DAYS
SIGHT DRAWN ON IMPORT EXPORT BANK, SEOUL KOREA AND ACCOMPANIED
BY THE FOLLOWING DOCUMENTS:

-FULL SET OF CLEAN ON BOARD BILLS OF LADING, MADE OUT TO THE
 ORDER OF IMPORT EXPORT BANK, MARKED 'FREIGHT PREPAID'
 AND 'NOTIFY KTS CORPORATION.'

-SIGNED  COMMERCIAL INVOICE IN THREE COPIES

-INSURANCE POLICY OR CERTIFICATE IN DUPLICATE, ENDORSED IN
 BLANK AT 110% OF THE INVOICE VALUE.  INSURANCE POLICIES
 OR CERTIFICATES MUST EXPRESSLY STIPULATE THAT CLAIMS ARE
 PAYABLE IN THE CURRENCY OF THE DRAFT AND MUST ALSO
 INDICATE A CLAIM SETTLING AGENT IN KOREA.  INSURANCE
 MUST ALSO INCLUDE: INSTITUTE CARGO CLAUSES: FPA

-PACKING LIST IN THREE COPIES

EVIDENCING SHIPMENT OF:
USED ENGINE PARTS PER PO 23487
ORIGIN USA
CIF BUSAN KOREA
```

Figure 11.2 Irrevocable Documentary Letter of Credit

```
SHIPMENT FROM: USA PORT
TO:               BUSAN KOREA
LATEST SHIPPING DATE      :MARCH 31, 1992
PARTIAL SHIPMENTS: PERMITTED
TRANSHIPMENT     : PERMITTED

ALL DOCUMENTS MUST INDICATE THE NUMBER OF THIS CREDIT
DOCUMENTS MUST BE PRESENTED WITHIN ZERO DAYS OF ISSUANCE
OF THE BILL OF LADING OR OTHER SHIPPING DOCUMENT

SPECIAL CONDITIONS:
    STALE B/L ACCEPTABLE.

INSTRUCTION OF NEGOTIATING BANK:

THE AMOUNT OF EACH DRAFT MUST BE ENDORSED ON THE REVERSE
OF THIS CREDIT BY THE NEGOTIATING BANK.  ALL DOCUMENTS
MUST BE FORWARDED DIRECT TO THE IMPORT EXPORT BANK,
SEOUL, KOREA.


WE HEREBY ENGAGE WITH DRAWERS, ENDORSERS, AND/OR BONAFIDE HOLDERS
OF ALL DPAFT(S) DRAWN UNDER AND IN COMPLIANCE WITH THE
TERMS OF CREDIT THAT SUCH DRAFTS SHALL BE DULY HONORED ON
DELIVERY OF DOCUMENT AS SPECIFIED.

EXCEPT SO FAR AS OTHERWISE EXPRESSLY STATED,
THIS CREDIT IS SUBJECT TO "THE UNIFORM CUSTOMS AND PRACTICE FOR
DOCUMENTARY CREDITS" (1983 REVISION) INTERNATIONAL CHAMBER OF
COMMERCE PUBLICATION NO. 400.

ALL BANKING CHARGES INCLUDING POSTAGE, ADVISING AND PAYMENT
COMMISSION OUTSIDE KOREA ARE FOR THE BENEFICIARY'S ACCOUNT
```

```
AUTHORIZED SIGNATURE
SIGNATURE VERIFIED
```

Figure 11.2 Continued

There are two dates in each letter of credit that require special mention. If a bill of lading is a required document, the Bill of Lading date (B/L date) is the date by which the shipment *must* be loaded on board the carrier named: ship, train, truck, or airplane. The expiry date of the letter of credit should be later than the bill of lading date. The UCP 400 sets a limit of 14 days unless a different limit is stated. The exporter *must* get the documents to the opening or negotiating bank by this expiration date.

Letters of credit can call for payment at sight or at some other time such as 90 days B/L date or 30 days sight. "Sight" means after receipt and review, which under the UCP means three working days. If your documents are in order, you should receive payment at one of the following times:

```
                    U.S. BANK OF WASHINGTON, NATIONAL ASSOCIATION
                         INTERNATIONAL BANKING DIVISION
                         1414 FOURTH AVENUE, P.O. BOX 720
                         SEATTLE, WASHINGTON U.S.A. 98111-0720
                         SWIFT USBWUS66   FAX (206) 344-5374

NORTHWEST EXPORTERS                USBW REF: X085127
8080 PARKWAY BOULEVARD             JANUARY 31, 1992
SUITE 400                         ISSUING BANK NUMBER:
SEATTLE, WASHINGTON 98005              M187609SE0002
============================================================
ORIGINAL AMOUNT: U.S. DOLLARS 31,445.50
  L/C APPLICANT: KTS CORPORATION
============================================================
AT THE REQUEST OF: IMPORT EXPORT BANK
                   SEOUL, KOREA

WE ENCLOSE FAX/COPY OF THE ABOVE MENTIONED LETTER OF CREDIT
AND HOLD THE ORIGINAL IN ACCORDANCE WITH YOUR INSTRUCTIONS.
WE HAVE AUTHENTICATED THE VALIDITY OF THIS CREDIT AND HAVE
ESTABLISHED A FILE UNDER OUR REFERENCE NUMBER. SHOULD YOU REQUIRE
ASSISTANCE OR SERVICE FROM US REGARDING THIS CREDIT, PLEASE
CONTACT US AT (206) 344-5447 OR (206) 587-7049.

THIS LETTER IS TO SERVE SOLELY AS OUR ADVICE TO YOU OF THIS
LETTER OF CREDIT AND CONVEYS NO OBLIGATION OR ENGAGEMENT ON
OUR PART. PLEASE EXAMINE THE ATTACHED INSTRUMENT CAREFULLY.
IF YOU ARE UNABLE TO COMPLY WITH ITS TERMS AND CONDITIONS,
PLEASE CONTACT YOUR BUYER IMMEDIATELY TO ARRANGE FOR AN
AMENDMENT TO FACILITATE PROMPT HANDLING OF YOUR DOCUMENTS
ON PRESENTATION.

THE LETTER OF CREDIT STATES THAT BANK CHARGES ON THIS SIDE OF
THE TRANSACTION ARE FOR THE ACCOUNT OF THE BENEFICIARY.

THIS CREDIT IS SUBJECT TO THE "UNIFORM CUSTOMS AND PRACTICES FOR
DOCUMENTARY CREDITS" (1983 REVISION) INTERNATIONAL CHAMBER OF
COMMERCE PUBLICATION NO. 400 WE WOULD APPRECIATE RECEIVING AN
EXTRA COPY OF THE COMMERCIAL INVOICE AND BILL OF LADING WHEN YOU
PRESENT DOCUMENTS FOR NEGOTIATION

U.S. BANK OF WASHINGTON, NATIONAL ASSOCIATION
INTERNATIONAL BANKING DIVISION


------------------------------
AUTHORIZED SIGNATURE
```

Figure 11.3 Advice of Letter of Credit

1. From the confirming bank within three business days of its receipt of the documents.

2. From the advising bank within three business days of receipt *if* the advising bank elects to pay.

3. From the issuing bank within three business days from that bank's receipt of the documents.

If the required documents are not in order (contain discrepancies), they will be returned to you for correction. A good working relationship with your bank will go far in ensuring that documents are reviewed promptly so that discrepancies can be resolved quickly. If the paying bank is at some distance from your city, it is even more critical that the documents be in order. That distant bank will not telephone you to work out a discrepancy; it will mail the documents back for correction and resubmission.

One of the special instructions you may encounter on a letter of credit will trigger a little-known body of law that tends to penalize exporters after the fact. The antiboycott laws of the United States are two sets of laws with different rules and regulations administered by the Department of Commerce and the Department of the Treasury.

Section 8 of the Export Administration Act is one of these laws. The Ribicoff Amendment to the Tax Reform Act of 1976, adding Section 999 to the Internal Revenue Code, is the other. The Office of Anti-Boycott Compliance in Commerce is there to see that you, the exporter, do not comply with a boycott. (The IRS operates under separate rules and has its own set of penalties.) If an exporter receives an order, a request for quote, or a letter of credit containing statements, terms, or conditions that relate to a boycott of a country or its products (usually Israel), the exporter is subject to fines, penalties, and imprisonment if the situation is not reported immediately. The advising bank on a letter of credit transaction is in equal jeopardy.

An interesting feature of the antiboycott regulations is that an exporter cannot obtain written acknowledgement or confirmation from the Office of Anti-Boycott Compliance of its own instructions on how to comply with its own rules. The office will provide advice, by telephone at 202-482-2381, between 9 A.M. and 5 P.M. EST, but it will not acknowledge or confirm its advice in writing.

The exporter is not protected by a bank's failure to advise of boycott-related wording in letters of credit. The antiboycott laws inhibit exports, intimidate smaller companies, and increase the costs of U.S. exports. They are bad laws, but you must be aware of them, particularly if you sell or plan to sell into Middle Eastern or Arab countries.

Understanding Sight Drafts and Time Drafts

Sight and time drafts are the instruments of payment under letters of credit. Also, they are a mechanism for payment under documentary collections, a practice separate from letters of credit.

Under a **documentary collection**, the sight or time draft, drawn on the buyer is accompanied by the bill of lading, packing list, invoice, and any other agreed documents. Your bank, as your agent, will send these documents to the buyer's bank for collection. Commercial banks around the world have a set of rules for handling documents submitted to them for *collection* (the process of presentation of a demand for payment). The Uniform Rules for Collections, ICC Publication No. 322, effective January 1, 1979, are the standards by which your bank will handle your documents on a sale under sight draft, time draft, or other terms and conditions. Your bank has no financial interest in this type of transaction and, therefore, acts only as agent for you, the principal.

For a **sight draft** sale (also called sight draft documents against payment, D/P, SD, or SDDP), the recipient bank will contact the buyer and advise him or her that documents have arrived for payment. These documents will be released to the buyer only against payment of your sight draft. When funds are received by the collecting bank, they are sent back to your bank for your account. The apparent risks are as follows:

1. The buyer changed his or her mind and will not pay. You then have your goods at his or her dock and will incur the cost of generating another sale there (of distressed goods) or the cost of returning the goods to the United States. You have a new insurable risk; contact your insurance broker. Some buyers may use this as a strategy to force a price reduction.

2. The recipient bank errs and gives the documents to the buyer without payment. This is unusual, and you have recourse to that bank. Depending on the country, that may be of little comfort.

3. The buyer will wait until the ship is unloaded to pay for the goods. This is the norm and, regrettably, little can be done to eliminate this type of delay. In your collection instructions, you can require the collecting bank to *protest* nonpayment. This legal process requires the buyer to acknowledge that he or she will not pay on the terms of the draft. In a few countries, mainly in western Europe, this protest carries a powerful commercial stigma. Buyers there will try to avoid protest.

When you grant **time draft** terms (also called time draft documents against acceptance or D/A), you have agreed to accept the buyer's promissory note in payment for your shipment. You have added the risks of extended time and loss of control to the risks of a sight draft shipment. In a time draft situation, the buyer will not necessarily be motivated to sign the draft any earlier than on a sight draft sale. To control the transaction time, an exporter can fix the payment date by tying it to

- the bill of lading date,
- the date of the draft,
- a certain date in the future (e.g., 22 January 19XX), or
- another readily identified date,

so the buyer cannot extend the time by inaction.

With a sale on time draft terms, you have given the buyer access to the goods. Once the buyer accepts the draft, the collecting bank gives the buyer the documents of title to the goods. The buyer is then free to do as he or she will. You do have evidence of debt, the signed draft, and you have the right to pursue the buyer in the courts of his country if he does not pay.

Figure 11.4 is an example of a collection letter, the form used by U.S. banks to send your sight or time draft and title documents to the collecting bank. Figure 11.5 is the transmittal form you would use to send the collection instructions to your bank.

Documentary collections are increasing in use because they reduce the total transaction costs for both parties, maintain suitable levels of control for experienced exporters, and speed the flow of transactions. In addition to the documentary collection services noted above and shown in Figures 11.4 and 11.5, many larger banks offer direct collection services. A **direct collection** is a documentary collection initiated by the exporter, who sends the necessary documents directly to the buyer's bank. This saves up to five business days of transaction time. It also keeps the exporter's bank in the loop; the bank receives a copy of the direct collection letter (Figure 11.6) and becomes the exporter's agent for follow up and collection. If your firm has numerous shipments to each foreign buyer, direct collections may reduce some of your costs and speed the process. Note that the draft (bill of exchange) is part of the direct collection letter.

Figure 11.7 is a sight draft drawn by the seller on the buyer and sent with the collection letter. Figure 11.8 is a time draft drawn by the seller on the buyer and sent with the collection letter.

Figure 11.9 is a time draft drawn under a letter of credit. Note that this draft is drawn on the negotiating or paying bank that was specified in the letter of credit. The draft is for less than the letter of credit because it represents a partial shipment. Partial shipments were permitted in the L/C.

A trade acceptance or a bankers' acceptance is created when a time draft (also known as a *usance* draft) is accepted by the drawee. A time draft accepted by the buyer is a *trade acceptance*; a time draft accepted by the bank

```
                    U.S. BANK OF WASHINGTON, NATIONAL ASSOCIATION
                    INTERNATIONAL COLLECTIONS DEPARTMENT
                    1414 FOURTH AVENUE, P.O. BOX 720
                    SEATTLE, WASHINGTON, U.S.A. 98111-0720
                    SWIFT USBWUS66 FAX (206) 344-5374
                    TELEPHONE:  (206) 344-3732

TO   IMPORT EXPORT BANK
     SEOUL, KOREA

FEBRUARY 12, 1992                       OUR REF: 0445500
================================================================
  D O C U M E N T A R Y   C O L L E C T I O N
================================================================

PRESENT TO DRAWEE:   KTS CORPORATION
                     SEOUL
                     KOREA

DRAWER:  NORTHWEST EXPORTERS
SHIPMENT OF ENGINE PARTS              VIA OCEAN SHIPMENT
==========================================================
  D O C U M E N T S  --  T E R M S  --  C H A R G E S
==========================================================
DRAFT  INVOICE  PKG LST    PHYTO    B/L
==========================================================
  1     2/2      2/2                 3/3


------------------------------------------------------------
TERMS:
      D/P          AT SIGHT

      DELIVER DOCUMENTS AGAINST PAYMENT
_____

      DRAFT/INVOICE AMOUNT:    USD  $2,050.00

CHARGES                   PAID BY              AMOUNT
==========================================================
COMMISSION                DRAWER    USD     50.00
POSTAGE                   DRAWER             8.50
==========================================================
  I N S T R U C T I O N S
==========================================================

- PLEASE ACKNOWLEDGE RECEIPT OF DOCUMENTS

- TELEX/SWIFT ADVISE NON-PAYMENT GIVING REASONS

- YOUR CHARGES ARE FOR ACCOUNT OF THE DRAWEE
==========================================================
  S E T T L E M E N T   I N S T R U C T I O N S
==========================================================

- PLEASE REMIT PROCEEDS BY SWIFT/CABLE TO
  OUR ACCOUNT WITH THE FED ABA NUMBER 1250000105.

THIS COLLECTION IS SUBJECT TO THE'UNIFORM RULES FOR COLLECTION'
  PUBLISHED BY THE INTERNATIONAL CHAMBER OF COMMERCE
     IN EXISTENCE AS OF THE DATE OF THIS LETTER
```

Figure 11.4 Documentary Collection Letter

U.S. BANK Transmittal Letter Covering Outgoing Foreign Documentary Collection

U.S. Bank of Washington, National Association • International Banking Division • 1414 Fourth Avenue • P.O. Box 720 • Seattle, Washington 98111-0720 USA • Phone (206) 344-4629

SHIPPER/DRAWER

ACCOUNTEE/DRAWEE

ACCOUNTEE'S BANK (IF KNOWN)

AMOUNT TO BE COLLECTED: _____

DOCUMENTS AGAINST: ☐ PAYMENT ☐ ACCEPTANCE

TENOR: _____

NAME OF VESSEL OR CARRIER: _____

DOCUMENTS ENCLOSED

DRAFT	COMMERCIAL INVOICE	PACKING LIST	CERT. ORIG.	INSURANCE	BILL OF LADING	AIR WAYBILL	INSPECTION CERTIFICATE		

WE REQUEST THAT THE FOLLOWING INSTRUCTIONS BE FOLLOWED:

(Mark spaces "X" where appropriate)

☐ Send by registered airmail
☐ Do not protest
☐ Protest in case of non-acceptance/non-payment
☐ Advise non-acceptance or non-payment by cable giving reasons
☐ Advise non-acceptance or non-payment by airmail giving reasons
☐ Remit proceeds by airmail
☐ Remit proceeds by cable

☐ Hold pending arrival of merchandise
☐ All charges will be for our account
☐ Foreign bank charges for account of accountee/drawee
☐ Your charges for account of shipper/drawer
☐ Waive all charges if refused — shipper will pay
☐ Do not waive charges

PROCEEDS TO BE REMITTED TO: ☐ Account No. _____ under advice to us ☐ By Cashiers Check

SPECIAL INSTRUCTIONS

TERMS AND CONDITIONS

APPOINTMENT OF AGENT Drawer authorizes U.S. Bank of Washington, National Association ("Bank") to act as Drawer's agent to send the above item(s) for collection. Bank may send the item(s) in any manner, including through any intermediary agent, acceptable to Bank. Bank agrees to notify Drawer when Bank has received a response to the collection request.
CHARGES Drawer agrees to pay Bank a collection fee for sending the item(s). Drawer also agrees to pay any additional fee(s) which may be assessed by any intermediary agent. Should Bank give Drawer provisional credit for a collection item which is later returned unpaid, Bank may revoke the credit.

LIMITED LIABILITY Drawer agrees Bank's liability shall be expressly limited to the amount of the assessed charge(s) should the collection item(s) be delayed, lost, mutilated, or destroyed for any reason. Under no circumstances shall Bank be liable for any incidental or consequential damages including those resulting from the actions of any intermediary agent. Drawer agrees to indemnify and hold Bank harmless from any claims made by any party arising from this collection request.
INTERNATIONAL COLLECTIONS Drawer understands an international collection request will be subject to the foreign currency exchange rates and the Uniform Rules for Collections established by the International Chamber of Commerce, applicable on the date of this collection.

Shipper's Signature _____ Date _____

BANK USE ONLY	RECEIVED BY	DATE RECEIVED	DATE DOCUMENTS MAILED & PROCESSED	OUR REFRENCE NUMBER C277—

277-038T (2/88)

Figure 11.5 Transmittal Form

U.S. BANK. International Direct Collection | **D 532401**

(PLEASE ALWAYS REFER)
OUR REFERENCE NUMBER

U.S. BANK OF WASHINGTON, NATIONAL ASSOCIATION
INTERNATIONAL DIVISION
1414 FOURTH AVENUE, EIGHTH FLOOR
SEATTLE, WA 98101, U.S.A.

SWIFT   USBW US 66
TELEX   379 4052 USBW US
TELEFAX   206 344-5374

REGISTERED AIRMAIL ☐   COURIER ☐

DATE

COLLECTING BANK

DRAWER (NAME & FULL ADDRESS)

REFERENCE NO.

DRAWEE (NAME & FULL ADDRESS)

Enclosed for collection are the following described draft(s) and/or documents for account of U.S. Bank of Washington, National Association, International Division. Please send your acknowledgement, all reports and advice of payment direct to U.S. Bank of Washington, National Association at the address shown above quoting our reference number.

DOCUMENTS	DRAFT	INV.	INS.	PHYTO	CERT. ORIGIN	B/L	INSP. CERT.	WGHT. CERT.	PACKING LIST	OTHER	TENOR	AMOUNT
ORIGINAL												
DUPLICATE												

FOLLOW INSTRUCTIONS MARKED "X" BELOW

☐ Deliver documents against Payment }
☐ Deliver documents against Acceptance }

☐ on first presentation
☐ may be deferred until arrival of goods

☐ Advise Date of Acceptance and Maturity of Time Bills by Airmail/Telex/S.W.I.F.T.
☐ Advise Dishonor by Cable giving reasons
☐ Protest if Unpaid }
☐ Do Not Protest } ADVISE US BY:

☐ Airmail
☐ Telex/S.W.I.F.T.

☐ Collect all your Charges and Expenses from Drawee
☐ Collect $ _____ for our Charges
☐ Collect Interest from Date of Draft at Rate of _____ % P.A. to approximate date funds will reach us.
☐ Do Not Waive Charges
☐ Waive Charges if refused
☐

PAYMENT INSTRUCTIONS

☐ Remit Proceeds by S.W.I.F.T./Telex
☐ Remit Proceeds by Air Mail.
☐ Authorize us to charge your account by S.W.I.F.T./Telex
☐ Credit Proceeds to our account and advise us by S.W.I.F.T./Telex
☐
☐

IN CASE OF NEED REFER TO:

AUTHORITY: ☐ Unlimited   ☐ Limited To:

FURTHER SPECIAL INSTRUCTIONS

THIS COLLECTION IS SUBJECT TO THE UNIFORM RULES FOR COLLECTIONS, INTERNATIONAL CHAMBER OF COMMERCE, IN EFFECT AT DATE OF THIS COLLECTION.

NAME & TITLE OF DRAWER'S REPRESENTATIVE

AUTHORIZED SIGNATURE
X

U.S. BANK. Sole Bill of Exchange | **D 532401**

U.S. BANK OF WASHINGTON, NATIONAL ASSOCIATION • INTERNATIONAL DIVISION • 1414 FOURTH AVENUE • EIGHTH FLOOR • SEATTLE, WA 98101, U.S.A.

AT _____ SIGHT   DATE _____

PAY TO THE ORDER OF   U.S. BANK OF WASHINGTON, NATIONAL ASSOCIATION _____ U.S. $ _____

_____ U.S. DOLLARS

TO

DRAWER'S NAME

AUTHORIZED SIGNATURE

16-7588 WA 9/91   **WHITE** – 1st Mail   **CANARY** – 2nd Mail   **PINK** – Customer Copy   **GOLDENROD** – Bank Copy

Figure 11.6 Direct Collection Letter

155

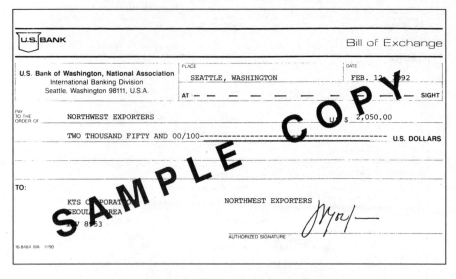

Figure 11.7 Sample Sight Draft

is a *bankers' acceptance*. Chapter 12 will identify the importance of this instrument to the exporter.

An **open account** sale in international trade has the same basic features as an open account sale in the United States, with increased risk. The risk increases because of different legal systems, currencies, and cultures; time; distance; and the cost of fixing any problems that arise.

Although not in frequent use, **consignment** is another term of payment that may be appropriate for some exporters. Introducing a new product line to a well-established stocking distributor may require an initial consignment sale. Agents may require a ready source for immediate delivery, best met by an inventory of consignment goods. The risks under a consignment sale are greater than those under an open account sale because you have moved your inventory into the buyer's control and will be paid only when a sale takes place. You still must deal with inventory control issues such as insurance, deterioration, pilferage, and the like, all in a different country.

RISKS AND PAYMENT TERMS

If you sell for *cash*, you have virtually no risk. You receive U.S. dollars before you ship the goods. The nominal risk you may assume is that associated with the timing of the order compared to receipt of the payment. If you initiate a

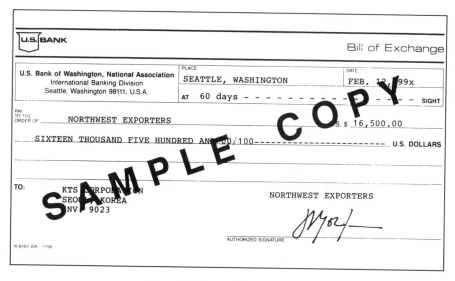

Figure 11.8 Sample Time Draft

manufacturing or acquisition process prior to receipt of the funds, your risk is that payment will not come; you have excess product or inventory manufactured for a specific transaction that did not come off.

A sale on a *confirmed irrevocable letter of credit* has slightly more risk. The confirmation places a U.S. or other known bank in front of the buyer's bank. This confirming bank can be from or in any country acceptable to you. If the sale is in foreign currency, you have the risk of a decrease in the value of the currency to be received.

An *unconfirmed letter of credit* (the usual type of letter of credit used in international trade) exposes you to the creditworthiness of the buyer's bank, the value of the foreign currency (if the sale is not in US$), the risk that the payment cannot be transferred to the United States, and the risk that political conditions in the buyer's country will change to your detriment.

Sales on *sight draft* terms increase the credit risk in the transaction and increase the foreign exchange risk in that a payment may occur later; the passage of time increases the foreign exchange risk and the political risk.

A *time draft* sale increases the credit risk because the buyer, by "accepting the draft," will receive the title documents and can pick up the goods without payment. Your foreign exchange and political risks, if any, will increase as more time may lapse.

An *open account* sale has all the risks one associates with open account sales; there is no evidence of the debt (promissory note, draft, etc.) and the payment due date may be effectively unenforceable (i.e., the cost of a trip from

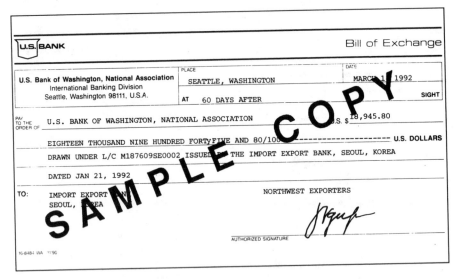

Figure 11.9 Sample Time Draft (under letter of credit)

Chicago to Sydney *is* expensive). This uncertainty of timing also could increase the foreign currency transaction risk and political risk.

For risk evaluation purposes, a *consignment* sale is similar to an open account sale with infinite dating. It's done, with caution.

FINDING A BANK

Your banker, lender, or financier is an important partner in your business. This role is key to your success in export marketing and sales. Lack of financial support can leave you unable to compete with your adversaries, from the United States or abroad. Darren Schulman, of MTB Banking Corporation, offers his perspective:

> Global reach is no longer the preserve of large multinational corporations. In fact, the best segment for growth in international trade is not in the Fortune 500, but in companies with US$250,000 to US$2 million in annual sales. Saturated domestic markets and the improved ability to move products to and from foreign markets quickly are the main reasons why growth companies have become attracted to international trade.
>
> Despite this potential, there is a severe shortage of export trade financing for growth companies. Many banks are closing their doors to international trade financing applications. Larger banks still interested in trade finance are holding their capital for larger customers simply because the mechanics of a US$25,000 deal are the same as those for a US$1 million deal—the latter significantly more profitable to the bank.

Companies need to shop for financing just as they would for a supplier. It's important to look for a bank that wants to establish a long-term relationship and help your business expand. Before you choose, ask:

1. How extensive is the bank's network of corresponding banks?

2. How quickly does the bank approve loans, handle letters of credit, and turn around correspondence from overseas banks?

3. Does the bank specialize in currency conversions?

4. Does the bank offer specialized services, such as foreign currency deposit accounts?

5. Does your prospective banker show an understanding of foreign cultures and international banking systems?

A bank with expertise and history in trade finance is best positioned to help carry out your international business plan. Some banks with a niche in the field—gained through operating in specialized areas such as, for example, foreign exchange or foreign currency lending—are strong candidates. How creative a bank is in seeking real financing options will determine whether a trip to the bank is worthwhile.

When a growth company begins to search for financing, it should be aware that there isn't only one bank, or one method of trade finance. A great deal of information is available to fuel an intelligent inquiry into trade financing options. As your first deal turns into your second and third, use these services to unlock the world market. It is the business of these trade finance specialists to help growth companies find the right footing for global economic success.

Your bank will be a major player in your export program, because it is in every transaction with you. The bank may make advances for production, negotiate drafts or letters of credit for collection, respond to credit inquiries on your company, obtain information on buyers for you, and perhaps give you solid advice.

When planning to begin or expand your export business, have a thorough discussion of your objectives and strategies with an international trade professional, your accountant, and the lending officer(s) and executive(s) at your bank. You need a bank officer that understands what you have in mind. Be prepared to discuss in some depth the plans for the business and the financing requirements you foresee. Try to learn from your banker the maximum line of credit you may arrange for your export business based on your track record, the collateral you can provide, and the type of business you will be doing. With this foreknowledge, you can approach business situations from a position of strength, pursue the opportunities of the right size, and not waste time on the deals that are beyond your capacity.

Export finance is of limited interest to the majority of U.S. banks. It has been a small segment of the bank lending market and has received little attention or encouragement. Banks have put their attention into real estate, consumer lending, and traditional domestic commercial lending. This is not expected to change. Mergers, consolidations, and bank failures in the late 1980s and early 1990s have brought retrenchment and an increased focus on "safe" loans. Therefore, you may need to search for a bank interested in financing your export requirements. Some banks in larger metropolitan areas do an excellent job, while most others pay lip service to the whole field of trade finance.

You need to find out if your bank is willing and able to work with you to some degree. If your bank is not interested in handling your export finance requirements:

1. Talk to other bankers in your area.

2. Talk to the managers of other firms that export.

3. Ask your chamber of commerce for recommendations.

4. Ask your state economic development department for recommendations to the banks they know are in the business of trade finance.

5. Ask your international trade consultant for introductions and assistance in dealing with bankers.

Be sure to ask your associates and competitors. Your trade association may have useful contacts.[5] Don't hesitate to take all of your business to the bank that will help.

A Line of Credit

In the export business, a line of credit is invaluable. Business opportunities may arise that offer ongoing profits significantly in excess of the costs of the needed financing, provided you can immediately take advantage of the situation by having the necessary financing available. This situation exists in differing degrees and forms for the producer/manufacturer and the trader/broker.

Your line of credit or the amount of credit you can obtain will be based on two main factors: the amount of financial security you can pledge and your experience and reputation in the business. One is as important as the other, and the line of credit can expand or contract drastically depending on the quality and level of collateral and your past performance. With this in mind, before you meet with your banker on a line of credit or loan, calculate exactly

---

[5]For example, the National Machine Tool Builders Association has formed an Export Trading Company for the benefit of its members. It may direct its members to banks that are interested in export financing.

how your repayment program will work, including dates, amounts, and alternatives. Be sure to calculate a financial and time margin for safety (your best guess may be wrong). Then keep your word implicitly on each transaction.

Banks will invariably want to discuss individual transactions with you and review the creditworthiness of your customers and their countries. This is an area where a more experienced loan officer can be invaluable to you; junior officers will be in new territory and of little value to you. With experienced officers, you may be able to finance individual transactions in addition to those carried out under your line of credit. Experienced bankers, outstanding performance on your part, and well-thought-out transactions make for excellent bank relations.

A knowledgeable bank can add to your business, as if it was another member of your top management team. Use the banker's skills and knowledge to keep your risks to a minimum and to make the best of your successes and opportunities. Again, if your bank doesn't support you in this field, and you honestly feel that support is warranted, find a bank that will.

Exporting and export financing are highly specialized business activities. Many of the smaller banks do not have the expertise or capacity. These banks can give you some level of service through a *correspondent bank,* a major regional or national bank that has the needed capabilities. Be sure your bank understands your needs for your exporting business. Only in this way can you assure yourself that the needed services are available to you in a timely and efficient manner. Smaller banks and those without the services you require usually are quite good at directing their customers to larger banks when it is necessary to preserve a good customer relationship.

Many foreign banks have established subsidiaries, branches, agencies, and representative offices in the United States in order to finance trade transactions between the United States and their home countries. They follow their customers and they actively look for new business in and around the location of their U.S. branches. These banks and bankers, from Europe, Asia, Canada, and Latin America, bring many different skills and different perceptions to our financial marketplace. The focus of foreign banks is the larger transactions (US$500,000 plus). For the small company or the small transaction, a foreign bank may only help by being a source of credit information for a company from their home country. Your associates, the library, your international trade consultant, and the chamber of commerce can help you find a bank from your buyer's country. In addition to credit information, this bank may want to finance the deal outright, that is, buy your draft drawn on and accepted by the buyer. The bank may pay on the letter of credit and thus save you a substantial amount. Focus your initial efforts on banks from your target country.

HOW TO GET EXPORT FINANCING

With few exceptions, export financing is provided by a commercial bank. If your bank is interested in export financing, it will follow a few inviolate criteria:

1. Your company is financially sound; company performance is in line with industry standards on equity, debt, liquidity, profitability, and other performance ratios.
2. The export transaction is collateralized.
3. The source of payment is assured or guaranteed.
4. The transaction is within your normal operating parameters.
5. Your company is a meaningful long-term prospect for the bank.

There are six traditional avenues for financing your exports. Listed below, the first four require the active participation and support of your bank. The other two do not, although payments may pass through your bank. Not listed here is countertrade, an option and strategy that is covered in Chapter 14. The six traditional avenues of export financing are:

1. Your existing or negotiated operating line of credit.
2. Exports under export letters of credit.
3. Exports insured by Eximbank or other export credit insurers.
4. Exports guaranteed by Eximbank.
5. Exports financed by the buyer's bank.
6. Other financing intermediaries.

An Existing or Negotiated Operating Line of Credit

Most companies in business over three years have established some form of line of credit with their bankers. This line of credit (it may be a loan facility, renewable annually, for the purchase of assets or equipment for use or resale) is generally collateralized by some ratio of accounts receivable and inventory. Collateral may also include real property, other fixed assets, and guarantees. The bank's objective is to hold an immediately liquid source of repayment in the event that the company fails to generate sufficient cash flow to pay its obligations in a timely manner.

The exporter may sell on letter of credit, collection, or other terms. Financing is probably required for the purchase of materials for export, the processing of the goods, delivery, and collection of the proceeds of the export sale. In most industries, this cycle can close within 12 months, often within 3 to 6 months. The bank may not consider as eligible collateral the export-destined assets purchased with the export finance loan. Bank logic is that these loans have a questionable source of repayment and, therefore, demand separate collateral.

Some lenders will look to your shipments on sight draft or time draft terms as collateral for short-term loans. The financing is straightforward. Your D/P or D/A receivable is treated as any other account receivable, and a loan is made based on a standard formula. Alternatively, the draft may be discounted (often called *bills purchased* or *bills discounted*) and the net amount paid to your account. Recourse is to the exporter for principal and interest or for any interest shortfall. Experienced companies and knowledgeable banks use these methods with a high degree of satisfaction.

Exports under Export Letters of Credit

When you receive a letter of credit, a number of options are open to you. You have received a firm and irrevocable promise to pay issued by a (supposedly) responsible bank. If you provide the documents required, when required, *you will be paid.* Based on this and your track record, your bank may lend you the funds (or some percentage) to acquire the goods to export, to manufacture or modify goods, or to otherwise get your product into the export channel. If you have a poor or unknown track record, your bank will only lend against other collateral and only to a percentage of its value. It will urge you to make the letter of credit transferrable or back to back or to get a guarantee from the Small Business Administration. If your documents on the letter of credit are in order, your bank may be willing to make a loan to cover the period between negotiation of the documents and receipt of funds from the paying bank. An alternative loan source might be a finance company. For example, Westinghouse has an export finance subsidiary that will make you a loan for this brief period, for a healthy fee plus interest.

A **transferrable letter of credit** transfers the payment provided by the letter of credit to a third party, your supplier. The dollar amount and shipping and expiry dates are changed. With this instrument, your source of supply will receive a letter of credit (the transfer) from your buyer, instructing him or her to carry out a transaction on which you will be paid. You have used the credit of the buyer's bank to effect your purchase. A transferrable credit is effective, although it can be unattractive to all parties for various reasons. To a bank, it is a satisfactory solution for its inability or unwillingness to provide you with the financing necessary to purchase goods for resale. It may be unsatisfactory to you because there is a good possibility that your supplier and your buyer can identify each other and take you out of the next sale.

A **back-to-back letter of credit** is one in which the terms of two letters of credit, the primary or backing credit and the secondary credit, must be identical. Each credit must require *the same* shipping documents, inspection certificates, insurance papers, and customs declarations. Other than the dollar amounts and the beneficiary of the primary and the secondary credit, *everything* must be the same. This type of credit can be a boon to the undercapitalized exporter and the bane of his or her bank. Banks are very cautious in handling back-to-back credits because a clerical error or oversight on their part may result in nonpayment by the opening bank. Because of this type of risk, the lack of additional collateral, the one-time nature of the transactions, and the minimal fees banks have traditionally charged, many banks are very reluctant to handle back-to-back letters of credit for all but the very best and most substantial customers.

An **assignment of proceeds** is a quick and viable way for an exporter to use the proceeds of any letter of credit as a source of payment to his or her supplier. The process is a three-party agreement between the exporter, his or her supplier, and the bank. The bank assures the supplier that when the bank receives payment on the letter of credit, the supplier will be paid the agreed amount, the balance being paid to the exporter. Banks like this business because it generates fees with no risk to them.

Exports Insured by Third Parties

When an exporter has exhausted his or her own bank lines of credit, but needs credit to carry export receivables or to extend financing to compete for international sales, there are some additional resources available for that needed financial support. A number of commercial credit insurance companies have extended their activities outside the United States. The focus has been on Europe because European standards of financial reporting are more acceptable than those elsewhere in the world.

From 1961 the U.S. government provided export credit insurance to United States exporters through a service contract and reinsurance arrangement with the Foreign Credit Insurance Association. In 1991 the Export Import Bank of the United States became the underwriter for Eximbank commercial and political risk insurance policies serviced by FCIA Management Company, Inc., a new arrangement of the prior association. On September 14, 1992 Eximbank cancelled its contract with FCIA Management Company, Inc. and now services its own policies through regional offices formerly operated by FCIA Management Company, Inc. FCIA Management Company, Inc. now offers private export credit insurance.

Government-supported export credit insurance policies are issued solely in the name of the Export-Import Bank (Eximbank). A number of programs are available directly to the exporter or through the exporter's bank. Eximbank export insurance coverage is available for sales on terms of up to five years to buyers in most countries of the world.

Eximbank issues policies that insure against nonpayment of foreign receivables due to certain defined political and commercial risks. Because Eximbank insurance policies and their proceeds can be assigned in full to a commercial bank or other financial institution, a bank may be willing to finance that receivable. At this writing, Eximbank has 39 types of insurance policies available to exporters. They are within four policy types: short-term comprehensive, short-term political, bank letter of credit, and medium-term. The nine principal policy structures are summarized here.

1. *The Eximbank New-to-Export Insurance Policy* is a one-year blanket policy insuring short-term export credit sales. Coverage is 100 percent for political risks and 95/90 percent for commercial risks. The maximum repayment period is 180 days. Insurance fees vary with country, repayment term, and buyer. The minimum annual premium is US$500.

2. *The Eximbank Umbrella Insurance Policy* is a one-year blanket policy insuring short-term export credit sales by exporters with annual export credit sales of less than US$2 million within the past two years. Coverage is 100 percent for political risks and 90 percent for commercial risks (98 percent for bulk agricultural commodities). The maximum repayment period is 180 days. Insurance fees vary with country, repayment term, and buyer. The minimum annual premium is US$500.

3. *The Eximbank Bank Letter of Credit Insurance Policy* is a one-year blanket policy insuring commercial banks against loss on irrevocable letters of credit issued by foreign banks for U.S. exports. This coverage will assist a bank that is reluctant to finance an export made on an irrevocable letter of credit.

4. *The Eximbank Financial Institution Buyer Credit Insurance Policy* is a single-buyer policy insuring short-term loans by financial institutions made to foreign buyers of U.S. exports. This insurance coverage is protection for a bank that makes a loan to a foreign buyer who uses the loan proceeds to pay for imports from U.S. exporters. In practice, the financial institution purchases your receivable at face value on a specific date (when a draft is accepted), credits your account, and creates a loan in the buyer's name.

5. *The Eximbank Multi-Buyer Insurance Policy* is a one-year blanket policy insuring short-term export credit sales. The maximum coverage varies from 100 percent political risk and 90 percent commercial risk, up to 100 percent political and commercial risk coverage (varies with type of buyer). Insurance fees vary with country, repayment term, and buyer. The minimum annual premium is US$500.

6. *The Eximbank Short-Term Single-Buyer Insurance Policy* insures individual short-term export credit sales. Coverage varies with the buyer, from 90 percent political and commercial risk to 100 percent for political and commercial risk. The maximum repayment period is 180 days. Insurance fees vary with country, repayment term, and buyer. The minimum annual premium varies from US$2,500 up to US$10,000.

7. *The Eximbank Medium-Term Export Credit Insurance Policy* insures single-buyer, medium-term export credit sales. There are three policy types: single-sale policy, a repetitive sale policy, and a combined policy. The maximum coverage is 100 percent for political risks and 90 percent for commercial risks. The repayment term varies up to five years by contact amount. Insurance fees vary with country, repayment term, and status of the buyer.

8. *The Eximbank Short-Term Political Risks Multi-Buyer Export Credit Insurance Policy* insures short-term sales with repayment terms of up to 180 days. The Political Risks policy covers currency transfer risk as well as other political risks. Other political risks include the following events taking place after shipment:

- Cancellation or nonrenewal of an export license.

- Imposition of export restrictions not in place prior to the shipment date.

- Cancellation, not due to the buyer's fault, of valid import authority.

- Imposition of any law, order, decree, or regulation that prevents importing products into a buyer's country.

- War, hostilities, civil war, rebellion, revolution, insurrection, guerrilla activity, civil commotion, or other like disturbance on or before the due date.

- Requisition, expropriation, or confiscation of the specific business of the buyer.

A country limitation schedule is made part of the policy and indicates which countries are eligible for coverage and any limitations on the terms of sale. A minimum annual premium of US$500 is paid for each annual policy period.

9. *The Eximbank Lease Insurance Policies* insure lease payments receivable under operating and finance leases on a single transaction basis. The maximum coverage varies from 90 percent to 100 percent for political and commercial risks. The repayment period varies up to five years; longer terms will be considered. Fees vary by country, lease term, and type of lessee.

Government Support for Export Finance

Richard Barovik, editor of *Washington Export Letter* and *ExImbank Letter*, explains two valuable sources of government financing support:

> For exporters of all sizes, the U.S. government offers an increasingly diverse array of export finance resources. Government programs provide credits to foreign buyers and guarantees on bank loans to overseas customers, as well as [the aforementioned] credit insurance.

The **Export-Import Bank** offers a program of export credit insurance that covers credit arrangements between U.S. exporters and their foreign customers. Specifically, Eximbank arranges lines of credit in several key markets that can be tapped by overseas buyers. For example, in India, Eximbank has set up a line to a local bank that funds leasing transactions for U.S. capital equipment.

In Mexico, and a few other Latin American countries, Eximbank has set up "bundling" arrangements through which it guarantees a line from a U.S.-based bank to the Mexican bank to cover U.S. exports. In Mexico these lines are typically in the US$100–200 million range, and finance many smaller transactions, "bundled" into a single security and sold on the U.S. capital markets, thus bringing fresh money to the trade finance scene.

The agency also works with a growing number of state government export finance programs. These states in many cases serve as an outreach for the Eximbank facilities, arranging Eximbank cover for their local firms.

The **U.S. Agency for International Development**, a foreign aid agency, is increasingly active in export finance through three programs. One is to offer its guarantee on leasing transactions in Third World nations. A second is to guarantee transactions known as "forfait," in which specialized finance organizations invest in trade finance paper covering capital goods sales. The agency is also expanding its role in project finance, providing credits for infrastructure installations in telecommunications, environmental clean-up, energy production, and transport. These credits are available only for U.S. suppliers, thus generating important new markets.

These programs are directed to support large and small exporters in all world markets. Each program meets a different need. The principal export support program of the U.S. government is the Eximbank.

Exports Guaranteed by The Export-Import Bank (Eximbank)

Eximbank, a U.S. government corporation, has loan and guarantee programs that help U.S. exporters compete in foreign markets by offering financing to buyers that receive aggressive financing offers from competing suppliers from France, Germany, England, Japan, and others. Most exporters do not face financing competition because the average transaction is relatively small. However, for those firms that export big-ticket items (aircraft, railroad equipment, power stations, earthmoving equipment, and such), Eximbank programs are very important.

For the smaller firm or the firm with smaller scale export transactions, Eximbank is important for another reason. The Eximbank guarantee on a sale enables the exporter to sell the export paper, generate cash, offer expanded payment plans, and keep leverage off the balance sheet.

At this writing, Eximbank has four loan and guarantee programs, a preliminary commitment process, and a program that supports export loan guarantees by the Small Business Administration.

The *Eximbank Preliminary Commitment (PC)* is an offer from Eximbank detailing the terms and conditions of loan or guarantee support for a particular transaction, in advance of the transaction. This PC enables exporters to establish terms of financing for effective planning, negotiation, and marketing.

The Eximbank Working Capital Guarantee is a program designed to provide eligible exporters with access to working capital loans from commercial banks. The Working Capital Guarantee program is available only through commercial lenders. The guarantee is in favor of the lender making the working capital loan. The concept of this program is excellent. This guarantee may be combined with the SBA Export Revolving Line of Credit Program. The lender is guaranteed for 90 percent of the principal of the loan, and interest at the Treasury bill rate plus 1 percent. The object is to encourage lenders to extend credit so as to encourage exports. Experience suggests that the program as envisioned is of little interest to most lenders; they are not more flexible, and they require collateral for the loan amount in addition to the guarantee and the assets being guaranteed.

The Eximbank Guarantee ensures repayment of export loans made to foreign buyers of U.S. exports. The guarantee is in favor of the lender or assignable to the lender (U.S. or foreign). The transaction must involve the export of U.S. capital goods and services under medium- or long-term repayment arrangements. Exporters that are required to extend two-year or longer repayment terms to their buyers can enjoy the benefits of this program. The exporter's bank can receive the guarantee for up to 85 percent of the contract price (this can be 100 percent of the loan amount). With this guarantee, the lender is able to pay off the exporter in full. There is recourse to the exporter for product-specific performance and warranty issues.

The Eximbank Direct Loan is a loan from Eximbank to a foreign buyer of U.S. exports, exports that face officially subsidized foreign competition. The applicant must be the foreign buyer. Interest rates available to the buyer are those established by guidelines of the Organization for Economic Cooperation and Development (OECD). The members of OECD semiannually agree on a range of interest rates applicable to government-supported, long-term export financing to rich, intermediate, and poor nations.[6]

The direct-loan program is confined to situations where proof exists of subsidized finance by other nations. This evidence is required of small businesses where the loan is less than US$2.5 million and the term is seven years or less.

The Eximbank Intermediary Loan is similar to the Direct Loan except the loan is made to an intermediary lender as either a loan or a standby commitment for a loan.

Claims under Eximbank guarantees are paid in a prompt and timely manner, whereas insurance claims undergo an investigation process.

---

[6]The rich, intermediate, and poor countries are designations adopted in the OECD Arrangement on Officially Supported Export Credits.

Exports Financed by the Buyer's Bank

Most export transactions take place on letter of credit or sight draft terms. The buyer has made arrangements with his or her local bank for the letter of credit or other source of payment. Usually, the seller has little knowledge of what transpires. The buyer's bank has access to Eximbank programs and has loan arrangements with U.S. and foreign banks. (It is customary for banks to finance each other.)

It is unlikely that the buyer's bank will call on the exporter for assistance in financing a transaction. However, the buyer may need to arrange financing for his or her bank in order to make the purchase from you. This is usually true of buyers in eastern Europe, and it is often true of buyers in Latin America. The greater the exporter's understanding of export financing programs and options, the greater the opportunity to solidify an ongoing relationship in the targeted markets.

Other Financing Intermediaries

The **Small Business Administration (SBA)** offers an Export Revolving Line of Credit Program. Application for this line of credit is made to a commercial lender who must approve the application. The SBA guarantee is for up to 90 percent of the line. This is another good idea that receives little support from the banking community. The Export Revolving Line of Credit is offered in conjunction with Eximbank. SBA has a statutory limit on its exposure to any one company of US$750,000. For guarantee requests of between $200,000 and $1,000,000, Eximbank will co-guarantee with SBA, if SBA requests its participation.

The *United States Department of Agriculture (USDA)* is involved with the financing of exports of U.S.-produced agricultural commodities. Public Law 480 provides for U.S. government financing of sales of U.S. agricultural commodities to friendly countries. Sales are made by private businesspeople, usually on a bid basis in response to tenders issued by the importing country.

The Commodity Credit Corporation (CCC) has a slightly different program. The CCC is an agency within the USDA. It is the financing arm used for the implementation of export finance under the GSM-102 and GSM-103 programs of the USDA. Commodity exporters can be placed on a mailing list to receive P.L. 480 and CCC information. See the "Resources" section of this chapter.

A **confirming house** is another financial intermediary that provides financing for your export sales. A confirming house is requested to guarantee the export receivable of the seller, that is, to confirm the obligation of the buyer. If the buyer's obligation is confirmed, the exporter has a marketable document that can be sold to a third party willing to take the confirming house name as a risk. Alternatively, the paper can be sold to the confirming house (a separate transaction). There are fees and interest charges in all of this, often higher than a bank might charge. The offset is that the confirming house may be interested in situations that your bank has declined.

A bank-owned[7] **export trading company** can be an important financial intermediary. Bank holding companies that continue to operate ETCs look at an export finance requirement as a profit-making opportunity, while the ETCs' sibling bank may have little or no interest in the transaction. The ETC (not to be mistaken for a general trading company owned and operated for the benefit of a commercial enterprise) will usually arrange financing for an export transaction in return for an interest rate and a percentage of the gross margin on the transaction.

RESOURCES

1. To determine the creditworthiness of your buyer, review the survey or questionnaire and contact the references given. Ask your bank to do a bank credit report. Contact the closest office of the US&FCS and purchase a World Traders Data Report (WTDR) on the buyer; there's a fee.

2. Copies of the UCP 400 and the ICC 322 are available from ICC Publishing Corp., 156 Fifth Ave., Suite 820, New York, NY 10010.

3. Many states have active international trade development services, usually found within a department called "economic development." These departments can help you identify lenders interested in your export requirements. Many can also assist you in the development of a financing plan. Some states offer export finance or guarantee programs, although these are often more pomp (and politics) than circumstance.

4. The National Association of Credit Management/Finance Credit and International Business (NACM/FCIB) is a trade association of credit managers that actively deals with credit issues on an industry basis. The FCIB section is an 800-member association of corporate managers responsible for worldwide export financing, credit, treasury, and inter-

[7]Under the Export Trading Company Act of 1982, any bank holding company is, on approval, permitted to form and own an export trading company. This company is allowed to engage in export trade services prohibited to a commercial bank.

national subsidiary operations. Contact the FCIB at 520 Eighth Avenue, New York, NY 10018. Tel: 212-947-5368 or Fax: 212-465-8360.

5. Many of the larger banks have excellent publications that detail letter of credit and collection transactions.

6. A few leading insurance and commercial credit agencies insure commercial credit on export receivables. Some of these firms are The Credit International Associates, New York, NY; American Credit Indemnity, a subsidiary of Dun & Bradstreet; Pan Financial, New York, NY; and American International Group, Inc. To locate this type of firm, look in the yellow pages under "Insurance," or contact your commercial insurance carrier or broker for a referral.

7. Political risk coverage will vary depending on the country and the risk itself. The major private-sector, political risk insurers are Lloyds of London, American International Group (AIG), Pan Financial, Citicorp International Trade Indemnity (CITI), P.A.R.I.S., Trade Indemnity, Multinational Investment Guaranty Agency (MIGA), and Universal Investment Consultants.[8]

8. Contact information for Eximbank Insurance is available from:

Tel:			Fax:	
	New York	212-227-7020		212-513-4704
	Chicago	312-641-1915		312-641-2292
	Miami	305-372-8540		305-372-5114
	Houston	713-589-8182		713-589-8184
	Los Angeles	310-322-1152		310-322-2041

9. The address of Eximbank is 811 Vermont Ave., NW, Washington, DC 20571. The Business Advisory Service is a voice mail system for ordering program information; call 800-424-5201. To speak to a person, call 202-566-8990. The west coast office of Eximbank is at 11000 Wilshire Blvd., Los Angeles, CA 90024. Tel: 310-575-7425, Fax: 310-575-7428.

10. To receive P.L. 480 and CCC press releases that cover all commodities, write: Director of Information, Office of the General Sales Manager, U.S. Dept. of Agriculture, Washington, DC 20250-1000.

   To receive copies of purchase authorizations write and specify your commodity interest: Program Operations Division at the same address. Tel: 202-720-6211 or 720-6301.

---

[8]This listing provided by Mark Shemesh, Vice President, Northwest Region, March & McLennan, Inc., Seattle, WA.

Copies of the Title I, P.L. 480 financing regulations and related sample forms are also available from the Program Operations Division.

11. For a broad presentation of export financing techniques, see John S. Gordon, *Alternative Finance: Strategy and Techniques* (Dayton, OH: Global Training Center, Inc., 1992).

12 Financing in the Marketing Mix

Financing is a major feature of every export sale. One of the parties to each transaction has to arrange financing to cover at least the duration of the shipment of the goods from the port of export to the port of import. This financing, whether using internal funds or debt, decreases capital available for the rest of the business.

As we discussed in Chapter 11, the buyer will always prefer an open account purchase over any other payment term, while the seller will always prefer cash in advance. This chapter looks at financing as a feature of the marketing mix, a factor in the pricing or "packaging" of the product offered to the buyer. All else being equal, a financing program or package can alter the purchaser's decision in favor of the firm offering the financing. A financing program can also open doors otherwise closed to a firm just entering a market.

THE ROLE OF FINANCING

Financing is important because the cost of money is a significant cost of doing business anywhere in the world. The developed nations of the world have relatively comparable interest-rate structures; the differentials are a function of anticipated inflation rates, government deficits, and global positioning. Most other countries operate under the burden of higher interest rates that reflect excessive or inflationary government spending on development or other programs (or government waste, corruption, etc.). In Latin America, many nations suffer from monthly inflation rates in the double digits; local interest rates are based on these inflation rates, which are at levels unheard of in the United States.

When a U.S. exporter requires that the purchaser of his or her goods establish a letter of credit or pay in advance, the cost of money can be a significant burden or a barrier for the importer. In addition to the cost of this capital, the availability of capital can be another problem for the importer. Your target country may have a shortage of hard currencies. If so, that country will impose import or exchange controls to discourage imports or slow down the outflow of hard currencies. If the exporter appreciates the problems of an importer in a high-inflation country or a country with import or exchange controls, that exporter may be able to adjust the marketing mix to make the product offering more attractive to the buyer.

Exporting to the developed world requires a different level of sensitivity. Buyers in the Organization for Economic Cooperation and Development (OECD) countries[1] may be interested in the opportunities available from lower interest rates in the United States, but of more importance may be the expanded credit capacity that export financing may offer the buyer.

As you know by now, letters of credit are not always the standard for the conduct of international trade. Indeed, the majority of international trade takes place without letters of credit, and the use of letters of credit to finance international trade has been gradually decreasing over the course of this century.

There are many options in the financing of your export sales. Each of the terms of payment (other than cash in advance) contains options that can make the transaction more attractive to the buyer with little or no increase in risk to the exporter.

Issues for the Buyer

The foreign buyer, your importer, may be a dealer, distributor, or end user. Your product may be a consumer good (toys, food products, apparel); a commercial good such as office equipment, furniture, or fixtures; or an industrial good such as manufacturing equipment, machinery, or transportation equipment. Each type of buyer, and each type of good, have different time structures to their sales channels. For example, a distributor of off-road construction equipment has two issues. He or she needs to purchase the goods, bring them through customs, inventory the goods, and sell them to end users. In addition, each end user may request or require financing of that purchase from the distributor. A dealer in office equipment and furniture may have to maintain sizeable inventories throughout cycles in the selling seasons. His or her buyers may require extended payment terms. The distributor of consumer goods deals with retailers that experience cycles related to the specific goods and dating terms for that industry in that country or region.

Each of the firms in these examples has unique financing requirements. The exporter that can offer competitive quality, timely delivery, first-class service,

---

[1]OECD member countries are Australia, Austria, Belgium, Canada, Denmark, Finland, France, Germany, Greece, Iceland, Ireland, Italy, Japan, Luxembourg, the Netherlands, New Zealand, Norway, Portugal, Spain, Sweden, Switzerland, Turkey, United Kingdom, and the United States.

and terms of payment that support the buyer's overall objectives will be more successful than the firm that is less flexible as to financing.

Issues for the Seller

Every exporter wants to get paid, and no exporter wants to give up control of the goods without payment. Every exporter is in business to make a profit, at the minimum a reasonable return on invested capital given the risks associated with the business.

The issues that are important to the seller are:

1. Making a profitable sale.
2. Establishing a meaningful presence in the target market.
3. Controlling the quality of service and support given to the products in that market.

Each sale exposes the exporter to the myriad of business risks associated with a business transaction in another country. In addition to language, culture, and business practice, there are financial and legal risks. These uncertainties give the exporter reason to strongly consider cash in advance and letter of credit as the only acceptable terms.

The terms of payment listed in Chapter 11 (other than cash in advance) all offer the exporter the opportunity to achieve his or her objectives and still address the importer's issues. Each risk can be mitigated or otherwise managed to an acceptable degree.

STRATEGIES FOR SALES FINANCE

Your product and its channels of distribution in each country will dictate the type of sales financing strategy you adopt. The terms-of-payment methods listed in Chapter 11 focus primarily on short-term payment transactions. In some industries, it is necessary to consider a combination of short- and medium-term financing for the buyer(s). In others, only long-term financing programs are acceptable. This financing usually relates to exports for infrastructure development or very long-term capital projects.

Short-Term Financing Strategies

Short term is usually defined as terms of up to 180 days. Banks, insurers, and government agencies are comfortable with this usage, so you should adhere to it. Each of the traditional terms of payment can be structured to provide your buyer with some form of financing assistance.

Letters of credit require that the importer do at least two things in order to purchase from you:

1. Pay a fee for issuance of the letter of credit.
2. Tie up his or her line of credit for at least the amount of the L/C.

In addition, the buyer may have to make a deposit in advance of the issuance of the L/C as part of the exchange or import control procedures of the host government. A letter of credit is often one of the more onerous demands an exporter may make on a buyer.

You can encourage the use of a L/C, or reduce the cost of the L/C, by doing one or more of the following:

1. Agree to pay the cost of issuing the L/C.
2. Require the L/C for less than the full amount of the transaction.
3. Pay the confirmation fee on the L/C, if you require that it be confirmed.
4. Finance the time for payment (tenor) under the L/C (see below).

Letters of credit also have amendment, negotiation, and payment fees. All of these fees increase the cost of purchasing from your company. You may wish to negotiate with your buyer as to the payment of any or all of these fees if the buyer is reluctant to issue a letter of credit in your favor.

You may wish to consider accepting a *standby letter of credit* rather than a commercial L/C. The standby L/C may cost less, it requires fewer documents for payment, and ensures payment by the buyer's bank in the event that the buyer does not pay on the agreed open account or documentary-collection terms.

To acquire financing to purchase the goods you export, the SBA may be of some service. In 1992, the SBA introduced a pilot program to provide financing to small exporters who are in receipt of export letters of credit. It sounds similar to the program any good finance company would offer, the type of financing that's perhaps second nature to lenders like MTB Bank. A good company that is well managed, reputable, and responsible could look to this as an option. Under this program, the exporter recipient of a small letter of credit assigns the proceeds of the letter of credit to an export management company or finance company. This company finances the purchase of the goods to be manipulated and exported. Documents are presented to the negotiating bank and the L/C is paid. The EMC or finance company collects a 5 percent fee, the bank collects its L/C negotiating fees, SBA collects its fees, and the exporter may have a small profit from the deal (maybe not). This may be an excellent program, sorely needed by the smaller exporters. However, it may just be an old horse with a new blanket. Banks with international banking departments will negotiate export letter of credit documents for letters of credit of any size. They are paid for the service, not for the size of the L/C. Contact your nearest SBA office and discuss the Exporters Letter of Credit Facilitation Service (ELFS), a pilot program.

Acceptances are drafts that are accepted by the buyer (trade acceptance) or a bank (bankers' acceptance). The acceptance is a promissory note payable at a certain date in the future. The signature of the buyer, the buyer's bank, or your bank (more on this later) may enable you to sell (discount) the draft and capture the cash otherwise tied up for the term of the draft. This mechanism can be used with or without a letter of credit. Also, the discount rate applied when you discount the draft can be either the U.S. rate or the rate in the buyer's country. The currency of the draft can be the U.S. dollar or any other marketable currency.

If you discount a time draft, one of the parties pays interest from the date of discount to maturity of the draft. If you hold a time draft, you absorb the cost of being out of funds for the duration of the draft. This cost can be passed to the buyer either in the amount of the draft or by the addition of an interest rate clause to the face of the draft. Discount charges can be for your account.

Under a letter of credit sale, the exporter can provide the importer with U.S.-dollar-based interest rates by requiring that the draft be negotiated in the United States, that U.S. bank discount charges be for account of the buyer. U.S. banks also charge an acceptance commission of about 1.5 percent per annum, which could be for account of the buyer. This procedure does not relieve the buyer of costs associated with opening the letter of credit (tie up line of credit, etc.). Under any type of letter of credit in your favor, you do not provide credit to your buyer; you only offer an extended payment date and the opportunity to reduce the buyer's cost of money.

Under a documentary collection, unless your bank has a line of credit for your buyer, the discount amount credited to your account (booked as a loan and often called either "bills purchased" or "drafts discounted") will be with recourse to you. Your liability will be eliminated when the buyer pays at maturity.

If the buyer's bank has a line of credit with your bank (or another bank more interested in export trade finance), or if your bank is willing to discount drafts accepted by that bank, another option is open to you. Your time draft sent on collection would be either (1) drawn on the buyer and accepted by the buyer with an additional acceptance or *aval* by the buyer's bank, or (2) drawn on the buyer's bank and accepted by that bank. In either case, you hold a promissory note payable by that bank. Your bank, or another bank, may be willing to discount that draft without recourse to you. Because the draft and documents were sent on a collection from your bank, your collection instructions could require that the title documents not be released until after the draft is accepted by the bank.

Another way to use acceptance financing and its rate advantage on an export transaction[2] is to use a time draft on a documentary collection. On the date the draft is accepted for payment, draw your own draft on your bank. Under prior arrangement, your bank will accept the draft (this is called a bankers' acceptance) and discount it in your favor. You will receive the discounted proceeds immediately and owe your bank the face amount of the draft at its maturity. That maturity should coincide with the payment you will receive from your buyer under the previously accepted time draft. The advantages to this process are:

1. Your buyer received time to pay, that is, credit, from you.

2. The goods were released only against the buyer's accepted draft.

3. You obtained a low interest rate, which you were in a position to pass on in the face amount or add to your time draft under the collection, or absorb.

The risk is that the buyer will fail to pay when due. To mitigate that risk, the above process could be done with the buyer's bank as the drawee or additional acceptor on the draft.

In any of these situations, Eximbank or other political and commercial risk insurers could have been involved. When you provide adequate information and they approve the risk, you can insure letter-of-credit, documentary-collection, or open-account sales to buyers in most countries around the world.

An **open account** sale offers the greatest flexibility you can extend to your buyer. Your sale could be in U.S. dollars, the buyer's currency, or the currency of a third country. You can protect your foreign exchange exposure with a forward contract from your bank. You can protect your commercial and political risk with the appropriate coverage from Eximbank or one of its competitors. You can capture your funds in advance of the payment date by use of loans or acceptances. Acceptances offer you the least-cost alternative.

A **factor** can be a useful alternative for your short-term financing strategies. Often called a *confirming house*, an export factor is a company that, for a fee, guarantees payment by the buyer. You may be able to use that guaranteed paper as collateral for financing from your bank for cash-flow purposes. Or, the factor or confirming house may offer to purchase the guaranteed paper from you at a discount. Many domestic finance companies have shown an increasing interest in export paper or accounts receivable from reputable firms

---

[2]On September 18, 1992, the U.S. Bancorp Prime rate was 6.0 percent p.a., the Bankers Acceptance discount rate was 3.22 percent p.a., and the acceptance commission (always negotiable between borrower and banker) was about 1.5 percent p.a. A corporate borrower who normally pays prime +2 percent would have these options: a 90-day loan at 8.0 percent p.a. or acceptance finance at the BA rate + 2 percent p.a., which is 5.22 percent p.a. discount (5.285 percent p.a. actual).

in OECD nations. They will guarantee the commercial risk and, in some cases, purchase the accounts from the exporters. As with the factor, the guarantee of a reputable finance company may enable you to cash out of the export receivable.

Other Short-Term Financing Strategies

Many of the major U.S. banks have lines of credit to banks in less developed or newly industrialized countries or to smaller or less-well-known banks. The purpose is to finance those banks' clients' imports from the United States. These credit lines may be guaranteed or insured by Eximbank or other political and commercial risk insurers. Lines may be partly or fully collateralized.

Bank lines of credit of this type may be available in your buyer's country. Your buyer may be aware of these facilities and be able to make good use of them. If the buyer is not familiar with this type of facility, suggest that he or she contact his or her nation's major banks and ask if they have lines of credit to finance imports. The benefit of this type of line of credit is twofold:

1. The bank name will be readily accepted for letters of credit and other international payment mechanisms.

2. The bank may have access to extra funds or to funds at a lower cost than would ordinarily prevail in that country.

These preestablished import financing programs can save both you and your client a great deal of time and trouble.

Medium-Term Financing Strategies

In international trade, *medium term* is usually interpreted as a payment term between six months and five years (seven years or more for aircraft and similar high-value capital goods). The products for which medium-term financing is requested or required are intermediate capital goods, transport and construction equipment, industrial machinery and equipment, project management, construction and engineering, and similar goods and services. Product buyers are either distributors or end users. Service buyers are end users, governments, or developers. The financing requirements of distributors and end users or governments differ significantly.

The distributor or dealer would like to receive two types of financing from the exporter. First, he or she would like financing for the purchase and inventory of the goods. Second, he or she would like assistance in financing the end user. For example, the TORO Company is a recognized leader in the manufacture and sale of groundskeeping equipment for recreational and commercial environments. In the past, TORO has provided short-term or flooring financing for its dealers, and it has provided medium-term financing for the end users of commercial equipment. This has encouraged dealers to maintain broad inventories and has positioned TORO as a local product in its many international markets. TORO has subsequently established subsidiary and joint-venture operations in its major international markets.

After the commercial bank loan problems of the late 1980s and early 1990s, many banks have withdrawn from any form of extended-term trade finance. Emerging exporters find it increasingly difficult to place a medium-term dealer or end-user financing program for their buyers. Many traditional resources have dried up. If your bank will not assist you with this type of financing, the senior international banker or senior loan officer at your bank may be able to suggest money-center or larger correspondent banks that would be interested. It may be necessary to consult with your trade association, Eximbank, and others in order to identify banks or other institutions that are interested in the risks you offer. Many foreign banks operate in the United States as owners of U.S. banking companies or as branches, agencies, or subsidiaries of the foreign parent. A bank with its parent in your target country may have a proprietary interest in financing your transaction. For example, ABN-AMRO Bank, N.V., the largest bank in the Netherlands, has offices across the United States and is interested in financing sizeable international trade transactions with the Netherlands, in addition to its core U.S. corporate banking business.[3] The posture of ABN-AMRO is the norm for large foreign banks.

The short-term phase of the financing requirement can be met by any of the strategies listed under "Short-Term Financing Strategies." At the end of that term, which may extend to 180 days, the obligation would be payable or convertible. If the goods are still in inventory, you may require immediate payment or you may wish to extend this inventory-financing period. Eximbank is an export credit insurer that understands this can occur and it has a policy that permits an extension for an additional 90 days.

At the time the product is sold to the end user, the dealer or distributor may want your assistance in providing finance for extended payment by that end user. This may be important to the distributor's business due to the competitive nature of the market. It may be necessary in order to sell your products into a new, unknown, or less liquid market.

The medium-term portion of the financing requirement usually involves the buyer's bank, your bank, and one or more third parties. If you can afford to carry the medium-term paper, you may wish to hold a promissory note from the end user (one to five years) at an attractive interest rate. The note could be guaranteed by the buyer's bank. With this guarantee, you may be able to sell the note at a discount to a third party. This third party could be your bank, an international finance house, an *á forfait* (or forfait) company, or another investor.

Eximbank has insurance and guarantee programs tailored for these medium-term sales. It requires regular quarterly or semiannual payments of principal, plus interest. Interest can be on a fixed or floating-rate basis. To ensure continued performance, the exporter is required to maintain a financial interest in the transaction. Arrange one of these programs for your medium-term export sales *before the sale*. Any guarantor or insurer requires an application, financial statements and credit reports on the buyer, and other information. Approval from the third party is often dependent on receipt of full and timely information. Make the information-gathering process part of your negotiation with the buyer. Extended payment terms at attractive U.S. prime-rate-based interest rates can be important to your sales efforts.

Á forfait is a financing technique well known to those who trade with eastern Europe. It is offered in the United States by some of the major money-center banks, some foreign banks, and a very few others. In an *á forfait* transaction, an exporter of capital goods grants extended payment terms to a buyer, the buyer's obligation is guaranteed by a leading financial institution (generally in the buyer's country), interest is in the transaction's value (the sale amount) or is a negotiated add-on amount, and the resulting long-term receivable of the exporter is sold to the *á forfait* institution without recourse to the exporter. It is important to note that the exporter is taken completely out of the transaction, other than its service and warranty obligations. This specialized form of export finance is usually restricted to exports with a value in excess of US$1 million. It is most frequently done with exports to Latin America, Eastern Europe, or the countries of the former Soviet Bloc. Some specialized finance houses advertise that they offer this type of financing for smaller transactions. If your buyer can arrange for his or her bank to guarantee or aval (guarantee) medium-term, interest-bearing notes, this may be viable for your export financing requirements. It is an alternative to Eximbank.

Your buyer may be a well-established and financially responsible firm that has been purchasing from U.S. suppliers for a long period of time. As such, that buyer and its bank may have long-term financing programs in place. When you and your sales organization are negotiating capital goods transactions with sizeable foreign buyers, be sure to ask about their existing financing arrangements. These established financing relationships may enable the transaction to close quite rapidly. However, your buyer may want to increase its credit capacity and place the financing burden on your company. It is important to learn this early on in the negotiations so that your firm can react and work to put a financing program in place.

If you project a steady increase in your exports of capital goods, it is important that you establish good working relationships with a number of banks interested in financing this type of business. You should also schedule a training session for your export finance manager at Eximbank. Attendance at one of these programs will quickly familiarize your finance manager with Eximbank programs, and he or she will develop working contacts with other capital goods exporters, Eximbank officials, and export finance bankers. This preparation is important to your success; your competitors in the United States and abroad are prepared with quality products, service programs, marketing programs, and financing plans.

Long-Term Financing Strategies

Long-term finance generally means financing with repayment terms in excess of five years (five to ten, or longer). These terms are appropriate for large projects or large product acquisitions.[4] Financing for the buyer on these large or long-term projects can often be arranged by one or more of the following:

1. Eximbank.
2. The World Bank.
3. Regional development banks.
4. The Overseas Private Investment Corporation, as part of the project development finance.
5. *À forfait* financing organizations.
6. Bank syndication, for project financing.

Long-term financing requires that the buyer provide the financing agencies with comprehensive planning and financing documents, including cash-flow projections in both the local currency and the currency of the debt instruments. Inflation and currency value assumptions must be valid within the context of the forecasted international economic environment over the financing period.

The exporter may be required to support the financing of the project in at least two ways:

1. The exporter may be required to provide a performance bond to guarantee performance on the project. This bond could be for up to 20 percent of the value of the exporter's portion of the project. The bond would be released after the exporter has performed or it would be drawn on in the event the exporter fails to perform.

[4]Adapted from Export-Import Bank of the United States, *Medium and Long Term Export Loans and Guarantees,* Revised July 1990, p. 4.

2. Payments to the exporter may be subject to a retention by the buyer to ensure performance. The retention amount would be paid upon completion of the project.

The buyer, if a commercial enterprise rather than a government, may request that the exporter help place financing for the project. With the exception of the OECD nations and very few others, most nations of the world do not have effective capital or debt markets, and banking systems are often restricted in their capacity to finance long-term projects. It is important that you appreciate the possible expectations of your buyers.

SUMMARY

Over the recent past, a tremendous emphasis has been placed on product quality and service. Writers, gurus, and business and government leaders have placed quality and service at the forefront of America's failings and its path back to glory. The message is needed and hopefully will be heard by those who have rested on the success of earlier times.

Today's new, emerging, and successful companies produce quality products, deliver premium service, and focus their efforts on meeting their buyer's needs. An important part of the international marketing mix is the ease with which a buyer can make a purchase from an exporter. Exporters can enhance their product and service packages with financing programs attuned to the requirements of the buyer and his or her marketplace.

Financing may be short, medium, or long term. Exporters do not need to take on excessive risks in order to provide attractive payment terms and financing programs to their buyers. Effective risk-management programs are available from a number of public and private sources. An understanding of the market and the nature of the competition in each marketplace and a flexible posture will enable the exporter to build a strong presence in each target market.

RESOURCES

1. Eximbank and other political and commercial risk insurers offer quotations on risks to most countries of the world. Rates and fees vary by country, by type of obligor, by amount, and by sales term.

2. One example of a domestic credit risk insurer that has entered the international marketplace is American Credit Indemnity, a subsidiary of Dun & Bradstreet. It will insure the credit risk of your export sales to

buyers in most countries of western Europe. Once insured, these receivables can often be financed at a bank.

Nations Bank is another good example. It has an export factor program by which it factors the political and commercial risk of your export sales and, on application, finances those receivables. Other banks provide similar services.

3. The Export-Import Bank (Eximbank) of the United States is at 811 Vermont Ave., NW, Washington, DC 20571. Tel: 202-566-8990. Ask for the country officer or the loan guarantee department.

4. To contact the Eximbank Insurance Programs, see Resource 8, Chapter 11.

5. Many leading international insurance companies cover the risk of fraudulent drawing on performance bonds. Exporters should discuss their needs with their commercial insurance carrier, broker, or underwriter.

6. MTB Banking Corporation specializes in trade financing for growth companies across the United States. The bank maintains three offices in New York and a branch in the Cayman Islands. For further information, contact: MTB Banking Corporation, 90 Broad St., New York, NY 10004-2290. Tel: 212-858-3300; fax: 212-858-3448.

13 Foreign Exchange

The term **foreign exchange** (FX) means the exchange of the currency of one country for the currency of another. A foreign exchange transaction occurs with any international trade or investment activity. Either the buyer or the seller of goods, services, or an investment property such as land, buildings, or production facilities will be required to enter into a foreign exchange transaction.

A **foreign exchange rate** is the price of one currency in terms of another. The rate for British pounds sterling (£) might be US$1.7850,[1] meaning that the pound sterling sells for US$1.7850. It is useful to keep in mind that foreign exchange is a commodity and is priced like one.

This exchange creates both risks and opportunities for each party to the transaction. These risks and opportunities warrant further investigation and understanding as they are part of any export activity. Into the 1990s, the United States has experienced immense imbalances in its trade with other nations. In part, this continued imbalance has been due to the U.S. dollar being overvalued. "Overvalued" in this context means that the dollar buys more of other currencies than it theoretically should, based on the underlying economic performance of the country as compared to the economic trading performance of its trading partners.

Theoretically, a currency (monetary unit) of any country that experiences continued and uncorrected deficits in its balance of trade and balance of payments should decrease in value. That decrease would make imported items more expensive, thereby discouraging imports. The lower the value of its currency in terms of others, the cheaper its exports; over time, its exports will rise. The decrease in imports and the increase in exports would gradually result in more balance to that country's trade situation. For a number of reasons, the value of the U.S. dollar has not adjusted in accordance with this macroeconomic theory.

---

[1]Rates as of Friday, September 18, 1992, reported in *The Journal of Commerce*, New York, NY. Rates were provided to the paper by Citibank/New York. These rates apply to currency transfers of US$1 million or larger.

EVOLUTION OF FOREIGN EXCHANGE ACTIVITY

Foreign exchange is an outgrowth of the very beginnings of trade, and it has been one of the basic facilitators of that trade. In its crudest form, foreign exchange is the exchange of a unit of value from one person (a sand dollar, a knife, shoes) for a unit or units of value (shells, blankets, and so on) from another person, tribe, or nation . This bargaining for value and establishment of value in a free-floating interchange of needs and wants is the basis for the foreign exchange market as we know it today.

International trade evolved from the exchange of goods by barter to the exchange of goods for payment by means of a store of value. Initially, gold or other commodities in limited supply were stores of value. Today, those values are supported by the integrity of the country of issue, and the economic performance of that country as compared to the economic performance of other nations.

Keep Your Objectives in Sight

Corporations, financial institutions, and individuals engage in foreign exchange transactions. It is necessary to make a distinction between the corporation that is exporting, importing, or investing and a bank or financial institution. These different types of organizations have different objectives. However, the foreign exchange market itself has led some corporate managers to lose sight of their objectives. Many exporters have seen that decisions regarding foreign exchange can result in added profits, and they then begin to treat foreign exchange as a way to generate income. These companies forget, ultimately to their peril, their basic business.

Foreign exchange is a result of the business they are in, ancillary to their business, and a function in support of the production or sale process. Banks and other financial institutions are in the foreign exchange business as profit centers; foreign exchange is their product. They have the trained personnel and the administrative organization to properly undertake the activity. This is a point you should remember as you conduct business in the international marketplace.

THE GLOBAL ECONOMY AND THE DOLLAR

Exchange rates came under widespread and formalized control in 1945, when the Bretton Woods Agreement created the International Monetary Fund (IMF). At those meetings, the leaders of the industrialized countries established the value of all major currencies in terms of the U.S. dollar, the value of which was established in terms of gold. Gold was given the value of $35 per troy ounce. This system worked remarkably well for a number of years, until an imbalance in the system created by a string of U.S. balance of payments deficits and large and growing surpluses in Germany and Japan became too large for the United States to ignore. Although the U.S. trade balance was positive, capital flowing into these countries for investment made our balance of payments in the negative.

Since 1971, when the U.S. government ended convertibility of U.S. dollars into gold, many changes have occurred. There have been conferences and agreements, par values and bands of intervention, snakes[2] and double snakes, and varying degrees of control and agreement on currency values by the major trading nations.

The U.S. dollar began the 1980s overvalued in an inflationary economy. This was a textbook case. The theoretical solution would be for the United States to experience an immediate loss of the confidence of the international community, followed by a decrease in the value of the currency, imposition of controls on the internal economy, guidance and assistance on economic management and performance by the IMF and other international economic agencies, and a rapid dampening of the inflation in the country. That did not happen.

The United States has had the distinction of being perceived as the best place for foreign investors to invest their funds. This is due to the relative political stability, the size and diversity of the economy, and the country's position as the political leader of the free world. Therefore, inflation, overvalued currencies, and other significant negative economic performance factors have elicited nontraditional long-term responses, which have made the trade imbalance more difficult to correct.

Corrective actions taken by the Federal Reserve to reduce the value of the dollar, control the level and rate of inflation, and continue to facilitate the financing of the immense federal budget deficit have supported continued large amounts of foreign investment in the United States.

In the mid-1980s, the U.S. government and the Federal Reserve began taking steps to reduce the value of the dollar while at the same time keeping the U.S. economy growing at a positive rate. This was not an easy task. Reduction in the value of the dollar acts to decrease the rate of increase in foreign holdings of claims on the United States. Those same reductions may result in a decrease in portfolio investment by foreigners in U.S. government debt—a negative step that creates upward pressure on interest rates to finance the federal budget deficit.

The U.S. government has used the strong and overvalued dollar to finance the federal budget deficit. The strong dollar has encouraged foreign purchase

---

[2]*Snake* is the FX term that describes the allowed range of volatility of a currency within an agreed band of intervention.

of U.S. debt at relatively low and noninflationary interest rates. This level of foreign purchase had, up to 1991, insulated the U.S. population from the reality of the budget deficits, but the deficit must be dealt with. In addition, the United States must take a more balanced approach to trade negotiations at GATT (see Chapter 19) and other venues in order to bring long-term equilibrium to its balance of trade and balance of payments.

CONTROL OF FOREIGN EXCHANGE

Foreign exchange activity is not dependent on an organized market such as a stock exchange or commodity exchange. There is no single place where buyers and sellers meet to conduct their foreign exchange business. Each country does, however, have its own rules and regulations about what can and cannot be done with its currency. You can find these rules in the *Annual Report on Exchange Arrangements and Exchange Restrictions*, published by the International Monetary Fund, which provides information on countries that are members of the IMF.

Major trading nations such as the United States, Canada, Britain, Germany, Japan, France, Italy, and others have little or no restriction on the convertibility of their currencies, thereby facilitating trade and investment. Other countries do have varying degrees of control. These range from a fairly standard control such as requiring all imports to be on letters of credit (which enables government control of foreign exchange outflows) and limiting the amount of currency travelers may carry, to the more severe forms of control embodied in embargoes, blockages, and general inconvertibility such as those of many nonmarket economies. These controls serve the needs of the controlling country that wants to limit the import of goods or restrict the outflow of currency (capital flight). The United States had controls on capital flight in the early 1970s; there were restraints and restrictions on the amounts that could be invested outside the United States. There is still a reporting requirement on any transfer of funds to a foreign address in excess of US$10,000 unless this is a standard business practice.

TWO TYPES OF TRANSACTIONS

While there are many different terms and options in the foreign exchange markets, the exporter will be exposed to two general types of foreign exchange transaction: the spot transaction and the forward transaction.

A **spot** transaction involves the purchase of a foreign currency (the sale of dollars) for immediate delivery, or the reverse. We will use an exporter of industrial lubricants to Germany in an example of a spot transaction. In the sale transaction, the exporter has the opportunity to quote the terms of sale in US dollars (US$) or Deutsche marks (DM). If the exporter quotes and sells in US$, the buyer is assuming the exchange risk and on the payment date must convert DM into US$ for payment to the exporter. If the sale is in DM, the exporter will receive DM instead of US$ some time in the future. Thus, either the exporter or the importer (in Germany) can assume the foreign exchange risk. The buyer is at risk for the value (cost) of US$ from the date of order to the payment date.

If the exporter quotes and sells in DM, then the buyer will pay in his or her own currency (an exporter may find that offering to sell in the buyer's currency is an advantage in the marketing program for that country or region), and the exporter will receive the DM in payment. The exporter will then sell these DM to his bank spot, receiving the US$ equivalent on the date of the sale of the DM. The exporter is at risk for the value (cost) of the DM from the date of the order to receipt of payment.

Assume an exchange rate of DM1.5210/US$. Also assume that the exchange rates did not change from date of quote to date of receipt of funds (an assumption useful for illustration only). On his sale of the US$35,000 in lubricants, the exporter would receive DM53,235, which he would sell to his bank when received.

In this example, by quoting the sale in the buyer's currency, the exporter used a good marketing tool to promote the sale of his goods to that foreign buyer. This is an accepted practice by exporters of other nations, and is done in the United States by many of the major companies. Few of the smaller companies do so, possibly from a lack of understanding of the process or a belief that the transactions are too complex for them or their bankers. However, exporters will achieve success in their businesses if they can break down the barriers that stand in the buyer's way.[3] The transaction currency can be one of these barriers.

By selling in a foreign currency and converting spot, the seller did leave himself open to a foreign exchange risk. If the buyer's currency had gone down in value between the time of the quote and the time of receipt of funds, the seller would have received less than US$35,000 for the DM53,235. If the DM/US$ rate had gone to DM1.5490/US$, the exporter would have still received DM53,235, but that would now be worth only US$34,367.30. This is a transaction loss of US$632.70, or 1.8 percent.

The seller could lessen this risk by planning prior to making the quotation. Based on the terms of payment (Chapter 11), the seller can estimate fairly well

---

[3] "The Buck Stops Here: Accepting Foreign Exchange Risk," by Susan Arterian, the August 1991 issue of *CEO Magazine* (pp. 40, 42) is an excellent brief survey of the value of adapting a corporate policy regarding sales in foreign currencies.

the date on which payment will be received. The seller can use this information to base the quote to the German buyer on the value of the DM on the anticipated date of receipt of the DM.

Now assume 30-day sight draft terms. The exporter would have obtained a rate of DM1.5276 from the bank (note the difference from the spot rate of DM1.5210), and the quote in DM would have been DM53,466 (for the purposes of this illustration, still a competitive quote). When the sale takes place, the exporter will at that date *sell* the DM to his bank forward for delivery at the approximate date of his receipt of the DM. When the exporter receives the DM, it will deliver them to the bank and receive the contracted price of US$35,000.[4] If the exporter had based his quote on the DM rate of 1.5210, he would have received US$34,848.80 for a loss of US$151.20 of 0.4 percent. The opportunity to capture a sale to a new or growing buyer may be worth the 0.4 percent loss.

If the exporter is selling into a country whose currency is increasing in value relative to the U.S. dollar, the forward foreign exchange cover would eliminate an opportunity for *extra* profit on the sale. In the above transaction, if the DM was increasing in value relative to the US$ such that the DM had gone to DM1.5110/US$ on day 30 (settlement), the exporter would have forgone a *gain* of US$231.60 on the transaction. This gain resulted from the increase in the value of the DM relative to the cost of the US$.

Figure 13.1 is a foreign exchange transaction confirmation. This confirmation covers the purchase of GBP 30,000,000 (£ sterling; GBP is FX dealer terminology) at US$1.80000/£) on January 2, for value (delivery) on January 6, 1992. The GBP transaction was settled through Standard Chartered Bank, Los Angeles. This is the type of confirmation you will receive when you engage in spot or forward foreign exchange transactions with your bank. Review this confirmation carefully as soon as it is received. Be sure that it corresponds to your understanding of the FX transaction.

When you look to a forward rate as a basis for a price quote, consider the range of foreign exchange rates that may prevail during the time period for which the U.S.-dollar-based pricing schedule is valid. If export prices are subject to change on a 90-day basis, you may want to consider taking an average of the forward rates in effect for the next 90-day period and using that as a basis for the local currency quote. This will enable you to quote in local currency terms for fixed periods of time. This is an aid to the buyer(s). The exporter could also pick the highest rate for that 90-day period instead of an average.

Foreign exchange rates fluctuate constantly, and the price of a currency is valid only at the time it is given. The exporter cannot expect a rate quoted at

---

[4]The maturity date spot rate (unknown at the transaction date) for the DM was DM1.5325. This forward transaction saved our exporter an additional 0.5 percent p.a. (1.5325-1.5276).

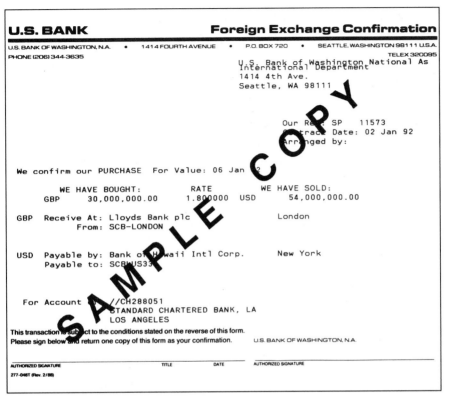

Figure 13.1 Foreign Exchange Transaction Confirmation

10 A.M. to be available at 2 P.M.; the 10:00 rate won't be available at 10:10. If markets are particularly volatile, due to uncertainties in the political arena or soon-to-be-announced economic data, rates may vary widely. In some circumstances, you may be unable to get a quote on a currency due to these uncertainties.

Options and Windows

Commercial banks also offer two alternatives that can assist you in protecting a forward exposure in a currency.

An **option** is a contract to buy or sell (call or put) a currency at a rate for an open period into the future. The option has a nonrefundable cost. The option provides you with the right to buy the currency in the future at the previously agreed rate or to sell the currency in the future at a previously agreed rate. Similar to option contracts offered on commodity exchanges, the banking option contract offers more flexibility in settlement dates and contract amounts.

A **window** is a period in which you either take delivery of a currency or deliver a currency. The window would be used when you have a sale in a foreign currency and you can pin down the date of receipt of the funds only within a range of time: a week, two weeks, a month, and so on. The FX contract gives you a rate of exchange for that period. You must deliver the exchange within that period or renew or cancel the FX contract. There will be a cost for renewal or cancellation. The rate you receive on the window transaction (it will be the sale of a foreign currency or purchase of dollars) will not be as attractive as a specific forward rate because the bank will pass on its cost of your uncertainty.

The size of the foreign exchange transaction is also a major consideration when dealing with your bank. Most banks can readily accommodate transactions in excess of US$150,000, but smaller transactions can be difficult to offset or match, difficult to absorb into the trader's own position, or unprofitable; therefore, they are not done.

The US$35,000 in the previous example, while very real for many firms, is somewhat small and may be difficult for most banks. Banks are compensated through the spread on the buy-and-sell rates of the currencies on any transaction. The spread on a small transaction does not cover the costs of the operation. Many banks will not consider transactions under US$50,000.

If you have small transactions and deal with a major bank, consider some alternatives:

1. A smaller bank may do your foreign exchange deals in hopes of acquiring your other business.

2. Group your transactions and cover your exposure in groups (e.g., 30 days' worth of receipts). This may create volume that is more reasonable, from a cost and operating standpoint, for you and your bank.

3. Set a floor on the transaction size for which you will quote in the buyer's currency. Below the floor, sales are in US$, and above the floor sales can be in the buyer's currency. Be sure it is a currency that has an active and viable market in the United States; for example, the Colombian peso, the Honduran lempira, or the Indian rupee do not have markets in the United States.

4. Be prepared to pay a minimum charge per FX transaction. Your bank may have a minimum revenue target per transaction which your small transactions do not generate. Determine your bank's target and agree to pay these transaction minimums as a flat fee or in the spread on each deal.

BANKS AND BROKERS

Over time, your need for foreign exchange services will change and become more complex. Decisions regarding foreign exchange exposure management require different considerations than those supporting an export marketing decision. The foreign exchange market can facilitate your response to these situations, through your banker or possibly through a brokerage firm on one of the major commodity exchanges.

Banks and brokerage firms differ in matters of foreign exchange. A commodity exchange deals with foreign exchange as a commodity, with fixed contract amounts and fixed trading or settlement dates, while the commercial bank generally handles foreign exchange as a product. The bank will trade almost any and odd amounts, with any maturity or settlement date. Each has its role to play. There are some principal differences you should be aware of in considering one or the other.

A **commodity exchange** has the following requirements:

1. You will have to make a nominal payment, called a *margin,* to be paid in as a percentage of each contract.

2. During the life of the contract, if the market moves against your contract position, you may be required to make added margin payments.

3. Transactions are limited to specific contract sizes, such as £50,000.

4. There are specific settlement or closing dates.

5. There are limits on the daily volatility of each contract. This is a positive feature not available through an open foreign exchange contract with a banking organization.

6. Compensation to the broker is by a commission on the contract, irrespective of degree or direction of movement in rates.

7. The commodity exchange contract may best be used to hedge a potential loss or fix a value in the currency denominating a foreign investment.

With a **commercial bank** contract, foreign exchange transactions have the following features:

1. It is an extension of credit by the bank to the contracting party.

2. The bank will allocate 10 to 20 percent of the contract amount to your line of credit, or require a cash deposit of 10 to 20 percent of the contract amount.

3. There are no limits on the dates a contract can cover, although anything over about six months is difficult and anything over one year quite difficult for most banks.

4. There are no lower or upper limits on contract size, although each bank will have an administrative minimum.

5. The maximum transaction limit or FX volume limit is a blend of the bank's comfort level and your credit line.

6. Income to the bank is the spread between the buy and sell rates in any transaction. The larger the transaction and the higher your credit standing, the finer the spread between those rates.

Commercial banks active in foreign exchange maintain foreign currency deposits with banks in foreign countries. The cost of those funds on deposit may dictate or contribute to the rates your bank offers. Banks holding these foreign currency accounts can make a market in your desired currency and be more competitive than a bank that does not actively maintain and manage its own foreign currency accounts.

Foreign exchange can play an important role in the success of any international company, and it is a subject that should be discussed with your bank when you review your export terms of sale and the credit quality of your foreign buyers. Advise your bank of your potential need for foreign exchange services; it can be prepared to assist you or direct you elsewhere for the service.

Other Considerations

Eximbank guarantees and insurance (Chapter 11) can provide coverage for transactions done in certain foreign currencies. First, you must get an Eximbank endorsement (approval) for sales in foreign currencies.

Your accountant must be told you are doing business in foreign currencies, as the accounting profession and the IRS have a number of rules that govern how you must report this phase of your business. The Financial Accounting Standards Board (FASB) has developed standards for reporting transactions that involve foreign currencies, and particularly situations that involve assets and liabilities denominated in foreign currencies. For the company that exports with receivables denominated in foreign currencies, the standard is straightforward; FASB 8 requires translation of those receivables at the US$ rate on the balance sheet date. For the company that has foreign currency liabilities (debt, payables, other) or foreign currency denominated investments such as inventory or fixed or other assets, the treatment is set out in FASB 52. Foreign currency translation accounting should be discussed with an international tax professional.

Other areas may be of interest to the reader. **Hedging** is a term often used in foreign exchange and generally means taking a speculative risk in order to offset or cover an equal and opposite speculative risk.

Eurodollar is a term often seen and easily understood. A Eurodollar is a U.S. dollar on deposit outside the United States, generally in Europe. Similarly, an **Asiadollar** is a U.S. dollar on deposit in Asia. A **Eurocurrency** (or Eurocurrency deposit) is a deposit denominated in a currency other than that of the country in which it is on deposit; Eurodeutschmarks are DM on deposit in London, Nassau, Singapore, or any other important international trading center for bank deposits.

Eurodollars and Asiadollars, conveniently known as Eurocurrencies, result from three principal types of event. In the U.S. context, they originate from

1. The transfer of dollars out of the United States. These transfers may be connected with payments for exports or imports or reflect the movement of investment capital.

2. Purchases of dollars in the foreign exchange market for investment abroad (e.g., Japanese buying dollars to buy U.S. government debt).

3. The redeposit function performed by international banks, just as your bank redeposits your deposit with others so as to generate income.

U.S. law now permits U.S. banks to offer foreign currency deposit accounts to their U.S. depositors. If your export sales are denominated in a foreign currency, the availability of this type of account may be valuable. Receipts of a strengthening currency deposited into your foreign currency account allow you to retain the upside potential in that currency. If you import components and have foreign currency payables, this account may enable you to avoid some FX transaction costs. There are strategic and speculative issues involved in the use of this type of account. These issues must be clearly understood by your management.

Foreign exchange services are available to you from your local or regional bank as well as from major U.S. banks and foreign banks operating in the United States. Consolidation of regional banks into *supraregionals* has enabled former small or medium-sized banks to handle the international banking needs of their local clientele. Talk with your bank about your requirements and objectives. If they are not helpful, go to another bank. Learn about the other banks in your area and the services they offer.

RESOURCES

1. Contact the IMF at: International Monetary Fund, Washington, DC 20431. Tel: 202-623-7430.

2. Regional and major banks have international banking service guides which include information on foreign exchange. Many of these banks will provide rudimentary FX training for client personnel.

3. *EUROMONEY* is a leading international financial affairs magazine available by subscription. Leading commercial banks subscribe and will make review copies available to customers.

4. *Basic Handbook of Foreign Exchange* by Claude Tygier (Euromoney Publications, London, EC4, England), published in 1983, is an excellent guide to foreign exchange operations and issues. Written for the guidance of bankers, it is a comprehensive learning tool for the interested corporate executive.

14 Barter and Countertrade

Barter (the exchange of goods for goods) has been the basis of trade throughout history. Countertrade is a series of refinements to this basic process and is widely used in the conduct of international trade. *Countertrade* is an umbrella term that includes all of the variations of the exchange of goods for goods. In its simplest form it means, "If I buy from you, you must buy from me," but with over 75 countries active in the field, it rapidly becomes more complex. Many events of the past 20 years have exacerbated the financial problems of weaker economies and forced an increase in the level of countertrade activity. It is still increasing. Countertrade is becoming an accepted method of carrying out sizeable international trade transactions. Some estimates place countertrade volume in excess of 25 percent of total world trade.[1]

Countertrade activity is not formally monitored as is currency-based trade; national export and import records may not reflect the true value of the goods or services involved in countertrade transactions. In addition, countertrade may comprise a portion of many international transactions, which are often underreported or not reported. Each country has its own practices and procedures. Even without hard statistics, there is no question that this trade increases annually.

REASONS FOR COUNTERTRADE

There are three general reasons for countertrade transactions to take place:

1. Governments of nonmarket economies, which control all international trade within that country, demand that an export occur as a result of, or to balance, an import.

[1]Office of Finance and Countertrade, International Trade Administration, 1991.

197

2. Developing countries lack the foreign exchange to pay for imports and require export sales to maintain production and employment and to foster economic development.

3. Countertrade is used as a form of protectionism, as a method of forcing home-country exports in exchange for the right to sell into that country.

In addition to these basic underlying reasons for countertrade, this business now takes place as a result of private agreement.

Nonmarket economies (NMEs), including the People's Republic of China (PRC), rely extensively on countertrade because their access to foreign capital markets is either restricted or politically unattractive. Countertrade forces exporters to the PRC and other NMEs to become importers of goods.

Other regions of the world have found countertrade a useful mechanism to diversify their economy. For example, an agricultural economy may require the purchase of its agricultural output, which has an otherwise limited market, as a *quid pro quo* for its purchase of industrial goods from a more developed country. The taker of the agricultural commodity then faces the dilemma of market development and sale of that commodity in order to come out whole on the transaction.

TYPES OF COUNTERTRADE

Countertrade is a term used to describe a variety of techniques for the exchange of goods in international trade and can be thought of as a framework for a trade transaction. There are many options, and definitions vary depending on the perspective of the traders. These definitions are industry standards, to the extent that standards exist.

Barter is the exchange of goods for goods, or services for services, without cash payment either way. Barter transactions have the following characteristics:

1. The exchange is set out in a single contract.

2. The goods are specified in quantity and quality without a value assigned in any currency.

3. Payment is solely in the exchange of goods or services.

4. The exchange takes place between two partners.

5. There are no third parties.

6. The exchange usually takes place simultaneously.

Pure barter transactions are a rarity today. A model of a barter transaction is shown in Figure 14.1.

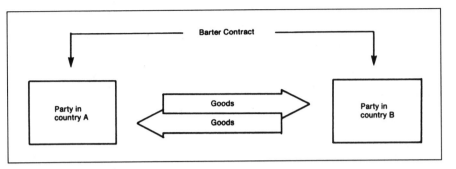

Figure 14.1 Model of a Barter Transaction

A **clearing agreement** is often the basis for barter transactions between governments. Two countries decide on the types and quantities of goods they want to obtain from each other and agree on the ratio of the exchange, the period of the exchange, and the basis for settlement. Clearing agreements are generally made between NMEs to facilitate specific product requirements. (The former Soviet Union traded oil for manufactured goods with its east European satellites under a clearing agreement.) The agreement is the basis for the trading, and settlement of accounts can take place in a number of ways. At the end of the period covered by the agreement, one country will be a creditor and one will be a debtor. The debtor may have the option of making a hard currency payment of the shortfall, or the debtor may issue a credit against the following year's clearing agreement, if there is to be one. Settlement with hard currency payment is doubtful and an unattractive solution given the initial reason for the agreement. Figure 14.2 shows a model of a clearing agreement.

Compensation is a countertrade procedure frequently used to finance and support major projects. In *project finance,* an industrial facility or infrastructure project is developed with domestic and imported resources; payment for the project is from the output of the facility or project. For example, a power station developed in a country that is deficient in hard currency sells power to another country, and the receipts for the power sales provide the funds to pay for the power plant. Compensation is also known as *buyback.*

In most compensation transactions, the tie between units of output and payment is less direct than in this example. Compensation relationships have the following characteristics:

1. Delivery and counterdelivery are covered by one contract.
2. The exchanged products are not dependent on one another.
3. The transactions are priced in money value.

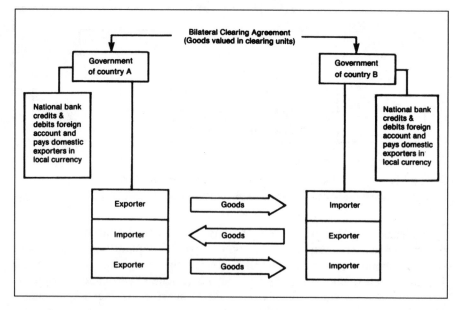

Figure 14.2 Model of a Bilateral Clearing Agreement

4. Delivery and counterdelivery are invoiced.

5. The counterparty's purchase commitment is usually transferrable to a third party.

6. Deliveries do not have to take place simultaneously. (The term could run for up to three years.)

7. Two or more parties can participate, resulting in triangular compensation arrangements.

Figure 14.3 is a model of a direct-compensation transaction involving only two countries.

There are full-compensation transactions and partial-compensation transactions in which the western or developed country exporter is free from a full counterpurchase commitment. In the United States, the International Trade Administration and other writers on the subject refer to a compensation arrangement as one in which the output of the exported facility is used to pay for the purchase of the facility as a *buy-back* or *take-back* arrangement. You, the exporter, should be aware of this inconsistency and ask for clarification in any instance where you are uncertain about the nature of the transactions under discussion.

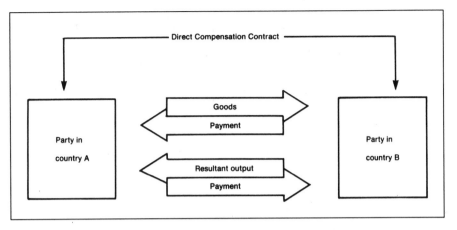

Figure 14.3 Model of a Direct-Compensation Transaction

These arrangements are not to be confused with **offset,** a practice in which the country of the importer of capital goods requires that its manufacturers be permitted to produce parts and components to be included in the capital goods. An example of this is the arrangement that the Boeing Commercial Airplane Company has with manufacturers in Japan, Canada, and Italy. Firms in these countries manufacture parts and components that are sold to Boeing and are installed into the airplanes, which are in turn purchased by the air carriers in those countries. The purchase of the airframes is in part offset by the exporter's purchase of inputs to the product that will be exported.

Counterpurchase links the value of exports to the value of imports of unrelated products. While compensation deals have one contract, counterpurchase transactions have two separate contracts that are technically independent of one another. Counterpurchase transactions have the following characteristics:

1. There are separate stand-alone contracts for delivery and counter-delivery.
2. Invoicing is done in an agreed currency.
3. Payments are independent for each delivery.
4. Goods are not a result of a primary delivery (compare to buy-back above).
5. Delivery and counterdelivery can take place over an extended time span of up to five years.

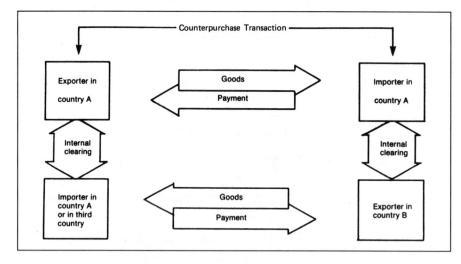

Figure 14.4 Model of a Counterpurchase Transaction

Because of the separate contracts under a counterpurchase arrangement, it is common to have the intervention of a third party. Figure 14.4 is a model of a counterpurchase transaction.

In a parallel counterpurchase transaction, the deal is structured in such a way as to take advantage of state export finance and insurance programs, such as Eximbank (see Chapter 11). Because the deals are like separate commercial transactions, these government-sponsored export finance programs can be used to the benefit of both parties.

A number of emerging or newly industrialized economies (NICs) exercise control over the type and volume of imports allowed. Brazil has been one of the most strident in this practice; Brazil will establish counterpurchase requirements for industry segments it wants to develop. Firms that want to export to Brazil may have their exports restrained by the level of export of Brazilian products of a related or unrelated type.[2]

In a linked counterpurchase arrangement, the sequence of the transactions are reversed. The western exporter first buys as an importer on the condition that the import meets the counterpurchase condition the exporter will be required to meet for future exports. There is a link between the initial import and the ability to export into an otherwise restricted market.

[2]In 1991, the Collor administration loosened many of Brazil's import controls, among other actions. The economy responded well for a brief time, then returned to triple-digit annual inflation rates. Brazil may reimpose a number of import and exchange controls in the 1990s in order to control inflation.

SWITCH TRADERS

Most companies specialize in a product line or product group (as a parent or subsidiary). They export these products. These companies, like yours, are usually *not* in the import business and not in the general merchandising business. These exporters, therefore, can make use of a third party that can create value out of a good received in a countertrade transaction.

Switch trading is a term often heard when discussing countertrade. When counterdeliveries of product occur, you may not be able to dispose of these products in your own market or in the international marketplace. This is not your primary business. At this point, with product representing payment for your export on its way to you, you need to make arrangements to turn those goods into cash. This is the role of a switch trader. The switch trader will find a market for the goods. The market could be in a hard-currency country, a country with restrictions on hard-currency payments, a soft-currency country, or another country where the switch trader may have connections. To carry out this market-finding and -clearing function, the switch trader will demand, and command, a sizeable fee in the form of a discount on the value of the goods being handled. This comes out of your pocket, off the top of the value of the goods you had previously agreed to take as payment in the counterpurchase or compensation transaction.

Because very few companies are professional switch traders, and most companies do not have the expertise or capacity to profitably dispose of the products received in a counterdelivery, it is imperative that the exporter look into the switch-trade costs at the time the initial transaction is being structured. This must be done to factor in the relevant costs. Even the largest U.S. companies have difficulty in this area. For example, a compensation transaction required that a leading U.S. airframe manufacturer take canned hams in partial payment for its aircraft sales to a buyer in a soft-currency country. The exporter incurred a substantial *and unanticipated* cost on the transaction because the value of the hams was less than anticipated, and the exporter was not a marketer of hams.

TERMS OF COUNTERTRADE

A would-be exporter, when first asked to consider a countertrade offering, will find that, as in other business transactions, the terms demanded are often weighed heavily in favor of the foreign importer. This should not deter you; terms are always open to reasonable negotiation. When countertrade is the requested means of business, the buyer is probably in need of your product and there may be a very limited market for his or her product. Therefore, your negotiating position could be much stronger than you initially believe.

Countertrade may conjure visions of dickering back and forth for the type and quantity of goods to be traded for those offered until agreement is reached. This vision does in fact hold true for countertrade, and the negotiation includes standard export contract considerations, such as:

1. Required inspections, by which party, payment of costs.

2. Freight arrangements, costs, control.

3. Insurance, from where to where, coverage, costs.

4. After-sale service and warranty requirements, repairs, and upgrades.

5. Jurisdiction of the agreements and arbitration provisions.

Even more thought and planning must be given to countertrade agreements than to exports handled in a more straightforward manner.

You must take care to substantiate values in the transactions, as you must be able to prove your purchases are not being dumped or sold for less than cost in the home market or on the U.S. or other import market. You must also know if a subsidy has been paid to the foreign exporter by his or her government. If a subsidy has been paid, your import may be subject to a *countervailing duty* to offset that subsidy. You should require a disclaimer in your agreements in which your counterparty confirms that no subsidy was paid to him or her or the foreign exporter.

U.S. Customs is another area of concern for the U.S. exporter. In the past, U.S. Customs has considered the full countertrade transaction for customs purposes when valuing the imported goods. The rationale is that duty on imported goods is based on the transaction value of the goods, which is a result of an arm's-length transaction. In Customs' view, countertrade goods are *not* a result of an arm's-length transaction. The import is tied to the export; therefore, the total transaction constitutes its value and is the basis for duty assessments. You may believe it is not necessary to report an import as part of a countertrade transaction. This is incorrect. Failure to report this side of the deal could result in action by U.S. Customs against the importer for fraud. Be careful.

SUMMARY

There are advantages and disadvantages to both parties to the countertrade transaction. For the NMEs, NICs, LDCs, or emerging states of eastern Europe and the former Soviet Union, countertrade offers the obvious benefits of foreign exchange savings and an improvement in the balance of payments. In addition, developing countries see countertrade as a way of developing their own manufacturing base. Countertrade can result in the more efficient provision for domestic needs and the improvement in quality that enables those countries to become fuller participants in international markets. Countertrade also provides a method of transferring significant marketing and distribution problems to the western or developed-country purchaser. A further advantage to NMEs is that a countertrade operation can easily be integrated into the long-term economic management programs of a managed economy, providing both a source of productive capacity and a captive market for planned production.

For a western or developed country, countertrade offers access to markets deficient in marketable foreign currency, and it opens new sources of supply. This is particularly important in the field of raw materials, where a spread of supplier risk is desirable. Participation in these difficult market procedures may over time provide a good stable and growing source of business for the knowledgeable western exporter. A protected niche can be developed as a result of this forced cooperation; the supply and resupply that occurs will build custom and familiarity. Finally, countertrade dealings will lead to the development of diverse markets or marketing mechanisms (switch traders and the like) for the counterparties' output.

With all the complexities of countertrade, you may reject this type of contract and mode of business entirely, but as countertrade is increasing rapidly, such business should be given serious consideration. Any company that negotiates carefully, covering all points before finalizing a contract, should see an increase in exports. That increase in export volume may add to the firm's bottom line by, among other things, decreasing marginal production costs, increasing production runs, using your work force in the off season, and stabilizing supply costs.

These advantages cannot obscure the fact that countertrade is very unlike the western market system. It is complicated and drawn out. Over time, systems will evolve to better facilitate countertrade and eliminate or reduce some of the burdens the process entails, easing entry into and participation in this growing facet of international trade. The UN has begun the process of standardizing this very significant and poorly measured segment of world trade. The UN Commission on International Trade Law has oversight on this project. U.S. interests are being watched by the Department of State.

RESOURCES

1. The Office of Finance and Countertrade is available to provide advice, guidance, assistance, research, and contracting information. Contact this office at: The U.S. Department of Commerce, 14th & Constitution Ave., NW, Room 406, ITA/TD/TIA/OFITI/Finance and Countertrade Division, Washington, DC 20230. Tel: 202-482-3277.

2. The booklet *Countertrade and You* is available from the Superintendent of Documents, U.S. Government Printing Office, Washington, DC 20402. SN: 603-009-00435-7.

3. *International Countertrade: A Guide for Managers and Executives,* by Pompiliu Verzariu of the U.S. Department of Commerce, published in November 1984, contains an introduction to practices, forms of the trade, regulations, support services, and more.

4. Most U.S. district offices of the US&FCS (Appendix A) maintain an internal guide on countertrade. This continually updated loose-leaf binder contains:

   a. Statements of U.S. government policy.
   b. Legal considerations.
   c. Countertrade Country Profiles for countries with countertrade policies, including a summary of the policy, bilateral clearing agreements (if any), key foreign government organizations, and companies engaged in countertrade in that country (incomplete due to the nature of the business).
   d. U.S. government countertrade contacts, by department, address, and telephone.
   e. A bibliography on countertrade, listing articles, books, essays, and other publications.

5. The American Countertrade Association has as members over 175 U.S. corporations that engage in countertrade activities. Write to: American Countertrade Association, % Monsanto Corp., P.O. Box 31432, St. Louis, MO 63131, Attn: Dan West, Chairman.

PART FOUR
Movement of the Goods

Part Two identified customer service as one of the major thrusts of an effective export market development process. The quality of your service is strongly dependent on your ability to move your product, whether it's a good or a service, to the buyer in a timely and cost-efficient manner.
Movement of the goods includes

1. The process of physical movement, covered in Chapter 15,

2. Protection of the goods from loss or damage in transit and the mitigation of any losses that may occur, covered in Chapter 16.

3. The control of the product from the point of export through the point of import, covered by the documentation process set out in Chapter 17.

Part Four deals with many of the controllable elements in your export activity, those you can negotiate, manage, and direct. Compare these with features in your markets that are uncontrollable: governments, distribution systems, cultures, economics, politics, consumer- or user-buying patterns, and more.

Most of the difficulties encountered in the movement of goods to a foreign market derive from either lack of knowledge and preparation or lack of foresight.

Clear delegation of authority for the logistics functions, export inventory management or control, traffic, packing, marking, and freight management will result in decreased costs and improved operations.

Marine insurance should be included in the risk-management portfolio of your "risk manager," whether it's the CFO or another person. The marine insurance program, which covers all modes of transport, should be well developed and comprehensive. While the insurance fees are relatively low compared to the value of the transactions, failure to adequately cover your shipments for all known or identifiable risks can result in significant unforeseen losses. These losses are unnecessary. You can insure your shipments through the insurance programs offered by your freight forwarder; however, there is some risk in doing so. Your forwarder is not, generally, a trained marine insurance broker or agent; in-depth knowledge of policies, endorsements, and coverage will be lacking. The convenience of a forwarder's program must be weighed against the value of counsel and guidance by a trained and knowledgeable marine insurance broker. Chapter 16 points out most of the issues you must address in your marine insurance program.

Exporters must meet the documentation needs of three disparate groups. Every country has its own requirements for documents. Each country has a number of objectives it seeks to accomplish with its import documentation requirements. Some of these are control of the level of imports, identification of dumping or unfair pricing activity by exporting companies and countries, data capture, and the collection of duties and fees. These requirements demand that the exporter and the importer provide acceptable documentation to some level of government authority at the point of import.

The U.S. government has its own set of documentation requirements which ensure that exporters conform with U.S. laws and regulations. These documentation requirements are relatively straightforward, although some of the documents may be cumbersome to complete, such as certificates of origin under various trade agreements. Export licensing is a separate issue addressed in Chapter 17.

The third player in the document string is your buyer. This company has its own requirements, which are usually met quite easily. Once the *pro forma* invoice or quotation has been accepted, the exporter must provide the documents that have been negotiated into the purchase and sale transaction. These generally include a commercial invoice, bill of lading, packing list, inspection certificate, insurance document, and draft.

Each of the activities identified in this section can, for the most part, be turned over to third parties. For a new or inexperienced company, that may be an excellent way to get started. Overhead is kept low and expertise is acquired on a transaction basis. Functions can be internalized as export volume and costs warrant.

For those companies adding an export function to their ongoing operations, many of the activities discussed in these chapters can be performed within your existing structure and by your current personnel. Export volume will dictate when additional personnel need to be brought into the organization.

15 Logistics

Logistics, the management of your goods from the time components or products enter your company until they are in the hands of the buyer, is one of the keys to success in the export business. Larry Kiser, former director of International Marketing for Burlington Northern Railroad, shares some valuable observations regarding logistics:

> In today's transportation market, *logistics* service provides a total door-to-door package that may include all the functions necessary to move goods through the distribution pipeline from point of manufacture to point of consumption. This package of *value-added services* is composed of the following:
>
> - Transportation management
> - Product distribution
> - Information systems
> - Product labeling
> - Packing, crating, and "special" handling.
>
> *Logistics* is also the management of all inbound and outbound materials, parts, supplies, and finished goods. It involves purchasing, transportation, and storage. Many large corporations now include logistics in the corporate *quality* process. Logistics is the driving force behind service quality.
>
> The best managed companies recognize the role of logistics and use it to integrate all functions of their business to meet customer needs and satisfy those needs to the customer's requirements. This extends the logistics role to include customers as full partners in the overall process. Companies which have overlooked the logistics process have felt it on the bottom line. By involving top management, you extend your involvement with all your customers and enhance your and their bottom line, forming a closer relationship with those customers.

Logistics are activities that encompass the movement of a product from the manufacturer or exporter to the buyer, importer, or end user. The term covers packing, labeling, handling, and transportation. It includes the control of the goods during the movement from the seller to the buyer, up to the point of payment for the goods.

Transportation and transportation management are a major consideration in the export business. The cost of moving the goods from your place of business to the buyer's can be a major cost in relation to the total selling price (see Chapter 8). Savings in transportation, packing, marking, and control can influence your competitiveness. The perils associated with the movement of the goods can be mitigated by insurance and the proper exercise of control in the transportation process.

With any mode of transportation, a *freight forwarder* can be a valuable adjunct to your business. Licensed by the Federal Maritime Commission, a forwarder can provide a wide array of services to an exporter; most will be noted in this book. Forwarders are compensated by a fee for each specific service or by a commission paid by other service vendors such as truck, rail, air, or ocean carriers and insurance companies. Fees are relatively nominal, to the point that only high-volume exporters can justify the cost of in-house freight forwarder expertise.

MODES OF TRANSPORTATION

The exporter can use five methods of transportation to move goods to foreign markets. These five vary in cost, in the elements of control, and in speed. A successful exporter can certainly expect to use at least four of these methods and probably will use all five during the conduct of the export business.

These five methods, also called *modes,* are ship, train, truck, air, and parcel post. Often, a combination of these methods may be used not only to cover the distance involved but to do so in a timely and cost-efficient manner. Each method has its own basis of charging freight and its own documentation; because of these variations, each will be discussed in some detail.

Ocean Freight

Types of Carriers. Generally, ocean carriers operate within one of two categories: conference and nonconference. This is a bit of a misnomer, as one result of the deregulation in the early 1980s was a lessening of the strength of liner conferences, which are referred to as *rate agreements.* These rate agreements have responded with increased flexibility. The Shipping Act of 1984, woven into the fabric of the Shipping Act of 1916, established governing regulation for the operation of conferences. Within these regulations, conferences have the latitude to negotiate rates and service arrangements for shippers.

Agreements are formed to serve particular endpoints in a particular manner. Within each conference, there are a number of shipping lines, each with a particular interest or motivation. To participate in a conference, a line must agree to abide by the rules of that conference. These rules cover vessel performance in the broadest sense, adherence to published schedules, and maintenance of rates to be charged (tariffs) by type of good and type of service.

Nonconference or independent lines (also called *outsiders*) differ from conference or agreement carriers in that, while they do operate on a scheduled basis, they have not agreed to be bound by a set of rates or a particular schedule. The itinerant or tramp steamer of yesteryear is being replaced, due to deregulation generally, by a number of relatively modern, relatively efficient, and sizeable steamship lines. Westwood Shipping, a subsidiary of the Weyerhaeuser Company of Tacoma, Washington, and Evergreen Shipping, Taipei, Taiwan, the world's largest ocean carrier, are two examples of sophisticated nonconference liner services. Small nonconference lines, with less frequent service, may be low-cost providers of transportation services; the trade-off could be less reliable service than that offered by other larger carriers. You may wish to consider these, depending on the goods you sell, the seasonality and stability of the goods, and the arrangements you have with your buyers or representatives.

An *agreement* is a "one-stop" resource for information on shipping services. Each agreement has established rates and services for most products. Shippers can negotiate to amend these rates based on their actual or anticipated export volume and the differences in their products. Rates for commodities are quite firm. For example, resins account for approximately 6 percent of the total U.S. exports to Asia; any new shipper would probably not add appreciably to that total or otherwise justify a review and renegotiation of tariffs.

The TransPacific Westbound Rate Agreement members serve all U.S. ports shipping across the Pacific Ocean. Traffic from the U.S. to Asia is expected to grow at no less than 7.1 percent per year into the mid-1990s. This alone will put upward pressure on rates by conference and nonconference carriers.[1] The same upward pressure will likely occur in the trades to Europe as the Single Market becomes a reality (Chapter 20).

For a schedule of vessels that call at the seaport you will use and that serve your importer's designated port, you need only check with the appropriate steamship schedule. Two of the leading schedules are published weekly. For the West Coast, use the *Pacific Shipper.* For the East and Gulf Coasts, the leading publication is the *Shipping Digest.*

Each principal seaport or port region also has one or more publications that update shipping schedules and provide carrier advertising. They are *The*

[1]Adapted from an interview with Mr. Ron Gotshall, Managing Director, TransPacific Westbound Rate Agreement, January 8, 1991.

Daily Shipping News and *The Journal of Commerce and Commercial*. The *Journal of Commerce* is a national daily with detailed information on shipping lines and schedules. It can best be compared to *The Wall Street Journal* in that its content has a standard format and structure. However, the content is significantly different from the Dow Jones publication. Part A has current world trade news and sections on trade finance, exports and imports, commodities/futures/finance, and insurance. Part B covers maritime, air/rail/truck, energy/coal, and export opportunities. The daily *Shipcards* section lists all inbound and outbound carriers by U.S. and foreign port of origin and destination.

In a regulated environment, shippers (exporters) were encouraged to sign contracts with steamship lines. By doing so, shippers were able to obtain lower rates in return for making a commitment to move all of their freight with one line. As a result of deregulation and the quality of competition from the independent lines, the structure of these contracts has undergone some change. Shippers contract with *rate agreement* carriers to obtain a particular level of service over a set period of time. To obtain a different or preferential level of treatment, the shipper can enter into a contract with the carrier outside of or separate from the conference. Because all the rates (tariffs) for each carrier must be filed with the Federal Maritime Commission, and all deviations from the agreement tariffs must also be filed with the Federal Maritime Commission, knowledge of change travels quickly. Shippers and carriers are able to make these deviations from the rate agreement by differentiation in the goods being handled or services being provided. Nonconference carriers now compete quite effectively with rate agreement carriers.

A third shipping option available (if you ship by container) is the non-vessel operating common carrier (NVOCC). Also called an NVO, it is a third-party company that contracts with a shipping line for a certain number of containers or container "space" over certain named routes for a period of time, generally one year. By acquiring this container capacity in volume, the NVO receives a discount, much the same as you receive when you purchase in volume. This space is then sold to shippers of smaller lots at rates they would generally be unable to obtain from either agreement or independent lines. There are trade-offs in service that each shipper will experience in varying degrees. Generally, using an NVO can result in less frequent service or end-of-the-line service in high-volume seasons, when freight capacity is in high demand. Many freight forwarders operate NVOs as a consolidation service and additional profit center.

Rate Structures. You can obtain rates for your shipments over the telephone by contacting your shipping agent, freight forwarder, or steamship line. This is another place where you will use the Schedule B number mentioned in

Chapters 9, 10, and 11. Rates are based on the products being moved and are published in a tariff. If your product is not listed in the tariff for the route you need, your goods are then rated on a Not Otherwise Specified (NOS), Not Elsewhere Specified (NES), or Freight All Kinds (FAK) basis, unless you and the person doing the rating can agree on a classification your product line does fit. Under a NOS, NES, or FAK tariff, the rates tend to be higher as these product classes are less frequently handled. If you are going to be shipping in a reasonable volume, you should negotiate with the line or agent and establish a tariff for your product. (The definition of "reasonable volume" is also negotiable.) The time spent may well be worthwhile.

When an exporter contacts the agent of the shipping line for a specific rate, more often than not a definite rate will be readily available and quoted for "one ton." The agent should add the comment, "That is one ton weight" or "one ton measure," one of which will apply. The rate may also be quoted with a currency adjustment factor (CAF). This is an automatic adjustment added on to the tariff and is related to the country of destination.

The "one ton" comment can cause some confusion, as a ton differs from place to place around the world and also differs by industry within and around the United States. Some agreements use a 2,000 pound ton, some use 2,204 pounds, and others use 2,240 pounds. If using short-ton (2,000 pound) weight, the carrier will also use cubic feet as a volume measure. A ton may then be thought to consist of 40 cubic feet. A long ton of 2,240 pounds is used less frequently. If a metric ton (2,204) is the weight, a cubic meter will be the basis of measure (approximately 35.3 cubic feet).

Shipping tonnage is measured in registered tons of cubic feet and has no reference to weight. It is only a measure of the size of the vessel.

If you are shipping something bulky but not heavy and therefore cannot get a ton into 40 (or 35.3) cubic feet, your products will be rated by measure, and for every unit of space you will be charged the rate for a ton. Conversely, if your products are very heavy but take up less than the minimum, you will be charged by the weight. The fee basis that generates the greatest revenue for the shipping company is the rate that applies. Be aware that, when obtaining rate quotes, you may be quoted on a *weight* or *measure basis,* and on a *U.S.* or *metric system;* it is up to you to ask which is being quoted. Take care in contracting with an NVO; if your firm ships about 8 or 9 tons (weight) or 12 to 13 tons (measure), you may be near a volume break point and should compare NVO rates and service to that available through negotiation with a conference.

Containers. Containers (boxes in shipping idiom) have become the standard for the ocean shipment of goods, other than bulk commodities (e.g., wheat) and large, irregular-shaped goods (e.g., logs). They account for well over 70 percent of the volume of all goods shipped from and to the United States. Standard sizes are 8 feet wide by 8 feet tall by either 20 or 40 feet in length, with a 45-foot length available on some routes. Two "high cube" containers have also been well received, one 8.5 feet tall by 40 feet long, the other 9.5 feet tall by 45 feet long.

On small shipments under the volume that would fill a 20-foot container, you may find it necessary to move your goods to the warehouse of the carrier or your forwarder for loading into a container. If you do have full container loads, you can readily arrange to have a container delivered to your warehouse for loading. Your carrier or agent can advise you on how much of your product can be loaded, given the size of the packaging and number of packages you have. A standard 40-foot container will hold about 50 cubic meters of goods, depending on how your goods are packaged and how the container is stuffed. There is some skill to stuffing a container; because freight can be a serious cost factor, you will want it done the most cost-efficient way. You may want to use a service (carriers, forwarders, consolidators, or agents) skilled at getting more into less space, thereby reducing your shipping costs. If you do have a container delivered to your warehouse for stuffing, be sure to turn it around (load it and move it) promptly, as there is a charge if you have it "spotted" for more than 48 hours or so. The charge is daily, but can be for parts of a day.

"Roll on-Roll off" (RoRo) is another type of container shipment. In RoRo, an over-the-road or chassis-mounted container is driven into the vessel. This process ties a box to a chassis (a potential increased expense), but it also offers considerable savings because you are not required to handle the goods a number of times for trailer stuffing and destuffing when changing modes of transport.

A "road-railer" box is the latest innovation. Coming into general use in 1992, this is an over-the-road box and chassis with rail wheels attached. The objective is time and, therefore, cost savings by rapid switching from road to rail to road.

Paperwork. As your shipment moves along on its route from factory or warehouse to its final destination in the buyer's country, each party that handles it will give you or your agent a type of receipt, acknowledging that he or she has accepted control at that point and for a specific purpose. For ocean shipments, the checker or foreman issues a receipt that the goods have arrived on the dock for shipment and notes the condition of the goods on the receipt. If your goods are in a container and you make no alternative arrangements, your shipment will remain on the dock, exposed to the elements. A bulk shipment may, by arrangement and if space is available, be put into or under a shed or protective cover. If there are shortages or damage to the goods observed as they are being received, these are noted on the receipt. The receipt is then an "unclean document"; this may cause you trouble later. This *dock receipt* (an example is at the end of Chapter 17) is an official form in the export process and, in some cases, it is the document required in delivery on an export sale. The required dock receipt is usually required to be "clean," which means no apparent shortage or damage to the goods were noted on receipt at the dock. Dock receipts may be *negotiable* or *nonnegotiable*.

From the dock, the shipment is loaded onto the vessel and a *bill of lading* is issued by the shipping agent on behalf of the shipping line. It will be made out word for word according to the instructions the agent receives from the exporter. The bill of lading, often called a "Blading" or "B/L" in shorthand usage, is title to the goods, a receipt for the goods and a contract to move the goods to the named port of destination/discharge. When your goods are loaded on board, the agent stamps the B/L "laden on board," and the document is then called an "on-board bill of lading." Unless you've chartered a vessel for your export transactions, you will generally be expected to provide this document to complete this phase of the export sale. There are several types of bills of lading. Because this can be a vitally important document in exporting, more complete information on bills of lading can be found in Chapter 17, Export Documents.

Wharfage. When you export, you make use of port facilities such as roads, docks, warehouses, and cranes. The cost of maintaining these facilities for the use of exporters and importers can be substantial. In addition, harbor maintenance (dredging and the like) must be done to keep harbors and channels open to ship traffic. These costs are met in part by placing a charge per ton on the goods that move through the port. Wharfage, harbor dues, and loading are the services to which charges often accrue, and *terminals* or *terminal charges* are the terms often used for this type of charge. For container shipments, this charge is usually within the ocean freight rate quoted per container and therefore is not apparent. It is quoted separately for bulk commodity shipments. Your shipping agent can tell you the level of this charge so you can compute it as an added cost. If your agent is unable to do so, telephone the port offices directly and they will provide the information.

Rail (Train)

A significant volume of U.S. exports go by train to both Canada and Mexico, and rail transport is one of the most cost-efficient methods of moving heavy or bulky goods or commodities from inland points to export points. As a result of deregulation of the railroad industry, some significant changes have occurred that benefit shippers. The Interstate Commerce Commission (ICC) focuses on safety and has left the pricing of rail services to the marketplace. Competition from truck lines for the inland cartage of goods has increased. Innovation to reduce costs of rail services has been begun to make rail service a better option for the exporter (see "Road-railer" above).

In addition to the standard and well-known box car, railroads have made some container-based innovations. One example is the double-stack train. On-dock container-rail yards are another innovation shared by carriers and ports.

Two types of freight rates exist for rail service, the CarLoad or Full CarLoad lot (CL or FCL) and Less than Carload (LCL) lot. Rates are calculated per 100 pounds, and LCL rates are higher than CL rates.

Since 1980, railroads can set their own rates and can enter into contracts with shippers. These contracts cover meaningful periods of time and are generally found in commodity businesses such as coal, grains, and bulk liquids. Other shippers generally deal on a spot basis, meaning an arrangement for one shipment at a time without a contract. Rail contracts can be for any time period from six months up to five years.

A shipper with large cargoes may deal directly with the railroad on a Full CarLoad basis, while shippers of smaller lots are best served by their freight forwarder (Chapter 17). When you need to move your goods to the seaport, contact your forwarder. If you have a rail siding at your facility, you can arrange to have a rail car spotted for loading. The railroad will pick up the car within 24 hours of the spot (more time will cause an overtime use charge, called *demurrage*) and deliver it to the seaport for loading on the ship. (Your alternative mode of transport is truck, which you should have priced.) The railroad will charge for all the services it provides: the pickup, the movement to the harbor, the unloading, and the loading (if done). Your forwarder can advise you of these charges.

Competition has been a major factor in pushing rates generally downward. Export volumes have increased substantially in the last five years. Former empty backhauls from import deliveries have been filled. This has improved the round-trip profitability for carriers. As exporting has changed so has the rail movement of goods. Boxcar volume has been converted to trailer capacity (rail-pigs), enabling container traffic to grow. As noted, double-stack trains and on-dock rail loading are recent innovations, available nationwide in major markets. The double-stack system moves more freight at no significant increase in marginal costs, enabling the railroads to be competitive with the over-the-road trucking industry, which has grown rapidly in recent years.

When the rail carrier picks up your goods, you will be issued a *railway bill of lading,* which is a receipt for the goods and a contract for their movement. This bill of lading, like the ocean document, can be either clean or unclean. It is generally not an acceptable title document on an export sale because the consignee on the B/L will be a party in the United States such as the steamship line or the exporter's agent at the port, and conversion into another document of title must occur.

Trucks

The alternative to rail for the inland movement of goods, or for the movement of goods within the region to the port of export, is the trucking company. Canada and Mexico are also served directly by a number of trucking lines. Interstate, intrastate, and independent are the three principal types of truck lines. With deregulation, interstate carriers have a great deal of flexibility in rate setting. Now tariffs filed with the ICC are effective 24 hours after filing, a marked difference from the past. Intrastate carriers, still actively regulated by state regulatory commissions, must file a request for tariff with their commission to change rates. Independent truckers operate on a contract basis and do not file tariffs, so it is often feasible to shop these carriers against the intrastate or interstate carriers for rates and service.

With deregulation, trucking companies are able to vary their charges to the market conditions. You can arrange service with a trucking line directly, with a freight broker, or through your freight forwarder. Trucking lines are listed in your telephone book, as are freight brokers. Charges are generally "per container" from the point of pickup to destination; however, the basis of the charges is the choice of the customer (e.g., cubic feet, cubic yards, cubic meters, or weight). This is an interesting point. The total cost for movement of the goods will not vary; it will be calculated on the maximum load for the route. The *basis* of the charges may be useful to some exporters in computing the burdened unit costs of their exports. A freight broker, if used, is compensated by a commission built into the cost of the move to the shipper.

Truck lines issue a *truck bill of lading,* which is a nonnegotiable document of title stating the point of origin, destination, consignee, and other pertinent information. If you are using a truck line, be sure the goods are clearly marked to tie to the bill of lading (as with any other movement of goods). Goods that are mismarked or not marked are delivered to the carriers "dead parcel" depot. They cannot be sent on because of inadequate marking. A caution when marking your goods: Packages marked with the name of the vendor or the contents (videos, software, hand tools, etc.) are targets for pilferage and loss. Leave these identifiers off your export packing. Shipping marks, weights, and measures are adequate for transportation purposes.

You will get a B/L whether your shipment is a CarLoad (CL) or Less than CarLoad (LCL) size. One of the most efficient methods of making small shipments, subject to the time constraints you may have, is for your goods to be shipped to a consolidator for combination with other LCL shipments bound for the same destination. Freight forwarders either operate consolidators or know of them. In addition, a U.S. customs authorized function called a *container freight station* (CFS) is in business in part for the movement and consolidation of smaller shipments. CFS operators are known by your forwarder or can be located through the telephone book.

Nearly all types of goods can be moved by truck, and rates will generally vary by the type of goods you are shipping. If you ship goods that must receive special handling, like refrigerated products or produce, paper, wood products, or merchandise that will deteriorate with the weather or time, you must take extra care in arranging inland transportation. If, for example, you have products that must be refrigerated, be sure the reefer truck arrives at the port at the same time as the reefer vessel so your goods are not warming up while waiting on the dock. This is your responsibility. The carrier will not do this for you if you do not specifically request the service. Also be sure you are insured for the types of loss or deterioration that could occur because of an extended delay. If your goods do sit on the dock, you can also incur the extra cost of the goods being placed in a cold storage warehouse, which will charge for the space and the in-and-out handling service.

Trucks are an alternative to rail for inland movement of your goods and provide flexibility in timing and routing that may not otherwise be available. The charge for loading and unloading of the trucks is generally part of the rate charged by the carrier and is not set out separately.

Air Freight

Air is a mode of transportation many exporters overlook as it may be perceived as too expensive. This is not necessarily true. Air is particularly useful when shipping spare parts, when time-sensitive additions or modifications must be made, or when the last part of an order must be filled. Many perishables move by air, particularly fresh seafood and flowers. Other considerations may lead to the use of air freight, such as your agreed payment terms, your cash flow, or efficient market access.

Your *time value of money* is an important consideration when monies (your cash flow and, possibly, your line of credit) are tied up in inventory, inland freight, insurance, or packing, and there is the potential of a long accounts receivable period facing you in the best of circumstances. In some situations, it may be more cost effective to make smaller shipments more frequently than to wait until the end of a full production run—in addition to waiting for a ship that calls at the correct destination port. Air shipments generally take only a day or two in transit to nearly any destination. If you use a consolidator to handle your smaller shipments, this could stretch transit time to 5 to 10 days, still a significantly shorter time than most ocean shipments.

Air freight directly through the carrier or through a freight forwarder (consolidator) is quoted on a weight or measure basis, with break points. By kilo (2.2 lbs per kg), freight rate breaks occur at 45, 100, 200, 300, 400, and

500. Goods move in containers. Containers are composed of a standard aluminum pallet and a fiberglass hut fixed to the base, which varies by airframe. The most common size of carrier-owned air freight containers are:

1. LD2 or Type A   124 cu.ft.   2,700 lbs capacity
2. LD3 or Type 8   158 cu.ft.   3,500 lbs capacity
3. LD7 or Type A-2   355 cu.ft.   10,000 lbs capacity
4. LD8 or Type 8   253 cu.ft.   5,400 lbs capacity
5. LD11 or Type 6   253 cu.ft.   7,000 lbs capacity

Shipper-owned containers are:

1. Type E   500 lbs capacity
2. Type EH   250 lbs capacity[2]

In calculating rates, carriers use 10.4 lbs/ft^3. Less weight incurs a volume charge. This weight/volume calculation is derived from the industry standard that 166 cubic inches constitute a pound. You can obtain a container for your loading of CL shipments from your air carrier or its agent or through your freight forwarder. For LCL shipments, you must deliver your goods to the carrier's dock. This also can be arranged by your agent or forwarder.

Tariffs are based on the route of air shipment, the weight or volume of goods, and the type of good being shipped. The Schedule B number commodity classification can be used for this purpose. By using this Schedule B number, a shipper will have a common basis to compare the cost of service of any number of air carriers. There are minimum charges for air cargo, by shipment and by location. Discounts are available for volume and may be negotiated with the carrier or the forwarder. Contracts are generally not written but exist as understandings between frequent shippers and their carriers or consolidators. Handling charges may be assessed; these charges are nominal and cover the cost of handling the air export documents. Hazardous goods or materials require special packaging and handling. Many carriers will not handle hazardous goods. Tariffs for shipping this type of product are quite high.

When shipping by air, you are issued an *air waybill* by the carrier. This air waybill always identifies a destination consignee who can pick up the goods at the destination; air carriers will not hold goods at the airport of import. This means that on air exports, the importer can obtain the goods immediately on arrival, unless the exporter consigns the goods to an agent or other trusted third party. The air waybill is a nonnegotiable document. Exporters have been

[2]Adapted from an interview with Mr. J. Totah, Global Transportation Services, Seattle, WA.

known to name a bank in the importer's country as the consignee of the air waybill, in this way ensuring themselves of control and restricting access for an importer they may not know well. U.S. banks do not provide this service to importers.

In addition to air carriers, you may also deal with air freight forwarders. These companies provide a number of useful services, ranging from the pickup of your goods at your warehouse, through assistance with the documentation, to the packing and shipment of your goods. They charge nominal fees for the documentation services they provide and can assist the exporter of small shipments in obtaining more favorable air freight rates than might otherwise be available.

The International Air Transport Association (IATA) provides standardization of rules and a level of regulation for air carriers throughout the world. This is best exemplified by the workings of an interline agreement. For example, a carrier may not provide direct service from Memphis to Kuala Lumpur and other carriers must be used. An interline agreement provides the standard for the two (or more) carriers involved. In this way, you can obtain a rate for the whole route, while two or more separate carriers carry the goods.

Parcel Post

Parcel post is a viable option for smaller shipments and can be by air or ocean. The service is available at your post office, and services are spelled out in the *International Mail Manual*. There are limits on both size and weight in parcel post shipments. The U.S. limit is 44 pounds, or 108 inches in dimension (greatest length, plus girth). While within these limits, the shipper must also conform to the limits of the receiving country. For example, the Netherlands size limit is 79 inches, combined length plus girth, and a maximum of 42 inches in length.

Packages must be wrapped well and tied thoroughly and must be marked for export. In place of a bill of lading, a parcel post receipt accompanies the package(s). Once clear of customs at destination, the package is delivered to the buyer. As in the air shipment, you have no protection against nonpayment, and no way to halt the delivery of the goods.

Air Express Services

Small package delivery has become a major industry in the United States and internationally. These services use their own aircraft or contract with airlines, and offer fast door-to-door service for a competitive price. You will find them listed in your Yellow Pages directory under "Delivery" or "Express."

INTERMODAL AND MULTIMODAL SHIPMENTS

Innovations in the movement of goods have resulted in new techniques for the interaction of carriers and the control of goods in the process. An export from the United States may use any combination of truck, rail, air, and ocean services in the movement of goods to the buyer's location. While the exchange of modes of transport, or transshipment transactions, used to require the issuance of new transport (therefore, title) documents at each point, changes in the INCOTERMS and the advent of *Electronic Data Interchange* practices now enable the efficient documentation and control over these new shipping practices. Today, an export from your facility in the United States to almost any point can be handled under one combined transport document that encompasses all modes of transport, all transport vendors, and all of the services required by you and your buyer.

These intermodal and multimodal services have improved shipper efficiencies, reduced transit times, reduced total transport costs, and improved control for both parties. Consult your freight forwarder or the marketing personnel at your export port to discuss this type of service for your export requirements.

Caution

In arranging the transport of your products to the buyer, be sure that you take into consideration the facilities at the receiving end. Inadequate or inappropriate facilities can mean your goods will sit in the harbor and collect demurrage, spoil, and incur other added costs. Additional handling unanticipated in the sales quote may make the goods more expensive to the buyer and you may be asked (or forced) to absorb this cost.

TERMS OF TRADE

As part of the process of pricing and quoting on export transactions, you will negotiate a price that covers all of your costs up to a named point or event in the export transaction. This will be tied to one of the modes of transportation we have covered. You bear responsibility for the goods up to the point of title transfer, and the buyer assumes liability and responsibility from that point onward.

INCOTERMS

Originally known as International Rules for the Interpretation of Trade Terms, INCOTERMS are the basic international trade terms for contracts covering the movement of goods and the transfer of title in international trade.[3] The contract terms of sale covered by INCOTERMS are listed below. You and your representative or buyer must agree on the basis of the terms of trade that you will use in order to protect yourselves, understand your obligations to each other, and ensure proper performance under your contracts.

> The purpose of *INCOTERMS* is to provide a set of international rules for the interpretation of the most commonly used trade terms in foreign trade. Thus, the uncertainties of different interpretations of such terms in different countries can be avoided or at least reduced to a considerable degree.[4]

INCOTERMS provides a listing of the obligations of both the seller and the buyer, based on the contracted terms of a sale. INCOTERMS, developed by the members of the International Chamber of Commerce, are accepted by all member countries as the standard for interpretation of international terms of sale.

Group	Term	Meaning
Group E Departure	EXW	Ex works
Group F Main carriage unpaid	FCA FAS FOB	Free carrier Free alongside ship Free on board
Group C Main carriage paid	CFR CIF CPT CIP	Cost and freight Cost, insurance, and freight Carriage paid to Carriage and insurance paid to
Group D Arrival	DAF DES DEQ DDU DDP	Delivered at frontier Delivered ex ship Delivered ex quay Delivered duty unpaid Delivered duty paid

Note that each term provides a gradual progression from the seller's place of business to the buyer's place of business. The terms most frequently used in the export business are:

---

[3]An alternative to INCOTERMS is *The Revised American Foreign Trade Definitions* (1941 revision), terms of trade for international transactions developed and agreed, in 1941, by members of the National Foreign Trade Council, Inc., New York. They are in limited use today.

[4]From *INCOTERMS 1990* by ICC Services S.A.R.L., 38 Cours Albert 1er, 75008 Paris, France. Publication No. 460.

FAS: Free alongside ship. The goods are delivered alongside the vessel on the dock or **lighter** at the named port of shipment. The buyer assumes all costs and risks from that point.

FOB: Free on board. The goods have passed over the ship's rail at the port of shipment. The buyer assumes all costs and risks from that point.

CFR: Cost and freight. The seller pays all costs to deliver the goods to the named port of destination except insurance. The buyer assumes all costs and risks associated with loss or damage to the goods from the time the goods pass the rail at the port of shipment.

CIF: Cost, insurance, and freight. The seller pays all costs to deliver the goods to the named port of destination and has to provide marine insurance against risks of loss or damage to the goods. The buyer takes delivery at the named port of destination.[5]

These terms are an important part of your international business operation. Before you establish your terms of sale with any new buyer, involve your transportation, finance, marketing, legal, and insurance personnel. Each of the 13 INCOTERMS has a specific meaning and exacting rights and obligations for the exporter and the importer. The terms of payment (Chapter 12) are often married to the terms of sale.

Shipping guides, mentioned earlier in this chapter, can give you valuable information and guidance. You should subscribe to at least one and take the time to read it regularly. Your port and your carriers and forwarder can also provide a great deal of information and assistance in the movement of your product to its destination.

PACKING AND MARKING

Several factors must be taken into consideration when choosing the type of packing for export shipments. You want to protect the cargo against as many hazards as possible, but use the lightest weight cartons or packing to give this security. Next, consider the mode of transport. Rail or ocean require heavier packing than a shipment by air, and containerized cargo on ship does not require the same protective packing as cargo going by break bulk. The latter faces the most hazards, including breakage due to storms or heavy weather; damage by heavy or leaking cargo stowed above; being dropped or jolted in loading or unloading; rainwater when unloading, especially in ports that must use lighters (licensed vessels or barges used in unloading and loading ships) to

[5]Adapted from *INCOTERMS 1990*, published by ICC Publishing Corp.

get the goods ashore; and pilferage. Containerized cargo loaded on deck is also subject to many of these hazards due to its exposure.

Even with the safety of shipping by container, you must exercise care so that cartons, packages, bags, or crates are well and solidly packed to prevent movement within the container.

Consider the route that each shipment will take and any extra hazards to which it may be exposed. For ocean shipping, if you are not using containers, the cardboard cartons should have a minimum breaking strength of at least 250 pounds per square inch. To prevent pilferage, which occurs in every port and on many ships, double wire-strap all cartons, and unless they are very large, wire-strap every two cartons together. Never use nonreinforced tape to secure carton tops or bundles.

Plastic sheet wrap is now used in place of wire-strap in many applications. It's quick, less costly, and effective for stabilizing cartons on pallets. New pallet innovations further reduce the cost of packing for export. Pallet management, movement, cost, and storage are meaningful issues for most firms. One such innovation is the Duopad™, a fiberboard sheet with flexible bellows for the blades of a forklift. With standard wrapping of palletized freight, the Duopad™ replaces the bulky wooden pallet, saving both the cost of the pallet and the space consumed by the pallet. Use of these types of innovations can give exporters a pricing edge.[6] Some countries charge customs duty on the gross weight of a shipment, so the weight of the cartons and packing should be kept to a minimum (see above) while protecting the goods to their destination.

Most exports require two markings. One is the *country of origin* or manufacture. Your freight forwarder or the US&FCS can advise you if the importing country has size and language regulations regarding this mark ("Made in USA"). The second type of mark is the *export mark,* which designates all packages as belonging to one shipment. Export marks must be clear and distinct. If the buyer has not stated a mark he or she wants, you must choose one, such as "B.F.K. LONDON." Do not use cartons with your company logo or advertising on them. Letters made with waterproof ink or paint should be at least two inches high. The load plan for the container and the vessel will place your goods in the vessel in correct unloading order. The marks assist the loadmaster and the handlers in locating and moving your goods. The marks facilitate the movement and control of the export shipment at the port of destination and are useful in the event of an insurance claim.

A third type of marking is useful if your products require a particular type of handling. Cargo handling symbols and packaging information can be

---

[6]The Duopad™ is available from Down River Forest Products, Commerce, CA. Tel: 213-720-1655.

obtained from your forwarder, the carrier, or leading marine insurance carriers.

Container Control

Unless you have your own trucks to haul containers to and from the carrier, you will pay an inland freight charge called *drayage*. *Demurrage* is charged if you retain a container longer than the time stated by the agent.

You should use a locked container to prevent pilferage. Both the International Longshore Workers Union (ILWU) on the West Coast and the International Longshoreman's Union (ILU) on the East Coast have a *50 mile rule* that requires union workers to stuff and destuff containers when the cargo is destined for a location within 50 miles of the port of import or export. This is a make-work rule that enjoys uneven enforcement, so each shipper should look to the longshore union practices at the port of choice. The critical issue is the cost of the stuff/destuff process and the risk of pilferage by workers outside your control.

Caution

A few buyers may ask that the bill of lading be made out in their name. This would be a *straight* bill of lading. Because the buyer is named in the straight bill or as consignee on a negotiable B/L, the buyer owns the shipment even if he or she never pays. Either refuse the request or assure yourself of the buyer's creditworthiness before agreement. To protect yourself, always use a negotiable bill of lading and mark the consignee box with the word(s) "shipper," "order," or your company name. You can then endorse the B/L over to the buyer at the appropriate time.

RESOURCES

1. *The Journal of Commerce,* 445 Marshall St., Phillipsburg, NJ 08865-2695. Tel: 908-859-1300.

2. *The Pacific Shipper,* 562 Mission St., Suite 601, San Francisco, CA 94105-2919. Tel: 800-221-8633.

3. *The Shipping Digest,* P.O. Box 1129, Dover, NJ 07801. Tel: 201-366-0946.

4. Two shipping conferences account for over 85 percent of the tonnage of goods exported from the United States:

   a. The TransPacific Westbound Rate Agreement, P.O. Box 7574, San Francisco, CA 94120. Tel: 415-986-8100.

    b. USA North Europe Rate Agreement (USANERA), Meadows Office Complex, 201 Route 17N, Rutherford, NJ 07070. Tel: 201-804-9000.

    Other conferences or agreements exist to service specific trades, such as the Trans Pacific Freight Conference of Japan and the Japan Atlantic and Gulf Freight Conference.[7]

5. To obtain a copy of the *International Mail Manual*, write to: Superintendent of Documents, U.S. Government Printing Office, Washington, DC 20402-0001. The price is $14.00, payable by check, GPO Deposit Account, or VISA, CHOICE, or MasterCard. Your local post office may have a reference copy. It has an order form on the last page.

6. INCOTERMS, the International Rules for the Interpretation of Trade Terms, are published by ICC Services S.A.R.L., 38 Cours Albert 1er, 75008 Paris, copyright ICC 1990. A complete explanation of each term is available in the publication *INCOTERMS*, available from ICC Publishing Corp., 156 Fifth Ave., Suite 280, New York, NY 10010. Tel: 202-206-1150.

7. Cargo handling symbols and packaging information are well presented in the publication *Ports of the World: A Guide to Cargo Loss Control*, available from Insurance Company of North America, a CIGNA Company, P.O. Box 7728, Philadelphia, PA 19101.

[7]Adapted from an interview with Mr. Ron Gotschall, Managing Director, TransPacific Westbound Rate Agreement, January 8, 1991.

16 Marine Insurance

The insurance of maritime perils has been traced to 215 B.C. when the Roman government was required by the suppliers of military stores to accept "all risk of loss arising from the attacks of enemies or from storms to the supplies which they placed in ships." About 50 B.C., Cicero makes mention of guarantees effected to safeguard the public money or treasure from danger of loss in transit. About a century later, the Emperor Claudius provided guarantees to importers with respect to all losses arising from storms. In each of these examples, certain essential elements of marine insurance were present, such as the following:

- Insurable interest.
- Assumption of risk by other than the property owner.
- Payment of a premium as consideration for the indemnities offered.

Forms of marine insurance policies in current use closely follow the material particulars of their prototypes. The oldest known policy still in existence is dated October 23, 1347, and insures the ship *Santa Clara* on a voyage from Genoa to Majorca. This policy provided that deviation from its course shall void the contract.[1]

Each of the shippers and the ship owners share in the marine adventure, the movement of goods from point to point. All cargo owners and the ship owners are party to the adventure and as such share the perils in proportion to the percentage of total value owned by them. Although it is called *marine insurance*, such coverage is extended to all modes of shipping.

You will be unable to enforce the provisions of marine insurance coverage unless you hold an insurable interest in the transaction at the time of the loss. You have such an interest if the cargo is lost, damaged, or destroyed, and

- you then suffer a loss, or
- you fail to make an expected profit.

[1]Adapted from the undated note in *A Brief History of Marine Insurance* from Mr. T. W. Kennard. President, B.A. McKenzie & Co., Inc., Tacoma, WA, credited to Lloyds of London, undated.

Therefore, when the title to the shipment passes from the exporter to the foreign buyer, you, as exporter, no longer have an insurable interest in that shipment, even if the buyer has not paid for it.[2] At that time, the insurance must be endorsed over to the buyer (or his or her appointed agent) so the buyer will acquire your insurable interest in the cargo. The exact time when title passes is determined by the terms of sale, which operate within the framework of the INCOTERMS.

GETTING STARTED

The exporter should learn the basics of marine insurance to ensure understanding of the protections available and the nature of the perils covered. This knowledge will assist you when contracting for insurance and when negotiating sales transactions. You should understand the three basic types of policy, what they insure and leave uninsured, and what must be done in the event of a claim.

First, select a good marine insurance company, agent, or broker. Other exporters, your commercial insurance carrier, your banker, international trade consultant, or attorney can assist with this selection. Do not hesitate to ask the advice of the agent or broker about the type of coverage in every instance before sending a quotation to the buyer. If you ship infrequently or your annual export volume is under US$1,000,000, it may be more cost effective to utilize the insurance offered by your freight forwarder. Forwarders offer marine insurance on single shipments, at rates that provide them with a 40 to 60 percent margin over their cost. As with its NVO arrangements (Chapter 15), the forwarder once again purchases wholesale and retails the product to you.

By using the forwarder's policy, you avoid the up-front annual premium required when you purchase your own policy. Depending on the type of coverage and the commodities being insured, annual premium levels start at about $1,500, at a rate of approximately $0.10 per $100 of insured value depending on commodity and destination. A forwarder will charge the exporter about $0.40 to $0.50 per $100 of insured value, depending on the commodity and destination. If your export volume is in excess of about

---

[2]The following incident was reported in the *Journal of Commerce*. In 1991, an exporter delivered goods to the dock to be loaded for export to a foreign buyer. The terms of the sale were FOB (exporter's dock) and the seller received an on-board bill of lading. A fire engulfed the dock and the vessel left the dock to save itself before the goods were loaded. The buyer had insured the goods from the FOB point (on the vessel). The goods left on the dock perished. The seller's insurance company claims it is not liable as the shipper received the on-board bill of lading, and the buyer's insurance company claims it is not liable as the goods were never loaded. The claim is in dispute by all parties.

US$1,000,000 per year, you can significantly reduce your cost of insurance and increase your control over the coverage you own.[3]

Once you select your insurer, determine if it issues only policies or if certificates are an option. If a company or agency issues only individual policies, you will have to complete an application for insurance for each shipment and deliver it to the company before a policy is prepared and sent to you. This process can take a number of days due to mail and processing time at the agency. Insurance certificates under an open policy are much easier to work with. Get a pad of them from your agent. Each open policy is assigned a number and the certificates are stamped with the number, usually in triplicate. They are negotiable documents and must be used conservatively.

The open policy is a master insurance contract between your firm and the insurance company. Under the open policy, you contract to insure all shipments you are responsible for insuring, and the insurer guarantees to insure all such shipments. Even if, by oversight, you fail to notify the insurance company of a specific shipment, it is still insured.

If you provide the agent with a list of your products by type, the probable destinations to which you will be shipping, and the type of coverage you require, basic rates will be established and shown in the open policy. Without this basic information, the agent will quote rates one by one as you request them before quoting prospective buyers. Administratively, it is more efficient to have a basic rate available for your sales and marketing personnel. If special circumstances warrant, you can obtain a specific quote from your agent. Over time, your low-loss experience will warrant a reduction in your rate; this is a negotiating point at your annual policy review.

When you make an export shipment, write the details of the transaction on the certificate:

1. Destination of the shipment.
2. Description of the goods.
3. Value of the shipment.
4. Amount of insurance.
5. The name of carrier (vessel name or airline).
6. Type of insurance required.
7. Additional hazards to be covered.
8. Date of shipment.
9. Name of consignee.

---

[3]The cost of insurance coverage should never cause a shipment to go uninsured. A US$50,000 export has an insurance cost of US$250 if at the high end of forwarder policy rates, and if under your own policy, the rate could be as low as US$55, or 0.11 percent of the value of the goods.

The type of insurance and perils insured must be a part of your open insurance policy. The first page of the triplicate (or more) set is the *insurance certificate*. The second page is mailed to the insurance agency, and the third copy is for your files. You thus have the insurance certificate in your possession immediately. This is important for two reasons:

1. Letter of credit sales require the certificate as a document for payment. Each letter of credit has an expiration date before which all documents must be presented for payment. Late documents can result in nonpayment.

2. There may be a loss or trouble with the shipment and you or the consignee must act immediately.

Before you complete each certificate, ask for your agent's advice until you learn exactly what coverage is necessary to adequately insure your products to each destination. The agent will be pleased to explain your options and what you may cover under your existing open marine policy.

Under an open policy, you must settle your premium obligations on a regular basis. Frequency of settlement is negotiable between you and the agent. Match the agent's billings to the certificates you have tendered. Your prepaid premiums will be applied until depleted, at which time you are obligated to pay in a timely manner. On an individual policy basis, you will pay the premiums with the application for each unit of coverage.

TYPES OF POLICIES

The three basic types of marine insurance policies are as follows:

- All Risks (AR).
- With Average (WA).
- Free of Particular Average (FPA).

Each of these basic types of coverage insures for the risks of sinking, burning, or stranding of a carrier; beyond this, each coverage is quite different from the others.

Table 16.1 shows the coverage given by (1) All Risk policies, (2) With Average policies, and (3) Free of Particular Average policies.[4] Other than Constructive Total Loss, the perils covered in Figure 16.1 are self-explanatory. "Constructive Total Loss" takes effect if the shipment has been badly dam-

---

[4]A glossary of some of the most referenced marine insurance terms appears at the end of this chapter.

Table 16.1
Comparative Chart of Marine Insurance Policies

Types of Peril	AR	WA	FPA
Total loss of cargo by insured peril	X	X	X
Constructive Total Loss	X	X	X
Stranding of vessel	X	X	X
Sinking of vessel	X	X	X
Burning of vessel	X	X	X
Total loss of whole boxes while loading or discharging	X	X	X
Fire damage	X	X	X
Damage from explosion	X	X	X
General Average contribution and expenses	X	X	X
Damage from collision	X	X	X
Jettison	X	X	o
Sue and labor	X	X	X
Heavy weather	X	X	
Hooks; rainwater	X	*	
Theft, Pilferage, Nondelivery	X	*	
Sweat damage; Leakage	X		
Taint, from other cargo	o		
Heat damage	o		
Breakage	o		
Delay			
Inherent vice			

oThis peril may not be covered.
*A WA policy can be endorsed to include the coverage for (1) Hooks, rainwater and (2) Theft, Pilferage, Nondelivery.

aged and the report of the insurance surveyor states that the cost of repairs would exceed the value of the total shipment. Insurance is then paid as if it were a total-loss claim. Endorsements may be added against nearly any hazard.

Each type of coverage gives you a different degree of control and risk at a different cost. Insurance is a manageable part of the export transaction. The cost of coverage varies by destination and all destinations do not necessarily warrant the same type of coverage. This is another risk management issue to review with your financial, administrative, and international sales personnel.

In the marine insurance business, the phrase *free of* means the insurance company is *not liable* for whatever follows that phrase. In a PA policy, the words *particular average* mean *partial loss*. Therefore, an FPA policy does not pay a partial loss, with some exceptions. Usage and terminology in this field have evolved from hundreds of years of practice and case law; they may be cumbersome and complex, but they work.

Under a WA policy, the insurer is liable for a partial loss. This liability may be limited by a *franchise*, usually 3 percent of the policy amount (this may vary by insurer and policy). This franchise means the insurer is not liable if the partial loss is 3 percent or less. However, if the loss is greater than 3 percent, the insurer is liable for all losses. Therefore, a franchise is not a deductible. The basic premium for a WA policy is slightly higher than for an FPA policy.

The highest premium (used in the earlier examples) is for the All Risk (AR) policy. However, all risks are not covered. Some of the perils that are not covered include the following:

• Delay in delivery.

• Inherent vice.

• War, strikes, riots, seizure, detainment, confiscation, requisition, nationalization, and those perils excluded by the FC&S and SR&CC warranties listed on the policy.[5]

Some of these perils can be covered by endorsement, at a cost. Under an AR policy, breakage may be covered only if the exporter has used sufficient care and proper material in packing.

ENDORSEMENTS

None of the three basic policies covers loss by war or by strike. Policies state that they are *Free of Capture and Seizure* (FC&S) and also *Free of Strikes, Riots, and Civil Commotion* (SR&CC). On all shipments to destinations where "War and Strike" coverage is purchased, you would add those two coverages to the certificate. Those endorsements have a very low premium for most destinations. If you question a routing or destination, contact your agent for clarification. Review your premium notices from insurers. An increase in rates for particular coverage or destinations can provide excellent commercial intelligence as this indicates increased risk in this destination.

The *War clause* covers goods only while they are on ship, and coverage ends 15 days after arrival at the port of destination. If the goods are still on board, you are uncovered and subject to loss.

The *Institute Strikes, Riots, and Civil Commotion clause* is commonly called the *Strike clause*. It covers loss, or damage, or theft by locked-out workers, strikers, rioters, or anyone participating in labor unrest. Malicious damage also is insured. The Strike clause does not pay for damage from the

[5]Ask your marine insurance agent for a detailed explanation of these terms.

perils covered by the standard War clause. The Strike clause insures the goods from the time they leave the seller's warehouse until they arrive at the buyer's warehouse. The exporter is not covered for delay, even if such delay is caused by strikes; delay also is not covered under the War clause. Delay is excluded from all coverages.

The addition of both the War and Strike clauses will protect the shipment against war risks while it is at sea and against risks of strikes while it is at sea and on land, until arrival at the buyer's warehouse.

It is customary to insure exports for 110 percent of the CIF value. This is negotiated into the sales arrangement and will be stated on the letters of credit received by the exporter. At times, an order may require coverage in excess of 110 percent of CIF and shipments can be insured for this excess, within reason. The rationale for the 110 percent of the CIF value is to provide for the extra costs that may be incurred in the settlement of a loss and the cost of being out of funds or goods for the duration of the resolution.

OTHER CLAUSES

Over time you and your staff will become conversant with the three basic types of coverage just listed and with the endorsements particular to your requirements. To ensure your understanding, do not hesitate to meet with your agent or broker to review the coverage and clarify all of the perils for which you are insured.

The Sue and Labor clause and the Total Loss clause will be discussed under "Claims." Some of the other Institute of Marine Underwriters Cargo Clauses and their meanings are as follows:

- *Termination of Adventure clause.* This provides coverage if the voyage is ended or interrupted before the final destination is reached.

- *Change of Voyage clause.* For an extra premium, this continues the coverage if the voyage is altered.

- *Transit clause.* This lists the points of the voyage between which the insurance is in effect, such as warehouse to warehouse (the normal coverage offered by a freight forwarder certificate).

- *Seaworthiness Admitted clause* (American policies only). This guarantees that the insurer will not try to avoid a claim on the grounds that the vessel was not seaworthy.

- *Craft clause.* This insures the goods if the shipment is going to or from the ship in small vessels or lighters. (Your forwarder or steamship agent should advise you of the capabilities of the destination port.)

- *General Average clause.* This gives the steps to be followed to settle a (claim and also salvage charges.

- *Both to Blame clause.* This covers the insured against any claim he or ! may have as to a result of collision, regardless of blame.

- *Not to Inure clause.* This clause prohibits the insured from assigning a right of recovery in the policy to the vessel owners, dock owners, or a other party connected in any way with the adventure. If the insured (assign rights to any such party, the insurance company then could ! bring action against them as they now hold the rights given under ! policy and become the insured parties.

While interpretations of marine insurance coverage are generally standa ized, there are some minor differences between U.S. and British insuran companies.

The open policy states the maximum amount to be insured on one carr Be sure to check this amount if you have large shipments. The maximu usually US$100,000, can be increased if you make a written request well advance of the date of shipment. This extra time gives your insurer (opportunity to spread the risk with other insurers and arrange coverage to s your requirements. Limits in excess of US$10,000,000 are usually read available.

INSURANCE PURCHASED BY THE BUYER

Usually, the exporter is responsible for obtaining the marine insurance. Ho ever, on occasion you may be requested to quote FAS (free alongside ship) the port of export or CFR (cost and freight) to the destination port. In the situations, the buyer is to arrange insurance. To save foreign exchange hard-currency reserves, some countries require that marine insurance be pu chased from indigenous companies. Some buyers may control insurance co panies and prefer to place the coverage, and the premium revenues, with the firms. In any situation where the buyer is claiming to insure the shipme the exporter is cautioned to insure the shipment until title passes to t buyer. Passage of title is a function of the terms of sale, discussed Chapter 15.

Interim insurance can be obtained at very low cost. Then, if the shipme is lost, destroyed, pilfered, or damaged before passing title, you, as export will be fully insured. As an example, on an FAS New Orleans sale, you mu pack the shipment and send it to the port at New Orleans. It is taken to t ocean wharf where the carrying vessel will arrive. As soon as the shipment placed alongside the ship ready to be loaded, the insurable risk belongs to t buyer whether or not he or she has paid you for the goods. Insure the goods for 110 percent of the FAS value to that point to assure that you come out whole. Your insurance agent or broker can give you a rate for this interim insurance and point out other hazards for coverage.

You can receive protection as long as you have an *insurable interest* in the cargo. An insurable interest exists only if you would suffer a loss if the cargo were damaged or destroyed, or if you would fail to make an expected profit. Contingency insurance can be purchased to cover a buyer's failure to insure and your resultant economic exposure. The insurable interest exists only as long as the title is in your name. After title passes, the risk is then a payment risk, not a cargo risk. Have this interim insurance written *payable to order* of your company.

SPECIAL COVERAGE

Some products that move in specific trades require special coverage. The required coverage is well known to those active in such trades; consult your agent or broker for guidance in the selection of the appropriate coverage. For example, special coverage is required for bulk agricultural commodities, fruit, fish, coffee, hazardous chemicals, live animals, and so on.

If you are shipping by container for one shipment, and later ship less than a container load (LCL) to the same destination, that second shipment may face additional hazards. These could include leakage of odors or otherwise from other cargo, sea water damage from heavy weather, or breakage from loose packing or mispacking. Protection can be arranged against nearly any hazard imaginable. However, you do not want to overinsure and decrease your export margins with unnecessary premiums charges.

CLAIMS

When a claim does occur, you as the insured party must act with *reasonable dispatch*. This is defined as how a prudent owner of the shipment would act if no insurance were carried. This means that unless the claim is for a total loss, you would do everything possible to protect your goods from further loss or damage. Keep in mind the foreign buyer will have first knowledge of the loss and initiate the claim. The following steps are to be taken:

1. Do everything to minimize the loss. For example, if canned goods have been subjected to sea water, you must immediately get them to a place where they can be rinsed and dried to prevent rusting. If labels are damaged, the cans must be relabeled.

2. Notify the insurance agent of the loss at the first possible opportunity. Fax your notification rather than wait for voice communication, then follow up with person-to-person voice and written notification.

3. Make a claim against the carrier or any other party that could be fully or partially to blame. Put the claim in writing and send a copy to your agent.

4. Your insurance carrier will appoint a surveyor to find the cause of the loss. Follow his or her instructions exactly.

These are the main steps, but others may be demanded by some surveyors or insurance companies.

Sue and Labor

This is a feature of all types of policies. Under the Sue and Labor clause, the insured is guaranteed repayment of expenses incurred to protect cargo from further loss or damage. However, if the surveyor has told you that the loss is so great that a Constructive Total Loss will be paid to you, no further protective steps are required. Until that notification by the surveyor or your agent, you *must* take all protective steps possible, even if you feel the total cost would exceed the value of your cargo.

Total Loss and Partial Loss

When a claim is for a total loss, you must submit the following information to the insurance company, plus any other documents the surveyor requests:

1. The original insurance policy or certificate, endorsed.

2. A complete set of bills of lading, endorsed. A *complete set* usually is one negotiable copy plus three nonnegotiable copies. Ask your insurance company or the surveyor for the number they require.

3. The original shipper's invoice.

4. A copy of your claim against the carrier, the dock company, stevedore firm or port, or any other party you feel might be liable. Also include a copy of the replies to your claim(s).

5. If possible, a *Master's Protest*, which certifies to anything that may have contributed to the loss, such as heavy weather.

6. Complete details of the shipment.

When approved, a total loss claim is settled by payment in full of the insurance amount.

When the claim is for a partial loss (Particular Average), submit the documents listed for total loss, plus the following:

1. The report of the insurance surveyor confirming the loss and giving details of its extent.
2. A copy of the packing list or notes on weights, if possible.
3. The lading account and notes therein regarding weights. The shipping line should have these.
4. Port of Customs Landing Certificate.
5. A copy of the Customs Consumption Entry.

If the shipment can be repaired for less than the insurer would pay for a total loss, repairs will be made.

Particular Average

A Particular Average claim is handled in a specific manner. The insurance pays a percentage of the coverage, it does not pay the difference between the amount of the insurance and the value of recovery from a sale. An example of the settlement process will be useful. Assume a foreign importer bought 2,000 jute bags of grain, each weighing 100 pounds. The CIF price is US$24.00 per bag, for a total cost of US$48,000. The importer insures for 110 percent, or US$52,800.

The shipment arrives and inspection shows that it has been damaged by hazards covered by the policy. Inspectors insist it can be sold only as animal feed. It is then sold at public auction and nets US$10.00 per bag after all costs of the sale are paid.

The price on the day of arrival of the shipment was US$28 per 100 pounds for this type of grain, if in perfect condition. Thus, the importer has lost US$18 per bag as the sale netted only US$10 per bag. Therefore, he lost 18/28, or 64.3 percent, of the *potential* value. He is therefore entitled to receive from the insurance 64.3 percent of US$52,800. This amount, plus US$20,000 received from the sale, yields a total of US$53,942 or US$1,142 *more* than the face amount of the insurance.

The insurance settlement would differ had the market price for the grain been US$20 per bag (US$40,000) on the date of arrival, and the sale of the damaged grain netted the importer only US$8 per bag. The importer received US$16,000 from the sale. He therefore lost 60 percent of the *market* price on the day of arrival. He is entitled to 60 percent (40 − 16 = 24/40) of the total insurance of US$52,800, which is US$31,680, plus the US$16,000 proceeds from the sale, for a total of US$47,680. If the grain had been undamaged, he could have sold it for only US$40,000 and would have incurred a normal commercial loss of US$8,000; therefore, he lost only US$320. Particu Average compares (1) the net amount lost by the sale of the damaged shipm to the (2) wholesale price of the goods, if they had arrived undamaged, on date of arrival. Note that the insurance deals with the value of the good: the place of arrival, not the purchase price paid.

If a claim arises for loss of a part of the shipment by any insured peril, procedure is much simpler, especially if the goods are similar. For example 20 cartons of a shipment of 100 cartons were destroyed or lost, 20/100 or percent of the insurance is paid. In some trades, it is recognized that a sn percentage of loss occurs due to possible natural shrinkage or other cau while in transit. If your goods are in this class, a deduction is made for t normal trade loss before the final percentage to be paid is calculated.

If the goods lost are not all identical, the valuation becomes more com cated. Invoice values of the lost or destroyed goods are then applicable.

General Average

A General Average claim is entirely different from a Particular Average cla Under General Average, a loss to one or more parties to a marine advent is shared by all parties to the adventure. Today, owners of a vessel carry many shipments and the owners of each lot of cargo also are members of adventure. If part of the cargo is lost so that the property of all others in adventure may be saved, a GA claim arises. If, for example, a vessel g aground and can be floated at high tide only after the cargo in, say, forward hold is jettisoned to make the bow lighter, then all members of adventure (even if uninsured) must contribute to pay for the loss.

The principle of General Average is to spread the value of the los suffered by some among all parties to the adventure. The amount each v have to contribute is based on a percentage calculated by dividing the va of the individual interests by the value of the total adventure.

When a GA claim is filed, a surveyor is appointed as soon as the ve reaches port. The surveyor controls the vessel and goods. The value of e shipment is then calculated from the wholesale price of each type of good, handling, customs duty, and any other taxes. The total price of all cargo calculated, plus the value of the vessel, is called the *contributory value.* each fully insured cargo, the insurance company will immediately tender the surveyor an underwriter's guarantee covering any estimated contributi Note the term *fully insured;* unless the amount of insurance either equals exceeds the contributory value, no guarantee will be made by the insu (another reason for insuring at 110 percent of invoice). As soon as underwriter puts up the guarantee, the cargo is released.

GA claims can take months to settle, and shipments can be held until fi settlement is reached unless the underwriter's guarantee is given. If a shipm is uninsured, it cannot be claimed until settlement date, unless the owners put up cash to cover their estimated contribution or post a General Average bond. In practice, the surveyor will try to assist any uninsured cargo owner.

The claims-in-general insurer will ask that you sign a *subrogation* form at the time the claim is paid, which it needs before taking action against any party that may have been responsible for the loss.

SUMMARY

This chapter reviewed the basic coverage given by the three main types of policies and the major clauses within this coverage. With your agent or broker, you can arrange to insure your shipments correctly. By doing so, you will have better control over your shipments, enjoy cost savings, and see improved operations for your company. Review each insurable transaction with your agent or broker before the insurance policy or certificate is completed. Some destinations have specific hazards not faced at others.

PARTIAL GLOSSARY OF MARINE INSURANCE TERMS [6]

Assured. The purchaser or owner of the policy or certificate; the insured.

Average. Loss less than total.

Particular Average. Loss that affects specific interests only.

General Average. Voluntary expenditure or sacrifice on behalf of the cargo and the vessel for the common good.

Free of Particular Average (FPA) Clause. Provides that, in addition to total losses, partial losses resulting from perils of the sea are recoverable, but only in the event that the carrying vessel has been stranded, sunk, or burnt; but notwithstanding this, insurers will pay losses reasonably attributed to fire, collision, or the vessel's contact with any external substance, ice included, or discharge of cargo at a port of distress.

With Average (WA) Clause. Provides coverage for damage by sea perils, in addition to those covered by FPA clause; for instance, damage by sea water except to on-deck cargo.

All Risk (AR) Clause. An extension of the With Average clause, but excluding, nevertheless, the risks of war, strikes, riots, seizure, detention, and

---

[6]These definitions are general only. They are provided for perspective. Consult your marine insurance broker or underwriter for complete details on any of these or other terms applicable to marine insurance.

other risks excluded by the FC&S warranty and the SR&CC warranty in the policy, excepting to the extent that such risks are specifically covered by endorsement. It covers only physical loss or damage from *external* cause(s). It may also expressly exclude certain types of damage.

Currency of Insurance. The term for which coverage is provided, that is, the time of attachment to the time of termination.

Total Loss. When the goods are destroyed, when the assured are irretrievably deprived of their possessions, or when the goods arrive so damaged as to cease to be a thing of the kind insured.

Constructive Total Loss. When the expense of recovering or repairing the goods would exceed their value.

Perils of the Sea. Fortuitous accidents or casualties of the seas. This does not include ordinary action of the wind and waves.

Subrogation. The right of the underwriter, having settled a loss, to place itself in the position of the assured, to the extent of acquiring all the rights and remedies in respect of the loss that the assured may have possessed.

Jettison. The throwing overboard of part of the cargo to lighten the ship in time of peril.

Sue & Labor Clause. Briefly, it obligates the owner of goods or property to act as though uninsured.

17 Export Documents

Every export sale requires a series of documents to prove, among other things, that:

1. The order has been shipped to the buyer.
2. The quality is at the required standard.
3. The freight has been prepaid if this was one of the terms of sale.
4. The shipment was insured as agreed in the contract of sale.
5. That you are licensed to export.

An understanding of each document, its purpose, how to obtain it, and how to complete it or have it completed is necessary knowledge for you as an exporter. You will encounter at least seven different export documents in your export business. Depending on the buyer and the importing country, there may be more.

These documents must be completed in such a way that the title passes to the buyer at the time stated in the sales agreement. The exporter must also know that the importer will receive all necessary documents so that the shipment can be discharged and clear customs in the buyer's country. Export documents can be prepared by any of a number of persons, including the exporter, a freight forwarder, banker, agent(s), and specialists in the preparation of certain documents. All exporters can complete some documents quite easily. Your freight forwarder can be an important assistant in the completion of other documents with which you may be less familiar. The bank's letter of credit department is the best resource to guide you in complying with a letter of credit transaction. Depending on the products you export, their destination, and their ultimate use, you may need to deal extensively with the U.S. Department of Commerce's Bureau of Export Administration (BXA) for export licensing, with the U.S. Department of Agriculture if agricultural products are exported, and with the Department of State if weapons or goods with a military use are to be exported.

SHIPPER'S EXPORT DECLARATION

The Shipper's Export Declaration, also called an ExDec, SED, or Form 7527-V, must accompany each export shipment when

1. A validated export license is required (see Chapter 18).
2. The FOB value of any commodity being exported is over $2,500.
3. The value of the goods being exported by parcel post is US$500 or more.[1]
4. The shipment is to Canada and a validated license is required.

If, for example, your export was to the United Kingdom, for under US$2,500, and a validated license was not required, you would not have to provide an ExDec.

ExDec forms are available from commercial stationers, larger office supply stores, freight forwarders, local or regional offices of U.S. Customs, or from the Government Printing Office. Instructions on completion of the form are available from the Bureau of the Census.

The original ExDec goes to U.S. Customs at the time of your shipment and is usually sent by your forwarder. There are several terms on the ExDec that you need to understand. Refer to Figure 17.1.

1. Item 1b. The *Exporter EIN number* is an identifier assigned to you if you have been issued a *validated export license*. If you have not been assigned an EIN number by the Bureau of Export Administration, use your Federal Tax ID number.

2. Item 16. *D/F*. Place a *D* or *F* in this column to indicate whether your product is from a Domestic or Foreign source. If this is a re-export, you may be able to recover previously paid duties under U.S. Customs Drawback procedures.

3. Item 17. The *Schedule B number* is the Harmonized System product identifier used by the Bureau of the Census to track all export activity. This number, also called the HS or HTS number, has the same meaning as a product identifier to most countries of the world. This allows standardization (harmonization) of custom's duties and facilitates reference and negotiations such as GATT. Your local US&FCS office, your freight forwarder, or the major library in your area will have a copy of the Schedule B directory for your reference.

4. Item 19. *Shipping weights* are reported in kilograms.

5. Item 21. State the *Validated Export License* number or *General License* symbol in this box (see Chapter 18).

[1]U.S. Postal Service, *International Mail Manual*, Issue 9.

U.S. DEPARTMENT OF COMMERCE — BUREAU OF THE CENSUS — INTERNATIONAL TRADE ADMINISTRATION

FORM **7525-V** (1-1-88)

SHIPPER'S EXPORT DECLARATION

OMB No. 0607-0018

1a. EXPORTER (Name and address including ZIP code)				
Brown and Company 123 Samantha Road Toledo, OH	ZIP CODE 43264	2. DATE OF EXPORTATION 1-10-88	3. BILL OF LADING/AIR WAYBILL NO. 00—1234—5678	
b. EXPORTER'S EIN (IRS) NO. 12—345678901	c. PARTIES TO TRANSACTION ☐ Related ☒ Non-related			

4a. ULTIMATE CONSIGNEE
Kirk Sales, LTD
162 Belva Street
London, England

b. INTERMEDIATE CONSIGNEE
Tim Service Company
3456 Fred Lane
London, England

5. FORWARDING AGENT Sharyn Exports P.O. Box XYZ New York, NY 10047	6. POINT (STATE) OF ORIGIN OR FTZ NO. OH	7. COUNTRY OF ULTIMATE DESTINATION England
8. LOADING PIER (Vessel only)	9. MODE OF TRANSPORT (Specify) Air	
10. EXPORTING CARRIER Fairway Air	11. PORT OF EXPORT Kennedy Airport	
12. PORT OF UNLOADING (Vessel and air only) Gatwick, England	13. CONTAINERIZED (Vessel only) ☐ Yes ☐ No	

14. SCHEDULE B DESCRIPTION OF COMMODITIES.
15. MARKS. NOS.. AND KINDS OF PACKAGES *(Use columns 17 – 19)*

D/F (16)	SCHEDULE B NUMBER (17)	CHECK DIGIT	QUANTITY – SCHEDULE B UNIT(S) (18)	SHIPPING WEIGHT (Kilos) (19)	VALUE (U.S. dollars, omit cents) (Selling price or cost if not sold) (20)
2 Boxes (B/1 and B/2) of Model 525 Signal Generators					
D	8543.20.0000	3	2	6 Kg	2,375
1 Box (B/3) of Parts for Model 525 Signal Generator (probes, tees. defectors, and defector mounts)					
D	8543.90.9500	4	X	31 Kg	1,854

21. VALIDATED LICENSE NO./GENERAL LICENSE SYMBOL A 123456	22. ECCN (When required) 1529

23. Duly authorized officer or employee

H. Brown

The exporter authorizes the forwarder named above to act as forwarding agent for export control and customs purposes.

24. I certify that all statements made and all information contained herein are true and correct and that I have read and understand the instructions for preparation of this document, set forth in the "Correct Way to Fill Out the Shipper's Export Declaration." I understand that civil and criminal penalties, including forfeiture and sale, may be imposed for making false or fraudulent statements herein, failing to provide the requested information or for violation of U.S. laws on exportation (13 U.S.C. Sec. 305; 22 U.S.C. Sec. 401; 18 U.S.C. Sec. 1001; 50 U.S.C. App. 2410).

Signature *K. Sharyn*

Title President

Date 1-10-88

Confidential - For use solely for official purposes authorized by the Secretary of Commerce (13 U.S.C. 301 (g)).

Export shipments are subject to inspection by U.S. Customs Service and/or Office of Export Enforcement.

25. AUTHENTICATION (When required)

This form may be printed by private parties provided it conforms to the official form. For sale by the Superintendent of Documents, Government Printing Office, Washington, D.C. 20402, and local Customs District Directors. The "Correct Way to Fill Out the Shipper's Export Declaration" is available from the Bureau of the Census, Washington, D.C. 20233.

Figure 17.1 Sample Shipper's Export Declaration

6. Item 22. The *ECCN* is the Export Control Classification Number that identifies your product for export control purposes. Refer to Chapter 18.

In addition to the Shipper's Export Declaration and the Export License, there are a number of other documents the exporter must understand and be prepared to deal with in completing an export transaction. The other principal documents are as follows:

- Commercial Invoice.
- Packing List.
- Draft.
- Bill of Lading.
- Insurance Certificate.
- Beneficiaries Certificate.
- Consular Invoice.
- Dock Receipt.
- Shipper's Letter of Instruction.

There may be other, more specialized, documents depending on the nature of your export. If exporting food or agricultural products, a certificate from the U.S. Department of Agriculture or other agricultural product inspection office may be required. If dealing with petroleum products or other nonagricultural bulk commodities, a third-party inspection certificate may be required.

If you export to Canada, Mexico, or Israel, there are trade agreements that offer preferential duties for exports of U.S. origin. To benefit, you have to provide one or both of a Certificate of Origin and a (country-specified) Customs Invoice. See Chapter 22 for a sample of an Exporter's Certificate of Origin under the U.S./Canada Free Trade Agreement.

COMMERCIAL INVOICE

The commercial invoice is very similar to the exporter's ordinary commercial invoice in that it contains basic information such as the following:

- Name and address of the buyer.
- Quantity of each item.
- Description of the goods.
- Unit price.

- Extended price.

- Deductions.

- Total or net amount invoiced.

It also contains additional information unique to international trade:

- The marks, which identify the shipment, destination, buyer identification, and other information. Mark the parcel once, or twice if particularly large. Mark each package with sequential/set numbers (e.g., 1/5, 2/5, etc.) if there are multiple packages (or boxes) in each shipment.

- The weights and special notations concerning weight.

- The name of the carrying vessel, if possible.

- The consignee, which may be the buyer, the shipper, the shipper's bank, the buyer's bank as agent for the shipper, the buyer's customs broker, or another party.

- The order number or sales contract identification.

- The seller's invoice or order number.

- The total amount invoiced, accompanied by an indication of the terms of sale, for example, FOB Factory, Detroit; FOB Vessel, New York; CFR Manila, the Philippines.

- A notation that the product(s) has been licensed for export to a specific destination, that deviation is contrary to U.S. law.

The commercial invoice contains a wealth of information and includes much of the information required by other documents you may have to prepare. A *pro forma* invoice is used in response to a request for a quote or in a submission of an offer to sell. With the *pro forma* invoice, the buyer should know all details relevant to the export. The commercial invoice evidences the transaction. A *pro forma* with explanatory notes is shown in Chapter 10.

PACKING LIST

The packing list, a document very similar to the commercial invoice, sets out how the goods were packed. It contains information on the following:

- The number of packages in the shipment.

- How they are numbered.

- The weight of each.

- The net weight of each.

- Dimensions, by package and gross.

- The quantity of goods contained in each package.

Other information on the packing list is the same as that contained in the commercial invoice.

DRAFT

A draft is a demand for payment drawn by the seller (drawer) on the buyer (drawee) for the amount of the transaction. It is normally presented to the buyer through the seller's bank, which handles the document as an international collection or as a drawing under a letter of credit. The draft or *bill of exchange* is:

1. A means of collecting the money owed on the sale.

2. A method of offering credit terms and receiving acknowledgment.

The draft may be a *sight draft,* which means the buyer is obliged to render payment when demand for payment is made, or a *time draft,* which stipulates that the buyer is to pay at a future date that is set out on the face of the draft. There are unlimited options for the fixing of the date, such as 90 days sight or 60 days from a specific date. The active exporter may find that some buyers prefer that a draft not be used because their country levies a tax on the amount of the draft and not on the transaction itself. See Chapter 11 for a discussion of sight and time drafts.

BILL OF LADING

The bill of lading serves an important role in that it is usually the final receipt or acknowledgment of property or merchandise delivered into the custody of a common carrier (see Chapter 15). It is a contract between the carrier and the shipper for specific transportation services between two or more points. It is a binding and legal contract to anyone who acquires a legal interest or right to the merchandise while the merchandise is in the custody of the carrier. An Air Waybill cannot effectively be consigned to the shipper due to the short time between pick up and delivery of the goods. An ocean bill of lading can be consigned to the order of the shipper, thereby controlling the shipper's interest in the merchandise. Endorsed in blank, the bills of lading can be released to the buyer after the buyer has either paid for the shipment or accepted the draft for payment at a future date. In this way, the exporter either receives payment or a binding claim on the buyer for payment. Figure 17.2 is an example of an ocean bill of lading.

INSURANCE CERTIFICATE OR POLICY

The marine insurance certificate or policy of marine insurance is covered in Chapter 16. Evidence of insurance is an important part of the documentation package as both the buyer and the seller want to be assured that the value of the merchandise can be recovered in the event of a loss. Figure 17.3 is an example of a certificate of marine insurance issued under a special cargo policy in favor of the freight forwarder for the account of the exporter. This policy insures an export of hand tools from Seattle to Auckland.

BENEFICIARY'S CERTIFICATE

The Beneficiary's Certificate is a document increasingly used in international trade. It is used because buyers want assurance that the goods being shipped do in fact meet the specifications previously agreed between the buyer and seller. This certification process further obligates the exporter to perform exactly as agreed with the importer. The content of the certificate varies and will generally certify compliance. For example, a Beneficiary's Certificate might state: "The merchandise shipped hereunder conforms to the specifications set out in your purchase order number 23487." Often the wording of the certification is applied to additional copies of the Commercial Invoice, which is then labeled the "Beneficiary's Certificate." If the exporter and importer do not have the basis of trust to accept the Beneficiary's or Seller's Certificate, the buyer may require an Inspection Certificate.

An **Inspection Certificate** is provided by an unrelated third party which warrants that the goods, or a sample of the goods, meet the quality called for in the transaction.

CONSULAR INVOICE

The consular invoice can cause time delays and other difficulties for the exporter. This document is required by countries that want to control the outflow of foreign exchange, control the level of imports, or generate income to the consulate and the country from the fees generated. The document is a full description of the shipment, usually in the language of the country of

PACIFIC AUSTRALIA DIRECT LINE
OPERATED BY REDERIAKTIEBOLAGET TRANSATLANTIC
and PAD SHIPPING AUSTRALIA Pty. Ltd.—A JOINT SERVICE
BILL OF LADING

SHIPPER (Principal or Seller licensee and full address)	BOOKING NUMBER	B/L NUMBER
	EXPORT REFERENCES	
CONSIGNEE (Name and Full Address/Non-negotiable Unless Consigned to Order) (Unless provided otherwise, a consignment "To Order" means To Order of Shipper.)	FORWARDING AGENT (References, F.M.C. No.)	
	POINT AND COUNTRY OF ORIGIN OF GOODS	
NOTIFY PARTY/INTERMEDIATE CONSIGNEE (Name and Full Address)	ALSO NOTIFY (Name and Full Address) /DOMESTIC ROUTING/ EXPORT INSTRUCTIONS/PIER—TERMINAL/ONWARD ROUTING FROM POINT OF DESTINATION	

INITIAL CARRIAGE (MODE)*	PLACE OF RECEIPT*	
EXPORT CARRIER (Vessel, voyage, & flag)	PORT OF LOADING	
PORT OF DISCHARGE	PLACE OF DELIVERY*	

PARTICULARS FURNISHED BY SHIPPER

MKS & NOS /CONTAINER NOS	NO. OF PKGS	DESCRIPTION OF PACKAGES AND GOODS	GROSS WEIGHT	MEASUREMENT

DECLARATION OF VALUE IN ACCORDANCE WITH PARAGRAPH 6 OVERSIDE

B L TO BE RELEASED AT	OCEAN FREIGHT PAYABLE AT				
FREIGHT RATES CHARGES, WEIGHTS AND OR MEASUREMENTS (SUBJECT TO CORRECTION)	PREPAID U.S. $	COLLECT U.S.$	LOCAL CURRENCY		The Undersigned Carrier hereby acknowledges receipt of the sealed container or packages or other shipping units said to contain the Goods described above in apparent external good order and condition unless otherwise stated. The Shipper agrees and the Consignee and every person purchasing this instrument for value if negotiable or otherwise having an interest in the Goods is advised that the receipt custody carriage and delivery of the Goods are subject to all the terms and conditions set forth and incorporated by reference on this side and the reverse hereof whether written stamped or printed

A set of   originals of this bill of lading is hereby issued by the Carrier. Upon surrender to the Carrier of any one negotiable bill of lading properly endorsed all others shall stand void.

PACIFIC AUSTRALIA DIRECT LINE

BY
Authorized Rep. of Carrier or Master

		TOTAL PREPAID		DATE AND
VESSEL	VOYAGE	OFFICE	**TOTAL COLLECT**	PLACE ISSUED

*APPLICABLE ONLY WHEN USED AS MULTIMODAL BILL OF LADING.

The PAD Highway

Figure 17.2 An Ocean Bill of Lading

destination. The form is available from the consulate of the country in question or from better commercial stationers. It may be acceptable to use a duplicate original of your commercial invoice for this purpose. The time delay occurs because the consulate may be in another city, consuls normally have very short work days, and the mail is the mail. Your freight forwarder can assist you with this document.

DOCK RECEIPT

The dock receipt (Figure 17.4) is used to transfer the control of the merchandise from the domestic to the international carrier, at the ocean terminal or when the goods have been placed in short-term storage pending shipment. The dock receipt is prepared by the shipper, the forwarder, or the warehousing company. The ocean carrier or its designated agent signs and returns the receipt to the inland carrier, thereby acknowledging receipt of the goods. The format of the dock receipt is similar to a bill of lading, a commercial invoice, a packing list, and other documents. This standardization of format has been an important step forward in international trade documentation. The dock receipt is not negotiable.

A **warehouse receipt** is similar to a dock receipt in that it is a receipt for the goods. Like a bill of lading, it is a document of title. Goods are held in a warehouse, bonded or otherwise, and the receipt is evidence of title. If issued in negotiable form, it can be transferred like a bill of lading or a draft. The warehouse receipt instrument is actively used for trade in agricultural products, bulk commodities, seafood, and other products that can be readily identified, are fungible (interchangeable), and have a readily determinable value.

SHIPPER'S LETTER OF INSTRUCTION (SLI)

The shipper's letter of instruction (Figure 17.5) is one final and very useful form. The document is a structured message from the exporter to its forwarder, and it is also a cover page to the ExDec. Your forwarder will supply one at no charge, or you could use your own form or letterhead. The information requirements are the same for air or ocean shipments. Once you have determined (or obtained) the correct export license and have prepared the commercial invoice, you can complete this letter of instruction and deliver it to the forwarder for completion of the transaction.

Many exporters will provide the forwarder with all of the documents required to complete the export transaction. The forwarder will then ensure

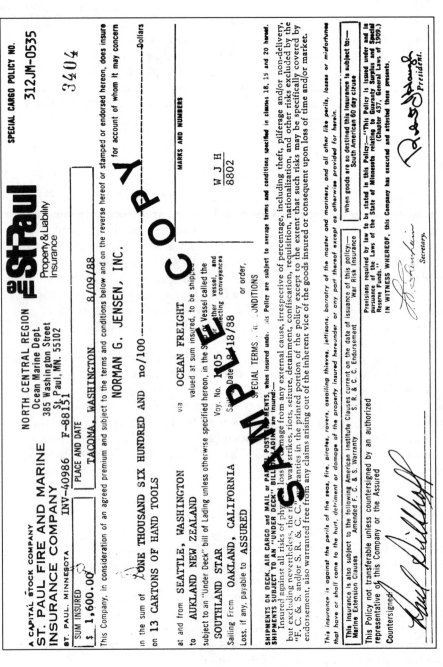

Figure 17.3 Sample Certificate of Insurance

250

Figure 17.3 Continued

DOCK RECEIPT

2. EXPORTER *(Principal or seller-licensee and address including ZIP Code)*		5. DOCUMENT NUMBER	5a. B/L OR AWB NUMBER
		6. EXPORT REFERENCES	
	ZIP CODE		
3. CONSIGNED TO		7. FORWARDING AGENT *(Name and address — references)*	
		8. POINT (STATE) OF ORIGIN OR FTZ NUMBER	
4. NOTIFY PARTY/INTERMEDIATE CONSIGNEE *(Name and address)*		9. DOMESTIC ROUTING/EXPORT INSTRUCTIONS	

12. PRE-CARRIAGE BY	13. PLACE OF RECEIPT BY PRE-CARRIER		
14. EXPORTING CARRIER	15. PORT OF LOADING/EXPORT	10. LOADING PIER/TERMINAL	
16. FOREIGN PORT OF UNLOADING *Vessel and air only)*	17. PLACE OF DELIVERY BY ON-CARRIER	11. TYPE OF MOVE	11.a CONTAINERIZED *(Vessel only)* ☐ Yes ☐ No

MARKS AND NUMBERS (18)	NUMBER OF PACKAGES (19)	DESCRIPTION OF COMMODITIES *in Schedule B detail* (20)	GROSS WEIGHT *(Pounds)* (21)	MEASUREMENT (22)

DELIVERED BY:

RECEIVED THE ABOVE DESCRIBED GOODS OR PACKAGES SUBJECT TO ALL THE TERMS OF THE UNDERSIGNED'S REGULAR FORM OF DOCK RECEIPT AND BILL OF LADING WHICH SHALL CONSTITUTE THE CONTRACT UNDER WHICH THE GOODS ARE RECEIVED. COPIES OF WHICH ARE AVAILABLE FROM THE CARRIER ON REQUEST AND MAY BE INSPECTED AT ANY OF ITS OFFICES.

LIGHTER
TRUCK

ARRIVED— DATE   TIME

UNLOADED—DATE   TIME   FOR THE MASTER

CHECKED BY

PLACED IN SHIP/ON DOCK LOCATION

BY

RECEIVING CLERK

DATE

'02
WHSE NO 0850

ONLY CLEAN DOCK RECEIPT ACCEPTED.

Figure 17.4 Sample Dock Receipt

SHIPPER'S LETTER OF INSTRUCTIONS

SHIPPER: COMPLETE ALL UNSHADED AREAS

AIR BILL NO.   92730735

1a. EXPORTER

ZIP CODE

b. EXPORTER EIN NO.

c. PARTIES TO TRANSACTION
☐ Related   ☐ Non-related

4a. ULTIMATE CONSIGNEE

TELEPHONE NO.

b. INTERMEDIATE CONSIGNEE

5. FORWARDING AGENT
BURLINGTON AIR EXPRESS, INC.

BURLINGTON AIR EXPRESS
P.O. BOX 19571
18200 VON KARMAN AVENUE
IRVINE, CALIFORNIA 92715-1027

6. POINT (STATE) OF ORIGIN OR FTZ NO.

7. COUNTRY OF ULTIMATE DESTINATION

8. LOADING PIER *(Vessel only)*

9. MODE OF TRANSPORT *(Specify)*

INTERNATIONAL SERVICE REQUESTED
☐ STANDARD AIR FREIGHT   ☐ IATA SERVICE
☐ EXPRESS   ☐ NON DUTIABLE   ☐ OCEAN SERVICES
☐ DUTIABLE

10. EXPORTING CARRIER

11. PORT OF EXPORT

12. PORT OF UNLOADING *(Vessel and air only)*

13. CONTAINERIZED *(Vessel only)*
☐ Yes   ☐ No

TERMS OF PAYMENT
☐ PREPAID   ☐ COLLECT   ☐ THIRD PARTY

INDICATE THIRD PARTY
ADDRESS IN SPECIAL
INSTRUCTION SECTION
BELOW - U.S. ONLY

Insurance requested
☐ Yes, if yes, amount $_____   No ☐

DECLARED VALUE
FOR CARRIAGE $_____

COD
AMOUNT $_____

14. SCHEDULE B DESCRIPTION OF COMMODITIES,   *(Use columns 17-19)*
15. MARKS, NOS., AND KINDS OF PACKAGES

VALUE (U.S. dollars,
omit cents)
*(Selling price or cost if
not sold)*
(20)

D/F (16)	SCHEDULE B NUMBER (17)	CHECK DIGIT	QUANTITY – SCHEDULE B UNIT(S) (18)	SHIPPING WEIGHT *(Kilos)* (19)	SHIPPER'S REF. NO.

CONSIGNEE'S P.O. NO.

Documents attached
☐ Commercial Invoice
☐ Packing List
☐ Certificate of Origin
☐ Banking (Sight Draft)
☐ Export License
☐ Letter of Credit
☐ Restricted Articles Statement

To be prepared
☐ Proforma Invoice
☐ Consular Invoice
☐ Certificate of Origin
☐ Banking (Sight Draft)
☐ Insurance Certificate
☐ Restricted Cargo Labels (only)

21. VALIDATED LICENSE NO./GENERAL LICENSE SYMBOL

22. ECCN *(When required)*

Received via

Pro No.

Received by

Date   Time

**PLEASE BE SURE TO LIFT UP THE TOP
COVER SHEET AND SIGN THE FIRST
BUFF COLORED EXPORT DECLARA-
TION IN PEN AND INK IN BOX 23.**

Condition (state exception)

Received at
☐ Shipper's door
☐ City Terminal
☐ Airport Terminal

SPECIAL INSTRUCTIONS:

NOTE: The Shipper or his Authorized Agent hereby authorizes Burlington Air Express Inc. in his name and on his behalf, to prepare any export documents, to sign and accept any documents relating to said shipment and forward this shipment in accordance with the conditions of carriage and the tariffs of the Forwarding Agent and carriers employed. The shipper guarantees payment of all collect charges in the event the consignee refuses payment. Hereunder the sole responsibility of the Company is to use reasonable care in the selection of carriers, forwarders, agents and others to whom, it may entrust the shipment.

Figure 17.5 Shipper's Letter of Instruction

that all of the necessary documents are on hand and do as instructed. A caution: Do not rely on the freight forwarder to do anything beyond what you specifically request in the SLI. If, for example, your container of potatoes must be refrigerated at all times, state on the SLI that the forwarder is to arrange for the refrigeration while the goods are in storage, on the dock, and in the ship.

Some exporters will elect to use all of the services of the forwarder, saving their own time and the cost of trained staff. The letter of instruction will tell the forwarder to prepare certain documents in completion of the transaction, based on the export license and the commercial invoice. If you prepare a forwarder-supplied SLI, do not pay for the preparation of an ExDec; the second page of the SLI is the Shipper's Export Declaration. Figure 17.5 presents a particularly useful SLI. Note the section where the exporter tells the forwarder which documents are attached and which the exporter wants the forwarder to prepare.

STANDARDIZATION OF DOCUMENTS

Under the auspices of the United Nations, simplification of many documents used in international trade is being achieved. The UN is coordinating the work of many private organizations in many countries to do this. Each participating country has set up a private organization to work closely with agencies of their own government to achieve this purpose. The U.S. organization is the National Council on International Trade Documentation (NCITD), organized in 1967. Membership in NCITD is open to private businesses and to government departments interested in foreign trade. NCITD is privately financed, and its objective is to simplify and improve trade documents and procedures, including information exchange by paper and electronic methods. The process is called electronic data interchange or EDI. Significant progress has been made; major corporations across the United States have taken up the EDI banner as it decreases costs and improves efficiencies on intranational and international transactions. Their use of EDI is forcing their suppliers and vendors to use it.

The first step performed by NCITD was the alignment of as many export documents as possible. Forms were designed so that when the commercial invoice was generated, other forms such as the bill of lading, packing list, dock receipt, and consular invoice would be a part of the same specially designed pad and would be prepared at the same time. These were named "aligned documents," and the document preparation time was cut considerably. As an additional benefit, the possibility of errors was greatly reduced. Your export department should look into EDI and its application to your international and domestic activities. Your traffic and logistics personnel should also look into the use of aligned documents to reduce costs and improve efficiency.

SUMMARY

Export documents appear complicated, but you will soon learn exactly which documents are required for each shipment and where to obtain each document in the most cost-efficient manner. Your freight forwarder and publications such as the *Exporter Encyclopedia* and the *Export Shipping Manual* can answer your questions about which documents are required (or may be required) for each particular situation.

International trade is a business constricted by documents. This chapter identified the principal documents you will be required to use in your export business. These documents can be prepared by your existing traffic, transportation, or distribution staff, or the work can be given to your freight forwarder. Familiarity with the documents and practices will enhance your control over an important step in the export process.

RESOURCES

1. *Correct Way to Fill Out the Shipper's Export Declaration*, Bureau of the Census, Washington, DC 20233.

2. U.S. law regarding sight and time drafts, otherwise called *Bills of Exchange,* are defined under the Negotiable Instruments Law, Section 126.

3. There are a number of third-party inspection agents available to the exporter, although they may be unknown to the importer who required the tests. One internationally known inspection service is Societé Generale Superintendents (SGS). This Swiss-headquartered international organization provides financial guarantees in support of its findings. SGS has offices throughout the world. There are a number of testing services in major cities across the United States; they are listed in the telephone book. Your industry association will also have the names of reputable inspection services for your industry.

4. National Council on International Trade Documentation, Suite 1200, 350 Broadway, New York, NY 10013. Tel: 212-925-1400.

5. U.S./Canada Free Trade Agreement Rules of Origin are available from the Office of Canada, International Trade Administration, Washington, DC. The address is in the "Resources" section of Chapter 22.

PART FIVE
Government Regulations

The U.S. government is an active participant in the export process from two distinct perspectives. These perspectives are not necessarily in opposition, although their objectives can often conflict. In addition, many of the government regulations affecting exports are to some extent politically driven.

Many members of the corporate private sector, professional and academic economists, consultants, and commentators have advocated the creation of a U.S. industrial policy. This policy would, theoretically, be a framework that could, to some extent, depoliticize the export business of U.S. firms who acted within the constraints of such a policy. Also, the existence of the policy would foster additional government support and attention on the market-entry or access problems many exporters claim they face.

This is a challenging question: What is the appropriate role for government in the health and success of the private sector in an increasingly competitive global economy? This issue will receive more attention as leading U.S. manufacturers claim they are unable to compete because of "unfair" competition and "lack of government support." Successful exporters should note these are often spurious claims, made by inept or incompetent managers. Successful exporters understand that other countries are different from the United States, and these exporters have managed to learn how to compete on the terms of their target markets.

Current government influence on export activity takes two forms. Chapter 18 reviews U.S. government export licensing requirements imposed on exporters. As a government policy, every export must be licensed. In practice, products, services, or intellectual goods the government believes could be used to the detriment of U.S. interests require a license or permit before they can be shipped to a foreign buyer. These requirements are set out in the Export Administration Regulations, which are promulgated and enforced by the Bureau of Export Administration at the U.S. Department of Commerce.

These regulations are subject to change by administrative edict, brought about by an alteration in the political objectives of the current administration. They also can be changed as a result of international agreement, through one or more of the multinational bodies in which the United States is a participant.

In Chapter 19, U.S. participation in the General Agreements on Tariffs and Trade (GATT) and the multilateral trade negotiating process is reviewed in the context of the barriers faced by exporters. These barriers are, with some exceptions, imposed by the importing country. GATT is the current multinational body that facilitates negotiations for the reduction and elimination of these barriers.

The United States is an active participant in GATT; however, its participation is tempered by a nominal exercise of its own self-interest. This is best evidenced by the United States' position within GATT regarding agricultural subsidies; a reasonable person might observe that the U.S. position on this issue is based on the administration and farm lobby's presumption that U.S. agricultural subsidies are acceptable while the agricultural subsidies of all other nations are unacceptable. The farm lobbies of other nations have equally strong attitudes about their right to get subsidies.

Government and other commentators have stated[1] that the Uruguay Round of GATT (in its sixth year in 1992) must succeed or the existing international trade regime will collapse. This is wrong in the author's opinion. Failure to complete the agenda of the Uruguay Round will leave the trade community with unresolved issues regarding trade in intellectual property, financial and other services, and agricultural products. Progress has been made on these and other issues. Progress is being made, outside of GATT, often bilaterally. Trade will continue. Existing tariff and nontariff structures will continue. They are not likely to increase, because retaliation by an affected nation (other than the United States) is swift and focused.

A new Multilateral Trade Organization (MTO) has been included in the last negotiating stages of the Uruguay Round. This MTO would replace GATT and enjoy some institutionalized powers for settlement of trade disputes among nations (lacking in the GATT). This MTO would change the rules of the road for the United States and other members. It is suggested that the MTO would be to the long-run benefit of U.S. interests. It would incorporate rules for services and intellectual property, and separate structures would exist within the MTO for these areas, placing them on a par with the manufactured goods sector.[2]

---

[1]These statements and commentary have regularly appeared in the general press, the business press, and other media from 1990 through the publication of the book.

[2]Claude Barfield, " 'New World Order' for Trade," *The Journal of Commerce*, February 6, 1992.

Strategies are recommended for the management of the export license process. The success of GATT (and the projected success of the MTO) has created a fluid and understandable trading environment that benefits every exporter. As Joel Junker of Graham & Dunn suggests on page 272, multinational trade regimes such as GATT can be of significant benefit to U.S. companies.

18 Licensing Your Exports

It's important to remember that the U.S. government treats exporting as a privilege rather than a right. The government requires that all exports be licensed. Export controls were formalized after World War II with the passage of the 1949 Export Control Act. This act has been amended and updated three times, most recently with the Export Amendments Act of 1985. In December 1990, the *Enhanced Proliferation Control Initiative* led to clarification and simplification of the export control process. This chapter identifies the rationale for export controls, explains how an exporter can work within the constraints of the Export Administration Regulations (EAR), and suggests a system for the management of export licensing activity. As Leann David-Valentine of Airborne Express explains, export controls are not insurmountable hurdles.

Exporters do not need to be overwhelmed when working with U.S. export regulations. Dealing with export licenses is only one factor within the planning necessary to make an international shipment successful.

1. Use the resources available. When faced with a disagreement over a regulation or interpretation of export controls, a face-to-face meeting with the government official may be in order. Although I have never gotten a government official to admit he or she was wrong, I have resolved many issues in my favor by meeting with the official and discussing the situation face to face. These contacts will also prove helpful if you are ever faced with an export violation or audit of your export records.

2. Don't assume. The Departments of Commerce and State (as well as other agencies) have their reasons for what products they control and why. Exporters cannot *assume* that their products do not require a license because they think their product could not be of interest or use in a defense situation, or be controlled because of foreign policy issues. Falling back on an assumption is not a good defense when you are involved with an export violation. Don't assume; educate yourself and export with confidence!

3. Be prepared. Do not wait until your product is on the shipping dock, scheduled for a 3:00 P.M. pick up, to check on export licensing requirements; you may be disappointed, face a delay, and face an angry customer. As soon as you begin negotiations, you can begin checking on the export licensing requirements to that customer and country. In addition, you can start checking how your product is controlled while it is still on the drawing board. Some manufacturers have incorporated design changes into their products in order to have their product decontrolled (released from the responsibility of obtaining a validated license) by State and Commerce.

4. Make the export controls part of your standard operating procedure for international business. Communicate the requirements with everyone involved in the export transaction, including your customer. Your customers will be much more understanding if you give them a clear strategy and timeframe for obtaining the proper licensing rather than a vague promise to "ship soon."

If you have a distribution network, you can plan ahead concerning what type of export licensing you will require. Planning for export licensing control should be a part of approaching every foreign sale.

In addition, having documented procedures in place will ensure an efficient handling of export licensing and controls. Every employee should know his or her responsibility and the procedures for working through government regulations. Put in the effort to train your people and document procedures. This will result in a smooth component of your whole export operation.

Export controls and licensing are as much a part of international shipping as understanding international finance terms and choosing an international carrier. It is just one more facet of shipping internationally that requires you to be prepared, educated, and committed.

EXPORT CONTROLS

Export controls are in place for four reasons. Each of these stated reasons is subject to interpretation by the President of the United States and the Bureau of Export Administration (BXA). This means that published policies and practices are subject to change for reasons other than those stated below. Exporters should exercise care in the license process, as the export of unauthorized shipments or the export to unauthorized end users (or end-user sale to unauthorized parties) can make the exporter liable for the loss of export privileges and possible prosecution for violation of Export Administration Regulations.

National Security Controls

These controls affect

1. East-West trade only.

2. Listed items that are controlled multilaterally by the Coordinating Committee for Multilateral Export Controls (COCOM).[1]

3. Items on the "Core List" of controlled military strategic goods and technologies in effect September 1991. These include electronics, advanced materials, materials processing, telecommunications, sensor/lasers, navigation, avionics and aircraft technology, marine technology, computers, and propulsion systems.

Foreign Policy Controls

As the name suggests, these controls are one method of implementing the foreign policy objectives of the United States. Our nation's foreign policy objectives change from time to time, often to the peril of exporters.[2] These controls deal with

1. Chemical and biological weapons.

2. Missile technology.

3. Regional stability.

4. South Africa.

5. Human rights.

6. Antiterrorism.

7. Countries under embargo by the United States.

Nuclear Nonproliferation Controls

These are subject to somewhat broad interpretation:

1. Controls are generally worldwide.

2. Controls are generally unilateral by the United States.

---

[1]COCOM is the organization that cooperates in restricting strategic exports to controlled countries. Members are: Australia, Belgium, Canada, Denmark, France, Germany, Greece, Italy, Japan, Luxembourg, the Netherlands, Norway, Portugal, Spain, Turkey, the United Kingdom, and the United States of America.

[2]For example, Ingersoll-Rand was prohibited from exporting a custom-made industrial assembly line to the Soviet Union, as a result of the Soviet activity in Afghanistan and a change in foreign policy objectives of the Reagan administration. The company was unable to remarket millions of dollars of machinery. Adapted from *Political Risk Letter,* Vol. 24, No. 8, August 1987, published by Shelby Publishing Corporation, Boston, MA.

3. Controls include items that may be destined for, or have the potential to be destined for, sensitive nuclear end users.

Short-Supply Controls

Controls exist to protect the United States's scarce or limited resources.

1. The controls are worldwide.
2. The controls include petroleum and its products, and Western Red Cedar, among others.

Exercise of Controls

While export control responsibilities are principally with the Office of Export Administration within the Department of Commerce, the Department of the Interior looks after endangered species, the Nuclear Regulatory Commission controls the export of nuclear-related items, the Department of State deals with military items through the Office of Munitions Control, and the Department of Agriculture has some additional jurisdiction.

THE EXPORT LICENSE PROCESS

The BXA manages the U.S. export license process. In 1991, the BXA Export Administration Regulations were modified to reflect the changing world environment. These regulations operate through a Commerce Control List (CCL), a list of all U.S. goods and services subject to export controls, other than items controlled by other departments or agencies of the U.S. government that are listed in Section 770.10 of the Export Administration Regulations. Export license applications that fail to use the current nomenclature will be rejected without action.

The Commerce Control List (CCL) [3]

The list of goods and services subject to export control is divided by four parameters: categories, subcategories, the nature of control, and the level of control. You must understand how the CCL is structured in order to determine if any controls apply to your item. An example demonstrates the new CCL system.

Let's say your company manufactures diesel engines for large pleasure boats. Your product would be listed in the Export Administration Regulations

---

[3]New nomenclature.

under a product category. Each product subject to control has a five-character Export Control Classification Number (ECCN).

1. Start in Section 799.1 of the Regulations; select the appropriate **category** (see below).

2. Next, go to the subcategory list. Select one and review the descriptions for the category and subcategory you have selected. If the products listed are not your products, change your selection (ECCN 9A02A is for marine turbine engines, not diesel).

3. Review the product descriptions under classification 9A; you will find that ECCN 9A94F covers Other Marine Engines, both inboard and outboard, among other items.

4. The 94 identifies the nature of the controls. This is a Foreign Policy control.

5. The F prohibits sales to SZ countries without a validated license. The SZ countries are Iran, Syria, and the South African military and police.

Therefore, you know that your product, ECCN 9A94F, has the following meaning within the CCL (see asterisks):

Category:

1. Materials

2. Material processing

3. Electronics

4. Computers

5. Telecommunications and information security

6. Sensors & lasers

7. Navigation and avionics

8. Marine technology

*9. Propulsion and transportation equipment

0. Miscellaneous

Subcategory:

*A. Equipment, assemblies, and components

B. Equipment to test or manufacture equipment

C. Materials to make the equipment

D. Software

E. Technology

Nature of the Controls:

01-19   COCOM Controlled

    18   International Munitions List

    19   International Atomic Energy List

20-39   Missile Technology

40-59   Nuclear Referral List

60-79   Chemical/Biological List

*80-99   Other

More than one reason for control may apply.

Level of Control

A. COCOM (all countries but Canada)

B. Non-COCOM (all countries but Canada)

C. Same as B with excepted countries

D. All countries including Canada

E. SZ and supplemental countries

*F. SZ plus specified countries

G. SZ and South Africa Military and Police

H. Z and South Africa Military and Police

I. No controls to any destination

This process identifies whether a validated export license is required, the reporting unit (for your Export Declaration), whether a general license is available, and whether other forms of license are required. Each ECCN specifies countries to which exports are prohibited. Countries are listed by *Country Group.* The groups are labeled Q, S, T, V, W, Y, Z. Members of a group may change from time to time, depending on the politics of the moment.

If you are uncertain about the correct classification of your product for export, do not hesitate to contact the Office of Technology and Policy Analysis for a commodity classification. It is staffed to assist you with this process. Include your recommended classification, your rationale for the classification, technical specifications in terms of control parameters, the anticipated end use and end user, and the country of destination.

TYPES OF EXPORT LICENSES

There are two types of export license issued by the U.S. government: the *general license* and the *validated license.* These are the only licenses you require to export. No other government organization, at any level, except as noted above, is empowered to license exports.

The general license is an authority to ship not evidenced by a document. Your license is evidenced by the correct completion of the Shipper's Export Declaration and appropriate record keeping.

The validated license is issued by the Office of Export Licensing. You must make written application, in a standard form and format, and receive approval *before* shipment takes place. Failure to do so will result in penalties that may include fines and imprisonment.

Before you export to any purchaser, be sure that buyer or his or her end user has not been denied access to U.S. goods and services. The Export Administration Regulations contains a *Table of Denial Orders* (TDO); companies on this list are not allowed to export from the United States. If a foreign firm or individual is named, U.S. exporters are not permitted to export to that entity.[4] The TDO is Supplement 1 to Part 788 of the EAR.

Types of General License

General licenses are defined and identified in Section 771.1 of the Export Administration Regulations. Use of a general license on the Shipper's Export Declaration "shall constitute a certification by the exporter that the terms, provisions, and conditions of the general license have been met."[5] There are 22 general license types. Use the Commerce Control List to select an ECCN. The ECCN will state which type of license is required, general or validated. For a complete explanation of the scope, definition, and prohibitions regarding each general license, refer to Part 771, General Licenses, of the Export Administration Regulations. These general license categories are:

1. G-DEST: Shipments of commodities to destination not requiring a validated license.

2. GIT: In-transit shipments.

3. GLV: Shipments of limited value.

4. Baggage: Includes personal and household effects, vehicles, and tools of trade.

5. Ship Stores: Dunnage and stow, fuel to operate the vessel, supplies.

6. Plane Stores: Dunnage and stow, fuel to operate the plane, supplies.

---

[4]The Office of Export Licensing recommends subscription to the *Federal Register* because exporters are obligated to comply with regulations in the *Federal Register* the same day it is published.

[5]*Export Administration Regulations,* U.S. Department of Commerce, April 1991, Part 771, page 1.

7. Crew: Personnel and household effects of a member of the crew of an exporting carrier.

8. RCS: Shipments to U.S. or Canadian vessels, planes, and airline installations or agents.

9. GUS: Shipments to personnel and agencies of the U.S. government.

10. GCG: Shipments to agencies of cooperating governments.

11. GTF-US: Goods imported for display at U.S. exhibitions or trade fairs.

12. G-NNR: Shipments of certain non-Naval reserve petroleum commodities.

13. GLR: Return or replacement of certain commodities.

14. GIFT: Shipments of gift parcels.

15. GATS: Aircraft on temporary sojourn.

16. GTDA: Technical data, see Section 779.3 of the EAR.

17. GTDR: Technical data, see Section 779.4 of the EAR.

18. G-TEMP: Temporary exports.

19. GFW: Low-level exports to certain countries.

20. G-COCOM: Certain shipments to cooperating countries.

21. GCT: Eligible trade.

22. Safeguards: International safeguards.

Each general license is very specific in its requirements. The license you use is dependent on the correct selection of an ECCN. Be sure to carefully identify your product and its components.

Validated Export License

A Validated Export License is often referred to as an Individual Validated Export License or IVL. Frequent exporters of goods or services requiring a Validated License may want to apply for a *Distribution License* that authorizes a number of export shipments to one or more destinations within a fixed time period. Contact your closest US&FCS office to pursue this issue.

Product Determination. If your product is very new, it may not be on the CCL, and you will need to get a determination from the BXA. If you cannot identify your specific product, this is another reason for a determination. I urge you to get a determination on your product if there is any question at all.

You apply for a Validated Export License with an Application for Export License. You get the form from the US&FCS office, which can consult with you on the completion of the form. For the more experienced and established exporter, the distribution license, mentioned above, may be appropriate. This license places a high degree of control in the hands of the exporter. It is available only after application and exporter interview with the Multiple License Control Officer.

You will find this export licensing process somewhat cumbersome and costly in terms of man-hours and record keeping. However, when you ship the same commodity classes to the same destinations, the process becomes routine over time. An IVL is now valid for up to two years, doing away with many amendment situations and increasing the flexibility of the U.S. exporter. In addition, much of the documentation in support of the application and license may be retained by the exporter, further simplifying the process.

Depending on the nature of your products, the countries to which you ship, and the sophistication of your export staff, the export license process can be a breeze or a nightmare. Don't hesitate to call on the available experts in the licensing process. A good starting place for referrals is the local office of the US&FCS. Introductory and advanced courses on the Export Administration Regulations and the licensing process are conducted in larger cities across the United States on a regular basis.

Tracing Your License Application

There are two ways to trace an export license application. You may telephone the Office of Export Licensing and request a report on the status of your application. Service and turnaround time have generally improved over the past three years; however, the increased volume of exports has made the automated application process much more important for tracing purposes. The computerized tracking system, STELA, can give you the status of your application(s). On a touch-tone telephone, dial 202-482-2752, then respond as requested. This system can give you a range of information regarding your application.

ELAIN is the Export License Application and Information Network. Exporters can electronically submit license applications for sales to most destinations. Your closest US&FCS office or the Office of Export Licensing (202-482-8536) can guide you in this process.

EXPORT LICENSE MANAGEMENT SYSTEM

The Bureau of Export Administration has been increasing its emphasis on the control of commodities that can be used to produce missiles and chemical and biological weapons. More responsibility is in the exporter's hands. It is important that exporters manage their export licensing activities in a way that meets the current, and the changing, requirements of the BXA.

The following *Export Management System Outline* is recommended by the BXA to assist companies that export under both general and validated licenses. It can protect exporters from errors and oversights and complement other management systems such as those for inventory control and customer financing.

Outline for an Export License Management System[6]

Administrative Elements

1. A clear statement of corporate policy regarding compliance with U.S. laws and regulations.

2. A clear identification of individuals and positions that have export control compliance authority and clarification of that authority both up and down the chain of command.

3. A program for clear and concise record keeping.

4. A continuing education program to assure export control personnel are informed and current on the regulations.

5. A system of internal review and audit to assure compliance.

6. A failsafe system to notify BXA if noncompliance is discovered.

Screening Elements

1. A screening procedure to assure compliance. This may include procedures on ECCN classifications, controls that apply to the firm's products generally, flagged countries, and so on.

2. A Table of Denial Orders update and screening process.

3. A screen for potential diversion of products.

4. A screening process particular to your products and their use in nuclear, nuclear-capable missile, chemical, or biological weapons, or goods destined for South Africa.

5. An order-processing system that captures relevant information at the front of the order-fulfillment process.

RESOURCES

1. The *OEL Insider* is published by the Office of Export Licensing. To subscribe, write to: Director, Office of Export Licensing, Bureau of

---

[6]Adapted from "An Export Management System Outline," *OEL Insider*, U.S. Department of Commerce, Vol. III, No. 3, Oct./Nov. 1991.

Export Administration, U.S. Department of Commerce, P.O. Box 273, Washington, DC 20044. A fax request should be sent to 202-375-3322.

2. To obtain a commodity classification, write or fax (202-482-5708) your *Request for Commodity Classification* to the Office of Technology and Policy Analysis, Technical Support Staff, Bureau of Export Administration, P.O. Box 273, Washington, D.C. 20044.

3. To subscribe to the Export Administration Regulations, order EAR 90 from the Superintendent of Documents, P.O. Box 371954, Pittsburgh, PA 15250-7954. The annual cost at this writing is US$87. This price includes all updates and changes to the regulations that occur during the term of your subscription. You may purchase by Visa or MasterCard. Facsimile credit card orders are accepted on 202-512-2233.

4. Each regional, district, or field office of the US&FCS has a current copy of the Export Administration Regulations. Government depository libraries, major public libraries, libraries at leading colleges and universities, and every freight forwarder will have a copy for your reference. Freight forwarders can often assist you in selecting the correct ECCN. *Caution:* You are responsible for the choice of ECCN and the subsequent license; your forwarder will not accept responsibility for an incorrect ECCN and license.

5. Report suspected export diversions to Export Enforcement Field Offices or 202-482-8208.

6. Airborne Express is a leading international air freight forwarder and shipping service, with offices across the United States and in major cities around the world. Ms. David-Valentine may be reached at Airborne Express corporate headquarters in Seattle. Tel: 206-298-3153; fax 206-282-2104.

19 Barriers to Export

It is important to learn the structure of tariff and nontariff barriers that affect the marketability of your products in your target country. Until this information is obtained, it is not possible to know whether your products can compete with exports from other nations or with similar or comparable goods made in the target country. Duty classifications and rates of duty must be ascertained. Quotas and other nontariff barriers must be identified. With this information, the exporter can alter pricing or export marketing strategies to optimize the opportunities of each market.

One supranational organization, the General Agreements on Tariffs and Trade (GATT), exists to deal specifically with the tariff and nontariff barrier issues. International trade attorney Joel Junker offers some background on GATT:

> The principal mission of the GATT after its formation following World War II was the reduction of the high tariffs that were impeding the free flow of goods in international trade. To its credit, the GATT through numerous rounds of multilateral negotiations has reduced tariff levels significantly. Further, the GATT codes on valuation and the Harmonized System for tariff classification developed under the Brussels Convention on Nomenclature for the Classification of Goods in Customs Tariffs have resulted in uniform rules for applying tariffs to goods. These rules give more certainty to international sales and shipments of goods.
>
> Successful reduction of tariffs, however, has led to new impediments to international trade in the form of nontariff barriers (NTBs). NTBs may have caused even greater obstacles to international trade than did tariffs. NTBs can take many forms and are limited only by human imagination. Examples include burdensome import licensing requirements, special testing in limited laboratories, extensive labeling requirements, and the like. NTBs are difficult to attack for several reasons. They often are thinly justified under the guise of legitimate protections such as national security, health, safety and welfare of consumers. Often NTBs will take the form of "unwritten rules" as well as formal regulations, e.g. unauthorized "grease" payments to officials. NTBs also may apply across the board to all imports or be very product- or industry-specific. Inevitably their net effect is discrimination against imported goods.
>
> The Uruguay Round of multilateral trade negotiations under the GATT is fashioning rules for raising and resolving NTB disputes. In addition, regional and bilateral trade agreements are creating mechanisms for disputing or negotiating

NTB problems. Because of the product- or industry-specific nature of many NTBs, government to government and industry to industry negotiations most certainly will remain an avenue for addressing market access problems.

NTBs will continue to be another element of the extensive "homework" necessary in international trade transactions. In the future, however, an international trader may have not only the option of learning to live with an NTB, but also the possibility of challenging the NTB through industry or government negotiations, or international agreement procedures.

TARIFFS

Tariffs or duties are charges assessed by the country of import on the value of the goods entering the country. Every country establishes its own rates of duty, subject to the multilateral, bilateral, or other agreements it has entered. On January 1, 1993, countries of the European Community will have a common external tariff and no internal tariffs (see Chapter 20). Under their Free Trade Agreement, the United States and Canada will have eliminated all tariffs between them by January 1, 1999 (see Chapter 22). There are other, smaller, trade blocs or associations that have made such arrangements. You must know what these tariff arrangements are and how they apply to your products. Some of these blocs or associations may be to your benefit.

Structure of Tariffs

A *multiple-column tariff* employs two or more schedules of duties for any article. The United States operates under a multiple-column tariff with three columns; therefore, goods are subject to three levels of tariff based on the source country.

Penalty tariffs apply to goods imported in violation of customs' laws or regulations of the importing country. The United States imposes penalty tariffs.

Antidumping duties are assessed if the cost of the imported product is determined to be below the cost of that product in the exporting country. The United States imposes antidumping duties.

Retaliatory duties are levied in retaliation for a real or perceived discrimination against the importing country's products by the exporter's country. The United States exercises retaliatory duties.

Preferential duties are used to promote or maintain close ties with a country. The United States offers preferential duties.

Most duties are *ad valorem*, levied as a percentage of the value of the shipment. Some countries charge duty on the CIF value of the shipment, others on the FOB value at the port of export. This is an important distinction. It is not uncommon for importers to ask that your invoices show the cost of the goods, the freight, and the insurance separately even though you quote

CIF or CIP to their destination. Follow these requests exactly because it is probable that duty is assessed only on the value of the goods.

You will want to institute the practice of stating the separate export costs as line items on your commercial invoice; these include the cost of your products packed for export, inland freight, forwarder's fees, banking fees, export freight, and insurance. Some of these fees will be included in the *transaction valuation* for duty purposes as agreed under GATT (discussed later); however, this breakout identifies the relative cost of your product and its associated export costs (see Part Four). With this knowledge, your buyer may be encouraged to purchase in larger quantities to reduce these "export transaction costs" and increase your respective efficiencies.

Specific duties are those charged by weight, volume, length, or any other unit (e.g., $0.10 per yard on bolts of cloth).

Compound duties call for both an *ad valorem* and a specific duty on the same item.

Alternative duties require that the customs officer calculate the *ad valorem* duty and the specific duty and apply that which is greater.

Two types of tariff exist to equalize perceived advantages granted by the exporting country to its exporters or to equalize costs at the consumption stage incurred by producers utilizing imported inputs. Each of these will affect the landed cost of U.S. exports.

1. A *countervailing duty* is used to offset a low price that results from the export country's subsidy of the exporter's cost of production. This is a form of retaliatory duty.

2. A *compensatory duty* is charged on the import of a manufactured good to equalize its final price with that of the home-country-manufactured product which utilizes imported inputs that are subject to duty.

This array of real and potential tariffs will increase the landed cost of exported goods. Information on the nature and structure of tariffs for each target country is available from the country officer at the U.S. Department of Commerce, the commercial officer of the target country's embassy or consulate in the United States, or from your potential representative in the target country. Knowledge of the tariffs, their rates, and how they are applied will enable you to correctly price your products for each market.

Learn which multilateral and bilateral trade agreements exist between your target country, the United States, and others. Overlapping bilateral agreements may give you an opportunity to reduce target-country tariffs by exporting through the mutual third party. If Certificate of Origin requirements exist, it may be necessary to assemble, modify, or add local content in order to benefit from these arrangements. That local cost may be nominal in relation to the net savings on target-country duties.

A few countries levy duty by weight, so the exporter must know if duty is on the gross or some other type of weight. If it is the gross weight, packing must be kept to a minimum, commensurate with sound protection of the shipment. Some definitions of weight are as follows:

- *Gross weight.* Total weight of the goods and all interior and exterior packing.
- *Legal weight.* The weight of the goods and the interior containers.
- *Net weight.* The weight of the goods only, with no packing material.
- *Tare.* The difference between gross and net weights.

NONTARIFF BARRIERS

When you investigate the tariffs that will apply to your goods on entry into the target country, you must also determine what nontariff barriers apply, if any. These barriers can be more complex and insidious than tariffs. They may be applied unexpectedly, usually when it is believed that the exporting country is violating a trade agreement or ethical trade rules. Nontariff barriers cause delay, raise costs or prices, limit market access, or force product modifications.

Nontariff barriers include the following:

- *Quotas.* A quantitative limit on the number of units of a good that may be imported.
- *Voluntary restraint agreements.* A "voluntary" quota such as exists between the United States and Japan regarding automobiles.
- *Embargoes.* Prohibitions on all trade, imposed by either country.
- *"Buy local" legislation.* Generally relates to government expenditures. This can trickle down to your products, which may be inputs later deemed "not local" under *national origin* requirements.
- *Standards.* These can apply to the product, its process, its operation or performance, or the labeling and marking of the goods.
- *Import licensing.* The importer is required to obtain permission to import.
- *Foreign exchange controls.* The importer must obtain permission to make the payment for the import in any currency that flows out of the country.
- *Language requirements.* The language of the importing or target country is required on the goods, the packaging, or the documents. For example,

export documentation for shipments to France generally must be in the French language. Products for sale in eastern Canada must have both English and French language in equal prominence on the label.

This list is not all-inclusive. It is imperative that you obtain accurate information on the target country before you initiate your export marketing strategy in that country. The existence of nontariff barriers can alter your approach to target countries or eliminate certain markets from consideration.

GENERAL AGREEMENTS ON TARIFFS AND TRADE (GATT)

GATT seeks to achieve a reduction of tariffs worldwide through multilateral conferences (the most recent is the Uruguay Round), a mutual guarantee of most-favored-nations' tariffs, elimination of quantitative restrictions (quotas), freedom of transit, simplification of customs procedures, and prevention of dumping.

Under GATT, nations are encouraged to provide preferential tariff treatment to less developed and developing nations and a common standard of tariffs among members. A demonstration of this is the Tariff Schedule of the United States. Under this schedule of tariffs, which has been harmonized as to product identification with that of the other GATT members, there are the previously mentioned three columns of tariff.

1. Column 1 is the MFN column. Under Most Favored Nation treatment, exports of MFN countries to the United States are treated the same for duty purposes. This equality of treatment is subject to amendment by fiat, as a result of bilateral trade agreements or other political decisions. MFN status is frequently a politically charged issue, focusing on the civil or personal rights records of applicant nations.

2. Column 2 is the GSP column. Under the Generalized System of Preferences, exports to the United States by certain countries are free from duty. GSP treatment is a political decision by the U.S. government. GSP status is granted to encourage the economic development of the grantee by allowing open access to the U.S. market.

3. Column 3 is the "other" column. This schedule of tariff rates was first established under the Smoot-Hawley Tariff Act of 1930. This pernicious level of tariffs led to retaliation and an extreme contraction of world trade in the 1930s. Countries subject to this schedule are those nations whose interests are not compatible with those of the United States. The list varies.

Valuation and Classification

GATT signatories have agreed to use *transaction value* as defined by GATT as the basis for customs valuation. The objective is to provide a fair, uniform, and neutral system for the valuation of goods for customs purposes. The relevant part of the lengthy and complex GATT agreement provides that customs valuation be based on the actual price of the goods shipped, as shown on the commercial invoice. This price, subject to certain conditions, is known as the transaction value. The United States adopted this system in 1981.

A Harmonized System (HS) of product classification was developed by the Customs Cooperation Council, Brussels, Belgium, and consists of a worldwide standardization of identifiers for various items. The United States was the last major nation to join this regime. We have used this Harmonized System since 1989. The Harmonized System used in the United States differs in scope for exports and imports.

- The HS for exports, the Schedule B, lists over 12,000 items, in order to minimize potential import duties.

- The HS for imports, the HTS (also HS or HTSUSA) lists over 5,000 items, which enables the grouping of commodities to optimize duties within the spirit of the system.

The HS system is a ten-digit numbering system with a check digit. All exporters are required to use this 11-digit number on the Shipper's Export Declaration (see Chapter 17). The first six digits are common to a product among all countries.

The United States is an active participant in GATT and negotiates strongly in support of positions deemed important by the administration.

RESOURCES

1. The United Nations Center for Trade and Development, known as UNCTAD/GATT, is an excellent resource for information on trade among nations, including trade statistics and tariff schedules of all member countries. The address is: UNCTAD/GATT, Palais des Nations, CH-1211 Geneva 10, Switzerland. The office is located at 54-56 Rue de Montbrilliant, Geneva, Switzerland. Tel: 34 60 21. Its publication, *International Trade Forum,* identifies export opportunities in the developing world and is available on a subscription basis. It is published in English, French, and Spanish.

2. The United States is actively represented at GATT and other international trade negotiating bodies by a number of government organizations. The principal negotiator of U.S. interests is the U.S. Trade Representative (USTR). The USTR has an office in Brussels, for both GATT and for participation in and observation of the Single-Market process of the European Community (EC). Contact information for these offices is listed in Appendix B.

PART SIX
Global Trading Blocs

The international business environment is rapidly changing. In addition to the success of newly industrialized countries and the dominance of Japan and Germany in international trade and investment, there has been a reduction in the rate of participation in multilateral trade arrangements. The role of GATT is under question as the means to bring about comprehensive global trading regimes. In this commentary, Robert A. Kapp, president of the Washington Council on International Trade, identifies the nature of the changes occurring in global economic and trade relationships and the concerns applicable to U.S. business interests.

As the world settles into the 1990s, global trading blocs are all the rage. Some observers fear them, others hail them, but people of many different perspectives share a sense that the "old" postwar world of nearly universal "equal" trade relations among the market economy nations of the world is now breaking apart into geographically defined regional trading associations. The evolution of the Single Market among the 12 nations of the European Community is perceived as the classic example of the new phenomenon. The North American Free Trade Agreement (NAFTA), now under negotiation by the United States, Canada, and Mexico—plus the U.S. administration's stated desire to extend free-trade relations throughout the hemisphere—appear to many observers to signify the purposeful pursuit of a trading bloc in the Americas. In the Asia-Pacific region, a geographically defined trade bloc has not emerged from international agreements or declarations of policy intent, but the trade and investment figures themselves tell an important story; increasingly, the nations of the Asia-Pacific region trade more among themselves than with extraregional trading partners, and capital flows (especially investments from Japan, but also including investments from the rapidly industrializing second tier of Asian economies) within the region are knitting the Asia-Pacific area more and more closely together.

Needless to say, some of the present excitement over the emergence of regional trading blocs paints the past in excessively rosy terms; at no time in the twentieth century, even at the moments of greatest postwar optimism about the emergence of a truly universal global trading system, was world trade completely even-handed and nondiscriminatory. The powerful geographically driven economic developments we see today require careful business attention, but they are not in and of themselves automatically favorable or unfavorable to U.S. business. The key question, that is, whether any of these regional trading relationships will prove intentionally exclusive to outsiders, has not been fully answered, but early predictions of disaster have not been borne out. The significance of the United States as a trading and investment partner of Europe, Latin America and Asia-Pacific nations is not in doubt, both in terms of the size of the U.S. market and the size of America's markets in these regions. The importance of transnational movements of investment capital, regardless of regional affinities, will continue in the future.

The true significance of regional special relationships will be measured more by developments in the world economy as a whole, into which trading blocs fit as only one dimension. The future of regional trade and investment will depend in part on the future of the overall multilateral trade and investment rules embodied in the General Agreement on Tariffs and Trade (GATT), whose six-year Uruguay Round of global negotiations is coming to a head in 1992. If the Uruguay Round succeeds in furthering the effectiveness of the GATT and in extending GATT rules of nondiscrimination to new fields of international business activity (investment, services trade, intellectual property protections, agriculture trade, and so on), the emergence of powerful regional trading relations is likely to be engulfed in a rising tide of global trade expansion beneficial to all nations. If, on the other hand, the GATT falters badly, and the nations of the world trading system begin to retreat to more intensely protectionist policies, then the regional trading relationships now in view may prove to be discriminatory to nonmember economies. That could contribute to a broad deterioration in many vital bilateral trading relationships worldwide and pose new challenges to U.S. companies already engaged internationally, or seeking to become part of the mosaic of U.S. international business activities.

Chapters 20, 21, and 22 provide overviews of the trading blocks of today and, perhaps, the future. Some areas of concern are identified and suggestions as to the most appropriate strategy are offered for your consideration.

Exporters must remember that within each bloc there are a number of individual countries with cultures, religions, languages, needs, and wants that are dissimilar from other members of the bloc. The nature of any bloc may offer interesting and unique market opportunities to the company that is well prepared, focused, and committed.

The following table[1] gives a regional breakdown of world gross domestic product (GDP):

Region	Percentage of World GDP, 1990
North America	29 %
Western Europe	25
Asia-Pacific	21

[1]The charts and information are used by permission of Mr. Robert Broadfoot, Managing Director, Political & Commercial Risk Consultants, Ltd., Hong Kong.

Region	Percentage of World GDP, 1990
East Europe and NIS*	11
Latin America	7
Middle East	4
Africa	3

*Newly Independent States, 1992 term for the former USSR.

The following figures provide for a ready appreciation of the relative relationships between the three major trading regions of the world. The first illustration demonstrates growth in GDP, in constant dollars, for 1980, 1990, and projected for 2000. The second shows the distribution of world population, by selected region, for 1989 and projected for 2000. The next figure reports the distribution of the world population, by region, as a percentage of total population. The fourth illustrates projected total growth rates for the world population for the 1990s.

East Asia and South Asia will experience the fastest growth. This region will also experience a 6.5 percent annual growth in GDP, which implies that growth in GDP per capita will be flat to nominal.

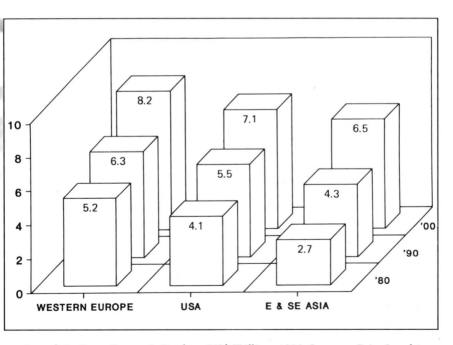

Growth in Gross Domestic Product (US$ Trillion, 1990 Constant Price Levels)

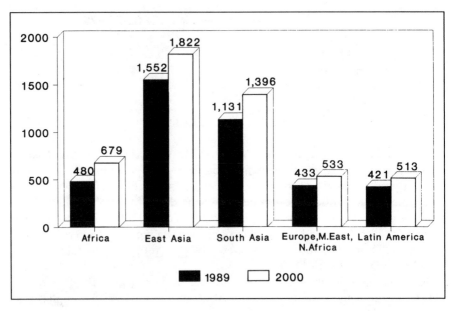

Population Growth by World Region in 1989 and 2000 (in millions)

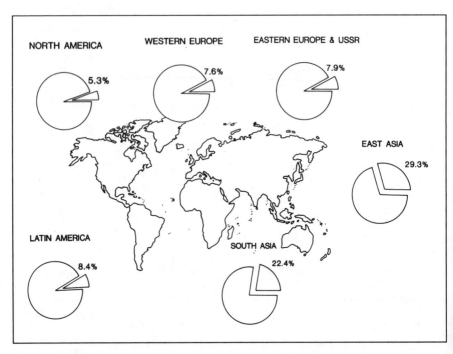

Distribution of World Population (Percentage of World Total)

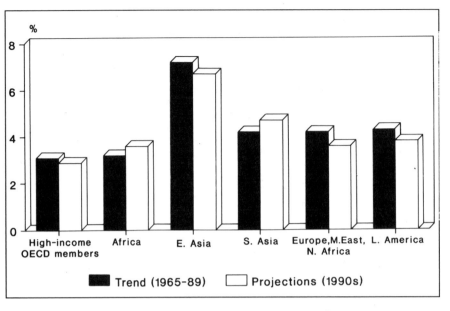

Population Growth of Selected Regions Through 2000

Western Europe is projected to experience nominal population growth while achieving GDP growth of approximately 8 percent. This portends a significant increase in per capita GDP. In general, nations and populations experiencing an increase in per capita incomes tend to spend those incomes on new products, imports, and other goods and services to improve the country's industrial capacity and individual standards of living.

North America will experience a similar relationship between population growth and growth in GDP, although not as dramatic as that projected for Western Europe. GDP growth will be uneven due to the recession of 1990–1992.

Growth in Developing Countries

The figures on page 284 illustrate the growth of real GDP per capita for developing countries in three regions of the world and within the Asia region. Starting from a significantly lower base, Asia has experienced much faster growth throughout the 1980s and into the 1990s. This increase in the rate of growth is expected to slow due to a number of factors.

Shifts in trade will result from the formal implementation of the EC's Single Market program and the NAFTA. Trade within each of these blocs and

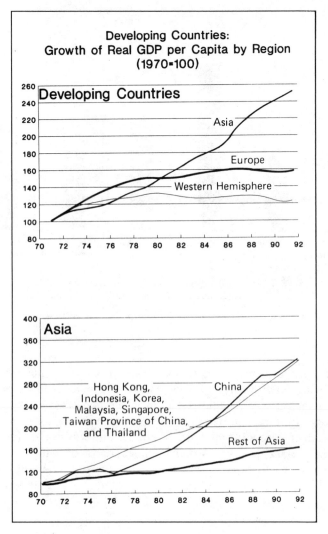

Growth of Real GDP Per Capita for Developing
Countries and Asia

between the two blocs will increase substantially. Developing nations of Asia
will continue to be suppliers and assemblers for Japan, North America, and
the EC. At the same time, they will experience a flattening of exports of
low-cost manufactures to the West. These low-cost labor activities will shift
in part to low-labor-cost countries in North America and Europe to take
advantage of the benefits contained in their trade agreements.

20 The European Bloc

The European Community (EC) holds tremendous potential for U.S. companies, as an export market and as a home for future investment activity. There is a wealth of information available to the interested businessperson or the inquiring academic. Peter Teare, London-based partner in the firm of Crowell & Moring, Ltd., is an active and lucid observer of this rapidly unfolding drama.

Europe is the United States' largest and fastest growing export market. The EC is already the world's largest trading bloc, accounting for around 40 percent of world trade and for nearly one-quarter of U.S. exports. The "1992" program of economic integration—the elimination of physical, technical, and fiscal barriers to trade—is largely complete. . . .

The emergence of a wider and deeper Europe and the development of a free-trade area between the United States, Canada, and Mexico is having a major impact on the landscape of international trade: The world's economic superpowers are about to shrink from a Group of Seven to a Group of Three—Europe, North America, and Japan—and the center of gravity of the global economy is about to shift back from the New World to the Old.

The Maastrict Treaty [for European Union, initialled in December 1991] has [subject to ratification] thrown the movement toward a federal Union of European states into fast forward. A single market of 345 million consumers will arrive at year-end 1992; a single currency and a Central European Bank may be introduced by 1999 at the latest; and the citizens of the 12 member states are now to be citizens of Europe with the right to live, work, and vote in any part of the Community, protected by a common security and defense policy.

For exporters of goods and services from the United States into the EC, fears of "Fortress Europe" have proven unfounded. The trade deficit with the EC steadily declined through the 1980s and is in a small surplus. Nevertheless, certain potential obstacles to market access for U.S. exporters remain. Heavy state subsidies give local producers in a number of industry sectors a significant competitive advantage over their counterparts in the United States. The systematic privatization of huge sectors of European industry is reducing the potential for market-distorting subsidies and creating significant investment opportunities for U.S. firms seeking a physical presence in Europe. Other features of the emerging single European market that have the potential to restrict access for U.S. exporters are rules of origin and local-content requirements—both of which feature in the EC's new public purchasing code—together with antidumping rules and the systematic approximation of national standards.

While technical and fiscal barriers to market entry remain in certain product sectors, careful strategic planning—gaining an understanding of local business conditions, practices, and cultures—can secure market share for every competitive exporter. For most U.S. companies, the single European market represents not a threat, but an unparalleled opportunity to increase global market share, to add value through the acquisition of new technologies and management skills, and to achieve greater economies of scale.

On January 1, 1993, the EC will institute programs and practices that will make it a *Single Market* in western Europe. To eliminate internal barriers to the movement of goods, services, money, and people, 282 initiatives have been developed. A great deal has been written about the EC and the opportunities or perils it presents to U.S. firms. This chapter is an overview of the Single Market—its scope and the factors that are important to a U.S. exporter when looking at this large and rapidly growing market. A number of resources are provided for your further investigation.

THE SCOPE OF THE SINGLE MARKET

The European Community has 12 member nations: Belgium, Denmark, France, Germany, Greece, Ireland, Italy, Luxembourg, the Netherlands, Portugal, Spain, and the United Kingdom. In addition, by agreements signed in October 1991, the European Free Trade Association (EFTA) members will become associates of the EC. This means that the seven nations of EFTA (Austria, Finland, Iceland, Liechtenstein, Norway, Sweden, and Switzerland) will attempt to bring their association practices in line with the mandates of the Single Market program. This new arrangement is called the European Economic Area.[1] The focus of this chapter is on the European Community of 12 nations and its Single Market initiative. A number of EFTA member states have applied for EC membership.

The Treaty of Rome, signed in 1957, set out the goal of the European Common Market in specific terms:

> The Community shall have as its task, by establishing a common market and progressively approximating the economic policies of Member States, to promote throughout the Community a harmonious development of economic activities, a continuous and balanced expansion, an increase in stability, an accelerated raising of the standard of living and closer relations between the States belonging to it.[2]

---

[1]"Pact Expands Europe's Common Market," *The Wall Street Journal*, October 23, 1991.

The EC is organized as a government. It has ambassadors and ministers posted in the United States, as do other nations. The EC bureaucracy (Eurocrats[3]) functions through:

1. *The European Council.* Composed of the heads of state of member states, it decides fundamental Community policy.
2. *The Council of Ministers.* This body consists of one representative of each national government, at the ministerial level. The Council meets in Brussels and Luxembourg and makes the legislative decisions necessary to achieve the aims set out in the EC treaties.
3. *The European Commission.* Often described as the EC's "executive branch," its main task is to develop proposals for the development of the EC and to ensure that EC regulations are observed. There are 23 directorates—general, comparable to government departments.
4. *The European Parliament.* Located in Strasbourg, this body has 518 elected members representing the citizens of the EC. This is the legislature of the European Community.
5. *The European Court of Justice.* The judicial arm of the EC interprets and applies the law of the Community treaties. Its decisions have extended Community law, which is comparable to the impact of the U.S. Supreme Court. The Court functions at two levels and its seat is in Luxembourg.

The EC is more than a group of nations that have agreed to reduce barriers between them. The EC is a new and powerful government, which over time may assume the mantle of power within the international community. Its structure is set and it works for the member states. The power sharing is effective and fair.

The EC offers many opportunities for U.S. exporters in all fields of endeavor. The countries of western Europe have long been our principal trading partners. To a large extent, we know them and they know us. There is a reasonable degree of homogeneity of culture and practice in our business and personal lives. As such, the EC offers U.S. exporters a market of 36 percent more people (345 million versus 253 million), with a total GDP 10 percent greater than the U.S. and per capita GDP at 80 percent of the U.S. level. Another comparison is useful: Total EC member international trade was

[2]*Europe Without Frontiers—Completing the Internal Market,* 3rd ed. (Office of Official Publications of the European Community, 1989).

[3]Barbara Jacob, West Coast representative, Commission of the European Communities, January 16, 1992.

approximately US$1.2 trillion in 1988.[4] For comparison, total U.S. international trade in 1991 was approximately US$1.0 trillion.

Other demographic statistics, including information on land area, cultures, languages, principal industries, employment, inflation, and other macroeconomic information, are available from the Commission for the European Communities or the appropriate consulate of an EC member state. The computer software PC Globe, among others, can also provide relatively current background information on population and geography.

PRINCIPAL AREAS OF INTEGRATION IN THE SINGLE MARKET

The Single Market process has dealt with a broad range of issues. These issues fall generally into one of the following areas. Each of these has been a focal point within the EC and often a contentious point with its trading partners.

1. Removal of technical barriers to intracommunity trade, that is, in the area of standards and their implementation.

2. Protection of industrial property and copyright.

3. Liberalization of public procurement.

4. Reorganization of post and telecommunications systems.

5. Freedom of movement.

6. Liberalization of capital movements.

7. A common market for services.

8. The liberalization of transport markets.

9. A consistent competition policy.

10. An open external trade policy.

11. Tax harmonization.

A number of these areas are important to exporters. One of the most important is that of standards. Others worth the early attention of management are protection of industrial property and copyright, public procurement, the post and telecommunications systems, liberalized transport policies, competition policy, external trade policies, and taxation.

---

[4]Press and Information Office of the Federal Republic of Germany, "Eurostate," in *The Completion of the Internal Market 1992.* The value of the ECU is approximately US1.32, or ECU0.759/US$. The value varies in the marketplace, just as that of the US$, DM, FF, and other leading currencies.

MAJOR ISSUES FOR EXPORTERS

By the EC constitution, EC member states cannot discriminate between companies established in Europe and companies established elsewhere.[5] This potential for discrimination has been the prominent issue in the business press. There is no reason to believe that U.S. exporters will be treated any differently than exporters from any other non-EC country. EC members are establishing a system to which they must conform; it is reasonable to require that same level of conformity of others. Each sector of U.S. industry also will have its own view on the effects of integration on its own access.

Standards

Product standards are the area where U.S. firms will feel the most pressure and pain. Under European standards practice, products are being placed in two groups: unregulated products not covered by an EC-wide directive and regulated products covered by EC-wide directives. Regulated products are classified as such because they must meet either, or both, a safety standard and a harmonized technical standard.

For unregulated products, mutual recognition of national standards applies for nonsafety aspects of a product. This applies to intra-European trade and to trade between the EC and other countries. A U.S. exporter of an unregulated product can certify to U.S. standards and, if these standards are accepted by at least one EC country, the standards will be accepted by the EC on the principal of mutual recognition. Most U.S. trade will benefit from mutual recognition because most U.S.-EC trade is largely unregulated.

Regulated products are those subject to European standards developed under EC directives. European technical standards for products are developed by the European standardization bodies set up by industry. These are:

1. The European Committee for Standardization (CEN). It deals with the nonelectrotechnical field. It is the largest regional standards group in the world.

2. The European Committee for Electrotechnical Standardization (CENELEC). This committee deals with the electrotechnical field.

3. The European Conference of Postal and Telecommunications Administrations (CEPT). It publishes recommendations to harmonize and improve administration and operational services.

---

[5]Barbara Jacob, West Coast representative, Commission of the European Communities, at a speech to the World Trade Club of Seattle, January 16, 1992.

4. The European Telecommunications Standards Institute (ETSI). The institute was established by CEPT to prepare standards for a unified telecommunications system.

An additional group, the European Organization for Technical Approvals (EOTA) provides technical assessments of the fitness of a product for its intended use. It grants approvals for products that have no European standards or recognized national standards.

Some in the U.S. have expressed concern that European standards may be established so as to exclude or restrict the entry of U.S. products into the European market. (Perhaps other nations felt the same about the development of many U.S. standards.) Exporters should recognize that all EC standards apply with equal force and effect on companies within Europe and companies from all nations outside Europe.

Many U.S. firms manufacture goods that conform to American Society for Testing Materials (ASTM) standards, many of which are accepted worldwide. In addition, the United States has long been an active participant in the International Organization for Standardization (ISO). This is the specialized international agency for standardization, comprising the national standards bodies of 91 countries. The ISO 9000 series is a set of five related international standards on quality management and quality assurance. Neither the ASTM nor the ISO are participating standard-setting bodies for the EC.

On June 21, 1991, the U.S. Secretary of Commerce and the EC Commission Vice President for Standards agreed that testing and quality assessment entities located in the United States will be able to perform the evaluations necessary to certify that U.S. products meet EC standards. These U.S. entities will be subject to certain EC conditions. The U.S. Department of Commerce (USDOC) named the National Institute for Standards and Technology (NIST) to assure the quality of designated U.S. testing and certification centers.

If your firm manufactures products that must conform to performance, safety, or health standards, EC standards must be addressed. There are a number of resources you should contact. They are listed in the "Resources" section of this chapter.

Industrial Property and Copyright

A major objective of the Single Market is to align patent, trademark, and copyright law throughout the Community. The European Patent Convention went into effect in 1977. That agreement made available a patent valid throughout the signatory countries. This "package of European patents" can be acquired by application to the European Patent Office in Munich.

Subsequently, a Community Patent Convention was agreed to by the member states. It provides a new uniform European patent for the Community. The objective is to have it enter into force by year-end 1992 by all 12 member states. This would be a point of negotiation and agreement between the EC member states and those applying for member or association status.

At the same time, protection of industrial and intellectual property rights is a subject of the Uruguay Round of the GATT. There is a push to bring this round to a successful conclusion in 1992. An agreement on this issue may not be achieved and could, therefore, be subject to multilateral negotiations outside the formal GATT framework.

Be sure you do a thorough investigation of the applicable laws before you enter into any agreements for the use of your industrial property by a company headquartered in the EC. U.S. law does not apply within the EC—a fact that many exporters forget.

Public Procurement

The European Commission has estimated that if internal *national* barriers to public procurement were eliminated, the savings could total well over ECU40 billion (approximately US$52 billion). Four directives (of the 282) deal with the procurement issue on general terms:

1. The Supplies Coordination Directive forces procurement to be more transparent.

2. The Works Coordination Directive also forces transparency and cooperation between the public and private sectors.

3. The Surveillance Directive ensures that Community rules are followed by all member states.

4. The Excluded Sectors Directive identifies economic sectors that had not been subject to liberalizing directives individually. These sectors are (a) water systems, (b) energy, (c) transportation, and (d) telecommunications. Under this directive, public procurement in these sectors must be announced in the *Official Journal of the European Communities*. The awarding public-sector entity must comply with certain principles and procedures such as nondiscrimination and reasonable deadlines. This directive does not deal with public procurement in services, which is also on the agenda.

The Postal and Telecommunications Systems

The European Commission has taken the communications sector beyond the issue of public procurement. The EC seeks a common telecommunications policy, within which EC rules of competition would apply. The policy on the post and telecommunications systems within the EC recognizes the need to separate the issues of sovereignty and administration. This translates into a more open market for access to supply, design, develop, and manage telecommunications projects within the EC.

European Commission directives seek to ensure access for private suppliers, under the appropriate standards regimes. It is important that U.S. exporters of equipment to these industry sectors assure that their products comply with the appropriate EC standards. These standards can be determined as noted in the "Standards" section.

Transport Policies

Transportation accounts for 7 percent of the EC's gross domestic product.[6] The Single Market program in transportation involves opening rail, air, road haulage, ocean cargo, and inland waterways to internal competition and competitive external access. U.S. companies complying with EC rules will have access to the EC as a market for their transportation services.

Of interest to exporters is the improvement in time, service, and the reduction in cost these harmonization programs will bring about. The Commission projects that this liberalized market will bring better and quicker services, and a reduction in shipping costs to customers of between 10 and 15 percent.

Use of a Standard Administrative Document has eased the documentation problems inherent at border crossings, and in 1993 the Commission reports that trucks will have to stop at borders only for such things as checks for illegal immigration.

Competition Policy

A concern of the EC is that the economic interests of the members operate within a common and consistent legal framework. Areas of concern include mergers and concentration of power, subsidies, and "unfair" competition that can result from a member's acts to protect an industry by aid payments, bans on cartels, access to member markets, and the prevention of market domination.

This internal competition policy is beneficial to U.S. exporters because it provides another area of common ground across the market. Exports to your representative (agent, rep, distributor, affiliate, or end user) under these competitive policies, and the other structures within the Single Market, can move across the Community as if they were produced within a member state.

The issue of member-state aid to those within its state is sensitive and is an uncontrollable issue from the exporter's perspective. It's important to recognize the situation, because market opportunities may result from these com-

---

[6]U.S. Department of Commerce, *The EC Builds an Integrated, Modern Transportation System,* October 1, 1991.

petitive policies. These could take the form of improved access, lower cost production or assembly services, and improved transportation, distribution, or other services because of state support (pointed out by way of the conflicts in the competition policies).

External Trade Policies

It is a stated policy of the EC to energetically resist any tendency toward isolation. "It would mean jeopardising Europe's success of integration if the Community were to want to offset the completion of the internal market by fencing itself in."[7] The EC has been an active participant in the Uruguay Round of GATT, and while no more obstreperous than the United States, it has by its nature made a positive contribution to the opening of world trade. The posture of the EC has established a tone and functional reality for other regions of the world seeking integration accompanied by expansion of external trade.

These external trade policies have improved the operating environment for U.S. exporters by adding certainty, or at least a sense of order, to the elimination of barriers and access to member-country markets. Exporters must be vigilant and attentive to EC regulations and interpretations of the EC Court of Justice, as these may over time impact the way business is done with and within the EC. You could compare this to the impact on foreign vendors to the United States of regulations, interpretations, and decisions by U.S. structures such as the International Trade Commission, the Interstate Commerce Commission, the Treasury, the Federal Reserve, and the Supreme Court, among others.

Taxation

One primary EC-oriented tax applies to U.S. exports to the EC: the Value Added Tax (VAT). This tax is added at each stage of the process of manufacture or distribution, and it is paid at each step in the production/distribution chain. The goal of the Single Market is to harmonize these VAT structures so as to eliminate advantages and disadvantages across geographic and national borders.

The different VAT rates will eventually equalize. Until that occurs, exporters should investigate the VAT rates applicable to their products. A significant disparity from the prevailing norm can raise the end price of your product and affect the marketability of your products. Exporting into a state with a lower VAT may enhance the marketability of your product throughout the EC, at least initially.

[7]Press and Information Office of the Federal Republic of Germany, *The Completion of the Internal Market 1992.*

Exporters should be aware of this structural difference. You will not see it directly in your costs or your receipts; however, the level of taxation, as in the United States, does affect purchasing decisions.

Plurality of Markets

The Single Market brings together 12 countries and establishes common rules, practices, and procedures for the flow of goods, information, money, and people between member countries. It will not change the languages of the members. It will not change the cultures, ethics, and mores.

The markets that existed in Western Europe before January 1, 1993, will continue to exist after January 1, 1993. This means that an exporter is faced with at least 12 different markets within the Community. Each of these markets has its own characteristics, including:

1. Cultural attitudes toward new products.

2. Business and consumer perceptions of U.S. products.

3. An attitude about importing from the United States or elsewhere.

4. A language different from our American English and an informal pattern of usage (idiom).

5. Accepted methods of advertising and product promotion.

6. A structure to its own internal market.

7. Preferences for products, whether industrial, commercial, consumer, or service.

These are not barriers. These are factors that "come with the territory" and are not likely to change to any significant degree.

Trade Barriers

Chapter 19 listed a number of laws and practices that can be barriers to trade. To a large extent, these barriers do not exist between the EC and U.S. business. There are issues particular to each market that you may have to address: labels in French or German, for example.

Duties and quotas are readily understood, because each of the member countries has agreed to a common external tariff and the eventual elimination of the few quotas that exist. Under GATT, there is an ongoing and gradual reduction of duties between countries. Agricultural product exports from the United States to the EC will continue to encounter difficulties for some time, because the farm interests in the EC have the same degree of political leverage within the EC as the political leverage enjoyed and exercised by the farm interests in the United States.

EXPORT STRATEGY CONSIDERATIONS

The EC is a tremendous marketplace, with immense purchasing power, economic growth rates in excess of those in the United States, stabilizing currencies,[8] a stable political environment, an educated population and work force, world-class communications systems, and an extensive transportation infrastructure. Government budgets are in control and adequate to meet the socioeconomic needs of the populations.

Each of these is a positive indicator for expansion of your export efforts into the EC. As noted earlier in the book, exporting can be a first step in the development of a joint venture or other investment activity in the EC.

Where to Start

Your market research on the member countries of the EC and EFTA will lead you to select one country that appears to offer the best opportunities for your products. Start with that one country. The elimination of internal tariffs, internal transport documents, and border checks and the free movement of people and capital mean that your target country can now be selected based on the clean market opportunity in that country. This is a significant improvement over the pre-1993 situation, when target-market considerations had to include transport times, number of border crossings and complexity, freedom of movement of capital, duties and drawbacks from transit countries, and treaties between countries so that your representative could sell outside his or her own borders.

Select the representative best suited to serve your needs within the target market and consider the representative's ability to grow with your products. For example, a leading U.S. manufacturer of lasers exports to the EC and has a principal distributor in one of the EC countries. This distributor has the capacity and the ability to distribute the product into most of the EC member states. The U.S. manufacturer reports that the relationship has been successful and is growing. A relationship with a lesser distributor would create difficulties over time, if the strategy was to cover the EC in the near term.

However, success today does not mean one should fail to plan for tomorrow. Your representative in any market should have the same long-term goals as your firm. Each firm should have the same relative importance to the other; a small U.S. firm cannot expect any meaningful attention from a major European distributor.[9]

[8] Barbara Jacob, West Coast representative, Commission of the European Communities, January 16, 1992. The Commission on the European Communities seeks a single European currency by 1999. It may be called the ECU. It will not be called the Deutsche mark.

[9] Adapted from an interview with Mr. Joseph Leonard, Regional Manager, ESCOM, Inc., and former Regional International Sales Manager, John Fluke Manufacturing, Inc.

In your interviews, discussions, and negotiations with your new representative, be very clear about your expectations for your product in Europe. At the same time, listen to what your representative has to say. He or she is (should be) successful in business, in the marketplace. He or she probably knows more than you about the market. Use this relationship to learn about the EC and how it works.

Problem Areas

Entry into each new market within the EC presents new challenges and new opportunities. Each different market offers a range of problems, often similar across markets. Some of these problems are:

1. The best marketing approach to overcome cultural resistance to your product.
2. The financing you may be required to provide to your representative or his or her buyer, to match the terms that are customary for the market. For example, French law encourages importers to insist on 90-day-draft terms, while German practice dictates sales on open account terms.
3. Blue laws in some countries mean that retailers are closed on Sundays and have limited hours on Saturdays.
4. Commercial or industrial goods warehousing and distribution practices differ by country.
5. Language and cultural practices overlap country boundaries or split countries with invisible lines. Marketing to Belgium requires two different approaches, France no less than two, Italy at least two, and Germany at least two different approaches. These regional identities may require specialized or separate representative arrangements.

Benefits of the Single Market

The elimination of internal barriers will make business life easier for exporters and their representatives. Initially, the U.S. companies that have been active or have a presence in the EC will have the benefit of that presence and the experience they have gained. However, it is never too late to enter the EC. The good deals will not slip away. The *big* deals will go to the big firms, but like the United States, the EC is a huge and deep market with tremendous potential for large and growing firms alike.

There is one standard for duty, one external tariff structure, an internal transportation system that requires only one internal transit document, free movement of capital so payments for your sales can be made efficiently, and an improving postal and communications system to facilitate mail order and

Table 20.1
Weighting and ECU Central Rates for EC Currencies

Country	Currency	Weight in ECU	Central Rate, 1 ECU =
UK	Pound Sterling	12.60%	0.697£
Netherlands	Guilder	9.49	2.316 hfl or Gld
Belgium/Lux	Franc	8.09	42.40 bfr/lfr
Denmark	Krone	2.52	7.841 dkr
France	Franc	19.32	6.895 FF
Italy	Lira	9.87	1538 Lit
Greece	Drachma	0.78	205.3 Dr
Ireland	Irish Pound	1.11	0.767 Ir£
Germany	Mark	30.36	2.056 DM
Spain	Peseta	5.15	133.63 Pta
Portugal	Escudo	0.78	178.74 Esc

other mass communications activities. European fulfillment companies will, on a contract basis, provide warehousing, order entry, fulfillment, pick and pack, and shipping activities for U.S. exporters. Your international executives can move freely within the EC (although the customs process has always been crisp and efficient when compared to even the best of U.S. entry points).

The EC Court of Justice and the implementation of EC business law provides a common legal framework for the conduct of your business arrangements. EC law even provides for incorporation as an EC company, subject to the laws of the EC rather than the laws of one particular city of incorporation. This facilitates trade between U.S. and European companies.

The Currency of the Community

As noted previously, there is no one currency of the EC at this time. There will probably be an EC currency before the end of the decade. In the interim, the European Currency Unit (ECU)[10] may be quite useful in your export marketing strategies. The ECU is a weighted basket of European currencies. Weighting and ECU central rates of the Community currencies (as of September 1992) are shown in Table 20.1.

This is the structure of the currencies in relation to each other and to the ECU. It is the EC common unit of account. The EC members have agreed to a "bilateral central course" or central rate around which each of these currencies can fluctuate. A deviation of +/- 2.25 percent on either side of this bilateral central rate is an intervention point; governments may step in as

---

[10]The historical Écu was named after the 1498 coat of arms of Louis XII of the Bourbon dynasty.

buyers and sellers of the deviant currency to bring it back into line. The upper and lower intervention points are at +/- 6 percent of the bilateral central rate. This is the point at which governments have to step in and adjust currency values. This recalls the "snake" of the 1970s, when the European Economic Community (EEC) first began to talk in terms of mutual monetary interests within the context of the EEC.

Because of these bands of intervention, quotations in terms of ECUs may be more palatable to your buyers and will be more manageable from your end. There is a forward market in the ECU. It can be accepted on an interbank basis for payments. The lack of a paper currency does not mean it cannot be used for payments.

The exporter and the buyer or representative would agree on a price of the goods or services in terms of the ECU. Payment dates and payment arrangements would be agreed. An export quote in ECU will be subject to less fluctuation and uncertainty than a quote and sale in any one of the member currencies.

The downside, to the extent there is one, is that your sale, in what would have been a nonfluctuating currency, would be in a currency (the ECU) that could fluctuate by, say, 2 percent because of the influence of other more volatile currencies.

The ECU can be used as an effective pricing vehicle for U.S. exporters. The benefits are manifold and include:

1. Quotation in the buyer's currency, demonstrating your flexibility, adaptability, and cultural sensitivity.

2. Ability to effectively cover your FX exposure.

3. Simplified bookkeeping across markets within the EC.

SUMMARY

The EC and the Single Market present both new problems and new opportunities for U.S. exporters. There are a number of excellent resources available to assist you in dealing with standards, markets, culture, and other issues you may face.

It's not too late to enter the EC, regardless of when you decide to do it (unless you want to be a major competitor in, for example, the airframe market and you are not Boeing or Airbus). Some major infrastructure industries may be subject to national or EC-wide controls, similar to the controls and constraints imposed on the U.S. nuclear power industry. These are exceptions.

Do the research recommended in this book. Take time to make reasoned and informed decisions. Export quality products with quality service and support. You will succeed in the EC.

RESOURCES

1. U.S.-based Offices of the Commission of the European Communities are in Washington, DC, and San Francisco, CA. In Washington, DC, the address is: 2100 M St., NW, Washington, DC 20037. Tel: 202-862-9500; fax: 202-429-1766.

   In San Francisco, CA, the address is: 44 Montgomery St., Suite 2715, San Francisco, CA 94104. Tel: 415-391-3476; fax: 415-391-3641.

2. American National Standards Institute, 11 W. 42d St., New York, NY 10018. Tel: 212-642-4900; fax: 212-302-1286.

3. GATT Inquiry Point/Technical Office, Office of Standards Code and Information, National Institute of Standards and Technology, Administration Building, Room A629, Gaithersburg, MD 20899. Tel: 301-975-4040. The National Center for Standards and Certification Information (NCSCI) is at the same address.

4. For standards, contact the Single Internal Market Information Service, Office of European Community Affairs, International Trade Administration, Washington, DC 20230. Tel: 202-482-5276.

5. ISO standards are available from ASQC, the ANSI ASC Z-1 Committee on Quality Assurance. Contact the ASQC at: 310 West Wisconsin Ave., Milwaukee, WI 53203. Tel: 414-272-8575; fax: 414-272-1734.

6. The U.S. Department of Commerce offers excellent information for U.S. firms looking at the European Community. The Office of European Community Affairs (number 4 above) has available a number of publications dealing with the EC directives, legislation, market opportunities, names and addresses of EC institutions, and more. This office can direct you to the country officers and industry officers familiar with your products and the EC to answer your questions or assist in the resolution of your issues.

7. Crowell & Moring is an international trade and business consulting firm with offices in Washington, DC, Newport Beach, CA, and London, England. It publishes the comprehensive monthly *EC-US BUSINESS REPORT* which follows and analyzes U.S. and EC events. Contact Crowell & Moring at:

1001 Pennsylvania Ave., NW	4675 MacArthur Court, Suite 1560
Washington, DC 20004-2595	Newport Beach, CA 92660-1851
Tel: 202-624-2500	Tel: 714-263-8400
Fax: 202-628-5166	Fax: 714-263-8414

8. KPMG Peat Marwick, one of the leading international accounting firms, produces a thorough quarterly on the EC. It is available through your local office of the firm.

21 The Asian Bloc

The creation of a common trading area comparable to that of the EC Single Market or the North American Free Trade Agreement area is not likely to occur among the major nations of Asia. The cultures, histories, and objectives are too diverse and resentments are perhaps too deep. Even geography is not compatible with significant integration.

Robert Broadfoot offered this cogent analysis of Japan's stature in his publication *Asian Intelligence:*

Japanese Influence in Asia

The consensus opinion has been that due to its sheer economic size and capital resources Japan is the natural center of gravity for Asia. Moreover, this same body of opinion holds that Asia will increasingly revolve around Japan as the U.S. looks more to domestic matters in the post-Cold War world while Europe preoccupies itself with the 1992 integration and with guiding the eastern part of the Continent out of the dark days of communism. In other words, an Asian bloc centering around Japan will evolve by default.

Such a view cannot be discounted entirely. There is no denying that Japan is very important to the region economically. Japan's GDP certainly dwarfs all other countries in the region both individually and collectively. Also, intraregional trade and investment is becoming increasingly important. However . . . we doubt that Japan's influence at the end of this decade will be very much larger than it is at present. It could be less if the recent tendency toward Japan bashing by the U.S. is picked up by Asian countries that resent Japan's exclusive position and imperial transgressions of the past.

According to one estimate, Japanese acquisitions of U.S. corporations and related investments plunged to US$3.8 billion in 1991 from US$11.9 billion in 1990, a fall of 68 percent. Asia lags considerably behind both the U.S. and Europe as a destination for Japanese direct investment. Although no official figures from Tokyo are available yet for 1991, it is clear . . . that Japanese direct investment fell back in most countries of the region in 1991.

So, why are the stock markets of other Asian countries still booming at a time when Japan is not simply down in the dumps but is pulling money back home? It is because Japan is not as important to the region economically as many observers would have us believe.

In part, this is due to the fact that the U.S. economy still has more influence on Asia than many give it credit for. There is no single place in the world, certainly not

Japan, that offers a real alternative to the U.S. as a market. The U.S. export position is much stronger than one would think from listening to the belly-aching of that country's over-paid automobile CEOs. The United States may not have a Sony or a Toyota, but Japan does not have a Microsoft or a Cargill or a Coca Cola. And whereas Japanese manufacturers are rushing to set up production facilities abroad, U.S. manufacturers are already there, having set up such facilities years ago.

There are other factors such as the international role played by the U.S. dollar; the yen has no such role. U.S. interest rates have far more important implications for the economies of Asia than do Japanese rates, and while the world worries about the size of the U.S. budget deficit (with good reason), no one voices similar concerns when it comes to Japan—not because Japan does not have fiscal problems, but because those problems are not perceived to be very relevant to the rest of the world or, for that matter, for the rest of Asia.

Nor should the influence of European companies in Asia be overlooked. European banks are second to none in the region . . . and both U.S. and European fund managers are far more aggressive in pushing for the opening and development of Asian capital markets than are comparable Japanese institutions.

As proud as Japan is of the quality of its consumer products, the Italians, French, Germans, and Swiss have set the standards in terms of luxury and quality for everything from fashion and fashion accessories to watches, cars, and even machine tooling equipment. There is not a Japanese food products company that can compare with Nestlé in any Asian market, and while Japanese manufacturers can make a darn good television and telephone, they are at a distinct disadvantage when it comes to building and maintaining the telecommunications systems that have to be in place for these electronic appliances to work properly. The big contracts in Asia in the coming decade will be in infrastructure, and although the Japanese will undoubtedly be aggressive bidders, the outcome is by no means a foregone conclusion.

While Japan may have the reputation in the region as the big boy on the block, in a very real way this perception is wrong. The biggest economic force in virtually every country in Asia outside of Japan and Korea are the Chinese. In every country in the region, including the Philippines, Thailand, Malaysia, Indonesia, and even Vietnam, the role of local, ethnic Chinese completely overshadows the role of the Japanese. In some countries, both are treated as outsiders. In others, the Chinese community has become so assimilated into the local population that it is treated as native—a position Japanese and Japanese companies will never enjoy.

At a time when interest rates are certain to remain low and major industrialized countries will be preoccupied with domestic problems, the Chinese dimension of Asia is likely to come into its own as one of the strongest, most positive forces shaping the region.

Mr. Broadfoot sets a broad framework for the question of an Asian bloc. In late 1990, the Prime Minister of Malaysia proposed an East Asia Common Market. In January 1992, the Association of South East Asian Nations (ASEAN)[1] began work to create a consortium of common interests tentatively called the East Asian Economic Caucus. Reports indicate a formal trade area, if any, will be in place by 2008.[2] These potential blocs are under discussion in

[1]Members of ASEAN are Brunei (1984), Indonesia, Malaysia, the Philippines, Singapore, and Thailand.

[2]*The Journal of Commerce,* January 29, 1992, page 5A.

response to the potential negative impact on member nations' exports by the formation of the EC and the NAFTA and fear of the barriers that may be erected.

The U.S. administration is concerned about an extensive Asian trading arrangement. Some in the administration believe that U.S. interests in the region would be weakened. To parry the initiatives noted above, the U.S. government is encouraging the Asia-Pacific Economic Cooperation Forum (APEC). This group includes the United States, Australia, New Zealand, Japan, *and* the ASEAN states.

However, neighbors to the north, west, and south of Japan are not excited about strengthening Japan's influence in the region, because of their past experiences with Japan.[3]

Major formal trading blocs may never form in Asia. Smaller subregional development blocs exist, and more will form as communities of interest are identified. ASEAN was established in August 1967 to strengthen regional cohesion and self-reliance, while emphasizing economic, social, and cultural cooperation and development.[4] In this chapter, Australia and New Zealand have been excluded from the discussion of a Japan/East Asia bloc.

Japan functions by choice in relative isolation from the world economy. It has remained largely apart fom the world community in order to further its universal national goal, its cultural imperative, and to protect its own self-interest.[5] In 1992, in response to world events and external political pressure, Japan cautiously began to moderate this posture of isolation. However, corporate Japan continues to place self-interest above all other considerations. Exporters should remember this at all times when they negotiate with their Japanese prospects, clients, or counterparts. As a nation and as a business community, the United States has failed to recognize this overriding passion.

THE JAPANESE SPHERE OF INFLUENCE

The Asian bloc of the future is a region under significant economic influence from Japan. This sphere of influence will probably not include Korea, Taiwan, China, or Hong Kong, for cultural and political reasons. Each of these countries is fiercely nationalistic and economically independent; each will act to discourage the expansion of Japanese interests in their country.

---

[3]Adapted from "No Future in a Fortress Asia" by Yoshihide Ishiyama of IBM Japan, reprinted in the *New York Journal of Commerce,* January 3, 1992.

[4]From the U.S. Department of State, *Background Notes: ASEAN,* March 1989.

[5]It is appropriate for a nation, like an individual or a business, to preserve its own self-interest. One must acknowledge any nation that can so clearly identify its interests and focus all its resources on its achievement. The United States has yet to identify its own self-interest.

However, Japan *will* expand its investments in the lesser developed nations of East Asia over the next decade, implementing a twofold objective.

1. Japanese companies are moving to new business strategies. Manufacturing work can be done in other Asian nations at a 10th of the wages paid in Japan, and the cost of training workers is minimal compared to training costs in Japan. This shift is being done to free the financial and mental resources necessary for Japan to retain its lead in product development and market share over the United States and EC nations. Peter Drucker calls this "control of brain power."[6]

2. Japanese companies are creating middle-income populations and middle-income nations, which will become consumers for their industrial, commercial, and consumer goods. Japanese investment in these countries brings economic development and employment, which result in improved living standards and expansion of discretionary incomes. These incomes will be spent on Japanese-controlled goods and services.[7]

This bloc—nations that are economically tied to Japan and reliant on Japan for technology, management, and finance—is the third major regional trading bloc to evolve this decade. Economic influence is the agenda. The isolationist, cultural-elitist nature of Japanese business will not translate into political power for Japan. Observers report that Japan does not believe it has a world role. As suggested by Mr. Broadfoot, the ethnic Chinese, entrenched throughout the region, will be another dominant economic influence.

Japan will have a major and silent influence in East Asia. U.S. exporters must learn to appreciate the impact of Japanese economic influence and prepare to deal with it head on.

THE SCOPE OF THE ASIAN BLOC

The Asian bloc is in fact two major informal groupings of long-term mutual interest. I use the term "Chinese states" in reference to the region populated by Chinese-speaking peoples with specific and strong ties to the People's Republic of China (PRC). These states are, therefore, the PRC, Taiwan, and Hong Kong. Chinese interests also abound in the other nations of the region.

The other major bloc is comprised of Japan and the East Asian states. Korea is a participant in the growth of the newly industrialized countries

---

[6]Adapted from Peter F. Drucker, "Japan: New Strategies for a New Reality," *The Wall Street Journal*, October 2, 1991.

[7]From an interview with Mr. R. Rardin, business consultant to Nisho Iwai America, Inc., December 1991.

(NICs) of the 1980s, but is not a strong participant in either of these structures.

The Chinese states of the People's Republic of China, Hong Kong, and the Republic of China (ROC or Taiwan) account for a growing proportion of trade with the United States. They offer investment markets that, while tightly controlled, are relatively stable and growing markets for U.S. exports. These countries are relatively stable for the following reasons:

1. The PRC and the ROC have held discussions on the merits of closer political and economic ties.

2. The PRC is now a sizeable market for subassemblies and other products manufactured in the ROC.

3. Young leaders in both countries appear willing to discuss a future less burdened by past conflicts. Current leaders in the PRC will pass on.

4. The transition of control of Hong Kong has been recognized internally. Hong Kongers have adjusted and the PRC appears to understand the value of Hong Kong to its split objectives of being both (a) exporter to the world and (b) relative isolationist.

5. The potential for another Tiananmen Square is slim. Although it was a political nightmare, it did not alter business arrangements in the important *enterprise zones*.

The business environment in the Chinese states will be receptive to the import of U.S. goods and services. The ROC needs to balance its burgeoning surplus with the West, the PRC must do the same, and Hong Kong is the center for all business in the region.

South Korea and North Korea have begun to discuss areas of mutual interest. Regional tensions continue to abate. South Korea (Korea) is a vibrant and growing economy with strong ties to the United States and with little use for Japan. U.S. economic relations with Korea have been and will be contentious: on imports and exports, on environmental issues, on foreign exchange issues, and on human rights issues. None of these points will keep U.S. exporters or investors out of Korea.

The countries of East Asia that are subject to increasing Japanese economic influence are Indonesia, Malaysia, the Philippines, Singapore, and Thailand. Readers who wish to investigate the potential for export business in Vietnam are directed to the "Resources" section at the end of this chapter.

Parameters of the Japan/East Asia Market

Statistical information on the scale and relative economic performance of each country of the region is useful. Each exporter should develop broad and useful background information on each potential target market. As noted in

Table 21.1
Statistical Data on the Japan/East Asia Market

Country	Pop., Millions (1991)	Pop. Growth Rate, %	GNP in US$ Billions (1990)	GNP Growth Rate, %	GNP per Capita	Literacy Rate, %
Brunei	.4	8.0	3.6	0.0	10,500	80
Indonesia	195	1.9	81.8	3.8	420	74
Malaysia	17	2.0	36.5	7.4	2,000	73
Philippines	68	2.7	41.6	5.0	610	89
Singapore	3	1.1	29.5	10.9	10,000	83
Thailand	57	1.7	67.2	11.0	1,100	89
Japan	124	0.5	2,830.0	4.8	21,900	99
USA	253	0.9	4,961.0	1.0	19,800	96

Chapter 3, a great deal of secondary research is readily available, including State Department Background Notes, USDOC Foreign Economic Trends, and Overseas Business Reports, in addition to the monthly updated information in the National Trade Data Bank.

The information in Table 21.1 was obtained from PC Globe, a PC-based global geography program, available at district offices of the US&FCS.[8] Other relevant information is given in Table 21.2.

A cursory analysis of this data leads to some useful observations. Conclusions may require more information. For example:

1. The influence of the ethnic Chinese does not appear in this data, as these populations are in the minority in most of these countries. They are, however, influential in the business communities of their respective nations.

2. There are very limited ethnic or cultural threads between countries, other than some concentration on the Buddhist religion.

3. English is not a native language. Product instructions, packaging, advertising, promotions, labels, and marks will have to be in languages that can be readily understood. The only possible exception could be U.S.-origin fashion goods, purchased for prestige. Sizing and care instructions must, however, be in the local language. In East Asia, you are dealing with at least 13 languages.[9]

---

[8]This program and other similar geography data bases are readily available nationally at nominal cost.

[9]The *global product,* popularized by Theodore Levitt of the Harvard Graduate School of Business Administration, requires extensive localization for each market.

Table 21.2
Other Relevant Information on the Japan/East Asia Market

Country	Composition of Economy % Agr.	% Indust.	% Serv.	Language	Religion	% Urban
Brunei	2	55	43	Malay Brunei	Muslim Buddhist	59.0
Indonesia	26	31	43	Indonesian English	Muslim	26.2
Malaysia	21	38	41	Malay Chinese	Muslim Buddhist	34.6
Philippines	26	33	41	Philippino English	Catholic	41.6
Singapore	1	35	64	Malay Mandarin	Buddhist	100.0
Thailand	17	31	52	Thai	Buddhist	17.9
Japan	3	44	53	Japanese	Shinto Buddhist	76.7
USA	2	38	60	English Spanish	Protestant Catholic	73.7

4. There are at least seven cultures with their own mores, beliefs, and practices.

5. Each country is growing faster than the United States. This means that external markets are, on average, growing faster than U.S. markets. Per capita GNP is also growing rapidly. Purchasing power is under US$1,000 for 280 million people, and over US$1,100 for the other 201 million. This diversity of purchasing power suggests that niche or target marketing will be necessary. Products will have to be tightly focused for the rich, the middle class, or the poverty markets. Industrial goods will have markets across countries, where the appropriate base of technology is in use or being introduced.

These are some of the determinations exporters and their marketers can make from a very cursory look at minimal secondary data. The East Asia market is large, growing at a rapid rate, and has significant markets for manufactured goods, services, and agricultural technology.

Figures 21.1 and 21.2 illustrate the Asian share of world imports and exports for 1980 and 1990. Total imports from the rest of the world increased by US$350.9 million or 121 percent, while exports to the rest of the world increased by US$433.4 million or 159 percent. The nations of East and Southeast Asia continue to be users of capital- and export-driven economies.

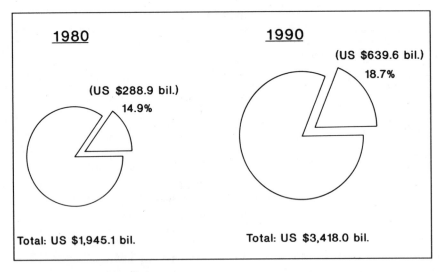

Figure 21.1   East Asia/Japan Imports as a Percentage of World Imports

Note also that this region's share of world exports increased by approximately 10 percent over the decade of the 1980s, and increased by 59% in absolute terms.

MAJOR ISSUES FOR EXPORTERS

Diversity of Markets

Unlike the European Community, the Japan/East Asia bloc presents the exporter with seven markets that are not bound by a common border, do not share a common legal and administrative system, and do not move forward with the same political, social, or economic objectives.

The community of interest that is forming in East Asia will serve a narrow range of self-interests on a subregional basis. Therefore, target countries within the Japan/East Asia bloc can be developed as individual markets. Your research, development, promotion, and product adaptation efforts should focus on markets rather than regions. Success in one market will facilitate expansion throughout the region.

Each exporter must answer this question: What have Japanese interests done to influence the market for my product in this target market? Japan has, and will, spread its economic influence throughout East Asia to accomplish Japanese objectives. Those objectives are:

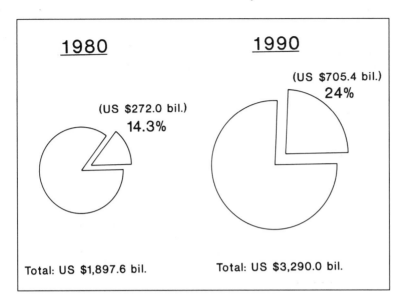

Figure 21.2 East and Southeast Asian Exports as a Percentage of World Exports

1. Low-cost production platforms.
2. Export platforms to enter the U.S., EC, Eastern European, and Latin American markets. Exporting under the flag of the host country is a strategy Japanese firms will use to divert the attention of governments in their target markets. For example, a synchronous electric motor made in Malaysia is a product of Malaysia, regardless of the owner of the plant or technology. This is true for GE telephone handsets made in Malaysia and for Japanese cars built in the United States.
3. Optimization of the cost of the factors of production. Land, labor, and capital, the three factors taught in Economics 101, each command a premium in Japan. As Peter Drucker suggests, the production function is being moved to low-factor-cost locations.
4. Optimization of the value of Japanese *brain power*, by directing the "intellectual" factor to
   a. Zero Defects Management, and
   b. Tripling the pace of product development and introduction to capture more of the "innovator's profit."[10]

---

[10]Adapted from Peter F. Drucker, "Japan: New Strategies for a New Reality," *The Wall Street Journal*, October 2, 1992.

Trade Barriers

Tariffs and quotas exist in each export market. Those countries that are signatories to GATT have agreed to the GATT quota-elimination and tariff-reduction schemes. Signatories demonstrated good will by complying with GATT provisions, and the burst of world trade of the late 1980s was the result. This will continue; Japan and the East Asian countries under discussion are GATT signatories. Japan has a fairly low average tariff; other East Asian nations have agreed to lower theirs from averages of up to 30 percent.

Japan is consistently denounced for its import barriers. Exporters should note that the United States has import barriers on at least 45 different groups of manufactured goods;[11] this is more than any other major country. Japanese business and cultural practices are different from ours. As a result, many U.S. companies believe them to be trade barriers, barriers that are more subtle and more pervasive than ours, therefore unfair.

These "barriers" come in many forms:

1. Monopolistic business practices. *Keiretsu* are business groups that share business among each other. Members, small and large, are discouraged from purchasing or dealing with those outside the group.

2. Government practices to encourage specific industries. These take the form of laws, business practices, and quiet encouragements to purchase from Japanese suppliers rather than from others.

3. Questionable business practices. The government of Japan has been accused of bid rigging, collusion, and failure to enforce commercial trade laws.

4. Cultural barriers. The culture of Japan, often incomprehensible to the West in its beliefs and practices, can be a barrier to markets. The exporter must accept the fact that the culture of Japan will not change to accommodate U.S. business practices.[12]

These obstacles should be of concern to U.S. exporters. At the same time, we should not set ourselves too high in passing judgment on Japan or any other nation. The world community sees a rising degree of protectionism in the actions of the U.S. government and in the attitudes of some of our more outspoken businesspeople.

As Japanese influence is to some extent imbedded into host countries in East Asia, business practices will change. The scope of change will not be nationwide, but it may affect your company and your industry.

[11]Reported in P. R. Cateora, *International Marketing*, 7th ed. (New York: Irwin, 1990).

[12]Adapted from "Barriers to More Trade with Japanese Are Formidable," *The Seattle Times*, January 6, 1992.

EXPORT STRATEGY CONSIDERATIONS

Many American companies have been successful in Japan and East Asia. These companies have manufactured quality products; sold the products at a price reflecting that quality; provided consistent, competitive, full-time service; and managed their activities so as to fit into the culture of the particular market.

Where to Start

Your company will not overcome the real and perceived barriers listed above. Understand what they are, develop a plan to deal with them for your product, and move on.

Each country in Asia that has accumulated a sizeable surplus with the United States has taken steps to reduce the magnitude of the surplus. Taiwan, for example, has buying missions that regularly come to the United States with an agenda and a US$1 to 3 billion checkbook they plan to clean out in a few weeks. Korea has often taken this same approach.

The PRC receives attention out of proportion to its US$10+ billion surplus with the United States; Congress doesn't like the politics of the PRC. Japan, with a surplus that has approached US$100 billion on occasion, has yet to bear the brunt of a truly irritated U.S. Congress. (One hopes it translates into constructive self-interest rather than into protectionist measures.)

Some Asian nations have established government offices in the United States to help U.S. companies export to their countries. Japan, through the Japan External Trade Organization (JETRO), is at the forefront of this effort (see "Resources").

The market research process in Part One is straightforward and can generate quick results. Good information is readily available on Japan and the ASEAN members. Pay attention to the culture of each separate market. Do not make the assumption that, for example, Chinese-speaking markets are similar, or that countries with similar dominant religions are culturally similar. This is a lesser issue for manufacturers or distributors of industrial goods.

The National Trade Data Bank (NTDB) can provide timely information on many segments of your market research. In addition to country information Overseas Business Reports (OBRs) and Foreign Economic Trends (FETs), it has Background Notes from the State Department, country information from the CIA, and over 3,500 industry research reports. These reports cover the export potential for certain industrial goods by market, product, competition, and other factors. Census data can give you trends and patterns for exports of your product type by country, quantity, and price or value.

Follow the steps in this book, weigh your decisions by the implications of the culture of the target country, identify the markets where Japanese influence (from financing, investment, population concentration, trade, or control) is pervasive, and make decisions accordingly.

Problem Areas

The problem that most U.S. exporters encounter in the Japan/East Asia marketplace is keeping up with the demand for new products. Japan sets the pace in the introduction of new products, and competitors who do not keep pace will fall behind. "New products" can be variations in form, texture, design, color, packaging, or promotion. New product *leaps*, exemplified by Sony's leap from a portable tape recorder to the Walkman™ opened a vast market with tremendous growth and spinoff opportunities. This is the Japanese objective with each innovation.

A second problem area is related to the target market. Every exporter in every market must select the right or best representative. This process was covered in Part Two. There are seven different countries with their own culture(s), barriers, economic systems, currencies, and perceptions of U.S. products. The region requires maximum flexibility in your approach and consistency in your efforts.

RESOURCES

1. Background Notes on Asian countries, from the U.S. State Department are available by single copy and by subscription. The single-copy price is US$1.00 for each of the 63 nations or political entities covered. The annual subscription is US$20.00. Order Background Notes from your closest U.S. Government Bookstore or from the Superintendent of Documents, U.S. Government Printing Office, Washington, DC 20402. Additional country information is available as noted in Part One.

2. For information on Vietnam, contact the Country Desk Officer at the International Trade Administration, Washington, DC. Tel: 202-482-3875.

3. The Japan External Trade Organization (JETRO) was created to increase Japanese exports; now it almost exclusively assists U.S. firms who seek to export *to* Japan. JETRO has offices in Atlanta, Chicago, Dallas, Denver, Houston, Los Angeles, New York, and San Francisco. Addresses and telephone numbers are listed under JETRO in the business pages of each city's telephone book. The closest Japanese consulate also can give you this information.

4. The February 10, 1992, edition of *Business America* has some very useful information on government programs to assist in your efforts to

export to Japan. It also contains a listing of market research reports on Japan published by JETRO and the USDOC.

5. The Japan Export Information Center (JEIC), formed within the USDOC, is directed to assist U.S. companies with Japan-related information on market entry, market data and research, product standards and testing requirements, intellectual property protection, tariffs and nontariff barriers, and more. Contact the JEIC at: Office of Japan, U.S. Department of Commerce, Room 2318, Washington, DC 20230. Tel: 202-377-2425; fax: 202-482-0469.

6. The JEIC published *Destination Japan: A Business Guide for the 90s*. It is available on the NTDB or through the U.S. Government Printing Office (Call No. SN: 003-009-006-3).

7. PC Globe is published by PC Globe, Inc., 4440 South Rural Rd., Tempe, AZ 85282. Tel: 602-730-9000; fax: 602-968-7196

8. Those companies seeking timely, incisive intelligence on the politics, economies, and workings of the Asian states are urged to contact: Political and Commercial Risk Consultancy, Ltd., Mr. Robert C. Broadfoot, Managing Director, GPO Box 1342, Hong Kong, Room 1603-1604 Hollywood Centre, 233 Hollywood Rd., Hong Kong. Tel: 852-541-4088; fax: 852-815-5032; telex: 46926 RISK HK.

22 The North American Bloc

The United States and Canada share the largest two-country trading relationship in the world. Combined, they trade about US$198 billion with each other. Japan is second at about US$163 billion, and Mexico is the United States' third largest trading partner. The following comparison is useful:

Country	U.S. Exports (billions)	% of Total	U.S. Imports (billions)	% of Total[1]	US$ Total
Canada	US$93.2	21.6%	US$104.7	18.7%	197.9Bn
Japan	52.5	12.2	110.9	19.8	163.4
Mexico	29.8	6.9	32.5	5.8	62.3

The *New North America,*[2] as these three countries can be called collectively, has a population of 362 million, a combined GNP of US$5.7 trillion, and total 1991 inter-NAFTA trade of over US$263 billion.[3]

This immense market brings together the productive and human resources of two leading industrial nations and one of the emerging newly industrialized countries (NICs) of the 1990s.

THE SCOPE OF THE NORTH AMERICAN FREE TRADE AGREEMENT (NAFTA)

International trade attorney John Peterson offers this valuable perspective:

[1]1989; Source: U.S. Department of Commerce, reported in CANADA 1991, *An International Business Comparison.*

[2]From "Will a North American FTA Become a Reality?" in *Global Trade,* March 1991.

[3]Source: U.S. Department of Commerce, and Consul General of Canada, Seattle Office, from *Statistics Canada,* 1991.

The proposed North American Free Trade Agreement (NAFTA) between the United States, Canada, and Mexico will present international businessmen with challenges and opportunities in the decade ahead. The centerpiece of NAFTA will be the gradual elimination by the participating countries of customs duties assessed on each other's products. Duties for most items will be reduced gradually at first, with complete free trade being achieved within a decade after the pact becomes effective.

NAFTA is intended both as an extension of the United States/Canada Free Trade Agreement (CFTA) and as a North American response to the creation of the European Community's "**Single Internal Market.**" As a trading bloc, NAFTA countries will try to harmonize their product standards and trade policies, but envision nothing quite so ambitious as the EC's Single Internal Market.

Rules of origin will be the key to administering NAFTA. It is one thing for a NAFTA country to say that it will eliminate duties on products made in another signatory; it is quite another to determine when products manufactured with the use of imported components or ingredients have been sufficiently transformed in a NAFTA country to qualify them for NAFTA's reduced-duty or duty-free status. NAFTA's rules of origin will probably resemble those in the CFTA and be based on determining whether operations performed in NAFTA countries effect certain changes in tariff classification. International businessmen seeking to take advantage of NAFTA will need to become intimately familiar with the rules of origin applicable to their goods.

During the first decade of NAFTA, as duty elimination is "phased in," international businessmen will also want to be aware of how they might be able to achieve comparative advantages in the North American market through the use of duty drawbacks, tariff preference programs other than NAFTA (such as "maquiladoras"), and tariff-advantaged facilities, such as Customs-bonded warehouses and Foreign Trade Zones.

Life under NAFTA should involve greatly expedited North American trade, but by no means will that trade be totally "free." NAFTA signatories will be nervous in the pact's early years and may invoke "safeguards" designed to temporarily set aside NAFTA rules and protect domestic industries. Adoption of the CFTA pointed out some deficiencies in the competitiveness of Canadian manufacturing industries. The United States and Canada are concerned that adoption of NAFTA will result in an exodus of manufacturing jobs from both countries to Mexico. All three NAFTA members will be carefully monitoring and enforcing the agreement to ensure that ingredients and components originating in "fourth" countries do not use the agreement to obtain unfair preferential access to the North American market.

Every business interested in competing in the North American marketplace should already be examining the outlines of the NAFTA agreement (CFTA is a good working model) and determining how to adjust its operations to take advantage of the pact.

The United States/Canada Free Trade Agreement (CFTA)

CFTA went into effect on January 1, 1989. The objectives of that agreement were manifold and included these goals, among others:

1. To eliminate all tariffs on all goods traded between these two countries over a short period of time.

2. To reduce artificial barriers to the free movement of labor and capital (people and money).

3. To give each nation's financial institutions equal access to the other market.

4. To improve cultural relations between the countries.

In practice, much of the agreement has been a success. Tariffs have gone down. In the planned three-phase tariff reduction, many tariffs were eliminated in 1989 on implementation. The five-year schedule is on track, and many industries have elected to drop tariffs ahead of schedule. This is done by industry application to each government, negotiations, testimony, and review.

The 10-year schedule of 10 percent reductions per year through 1998 is also on track, again with a number of industries seeking acceleration of these reduction schedules.

The overall effects have been positive from the U.S. standpoint, but not from the Canadian. U.S. corporations have a significant ownership interest in the natural resources of Canada. These interests have expanded; this increase in control of assets by foreign firms concerns many in the Canadian public and private sectors. There is strong feeling that the CFTA has and will have permanent negative effects on the Canadian economy. From the Canadian perspective, this is a reasonable concern.

In addition, expansion of investment activities by U.S. firms into Canada has decreased from the pre-1989 pace. It is no longer necessary for a U.S. company to have manufacturing or distribution facilities in Canada to effectively serve the market; it can be done from existing U.S. facilities because the border barriers have been reduced. (The same theory applies to the Single Market in the EC.) This decrease in the rate of increase in U.S. investment in Canada has dampened some of the growth in the Canadian economy, decreased GNP growth, impacted employment, and reduced the general revenues of the government.

Some industry sectors have not adapted to the word and spirit of the CFTA, particularly concerning agriculture and forest products. Both the U.S. and Canadian governments and private-sector producers have equally strong self-interests. Each nation believes that its timber-harvest and wood-products-industry support programs are fair and reasonable. Each nation believes its agricultural-support programs are needed. The result is continued disharmony in the affected industries and disputes that are not resolved within the context of the CFTA. These are problem areas for both countries. U.S. firms active in the forest products or agricultural products sectors may have difficulty expanding their activities in Canada.

The CFTA has opened Canada's strongly unionized cost structure to U.S. competition, with particular impact on the retail sector. Canadians regularly cross the border to purchase U.S. goods, leaving the shelves of Canadian retailers full. Many of the largest Canadian retailers are consolidating, pulling back, and shutting down operations.[4]

Competitive pressure from the United States may cause a change in the basic social programs of Canada. Canadian opposition to the CFTA is reported as high as 54 percent, and politicians that support free trade are in jeopardy.[5]

The United States/Mexico Free Trade Agreement

In December 1991, the presidents of the United States and Mexico met and agreed to establish the draft US/Mexico Free Trade Agreement, which was redirected to include Canada at its insistence and is now called the NAFTA. Fast-track negotiating authority was granted to the president of the United States in July of 1991. Final agreement among the President of the United States, the Prime Minister of Canada, and the President of Mexico was reached in August 1992 and was submitted to Congress for approval or rejection as a whole. The U.S. Department of Commerce states that the objective of the NAFTA is to improve export markets for U.S. goods and services, with emphasis on the export of services. The NAFTA will probably be similar to the CFTA. It also means:

1. Greater access to a potentially dynamic and growing market by the reduction and removal of tariffs and import permits.

2. Improved access for services and investment activities.

3. The protection of intellectual property rights.

4. Strengthening a U.S. competitive advantage not accessible by our international competitors.[6]

Mexico has one common language, which is also the second language of the United States (first for over 25 percent of the U.S. population). Demographers and others have projected Spanish to be the language of over 50 percent of the population of Southern California, Arizona, New Mexico, and Texas within the next decade. The U.S. has accepted the Mexican culture and its

---

[4]"International Outlook," *Business Week*, January 27, 1992.

[5]ibid.

[6]"North American Free Trade Agreement: Generating Jobs for Americans," *Business America*, April 8, 1991.

people. This is a major building block for increased interaction with the Mexican economy.

Mexico is rapidly recovering from the traumas of the 1980s, which brought triple-digit inflation, massive unemployment, debt abrogation and renegotiation, and deflation to an already poor country. Since 1989, there have been major changes in Mexican government policy in:

1. *International trade.* There are reduced import tariffs, quotas, and other restrictions.

2. *Foreign investment.* Many sectors of Mexican industry can now be majority or wholly owned by foreign nationals (petroleum industries excluded).

3. *The environment.* The government has joined with the United States and others in forums and agreements to move toward improved environmental standards and enforcement.

4. *The notion of economic interdependence.* The economy is more open to trade and investment. The Mexican drive for the NAFTA is a centerpiece of its government.

Parameters of the NAFTA

The reduction and elimination of trade barriers under the NAFTA will increase cross-border activity in goods and services and lead to improved mobility for people and capital. There is a tremendous spread in the size and wealth of these three economies. Both Canada and Mexico offer diverse and long-term opportunities for U.S. exporters. Tables 22.1 and 22.2 give a useful and quick view of many of the major characteristics of each economy.

The USDOC regularly updates its report on the "Best Export Prospects" for each U.S. export market. Recent reports suggest that Canada and Mexico will be good markets for the U.S. exports shown in Table 22.3. Other goods

Table 22.1

Country	Pop., millions	Pop. Growth Rate %	GNP US$ Billion	GNP Growth Rate %	GNP per Capita	Literacy Rate %
USA	253.0	.9%	4,961.0	1.0%	19,800	96%
Canada	26.7	.8	474.1	4.1	17,300	96
Mexico	86.0*	2.2	228.0*	3.0*	2,651*	90
Totals	365.7		5,663.1			

Source: Adapted from PC Globe 4.0, 1991. Published by PC Globe, Inc., Tempe, AZ.
*Source: IMF; U.S. Embassy, Mexico City.

Table 22.2

| | Composition of Economy | | | | | |
Country	% Agr.	% Indust.	% Serv.	Language	Religion	% Urban
USA	2	38	60	English	Protestant	73.7
				Spanish	Catholic	
Canada	4	36	60	English	Catholic	76.5
				French	Protestant	
Mexico	9	39	52	Spanish	Catholic	66.3

Source: PC Globe 4.0, 1991.

and services also have excellent market potential. These market potentials can be identified by conducting the research recommended in Part One.

MAJOR ISSUES FOR EXPORTERS

Distribution

The population centers of Canada are within 100 miles of the U.S./Canadian border. The six largest, in order, are Toronto (3.4 million), Montreal, Vancouver, Ottawa, Calgary, Winnipeg, and Edmonton (smallest of the six at

Table 22.3
Best Export Prospects

Product Group	Canada	Mexico
Apparel		X
Auto parts and service equipment		X
Chemical production machinery		X
Computer systems, peripherals, and services		X
Computer software	X	X
Cosmetics and toiletries		X
Electronic components	X	
Industrial chemicals		X
Industrial machinery	X	
Machine tolls and metalworking equipment		X
Medical equipment	X	
Oil and gas field machinery and equipment		X
Pollution control equipment	X	
Plastic materials and resins	X	X
Telecommunications equipment	X	X

Source: U.S. Department of Commerce, 1992. Industry sectors that offer significant export opportunities are not subject to rapid change. The prospects listed were reported in 1991 for each country market.

600,000). Truck, rail, and air transportation are excellent to all major centers. While Canada has only two Free Trade Zones for receipt of imports, many large and responsible customs brokers provide warehousing and distribution services from within Canada. Communications facilities are excellent. Business transactions do not require an on-site presence in Canada for effective completion. Use caution with mail to or within Canada, as the postal service is known for frequent and difficult strikes and work stoppages.

The population in Mexico is less concentrated than in Canada. The eight largest cities, in order, are Mexico City, the federal capital (8.8 million), Guadalajara, Monterrey, Puebla, Leon, Ciudad Juarez, Culiacan, and Mexicali (smallest of the eight at 500,000). National highways are not as well developed as in the United States or Canada. The rail system is government owned and less extensive than comparable systems in the United States or Canada. Major U.S. air carriers do not offer frequent cargo service to all larger cities, as they do in Canada. Communications is more problematic due to the quality and availability of telephone systems at all major points. Mail is less reliable than in either the United States or Canada.

Language

Canadian law requires bilingual marking and promotion. In western Canada, English can be prominent with French available on the package. In the east, French and English must be equally prominent. Service, operating, and other instructions must be in both languages. Communications with prospects, representatives, and others may require both languages. French is required in Québec and may be expected in Ontario.

Spanish is the language of Mexico, although most Mexican businesspeople speak, read, and understand American English. Your promotions, communications, packaging, and other printed information should always be in Spanish, with English added if you wish.

Legal Systems

Your export activities in Canada or Mexico are governed by U.S. law and may be subject to Canadian or Mexican law. This may seem apparent, but your sales and marketing representatives may not appreciate the ramifications. Sales contracts, distribution agreements, and other business arrangements should be negotiated to include dispute resolution provisions with *choice of law* and *jurisdiction clauses*. Different cultures present the opportunity for disputes and disagreements over things we may not appreciate.

Certificates of Origin

The CFTA requires that exports have a Certificate of Origin with each shipment. You must certify that your goods are of more than 50 percent U.S.

origin (70 percent in some instances) so your export can benefit from the CFTA duty treatment.

When the NAFTA is approved and comes into force, the U.S. Department of Commerce, the U.S. Treasury Department, and U.S. Customs will conduct regional training programs in the use and completion of origin documents and other provisions of the NAFTA. The Certificate of Origin will be similar to that required by the CFTA.

Foreign Exchange

Most U.S. exporters do not quote or sell in the buyer's currency. This is a mistake. Our competitors do it, because a price in the buyer's currency makes the purchase decision easier. See Chapter 13 for a discussion of how this factor can improve your competitive posture in export markets.

Canadian exporters quote and sell in U.S. dollars. Catalogs, promotions, and other materials have prices in U.S. dollars. It's customary and expected. The relationship between the U.S. dollar and Canadian dollar is pretty stable. With the added stability of the CFTA, it is likely that over the near term the currency values will remain within a relatively narrow trading range. The perceived risks of export transactions denominated in the Canadian dollar will diminish.

The Mexican peso (M$), currently at M$3,106/US$,[7] will continue to devalue. This fairly regular devaluation is a government objective, to keep Mexican goods and services competitively priced in the world market. A low peso encourages exports, supports slow growth of imports, and discourages private external debt.

There is no forward market in the Mexican peso (M$). Exporters who wish to quote in that currency will be "open" or exposed to some uncertainty, which increases as the length of the payment term is extended (see "Export Strategies" below).

Trade Barriers

A free trade agreement does not create a common market, so some internal barriers will remain. The NAFTA will not address:

1. The free movement of people from country to country.
2. The general equivalence of commercial laws and their applications across borders.
3. Taxation on incomes, sales, and other transactions.
4. Ownership of land, natural resources, or factors of production.
5. The free movement of capital.

[7]*The Journal of Commerce,* September 29, 1992.

EXPORT STRATEGY CONSIDERATIONS

Canada is a sophisticated, industrialized, and technologically literate market. Commercial, industrial, and consumer products that have been accepted in the United States generally will find ready acceptance in Canada.

Mexico is a rapidly developing country with significant demands for industrial goods. The market for commercial goods is strong but that sector will be quick to develop internally. Consumer demand is strong across the country, driven by the improved economic environment. The structure of consumer distribution is changing toward more mass merchandising and shopping centers, from village shops and small, widely dispersed general retailers. The population is becoming more urban. The service sector is growing rapidly.

Where to Start

History, culture, government attitudes and policies, and economic realities encourage your exports to Canada and Mexico. Carry out the research program discussed in Part One. Use the resources of the Office of Canada and the Office of Mexico at the USDOC in Washington, DC.

Canada and Mexico have consular offices in a number of U.S. cities. They will not specifically encourage your exports to their country but they can provide you with industry and country information that will be useful.

The U.S. government has consulates and commercial offices across each country. For Canada, offices are in Ottawa, Calgary, Halifax, Montreal, Quebec, Toronto, and Vancouver. For Mexico, offices are in Mexico D.F., Ciudad Juarez, Guadalajara, Monterrey, Hermosillo, Matamoros, Mazatlan, Merida, and Nuevo Laredo.

The U.S. government actively sponsors trade shows in each country. Contact your industry or trade group and ask about trade shows, meetings, conventions, and other activities it may have planned for either market over your near term.

Problem Areas

The problems that U.S. exporters encounter in Canada center on origin-of-goods issues, communicating in French, and managing the costs of distribution to geographically dispersed markets.

In Mexico, language, cultural realities, credit, and internal distribution are the dominant problem areas. Banking and finance is one problem on this short list where you must turn to a third party for help; that's the problem.

Financing your export activity can be a problem, depending on the market, the size of your company, and other factors. Mexico is seen by many lenders as a foreign and therefore "risky" market, while U.S. banks generally look on Canada as additional domestic business. Mexico began its recovery from the financial nightmare of the mid 1980s just as U.S. banks entered the real estate and leveraged buyout business. Foreign was out, large and local was in. Losses in these businesses, on top of prior losses in oil and gas, real estate, LBOs, REITs, leasing, credit cards, foreign loans, and consumer loans forced banks to consolidate to survive. Fewer and more risk-averse banks mean less trade finance, particularly to markets like Mexico.

In mid-1992, a few major U.S. banks began to offer highly structured export financing programs for U.S. exporters selling to Mexico. Lines of credit, for short-term and medium-term loans, to finance Mexican imports of U.S. goods and services were established by the U.S. banks in favor of Mexican financial institutions under the guarantee of Eximbank.

Interested exporters should contact their international banking department and inquire about Eximbank-guaranteed buyer credits for exports to Mexico.

Foreign exchange exposure management can be a problem area. The risk varies with the currency of sale and the terms of payment granted to the buyer. In Canada, your forward exposure can be covered for periods beyond six months. If you have a good or working credit relationship with your bank, it takes only a telephone call. In Mexico, you must be more creative to deal in pesos:

1. Price your product at an inflated peso rate, that is, adjusted for the exchange rate devaluation you believe may occur over the payment term. An example of a simple FX adjustment calculation is:

Value of the M$ today	3,108/US$
Projected devaluation in three months	10% p.a.
This is your best guess:	
Formula: 3,108 + ([3,108 x 0.10][90/360])	
Your projected M$ rate in 90 days is:	3,185.70/US$

2. Accept other goods or services in exchange. If you or an associate import from or invest in Mexico, this may be an excellent arrangement, which also demonstrates your creativity and flexibility—important attributes for an international businessperson.

American businesspeople often overlook or ignore the differences in culture between Mexico and the United States and between Canada and the United States. Mexico has a cultural heritage much different from the rest of North America. Failure to understand the cultural perspective of your representative and his or her clients can cost you sales and long-term success. Latin business styles are different. Personal interaction is different. Negotiating styles are different. Learn about these differences and take advantage of the opportunity to enjoy a very different society when you travel to Mexico.

Although the growth and development of the United States and Canada has been largely parallel, we differ markedly in politics, economic persuasion, social perspective, and motivations. Canada is a different country and the U.S. exporter is well served by understanding this. Canadian businesspeople are more English, French, or European than American. This means there is a difference in the level of formality, negotiating style, expectations, timing, and other business factors.

SUMMARY

The benefits of the NAFTA for U.S. exporters have been identified. The NAFTA expands the borders of the United States, both north and south. A 253-million-person market becomes a market of 367 million people with a per capita GNP of US$15,400. The NAFTA market is similar to the EC's Single Market in wealth, purchasing power, and export and import trade.

For manufacturers, Mexico offers a low-cost, close, adaptable work force—a work force often employed by Japanese and other Asian and European manufacturers as a low-cost labor pool for goods that will be sold into the United States and Canada.

The NAFTA will eventually eliminate tariff and quota barriers among the member countries. During this time, there will be some difficulty with Canada and Mexico because of the disproportionate size and influence of the U.S. economy. Agricultural interests in the United States and Canada are concerned about agricultural productivity in Mexico. Mexico and Canada are concerned about U.S. multinational ownership of their industries and resources. The United States is concerned about Canadian agricultural and forest products industries. The United States and Canada are concerned about Mexican environmental laws and health services. These problems are part of growth. They will be resolved.

Each market is an opportunity. The NAFTA places U.S. firms in an excellent position to gather resources, increase productivity and marginal efficiencies, decrease production costs, and export to other markets more effectively. External barriers—the duty and quota structures that exist in Canada, the United States, and Mexico—will not change. However, the scope of the intranational market and enforcement of its North America policies will change the nature of exports to North America. This change breeds opportunity for U.S. exporters.

RESOURCES

1. Key Mexican contacts, by agency of the U.S. government:

   Commerce   202-482-4464
   Agriculture   202-447-3221

Eximbank	202-566-8234
Labor	202-523-8538
State	202-647-9292
U.S. Trade Rep.	202-395-5663

For an up-to-date listing of key contacts, telephone the Office of Mexico at the U.S. Department of Commerce (phone number above).

2. Key Canada contacts are available from the Office of Canada at the USDOC. Tel: 202-482-3101; fax: 202-482-3718.

3. The Office of Mexico and the Office of Canada in the USDOC collect, maintain, and distribute a wide variety of information regarding business with and in each country.

4. Laredo State University, a part of the Texas A&M system, publishes a well-researched, monthly update on Mexico-U.S. trade and the NAFTA called *Free-Trade Winds*. Subscribe by letter, telephone, or fax to: The Office for the Study of U.S./Mexico Trade Relations, Laredo State University, One West End Washington St., Laredo, TX 78040-9960. Tel: 512-722-8001 x338; fax: 512-725-3348.

5. The USDOC booklet *US-Canada Free Trade Agreement Guide to Exporting Procedures*, April 1989, provides direction on the rules of origin and completion of the CFTA Certificates of Origin forms. For assistance or training in completion of the forms, contact your freight forwarder or international trade consultant.

6. Neville, Peterson & Williams, Counselors at Law, with offices in New York and Washington, DC, specialize in international trade and customs law. The firm publishes the *Global Trade Report*, an excellent monthly newsletter that addresses import, export, and customs issues. Their address is:

Neville, Peterson & Williams
39 Broadway
New York, NY 10006
Tel: 212-635-2730
Fax: 212-635-2734

Dickey, Neville, et al. . . .
2300 N St., NW, Suite 600
Washington, DC 20037
Tel: 202-663-9036
Fax: 202-223-1512

PART SEVEN
Summary

In early 1992, the American Management Association (AMA) issued a report on its 1991 Survey on International Management. Of the top ten organizationwide issues that command the attention of the senior international executives, respondents stated that five of these issues concerned marketing to economies outside the United States. Three of the top issues concerned the international strategy of the firm. Operations and finance round out the top ten. In his summary of the findings, Spencer Hayden, founder of the Center for International Management Studies and consultant to the AMA, states that the findings zero in on the three most troublesome needs: to have a sound strategy, do good marketing, and exercise strong financial and quality controls.[1]

This book has identified the major factors in the development and implementation of an export business. Chapter 23 identifies the planning issues you must address. It provides a framework for, but will not tell you how to write, a business plan—that information is available from a library and bookstore. Business plans in various forms have been with us for well over a hundred years. The general goals of the plan have not changed; the contents and presentation are different and more sophisticated.

Success in the export business does not depend on the size of your company. It does depend on a number of factors that have been identified, starting with commitment. Other factors are the quality of your product (a good or service), the after-sale service you provide, the pricing of the product, the quality of your in-country representation, and your flexibility.

Sole proprietorships, partnerships, corporations, joint ventures, and associations can all be successful in the export marketplace. Structurally, export activity can be conducted and managed as a department, division, subsidiary,

---

[1]Adapted from *The 1991 AMA Survey on International Management,* copyright 1991, American Management Association, New York, NY.

independent reporting unit, or as the sole activity of the firm. In its infancy, exporting can occur within an existing general sales structure under the caveat that it will receive the necessary support so that exports can grow and contribute to the profitability of the company as a whole.

Many new companies have recognized the potential sales and profit opportunities available by expanding their market scope beyond the United States. One example is Aldus Corporation, a young company and a leading developer of desktop publishing software. Its international managers report that, from day one, it was going to be a global company. As a result of that decision and the commitment of executive management, Aldus acts like a global company. The international marketability of its products is on the agenda from the concept stage, through packaging, positioning, and marketing. These are keys to success.

Your products can be simple or sophisticated. The issues are the same. However, the nature of your product(s) will dictate your approach to the resolution of each issue. For example, an exporter of consumer goods such as table-top items must deal with the issue of export licensing from a different perspective than a manufacturer of computer data storage devices.

Each type of company must understand the nature of its product and the realities of the markets into which the product will be marketed. Ethnocentrism and a self-reference criterion will blind you to the realities of your target markets. Do not let them. Each market is always different in some way. Product adaptation— in packaging, language, size, color, or promotion—may be necessary. These types of decisions cannot be made without an understanding of the needs and perspectives of your selected markets.

Another example of a working and profitable export market entry is that of Recreational Equipment, Inc. REI is a leading retailer of outdoor recreational clothing and equipment. It is a consumer cooperative. In early 1992, it reported significant growth in its sales to Japan, an increase of 70 percent over the prior year, with projections of 50 percent growth rates for the next few years. All sales were by mail order, and early sales were unsolicited (recall the comments by Mike Giambattista in Part Two). To expand its sales to Japan, REI hired a Japanese consultant. This person provides on-site, after-sale service in Japan, assists with media and public relations activities in Japan, assists in the development of effective marketing brochures, and works with Japanese outdoor groups (whose members represent the target market).

REI has adapted its Japan strategy to the expectations of the market. Most of its Japanese members want English-language catalogs with prices in U.S. dollars, to see that they are getting the same goods at the same price as U.S. members. A special brochure was developed for the Japan market describing, for example, which U.S. sizes might be appropriate for Japanese buyers. It added designer logos to some items because designer logos are popular in Japan.

REI accepts payment by credit card in Japanese yen (¥) or U.S. dollars. They make express delivery arrangements with DHL, an international air freight company, so packages arrive in the customer's home in Japan within seven days.

None of these actions is a major or costly disruption in the activity of REI. These sales provide a new and potentially important market for its products. This strategy is entirely appropriate for REI. It works for the company because "you can't just have the same strategy you have in the U.S. and apply it to Japan," states Jim Cross, manager of mail order for REI.[2]

Chapter 23 provides guidance on the nature and structure of an export business plan. There are many resources available to guide you in writing a business plan. The critical issue of your export plan is the critical issue for your company: commitment by executive management.

[2]Adapted from Tom Brown, "A Yen to Mail Order," *Seattle Times,* February 10, 1992, p. C1.

23 Your Export Plan

Any business activity you undertake warrants some degree of planning. The type of planning covered in this chapter is specifically for your export business. It does not include issues of budgeting, an expenditure plan for personnel, capital goods, or operations. Nor does the procedure discussed here deal with raising capital from the public, venture capitalists, or lenders. What follows is a market identification, entry, and development plan for what could be the most important market for your business.

Export activity can require a significant allocation of your resources. Amounts and percentages of these resources will vary by company, by target market, and by product. Parts One through Six presented material on the nature of the resource commitment you need to make. That commitment will be tempered by the nature of your involvement; indirect export activity requires less from the company than direct export market development and sales.

Corporations plan at three levels. The first, and traditionally the most important, is at the corporate level. As suggested later in this chapter, top-down planning doesn't work. It is not responsive to the world of the 1990s and beyond. A second level of planning is strategic, and the third is the tactical.

This export plan process must be imbedded in each of these levels. At the corporate level, leaders must look to the long term and establish goals for the whole firm. Exporting, and positioning the firm to compete with all comers, must receive a significant amount of attention if it is to be a successful segment of the business. As noted throughout, commitment by the owners, directors, and senior executives of the firm is the foundation for success in exporting or any other company activity. The ability to compete at home will increasingly be determined by how well any firm can compete in the global marketplace.

The strategic plan must deal with the accomplishment of the corporate objectives. These long-term strategies include research and development, production, market development and expansion, strategic partnering, finance, legal, personnel optimization, market research, and survival strategies.

Your tactics are the specific actions your firm will take to implement the strategies. Resources—personnel, financial, and operating—must be allocated. Exporting requires a long-term strategy and tactics based on experience and capabilities. You can acquire the experience (it's a make-or-buy decision). You must fairly assess the capabilities of the firm for export or for any new or expanding business venture.

PLANNING ISSUES

There are six issues you must resolve:

1. Commitment to exporting.
2. Capacity of the firm to support an export effort.
3. Accountability for the export effort.
4. Foreign markets for your product.
5. Market entry.
6. Progress review.

Commitment is the starting point, and each step builds on the previous one. Review, evaluation, criticism, and adjustment are vital to any business, particularly one that deals in foreign environments.

Commitment to Exporting

The critical issue for the success of any export program is the commitment to the export business by the owners or managing executives. The companies with the greatest degree of success in export are those that position exporting as an important business segment capable of broad contributions to the whole company.

This commitment means that the company will allocate necessary resources, including people, capital, production capacity, and time. The commitment means the company will organize for success and establish the export business as a full-time, continuous activity that will receive support and attention through all stages of each business cycle.

Capacity of the Firm to Support an Export Effort

Your business plan must address your company's capacity to enter the export business. Keep in mind these important considerations:

1. Export sales will require increased production capacity, because you are not replacing U.S. sales.

2. Increased volume will require longer production runs or longer work days.

3. Inventories will increase, so storage requirements will increase. Export shipments will occur less frequently to optimize the cost of transportation and documentation.

4. Outstanding accounts receivable will increase. Days sales outstanding (DSO) may increase. Account follow up will be necessary.

5. Adequate funds to research, develop, and penetrate new markets must be made available.

6. The market-entry process can take longer than the expansion of your business to another domestic market. Prepare for this and allocate sufficient resources.

Accountability for the Export Effort

Assign responsibility for the export business to one person. Give that person the authority to do the job. Hold that person to strict and quantifiable performance measurements. The export executive should be senior, a peer with line managers of other important business segments, in a position to expect and receive the support of the whole company and negotiate accordingly. That person must have your full support unless performance does not occur. A serious commitment to exporting means a serious commitment of management talent, not a part-time or "additional" assignment. This is not the time to see if the new hire will work out. Exporting is probably the most important market-entry project your company will ever take on.

Foreign Markets for Your Product

The market research process and procedures covered in Part One will quickly direct your company to a number of markets for your goods or services. This research will confirm your opportunities, opportunities based on the unsolicited inquiries you receive in response to word-of-mouth or your advertising to the trade.

Foreign buyers are interested in U.S. products. Demand is good to high in almost every country for most U.S. products. Your challenge is to quantify the demand, identify the potential buyers, contact them, and establish relationships. Establish a structure to do this. Part Two will help you develop that structure.

Market Entry

You will identify representatives (reps, agents, distributors, or joint-venture partners) who will market your products in the foreign country. Your representative(s) will require your full support in a number of important areas. These include:

1. Pricing to the particular market.
2. Customer service, on site or on demand.
3. Financing: you may have to grant terms to compete.
   a. Your distributor will want terms.
   b. The end user will want terms.
4. Cost-effective and timely transportation from the United States to the buyer.
5. Packaging, marking, and labeling.
6. Translations, promotional material, trade show support, training, and more.

Every market will have its own requirements. Start with one market. Develop your skills and systems. Then expand. Succeed in one market; use that success as a steppingstone, a reference, a building block. This success breeds confidence, which supports the management commitment, which leads to the next success.

Progress Review

If you own or manage the company, review the performance of your export executive on a regular and frequent basis. Negotiate milestones and timelines. Review progress and performance at least quarterly; world economic and political environments change, which will impact your business.

If you are the export executive, establish goals and timelines by negotiation within your chain of command or management structure. Discuss these goals and expectations with your personnel. Delegate or dispose of everything that does not help you move toward those goals.

Focus is important in the export business; there are so many opportunities that you may easily find yourself chasing them all. This dissipates your energy, wastes time, and wastes money.

AN EXPORT BUSINESS PLAN OUTLINE

"Keep it simple. Strive to keep your plan to 10 pages or less."[1] This is good advice. Without care, the business plan can take on a life of its own. A business plan is a document that tells you two basic things:

[1]Paul Parish of Grant Thornton, CPAs, in "Business Plans: Blueprints for Success," *Your Company* (New York: American Express Publishing Corp., Winter 1992).

1. Where you are.

2. Where you are going.

Variations on the plan deal with how you are going to get there. These include financing, personnel, technical data, and so on.

The value of the business plan lies in how you use it. If you write a business plan because this book, a mentor, a consultant, or your bank tells you to, you won't buy into the value of the plan. Write the business plan because you want to understand:

1. Where you are.

2. What you are positioned to accomplish.

3. What goals you have established.

4. What you have decided not to do.

5. How you have allocated duties and functions.

6. What your objectives are for the short-term and the near term.

The business plan can have life and meaning and will be a valuable management tool for your business. Going through the process "forces you to rethink all aspects of your enterprise—always a valuable exercise."[2] If you do not agree with this, don't write a business plan for the export business—or any other activity.

Outline of Your Export Plan

Following is a summary outline of a plan for your export business. Draw on the other members of your management team, your directors, and your outside advisors or mentors for suggestions and criticisms. A top-down plan, without the "buy-in" of the collaborative process, can easily fail. Division or department heads, functional managers, and line personnel can make valuable contributions at the front end of the plan and throughout the process. Use their knowledge of their piece of the company. (You should have hired the very best people you could find for the tasks to be accomplished. If you did, they know far more about their area of responsibility than you do!)

Your directors or advisory board (your mentor group) may have a wealth of experience in international business or exporting.[3] They are interested in your success and will be pleased with the opportunity to contribute their perspectives to your plan.

---

[2]Ibid.

[3]If your board or advisors do not have hands-on experience in this field, seek out and acquire one or more board members or advisors with this type of knowledge.

With this type of active participation, the plan will be assured of a positive reception. There will be companywide enthusiastic efforts to make it work. Exporting should be a companywide process, just like cost control, quality, and customer service.

Framework for the Export Plan

The export business plan includes the following:

1. The objective of the plan. Why the plan is being written, the purpose it will serve.
2. Your company and product and your place in your industry, in the United States and worldwide.
   a. Organizational structure, commitment, accountabilities.
   b. Competitive advantages of your product.
   c. Company resources available for dedication, or allocation, to the export business segment.
   d. Goals and objectives for export business.
      (1) The objective performance parameters for this business segment, in terms of such factors as increased unit sales, decreased marginal cost of production per unit, increased sales by dollar volume or units sold, by product type.
      (2) Market share or new markets entered.
   e. Date for performance review, plan review, and rewrite.
      (1) A written schedule for review of personal performance for those in charge of this business segment.
      (2) A written schedule and procedure for review of performance compared to the plan.
      (3) An institutionalized mechanism to modify the plan as needed, to adjust for the success that has been achieved, to adjust the plan parameters to the realities of the target markets, to adjust to the demonstrated capacities of the personnel involved.
3. Market factors.
   a. Parameters of the "ideal" target market.
      (1) Characteristics of those markets best suited to your product. These will vary by type of product but could include, for example:
         (a) Per capita GNP.
         (b) GNP growth rate.
         (c) Size of the prospect segment, in population, purchasing power, number of units per market, and so on.

(d) Disposable income per person, or liquidity within the commercial market.

(e) Level of education or degree of literacy.

b. Target market research plan.

(1) Secondary research.

(a) Research resources.

(b) Research requirements.

(2) Primary research.

(a) What information do you need?

(b) Who will conduct this research?

c. Risk-analysis process.

(1) Financial risks.

(2) Country risks.

(a) Political.

(b) Commercial.

(c) Exchange.

(d) Transfer.

(3) Product risks.

(4) Capacity of the firm to absorb, mitigate, or eliminate these risks.

d. Selection of direct or indirect market entry strategies, based on findings of 2c.

(1) Direct, if the company has the capacity to effectively manage these risks.

(2) Indirect, if the company does not have the capacity, or if the company elects to concentrate on certain markets and use indirect programs for other markets.

4. Marketing strategy.

a. Representative development (direct or indirect).

(1) A function of 2d, the answer to which will drive the balance of the plan through item 6.

b. Pricing policies.

(1) Based on selection of one or more of the pricing strategies presented in Part Two.

c. Promotion strategies.

(1) Available media.

(2) Requirements of the marketplace.

(3) Services required to implement promotion strategies.

d. Buyer-financing strategies.

(1) Availability of international banking expertise to the company.

(2) Export guarantee or risk insurance programs.

(3) Competitive requirements.

(4) Other buyer or transaction finance options.

    e. Logistics management.
      (1) Internal controls on inventory.
      (2) Transportation services and capacities.
      (3) Special handling requirements of the goods.
    f. Service strategy.
      (1) Service in-country or remote.
      (2) Service company or representative.
        (a) Required capabilities.
      (3) Train representatives in-country.
      (4) Support: equipment, manuals, communications.
      (5) Training updates, in-house programs, frequency.
    g. Performance evaluation parameters and procedures.
      (1) Determination of objective measures of performance.
      (2) Institutionalized evaluation procedures.

5. Budgeting.
    a. Sales forecasts.
      (1) Basis for forecasts.
      (2) Variables.
    b. Sales finance requirements.
      (1) Capital or capacity available to support sales programs.
      (2) Cost of sales financing and recapture provisions.
    c. Financing requirements.
      (1) See 4a above. Requirements will differ based on entry strategies
         and channels selected.
      (2) Ability of firm to acquire export financing services and export
         credit facilities.
    d. Financial projections.
      (1) Baseline unit sales projections, adjusted down to acknowledge
         resistance from a new foreign market.
      (2) Experience-based projections.
        (a) Trade or industry experience in the marketplace.

6. Performance evaluation.
    a. Timetables.
      (1) Frequency of evaluations.
        (a) Markets.
        (b) Programs.
        (c) Personnel.
    b. Objective measurement criteria.
      (1) Dynamics of export markets.
        (a) Political change.
        (b) Economic change.
        (c) Competitor performance in same market.

(d) U.S. policy impacts.

(2) Unit sales, by product.

(3) Gross revenues.

(4) Performance compared to plan, acceptable range.

c. Action steps.

(1) Structure of the evaluation process.

(2) Level of evaluation (who does the evaluating).

7. Rewrite plan for next period.

a. Review the product line, make adjustments.

b. Review the market factors, adjust.

c. Review the market entry and marketing strategies.

d. Determine objectives for next planning period.

(1) Three planning periods.

(a) Near term, six months or one year.

(b) Two to three years.

(c) Five years.

e. Implement the new or revised plan.

This framework can be easily modified to suit the needs of your organization. The objective of the plan is to position the company for a new business activity or to expand and enhance existing offshore market activities. A business plan to seek debt or equity capital is a completely different issue.

SUMMARY

A business plan is not static. It is not a highway map with roads made of stone and concrete. It's a topographic map showing the hills and valleys you will encounter; it states how you will traverse the landscape and the processes you will use when you reach fixed or immovable barriers.

The export business can be an exciting walk across the world. It requires focus, commitment, and enthusiasm. Each culture is an adventure. Each client is a potential friend. Each market is a profit opportunity. Give your export business the same attention and commitment you give to your U.S. business and you will succeed.

RESOURCES

1. *Your International Business Plan, a Workbook for Owners of Small Businesses* is available from: Oregon Small Business Development Center Network, 99 West 10th Ave., Suite 216, Eugene, OR 97401-3017. Tel: 503-726-2250. This workbook provides a question/answer format

to create a business plan document. It is tailored to the small business community.

2. The U.S. Small Business Administration has an international department structured to provide information and assistance to small companies.[4] In addition, the SBA co-sponsors Small Business Development Centers across the United States. These centers provide assistance to small firms in the business planning process.

3. Large or emerging companies can acquire the assistance of international business experts to support their development of export plans. Many of these international trade consultants can assist your executives in marketing, market research, financing, and risk management. The US&FCS offices have been instructed to work with larger, established companies, those with a greater potential for success in exporting.

4. The US&FCS district offices will assist companies that seek to expand their export activity or make initial entry into the business. The Export Qualifier Program discussed in Part One can give you some basic background on issues you must resolve. It's good background, a firm starting point. It is not perfect, not comprehensive, and not authoritative, but it gives you and the US&FCS trade specialist a common ground for further discussions. Smaller firms may be directed to state trade development offices, community college programs, and other resources.

[4]The SBA definition of a small company varies by SIC code.

Appendix A
International Trade
Administration/US&FCS
District Offices

District offices are staffed with a director, one or more trade specialists, a trade reference assistant, and interns. Branch offices are staffed with a trade specialist. *Note:* Addresses and telephone numbers were accurate at the time this book was written; however, they do change periodically.

Each office can provide you with access to the complete range of U.S Department of Commerce International Trade Services.[1] These services include:

1. Market Identification and Assessment
   a. U.S. Merchandise Trade: Exports, General Imports and Imports for Consumption, FT-925; U.S. Exports and Imports—Commodity by Country
   b. Overseas Business Reports
   c. Foreign Economic Trends

2. Market Research Reports
   a. Market Research Extracts
   b. Industry Sector Analyses
   c. U.S. and United Nations Trade Data

3. Trade Contact Services
   a. Agent/Distributor Service
   b. New Comparison Shopping Service
   c. World Traders Data Report

[1]For export licensing, contact the Bureau of Export Administration. See Chapter 18.

    d. New Product Information Service

    e. Foreign Traders Index

    f. Trade Opportunities Program/TOP Leads

    g. Electronic Bulletin Board

4. Overseas Export Promotion

    a. Solo Exhibits

    b. International Trade Fairs

    c. Catalog Shows

    d. Trade Missions

    e. Matchmaker Events

    f. Video Catalog Exhibitions

5. Export Regulations, Documentation, and Licensing

6. Educational Workshops and Seminars

US&FCS DISTRICT OFFICES

ALABAMA
Birmingham—Berry Bldg., 2015 2d Ave. No., Rm. 302, 35203, (205)-731-1331

ALASKA
Anchorage—World Trade Center, 4201 Tudor Centre Dr., Rm. 319, 99508 (907)-271-6237

ARIZONA
Phoenix—Federal Bldg., 230 N. 1st Ave., Rm. 3412, 85025, (602)-379-3285

ARKANSAS
Little Rock—Savers Federal Bldg., 320 W. Capitol Ave., Rm. 811, 72201, (501)-324-5794

CALIFORNIA
Los Angeles—11000 Wilshire Blvd., Rm. 9200, 90024, (213)-575-7104

Santa Ana—116-A W. 4th St., Rm. 1, 92701, (714)-836-2461

San Diego—6363 Greenwich Dr., Rm. 145, 92122, (619)-557-5395

*San Francisco—250 Montgomery St., 14th Flr., 94104, (415)-705-2300

COLORADO
*Denver—1625 Broadway, Rm. 680, 80202, (303)-844-3246

CONNECTICUT
*Hartford—Federal Bldg., 450 Main St., Rm. 610-B, 06103, (203)-240-3530

DELAWARE—See Philadelphia, PA

FLORIDA
Miami—Federal Bldg., 51 S.W. First Ave., Rm. 224, 33130, (305)-536-5267

+Clearwater—128 N. Osceola Ave., 34615, (813)-461-0011

+Orlando—UCF, CEBA II, Rm. 346, 32816, (407)-648-6235

+Tallahassee—Collins Bldg., 107 W. Gaines St., Rm. 401, 32304, (904)-488-6469

GEORGIA
Atlanta—Plaza Square North, 4360 Chamblee Dunwoody Rd., 30341, (404)-452-9101

Savannah—120 Bernard St., Rm. A-107, 31401, (912)-944-4204

HAWAII
Honolulu—300 Ala Moana Blvd., 96850, (808)-541-1782

IDAHO
⁺Boise—J.R. Williams Bldg., 700 W. State St., 2d Flr., 82720, (208)-344-3857

ILLINOIS
Chicago—55 E. Monroe St., Rm. 1406, 60603, (312)-353-4450

⁺Wheaton—Illinois Inst. of Technology, 201 E. Loop Rd., 60187, (312)-353-4332

⁺Rockford—515 N. Court St., 61110-0247, (815)-987-8123

INDIANA
Indianapolis—One North Capitol Ave., Rm. 520, 46204, (515)-284-4222

IOWA
Des Moines—Federal Bldg., 210 Walnut St., Rm. 817, 50309, (515)-284-4222

⁺Cedar Rapids—424 First Ave., NE, 52401, (319)-362-8418

KANSAS
⁺Wichita—151 N. Voltusia, 67214-4965, (316)-269-6160

KENTUCKY
Louisville—Snyder Courthouse, 601 W. Broadway, Rm. 636B, 40202, (502)-582-5066

LOUISIANA
New Orleans—World Trade Center, No. 2 Canal St., Rm. 432, 70130, (504)-589-6546

MAINE
⁺Augusta—77 Sewall St., 04330, (207)-622-8249

MARYLAND
Baltimore—U.S. Customhouse, 40 S. Gay St., Rm. 413, 21202, (301)-962-3560

Gaithersburg—Nat'l. Inst. of Standards & Tech., Bldg. 411, 20899, (301)-962-3560

MASSACHUSETTS
Boston—World Trade, Rm. 307, Commonwealth Pier, 02210, (617)-565-8563.

MICHIGAN
Detroit—McNamara Bldg., 477 Michigan Ave., Rm. 1140, 48226, (312)-226-3650

⁺Grand Rapids—300 W. Monroe NW, 49503, (616)-456-2411

MINNESOTA
Minneapolis—Federal Bldg., 110 S. 4th St., Rm. 108, 55401, (612)-348-1638

MISSISSIPPI
Jackson—Jackson Mall Center, 300 Woodrow Wilson Bldg., 39213, (601)-965-4388

MISSOURI
*St. Louis—7911 Forsyth Blvd., Rm. 610, 63105, (314)-425-3302

Kansas City—601 E. 12th St., Rm. 635, 64106, (816)-426-3141

MONTANA—See Portland, OR

NEBRASKA
Omaha—11133 "O" St., 68137, (402)-221-3664

NEVADA
Reno—1755 E. Plumb Lane, No. 152, 89502, (702)-784-5203

NEW HAMPSHIRE—See Boston, MA

NEW JERSEY
Trenton—3131 Princeton Pike Bldg., #6, Rm. 100, 08648, (609)-989-2100

NEW MEXICO
⁺Albuquerque—625 Silver SW, 3d Flr., 87102, (505)-766-2070

⁺Santa Fe—Econ. Devel. Dept., 1100 St. Francis Dr., 87503, (505)-988-6261

NEW YORK
Buffalo—Federal Bldg., 111 W. Huron, Rm. 1312, 14202, (716)-846-4191

⁺Rochester—111 East Ave., Rm. 220, 14604, (716)-263-6480

New York—Federal Bldg., 26 Federal Plaza, Foley Sq., Rm. 3718, 10278, (212)-264-0600

NORTH CAROLINA
*Greensboro—324 W. Market St., Rm. 203, 27402, (919)-333-5345

NORTH DAKOTA—See Omaha, NE

OHIO
*Cincinnati—Federal Bldg., 550 Main St., Rm. 9504, 45202, (513)-684-2944

Cleveland—668 Euclid Ave., Rm. 600, 44114, (216)-522-4750

OKLAHOMA
Oklahoma City—6601 Broadway Extension, 73116, (405)-231-5302

+Tulsa—440 S. Houston St., 74127, (918)-581-7650

OREGON
Portland—121 S.W. Salmon St., 1 World Trade Center, Rm. 242, 97204, (503)-326-3001

PENNSYLVANIA
Philadelphia (King of Prussia)—475 Allendale Rd., Rm. 202, 19406, (215)-962-4980

Pittsburgh—Federal Bldg., 1000 Liberty Ave., Rm. 2002, 15222, (412)-644-2850

PUERTO RICO
San Juan (Hato Rey)—Federal Bldg., Rm. G-55, 00918, (809)-766-5555

RHODE ISLAND
+Providence—7 Jackson Walkway, 02903, (401)-528-5104

SOUTH CAROLINA
Columbia—Federal Bldg., 1835 Assembly St., Rm. 172, 29201, (803)-765-5345

Charleston—J. C. Long Bldg., 9 Liberty St. Rm. 128, 29424, (803)-724-4361

SOUTH DAKOTA—See Omaha, NE

TENNESSEE
Nashville—404 Robertson Pkwy., Parkway Towers, Rm. 1114, 37219-1505, (615)-736-5161

+Knoxville—301 E. Church Ave., 37915, (615)-549-9268

+Memphis—22 No. Front St., Falls Bldg., Rm. 200, 38103, (901)-544-4137

TEXAS
*Dallas—1100 Commerce St., Rm. 7A5, 75242-0787, (214)-767-0542

+Austin—816 Congress Ave., Rm. 1200, 78711, (512)-482-5939

Houston—Federal Courthouse, 515 Rusk St., Rm. 2625, 77002, (713)-229-2578

UTAH
Salt Lake City—324 S. State St., Rm. 105, 84111, (801)-524-5116

VERMONT—See Boston, MA

VIRGINIA
Richmond—Federal Bldg., 400 N. 8th St., 23240, (804)-771-2246

WASHINGTON
Seattle—3131 Elliott Ave., Rm. 290, 98121, (206)-553-5615

+Spokane—W. 808 Spokane Falls Blvd., Rm. 625, 99201, (509)-353-2922

WEST VIRGINIA
Charleston—405 Capitol St., Rm. 809, 25301, (304)-357-5123

WISCONSIN
Milwaukee—Federal Bldg., 517 E. Wisconsin Ave., Rm. 606, 53202, (414)-297-3473

WYOMING—See Denver, CO

* Denotes regional office.

+ Denotes branch office.

Appendix B
US&FCS Overseas
Commercial Sections

The overseas commercial sections of the US&FCS provide incountry services for the International Trade Administration and the U.S. district offices of the US&FCS (listed in Appendix A).

Many of these offices provide the Gold Key service mentioned in the text. The commercial officers at these posts are, with appropriate notice and by prior arrangement, available to assist the US business executive traveling to a foreign location for a sales meeting, trade fair, or other business purpose. The offices are listed by country. The handbook titled *Key Officers of Foreign Service Posts,* available from the U.S. Government Printing Office, has a complete listing with street address and names and titles of personnel at each foreign service post.

US&FCS OVERSEAS COMMERCIAL SECTIONS[1]

ALBANIA
Tirana (AE)—PSC 59, APO AE 09624, Tel. 355-42-33-520/Fax 355-42-32-222

ALGERIA
Algiers (AE)—USDOS (Algiers) WDC 20521-6030, Tel. 213-260-1863/Fax 213-260-1863

ARGENTINA
Buenos Aires (AE)—UNIT 4326, APO AA 34034, Tel. 541-733-1063/Fax 541-775-6040

AUSTRALIA
Sydney (ACG)—UNIT 11024, APO AP 96554-0002, Tel. 612-261-9200/Fax 612-261-8148

---

[1]Contact the local US&FCS office for the location of the foreign commercial service office of any recently established or independent nation.

345

Brisbane (AC)—UNIT 11018, APO
AP 96553-0002, Tel. 617-832-
6247/Fax 617-831-1345

Melbourne (ACG)—UNIT 11011,
APO AP 96551-0002, Tel. 613-526-
5900/Fax 613-510-4660

Perth (ACG)—UNIT 11021, APO AP
96553-0002, Tel. 619-221-1177/Fax
619-325-3569

AUSTRIA
Vienna (AE)—APO AE 09108, Tel. 43-
222-315511/Fax 43-222-341261

BARBADOS
Bridgetown (AE)—BOX B, FPO AA
34054, Tel. 1-809-436-4950/Fax 1-
809-426-2275

BELGIUM
Brussels (AE)—PSC 82, BOX 002,
APO AE 09724-1015, Tel. 322-513-
3830/Fax 322-512-6653

BRAZIL
Brasilia (AE)—UNIT 3502, APO AA
34030, Tel. 55-61-223-0120/Fax 55-
61-225-3981

Belem (ACA)—APO AA 34030, Tel.
55-91-223-0800

Belo Horizonte (ACA)—APO AA
34030, Tel. 55-31-335-2250/Fax 55-
31-335-3054

São Paolo (ACG)—APO AA 34040-
0002, Tel. 55-21-292-7117/Fax 55-21-
240-9738

BULGARIA
Sofia (AE)—APO AE 09213-5740,
Tel. 359-2-884801/Fax 359-2-801977

CAMEROON
Douala (ACG)—USDOS (Douala)
WDC 20521-2530, Tel. 237-425-
331/Fax 237-427-790

CANADA
Ottawa (AE)—POB 5000, OGDENS-
BURG, NY 13669, Tel.
1-613-238-5535/Fax 1-613-238-8511

Calgary (ACG)—c/o AE Ottawa, Tel.
1-403-265-2116/Fax 1-403-264-6630

Halifax (ACG)—c/o AE Ottawa, Tel.
1-902-429-2482/Fax 1-902-423-6861

Montreal (ACG)—POB 846, CHAM-
PLAIN, NY 12919-0847, Tel. 1-514-
398-9695/Fax 1-514-398-0711

Toronto (ACG)—POB 135, LEWIS-
TON, NY 14092, Tel. 1-416-595-
5413/Fax 1-416-595-5419

Vancouver (ACG)—POB 5002, PT
ROBERTS, WA 98281, Tel. 1-604-
685-3382/Fax 1-604-685-5285

CHILE
Santiago (AE)—UNIT 4111, APO AA
34033, Tel. 562-671-0133/Fax 562-
697-2051

CHINA
Beijing (AE)—PSC 461, BOX 50, FPO
AP 96521-0002, Tel. 861-532-
3831/Fax 861-532-3297

Guangzhou (ACG)—PSC 461 BOX
100, FPO AP 96521-0002, Tel. 8620-
677-842/Fax 8620-666-409

Shanghai (ACG)—PSC 461 BOX 200,
FPO AP 96521-0002, Tel. 8621-433-
2492/Fax 8621-433-1576

Shenyang (ACG)—PSC 461 BOX 45,
FPO AP 96521-0002, Tel. 8624-220-
057/Fax 8624-290-074

COLUMBIA
Bogotá (AE)—UNIT 5120, APO AA
34038, Tel. 571-232-6550/Fax 571-
285-7945

COSTA RICA
San José (AE)—APO AA 34020, Tel.
506-20-3939/Fax 506-31-4783

CÔTE d'IVOIRE
Abidjan (AE)—USDOS (Abidjan)
WDC 20521-2010, Tel. 225-21-
4616/Fax 225-22-3259

CROATIA & SLOVENIA
Zagreb (AE)—APO AE 09213-5080,
Tel. 38-41-444-800/Fax 38-41-440-235

CZECHOSLOVAKIA
Prague (AE)—BOX 5630, APO AE 09213-5630, Tel. 422-536-641/Fax 422-532-457

DENMARK
Copenhagen (AE)—APO AE 09176, Tel. 451-423144/Fax 31-420175

DOMINICAN REPUBLIC
Santo Domingo (AE)—APO AA 34041-0008, Tel. 1-809-541-2171/Fax 1-809-688-4838

EC
Brussels (USM)—See AE Brussels

ECUADOR
Quito (AE)—UNIT 5344, APO AA 34039-3420, Tel. 5932-561-404/Fax 5932-504-550

Guayaquil—APO AA 34039, Tel. 5934-323-570/Fax 5934-324-558

EGYPT
Cairo—UNIT 64900 BOX 11, APO AE 09839-4900, Tel. 202-537-2340/Fax 202-355-8368

Alexandria—UNIT 64904, FPO AE 09839-4904, Tel. 203-491-1911/Fax 203-482-9199

ESTONIA
Tallinn (AE)—c/o AE Helsinki APO AE, NY 09723, Tel. 358-49-303-182/Fax 358-49-306-817

FINLAND
Helsinki (AE)—APO AE 09723, Tel. 3580-171-931/Fax 3580-635-332

FRANCE
Paris—APO AE 09777, Tel. 331-4296-1202/Fax 331-4266-4827

Bordeaux (ACG)—c/o AE Paris, Tel. 3356-526595

Lyon (ACG)—c/o AE Paris, Tel. 3378-246849

Marseille (ACG)—c/o AE Paris, Tel. 3391-549200

Strasbourg (ACG)—c/o AE Paris, Tel. 88-353104

GATT
Geneva (USM)—USDOS (Geneva) WDC 20521-5130, Tel. 4122-749-5281/Fax 4122-749-4885

GERMANY
Bonn (AE)—UNIT 21701 BOX 370, APO AE 09080, Tel. 49-228-339-2063/Fax 49-228-334-649

Berlin (AEO)—BOX E, APO AE 09235, Tel. 49-30-819-7888/Fax 372-229-6127

Dusseldorf (USCO)—c/o AE Bonn, Tel. 49-211-596-790/Fax 49-211-594-897

Frankfurt (ACG)—APO AE 09213, Tel. 49-69-7535-2453/Fax 49-69-748-204

Hamburg (ACG)—APO AE 09215-0002, Tel. 49-40-4117-1304/Fax 49-40-410-6598

Munich (ACG)—APO AE 09108, Tel. 49-89-2888-748/Fax 49-89-285-261

Stuttgart (ACG)—APO AE 09154, Tel. 49-711-246-513/Fax 49-711-236-4350

GREECE
Athens (AE)—PSC 108 BOX 30, APO AE 09482, Tel. & Fax 301-723-9705

GUATEMALA
Guatemala (AE)—UNIT 3306, APO AA 34024, Tel. 5022-348-479/Fax 5022/313-373

HONDURAS
Tegucigalpa (AE)—APO AA 34022, Tel. 504-32-3120/Fax 504-32-0027

HONG KONG
Hong Kong (ACG)—PSC 464 BOX 30, FPO AP 96522-0002, Tel. 852-521-1467/Fax 852-5-845-9800

HUNGARY
Budapest (AE)—APO AE 09213-5270, Tel. 36-1-1228600/Fax 36-1-1322529

INDIA
New Delhi (AE)—USDOS (New Delhi) WDC 20521-5000, Tel. 91-11-600651/Fax 91-11-687-2391

Bombay (ACG)—USDOS (Bombay) WDC 20521-6240, Tel. 91-22-821-3611/Fax 91-22-822-0350

Calcutta (ACG)—USDOS (Calcutta) WDC 20521-6250, Tel. 91-33-44-3611/Fax 91-33-283-823

Madras (ACG)—USDOS (Madras) WDC 20521-6260, Tel. 91-44-475-947/Fax 91-44-825-0240

INDONESIA
Jakarta (AE)—BOX 1, APO AP 96520, Tel. 62-21-360360/Fax 62-21-360-644

Medan (AE)—APO AP 96520, Tel. 62-61-322-2000

Surabaya—APO AP 96520, Tel. 62-31-67100

IRAQ
Baghdad (AE)—USDOS (Baghdad) WDC 20521-6060, Tel. 964-1-719-6138/Fax 964-1-718-9297

IRELAND
Dublin (AE)—USDOS (Dublin) WDC 20521-5290, Tel. 353-1-288-4569/Fax 353-1-608-469

ISRAEL
Tel Aviv (AE)—PSC 98 BOX 100, APO AE 09830, Tel. 972-3-654338/Fax 972-3-658033

ITALY
Rome (AE)—PSC 59, APO AE 09624, Tel. 396-4674-2202/Fax 396-4674-2113

Florence (ACG)—PSC 59 BOX G, APO AE 09624, Tel. 39-55-211-676/Fax 39-55-283-780

Milan (ACG)—PSC 59 BOX M, APO AE 09624, Tel. 392-498-2241/Fax 392-481-4161

Naples (ACG)—PSC BOX N, FPO AE 09624, Tel. 39-81-761-1592/Fax 39-81-761-1869

JAMAICA
Kingston (AE)—USDOS (Kingston) WDC 20521-3210, Tel. 1-809-929-4850/Fax 1-809-929-3637

JAPAN
Tokyo (AE)—UNIT 45004 BOX 204, APO AP 96337-0001, Tel. 813-3224-5000/Fax 813-3589-4235

Fukuoa (AC)—BOX 10, FPO AP 98766, Tel. 8192-751-9331/Fax 8192-71-3922

Nagoya (RO)—c/o AE Tokyo, Tel. 8152-203-4011/Fax 8152-201-4612

Osaka-Kobe (ACG)—UNIT 45004 BOX 239, APO AP 96337, Tel. 816-315-5953/Fax 816-361-5978

Sapporo (AC)—APO AP 96503, Tel. 8111-641-1115/Fax 8111-641-0911

KENYA
Nairobi (AE)—UNIT 64100 BOX 51, APO AE 09831-4100, Tel. 254-2-334-141/Fax 254-2-340-838

KOREA
Seoul (AE)—UNIT 15550, APO AP 96205-0001, Tel. 822-732-2601/Fax 822-739-1628

KUWAIT
Kuwait (AE)—UNIT 6900 BOX 10, APO AE 09880-9000, Tel. 965-242-4151/Fax 965-244-7692

LATVIA
Riga (AE)—c/o AE Helsinki APO AE, NY 09723, Tel. 358-49-311-348/Fax 358-49-314-665

LITHUANIA
Vilnius (AE)—c/o AE Helsinki APO AE, NY 09723, Tel. 7-012-2-222-724/Fax 7-012-2-222-779

MALAYSIA
Kuala Lumpur (AE)—APO AP 96535-5000, Tel. 603-248-9011/Fax 603-243-1866

MEXICO
Mexico (AE)—POB 3087, LAREDO TX 78044-3087, Tel. 525-211-0042/Fax 525-207-8938

Guadalajara (ACG)—POB 3098, LAREDO TX 78044-3098, Tel. 5236-25-0321/Fax 525-35-26-3576

Monterrey (ACG)—POB 3098, LAREDO TX 78044-3098, Tel. 5283-452-120/Fax 525-83-425-172

MOROCCO
Casablanca (ACG)—APO AE 09718, Tel. 212-264550/Fax 212-220259

Rabat (AE)—APO AE 09718, Tel. 212-762265/Fax 212-765661

NETHERLANDS
The Hague (AE)—PSC 71 BOX 1000, APO AE 09715, Tel. 3170-310-9417/Fax 3170-363-2985

Amsterdam (ACG)—APO AE 09159, Tel. 3120-664-8111/Fax 3120-675-2856

NEW ZEALAND
Auckland (ACG)—PSC 467 BOX 99, FPO AP 96531-1099, Tel. 649-303-2038/Fax 649-366-0870

Wellington (ACG)—PSC 467 BOX 1, FPO AP 96531-1001, Tel. 644-722-0686/Fax 644-781-701

NIGERIA
Lagos (AE)—USDOS (Lagos) WDC 20521-8300, Tel. 2341-616-477/Fax 2341-619-856

Kaduna (ACG)—USDOS (Kaduna) WDC 20521-2260, Tel. 234-201070

NORWAY
Oslo (AE)—PSC 69 BOX 0200, APO AE 09085, Tel. 472-448550/Fax 472-558803

OECD
Paris (USM)—APO AE 0977, Tel. 331-4524-7437/Fax 331-4524-7410

PAKISTAN
Carica (ACG)—UNIT 62400 BOX 137, APO AE 09814-2400, Tel. 9221-515-081/Fax 9221-568-1381

Lahore (ACG)—UNIT 62216, APO AE 09812-2216, Tel. 9242-870221

PANAMA
Panama (AE)—UNIT 0945, APO AA 34002, Tel. 507-27-1777/Fax 507-27-1713

PERU
Lima (AE)—UNIT 3780, APO AA 34031, Tel. 5114-33-0555/Fax 5114-33-4687

PHILIPPINES
Manila (AE)—APO AP 96440, Tel. 632-818-6674/Fax 632-818-2684

POLAND
Warsaw (AE)—co/AMCONGEN WAW, APO AE 09213-5010, Tel. 48-22-214515/Fax 48-22-216327

PORTUGAL
Lisbon (AE)—PSC 83 BOX FCS, APO AE 09726, Tel. 351-1726-6600/Fax 351-1726-8914

Oporto (AC)—APO New York 09678-0002, Tel. 351-263094/Fax 351-26002737

ROMANIA
Bucharest (AE)—APO AE 09213-5260, Tel. 400-104-040/Fax 400-120-395

RUSSIA
Moscow (AE)—APO AE 09721, Tel. 7095-225-4848/Fax 7095-230-2101

SAUDI ARABIA
Riyadh (AE)—UNIT G1307, APO AE 09803-1307, Tel. 966-1-488-3800/Fax 966-1-488-3237

Dhahran (ACG)—UNIT 66803, APO AE 09858-6803, Tel. 966-3-891-3200/Fax 966-3-981-8332

Jeddah (ACG)—UNIT 62112, APO AE 09811-2112, Tel. 966-2-667-0040/Fax 966-2-665-8106

SINGAPORE
Singapore (AE)—APO AP 96534-0006, Tel. 65-338-9722/Fax 65-338-5010

SOUTH AFRICA
Johannesburg (ACG)—USDOS (Johannesburg) WDC 20521-2500, Tel.
2711-331-3937/Fax 2711-331-6178

Cape Town (ACG)—USDOS (Cape Town) WDC 20521-2480, Tel. & Fax
2721-214-280

SPAIN
Madrid (AE)—PSC 61 BOX 0021,
APO AE 09642, Tel. 341-577-4000/Fax 341-575-8655

Barcelona (ACG)—PSC 64, APO AE 09646, Tel. 343-319-9550/Fax 343-319-5621

SWEDEN
Stockholm (AE)—USDOS (Stockholm)
WDC 20521-5750, Tel. 468-783-5346/Fax 468-660-9181

SWITZERLAND
Bern (AE)—USDOS (Bern) WDC
20521-5110, Tel. 4131-437341/Fax
4131-437336

Zurich (ACG)—USDOS (Zurich)
WDC 20521-5130, Tel. 411-552-070/Fax 411-383-9814

TAIWAN [2]
Taipei (AIT)—Letters: POB 1612,
WDC 20013; Packages: AIT,CU,
USDOS (Taipei) WDC 20521; Tel.
886-2-720-1550/Fax 886-2-757-7162

THAILAND
Bangkok (AE)—APO AP 96546, Tel.
662-253-4920/Fax 662-255-2915

TRINIDAD & TOBAGO
Port of Spain (AE)—USDOS (Port of Spain) WDC 20521-3410, Tel. 1-809-622-6371/Fax 1-809-622-9583

TURKEY
Ankara (AE)—PSC 93 BOX 5000,
APO AE 09823, Tel. 904-126-5470/Fax 904-167-1366

Istanbul (ACG)—PSC 97 BOX 0002,
APO AE 09827-0002, Tel. 901-151-3602/Fax 901-152-2417

Izmir (ACG)—APO AE 09821, Tel.
9051-149-426/Fax 9051-130-493

UNITED ARAB EMIRATES
Dubai (ACG)—USDOS (Dubai) WDC
20521-6020, Tel. 9714-378-584/Fax
9714-375-121

Abu Dhabi (AE)—USDOS (Abu
Dhabi) WDC 20521-6010, Tel. 9712-345-545/Fax 9712-331-374

UNITED KINGDOM
London (AE)—PSC 801 BOX 33, FPO
AE 09409-4033, Tel. 4471-499-9000/Fax 4471-491-4022

VENEZUELA
Caracas (AE)—UNIT 4958, APO AA
34037, Tel. 582-285-2222/Fax 582-285-0336

YUGOSLAVIA
Belgrade (AE)—APO AE 09213-5070,
Tel. 3811-645-655/Fax 3811-645-096

Zagreb (ACG)—APO AE 09213-5080, Tel. 3841-444-800/Fax 3841-440-235

[2]The American Institute in Taiwan is an important non-US&FCS commercial office.

Key:
AC = American Consulate
ACA = American Consular Agency
ACG = American Consulate General
AE = American Embassy
AEO = American Embassy Office
RO = Representative Office
USCO = US Commercial Office
USDOS= US Department of State
USM = US Mission
WDC = Washington, DC

Appendix C
Industry Specialists: U.S. Department of Commerce, International Trade Administration

Industry specialists are found within the Trade Development Division of the International Trade Administration. The Assistant Secretary for Trade Development reports to the Undersecretary for International Trade within the ITA.

Industry specialists exist to support the information needs of individuals, companies, associations, and others regarding international trade events and issues relative to their assigned industry. Each industry officer should be aware of current trends in the export and import of their product group, principal markets, major features of the trade environment for their product, and other information relevant to the international markets for his or her assigned product group. Industry officers are organized by "office." These offices are:

1. Office of Computers and Business Equipment
2. Office of Microelectronics and Instrumentation
3. Office of Telecommunications
4. Office of Automotive Industry Affairs
5. Office of Consumer Goods
6. Office of Textiles and Apparel
7. Office of Service Industries
8. Office of Export Trading Company Affairs

9. Office of Aerospace

10. Office of Chemicals, Industrial Materials, and Machinery

11. Office of Energy, Environment, and Infrastructure

12. Office of Finance

The following lists the industry sectors to which personnel have been assigned, along with their telephone numbers. Your closest US&FCS district office can give you current desk officer names.

Mail to individual desk officers should be addressed to the appropriate room at the U.S. Department of Commerce, 14th Street & Constitution Avenue, NW, Washington, DC 20230.

Industry Sector	Telephone Number 202–482–	Room	Industry Sector	Telephone Number 202–482–	Room
Abrasives	5158	4059	Aerospace Trade		
Accounting	0345	1110	Promo	8228	2130
Adhesives/			Agribusiness		
Sealants	0128	4033	(Major Proj)	2460	2013
Advertising	0345	1110	Agricultural		
Aerospace			Chemicals	0128	4029A
Financing			Agricultural		
Issues	4222	2124	Machinery	4708	2104
Aerospace			Air Conditioning		
Industry			Eqpmt	3509	2213
Analysis	4222	2122	Air, Gas		
Aerospace			Compressors	0680	2107
Industry Data	4222	2122	Air, Gas		
Aerospace			Compressors		
Information &			(Trade		
Analysis	4222	2122	Promo)	0558	2104
Aerospace			Air Pollution		
Market			Control		
Development	8228	2130	Eqpmt	0564	2211
Aerospace			Aircraft &		
Market Promo	8228	2130	Aircraft		
Aerospace-Space			Engines		
Market			(Market		
Support	8228	2130	Support)	8228	2130
Aerospace			Aircraft &		
Marketing			Aircraft		
Support	8228	2130	Engines (Trade		
Aerospace Policy			Promo)	8228	2130
& Analysis	4222	2122	Aircraft		
Aerospace-Space			Auxiliary		
Programs	2122	4221	Equipment		
Aerospace Trade			(Market		
Policy Issues	2124	4222	Support)	8228	2130

Industry Sector	Telephone Number 202–482–	Room	Industry Sector	Telephone Number 202–482–	Room
Aircraft Parts (Market Support)	8228	2130	Audio Visual Services	4781	1114
Aircraft Parts/Aux Eqpmt (Trade Promo)	8228	2130	Auto Ind Affairs Parts/Suppliers	1419	4044
			Auto Ind Affairs Parts/Suppliers	4019	4008
Airlines	5012	1120	Auto Ind Affairs Parts/Suppliers	1418	4044
Airport Equipment (Market Support)	8228	2130	Auto Industry Affairs	0554	4036
Airport Equipment (Trade Promo)	8228	2130	Aviation and Helicopter Services	5012	1120
Airports, Ports, Harbors (Major Proj)	3352	2011	Avionics Marketing	8228	2130
			Bakery Products	2250	4318
			Ball Bearings	3489	2210
Air Traffic Control (Market Support)	8228	2130	Banking	0339	1110
			Basic Paper & Board Mfg	0375	4016A
Alcoholic Beverages	2428	4320	Bauxite, Alumina, Prim Alum	0575	4053
Alum Sheet, Plate/Foil	0575	4053	Belting & Hose	0128	4033
			Beryllium	0575	4053
Alum Forgings, Electro	0575	4053	Beverages	2428	4320
			Bicycles	0348	4319
Alum Extrud Alum Rolling	0575	4053	Biotechnology	3888	4043
Analytical Instrument (Trade Promo)	2991	1015	Biotechnology (Trade Promo)	3090	1015
			Blowers and Fans	0564	2211
Analytical Instruments	8411	1015	Boat Building (Maj Proj)	3352	2011
Animal Feeds	2250	4318	Boats Pleasure Craft	0348	4319
Apparel	4058	3117	Books	0379	4316
Artificial Intelligence (TE15sKader, Victoria)	0571	1106	Books (Export Promo)	3640	4327
Asbestos/ Cement Prod	0132	4514	Builders Hardware	0132	4514
Assembly Equipment	0312	2014A	Building Materials (Trade Policy)	0132	4520
Audio Visual Equipment (Trade Promo)	5478	4327	Building Materials & Construction	0132	4024
			Business Forms	0380	4316

Industry Sector	Telephone Number 202–482–	Room	Industry Sector	Telephone Number 202–482–	Room
CAD/CAM	0314	2206	Commercialization		
Cable			of Space		
Broadcasting	4781	4112	(Services)	5820	1114
	5820	1114	Composites,		
Canned Goods	3346	4320	Advanced	5157	4059
Capital Goods			Computer and		
DAS	5023	2001B	DP Services	4781	1116
Capital Goods				5820	1116
(Trade Promo)	0560	2211	Computer		
Carbon Black	0128	4033	Consulting	4781	1114
Case	4936	1004	Computer Eqpmt	2053	1104
Cement	0132	4024	Computer		
Cement Plants			Networks	0572	1104
(Major Proj)	4160	2007	Computer,		
Ceramics			Personal	3013	1004
(Advanced)	0128	4033		2990	1104
Ceramics			Computer		
Machinery	3494	2204	Professional		
Cereals	2250	4318	Services	4781	1114
Chemicals			Computers		
(Liaison &			(Trade Promo)	4936	1006
Policy)	0128	4033	Computers		
Chemical Plants			(Trade Promo)	0396	1004
(Major Proj)	4877	2007	Computers &		
Chemicals &			Business		
Allied Products	0128	4033	Eqpmt (Office		
Chinaware	0338	4312	of)	0572	1102
Chromium	5158	4059	Confectionery		
Civil Aircraft			Products	2428	4320
Agreement	8228	2124	Construction,		
Civil Aviation	5012	1120	Domestic	0132	4026
Coal Exports	1466	4411	Construction		
Coal Exports	1466	4415	Machinery	0558	2104
Cobalt	0575	4053	Consumer		
Cocoa Products	5124	4027	Goods	0338	4312
Coffee Products	5124	4027	Containers &		
Columbium	5158	4059	Packaging	5159	4059
Commercial			Contract		
Aircraft (Trade			Machining	0314	2206
Policy)	4222	2122	Conventional		
Commercial			Fossil Fuel		
Lighting			Power (Major		
Fixtures	0682	2213	Proj)	2733	2015B
Commercial/			Converted Paper		
Indus Refrig			Prod	0375	4018
Eqpmt	3509	2215	Conveyors/		
Commercial			Conveying		
Printing	0379	4316	Eqpmt	4708	2104

Industry Sector	Telephone Number 202–482–	Room
Copper/Brass Mills	0575	4053
Copper Wire Mills	0575	4053
Copper	0575	4053
Corn Products	2250	4318
Cosmetics	0128	4033
Cosmetics (Export Promo)	3640	4327
Costume Jewelry Trade Promotion	5478	4327
Cotton Seed Oil	2250	4318
Courier Services	1134	1124
Current-Carrying Wiring Devices	0682	2213
Cutlery	0338	4312
Dairy Products	2250	4318
Data Base Services	5820	1114
Data Processing Services	4781	1114
Desalination/ Water Reuse	3509	2213
Diamond, Industrial	5158	4029
Disc Drives	0571	1106
Dolls	0338	4312
Drilling Mus/Soft Compounds	0564	2213
Drugs	0128	4033
Durable Consumer Goods	1176	4312
Earthenware	0338	4312
Education Facilities (Major Proj)	4160	2007
Educational/ Training	0345	1110
Electric Industrial Apparatus Nec	0682	2213
Elec/Power Gen/ Transmission & Dist Eqt (Trade Promo)	0560	2211

Industry Sector	Telephone Number 202–482–	Room
Electrical Power Plants (Major Proj)	2733	2015B
Electronic Prod & Test	3360	1015
Electricity	1466	4411
ElectroOptical Instruments (Trade Promo)	2991	1015
Electronic (Legislation)	5466	1015
Electronic Components	2946	1012
	1333	1012
Electronic Components/ Production & Test Equip	5014	1015
Electronic Database Services	5820	1114
Elevators, Moving Stairways	4708	2104
Energy & Environ. Sys.	5456	2213
Energy (Commodities)	1466	4415
Energy, Renewable	1466	4411
Engineering/ Construction Services (Trade Promo)	0359	2005
Entertainment Industries	4781	1116
Explosives	0128	4033
Export Trading Companies	5131	1800
Express Delivery Service	1134	1124
Fabricated Metal Construction Materials	0132	4026
Farm Machinery	4708	2104
Fasteners (Industrial)	3489	2206

Industry Sector	Telephone Number 202–482–	Room	Industry Sector	Telephone Number 202–482–	Room
Fats and Oils	2250	4318	Gaskets/Gasketing		
Fencing (Metal)	0132	4514	Materials	3489	2206
Ferroalloys			General Aviation		
Products	5158	4059	Aircraft		
Ferrous Scrap	0606	4414	(Industry		
Fertilizers	0128	4033	Analysis)	4222	2122
Filters/Purifying			General Aviation		
Eqmt	0564	2211	Aircraft		
Finance &			(Market		
Management			Support)	8228	2130
Industries	0339	1110	Gen. Indus.		
Fisheries (Major			Mach.	5455	2102
Proj)	2460	2013	Gen. Indus.		
Flexible Mftg			Mach. Nec,		
Systems	0314	2204	Exc 35691	3494	2204
Flour	2250	4318	Generator		
Flowers	2250	4318	Sets/Turbines		
Fluid Power	0680	2107	(Major Proj)	2733	2015B
Food Products			Germanium	0575	4053
Machinery	3494	2204	Glass, Flat	0132	4026
Food Retailing	2428	4320	Glassware	0338	4312
Footwear	4034	4318	Gloves (work)	3459	4323
Forest Products	0375	4016A	Giftware (Export		
Forest Products,			Promo)	5478	4327
Domestic			Grain Mill		
Construction	0384	4016A	Products	2250	4318
Forest Products			Greeting Cards	0380	4316
(Trade Policy)	0375	4520	Ground Water		
Forgings			Exploration		
Semifinished			and		
Steel	0609	4025	Development	3509	2213
Fossil Fuel			Guns &		
Power			Ammunition	0348	4319
Generation			Hand Saws, Saw		
(Major Proj)	2733	2015B	Blades	3494	2204
Foundry Eqmt	5956	2014A	Hand/Edge Tools		
Foundry			Ex Mach		
Industry	0609	4025	Tl/Saws	3494	2204
Frozen Fruits,			Handbags	4034	4318
Vegetables &			Hard Surfaced		
Specialties	3346	4320	Floor		
Fur Goods	4034	4318	Coverings	0132	4028
Furniture	0338	4312	Health	5131	1800A
Fuzzy Logic	0571	1106	Heat		
Gallium	0575	4053	Treating		
Games &			Equipment	5956	2204
Children's			Heating Eqmt		
Vehicles	0575	4053	Ex Furnaces	3509	2213

Industry Sector	Telephone Number 202–482–	Room
Helicopter Services	5012	1120
Helicopters	4222	2122
Helicopters (Market Support)	8228	2130
Helicopters (Trade Promo)	8228	2130
High Tech Trade, U S Competitiveness	3913	2225
Hoists, Overhead Cranes	4708	2104
Hose & Belting	0128	4033
Hotel & Restaurant Eq. (Export Promo)	3640	4327
Hotels and Motels	4582	1120
Household Appliances	1178	4325
Household Appliances (Export Promo)	3422	4327
Household Furniture	0338	4312
Housewares (Export Promo)	3422	4327
Housewares	1178	4312
Housing Construction	0132	4026
Housing & Urban Development (Major Proj)	4160	2013
Hydro Power, Plants (Major Proj)	4333	2013
Industrial Controls	0682	2213
Industrial Drives/Gears	3489	2204
Industrial Gases	0128	4033
Industrial Organic Chemicals	0128	4033

Industry Sector	Telephone Number 202–482–	Room
Industrial Process Controls	0411	1015
Industrial Process Controls (Export Promo)	2991	1015
Industrial Robots	0314	2204
Industrial Structure	4924	2224
Industrial Trucks	4608	2104
Information Services	5820	1114
Inorganic Chemicals Pigments	0128	4033
Insulation	0132	4514
Insurance	0346	1108
Intellectual Property Rights (Services)	4781	1114
International Commodities	5124	4515
International Major Projects	5225	2015B
Investment Management	0346	1108
Irrigation (Major Proj)	2460	2013
Jams & Jellies	3346	4320
Jewelry	1178	4325
Jewelry (Export Promo)	5478	4327
Jute Products	0132	4024
Kitchen Cabinets	0375	4022
Laboratory Instruments	8411	1015
Laboratory Instruments (Trade Promo)	3090	1010
Lasers (Trade Promo)	2991	1015
Lawn & Garden Equipment	0348	4319
Lead Products	0575	4053

Industry Sector	Telephone Number 202–482–	Room	Industry Sector	Telephone Number 202–482–	Room
Leasing: Eqmt & Vehicles	3050	1160	Mercury, Fluorspar	5157	4055
Leather Tanning Products	4034	4318	Metal Building Products	0132	4026
Legal Services	0345	1110	Metal Cookware	0338	4312
LNG Plants (Major Proj)	4146	2007	Metal Cutting Machine Tools	0314	2204
Logs, Wood	0375	4022	Metal Cutting		
Luggage	3034	4318	Tools Fr Mach		
Lumber	0375	4020	Tools	0312	2204
Machine Tool			Metal Forming		
Accessories	0314	2204	Machine Tools	0314	2204
Magnesium	0575	4053	Metal Powders	0575	4053
Mainframes	2990	1104	Metals,		
Major Projects	5225	2015B	Secondary	0606	4023
Management			Metalworking	0315	2202
Consulting	0345	1110	Metalworking		
Manganese	5158	4059	Eqmt Nec	0314	2204
Manifold			Mica	5158	4059
Business Forms	0380	4316	Millwork	0375	4022
Manmade Fiber	4058	3117	Mineral Based		
Margarine	2250	4318	Construction		
Marine			Materials		
Recreational			(Clay,		
Equipment			Concrete,		
(Export Promo)	5478	4327	Gypsum,		
Marine Insurance	5012	1120	Asphalt, Stone)	0132	4024
Maritime			Mini Computers	2053	1104
Shipping	5012	1120	Mining		
Marketing			Machinery	0680	2107
Promo (Basic			Mining		
Ind)	2493	4043	Machinery		
Materials,			(Trade Promo)	0552	2107
Advanced	0575	4053	Mobile Homes	0132	4028
Mattresses &			Molybdenum	0575	4053
Bedding	0338	4312	Monorails	4708	2104
Meat Products	3346	4320	Motion Pictures	4781	1114
Mech Power			Motor Vehicles		
Transmission			Auto Ind		
Eqmt, Nec	3489	2206	Affairs	0669	4040
Medical			Motor Vehicles	0669	4036
Facilities			Motorcycles	0348	4319
(Major Proj)	4160	2007	Motors, Elect	0682	2213
Medical			Music	4781	1114
Instruments	0550	1015	Musical		
Medical			Instruments	0338	4312
Instruments			Mutual Funds	0343	1108
(Trade Promo)	2010	1015	Natural Gas	1466	4413

Industry Sector	Telephone Number 202–482–	Room	Industry Sector	Telephone Number 202–482–	Room
Natural, Synthetic Rubber	0128	4033	Outdoor Power (Export Promo)	3422	H4327
Newspapers	0380	4316	Packaging and Containers	5159	4059
Nickel Products	5158	4059	Packaging Machinery	3494	2204
Non-alcoholic Beverages	2428	4320	Paints/Coatings	0128	4033
Noncurrent			Paper	0375	4018
Carrying Wiring Devices	0682	2215	Paper And Board Packaging	0375	4016A
Nondurable Goods	0341	4314	Paper Industries Machinery	0312	2204
Nonferrous Foundries	0610	4053	Pasta	2250	4318
Nonferrous Metals	0575	4059	Paving Materials (Asphalt & Concrete)	0132	4024
Nonmetallic Minerals Nec	0575	4059	Pectin	2250	4318
Nonresidential Constr (Domestic)	0132	4026	Pens/Pencils, etc.	0338	4312
			Periodicals	0380	4316
Nuclear Power Plants (Major Proj)	2733	2015B	Pet Food	2250	4318
Numerical Cntrls Fr Mach Tools	0314	2204	Pet Products (Export Promo)	3640	4327
Nuts, edible	2250	4318	Petrochem, Cyclic Crudes	0128	4033
Nuts, Bolts, Washers	3489	2206	Petrochemicals	0128	4033
Ocean Shipping	5012	1120	Petrochemicals Plants (Major Proj)	4877	2007
Oil & Gas Development & Refining (Major Proj)	2460	2073	Petroleum, Crude & Refined Products	1466	4413
Oil & Gas (Fuels Only)	1466	4413	Pharmaceuticals	0128	4033
Oil Field Machinery	0680	2122	Pipelines (Major Proj)	2460	2013
Oil Field Machinery (Trade Promo)	0552	2109	Photographic Eqmt & Supplies	0574	1106
Oil Shale (Major Proj)	2460	2073	Plastic Construction Products (Most)	0132	4026
Organic Chemicals	0128	4033	Plastic Materials	0128	4033
Outdoor Lighting Fixtures	0682	2213	Plastic Products	0128	4033
			Plastic Products Machinery	3494	2104

Industry Sector	Telephone Number 202–482–	Room	Industry Sector	Telephone Number 202–482–	Room
Plumbing Fixtures & Fittings	0132	4028	Pumps, Pumping Eqmt	0680	2109
Plywood/Panel Products	0375	4022	Pumps, Valves, Compressors (Trade Promo)	0558	2104
Point-of-Use Water Treatment	0564	2213	Radio & TV Broadcasting	4781	1114
Pollution Control Equipment	0564	H2211	Radio & TV Communications Eqmt	4466	1003A
Porcelain Electrical Supplies (Part)	2213	H2215	Railroad Services	4582	1120
Portable Computers	2053	1104	Recreational Eqmt (Export Promo)	5478	4327
Pottery	0338	4312	Refractory Products	0610	4053
Poultry Products	3346	4320	Renewable Energy Eqpmt	0556	2209
Power Hand Tools	0312	2204	Research & Development	4781	1114
Precious Metal Jewelry	1178	4325	Residential Lighting Fixtures	0682	2213
Prefabricated Buildings (Wood)	0132	4028	Retail Trade	5086	1120
			Rice Milling	2250	4318
Prefabricated Buildings (Metal)	0132	4026	Roads, Railroads, Mass Trans (Major Proj)	4642	2011
Prepared Meats	3346	4320	Robots	0314	2204
Primary Commodities	5124	4029	Roofing, Asphalt	0132	4024
Printing & Publishing	0379	4316	Roller Bearings	3489	2204
Printing Trade Services	0380	4316	Rolling Mill Machinery	0312	2204
			Rubber	0128	4033
Printing Trade Mach/Eqmt	5956	2204	Rubber Products	0128	4033
Process Control Instruments	8411	1015	Saddlery & Harness Products	3034	4318
Process Control Instruments (Trade Promo)	2991	1015	Safety & Security Equip (Trade Promo)	8410	1015
Pulp and Paper Mills (Major Proj)	4160	2007	Satellites, Communications	4466	1001A
Pulpmills	0375	4018			

Industry Sector	Telephone Number 202–482–	Room	Industry Sector	Telephone Number 202–482–	Room
Scientific Instruments (Trade Promo)	2991	1015	Soy Products	2250	4318
Scientific Management/ Control Eqmt	8411	1015	Space Policy Development	4222	2800A
Screw Machine Products	3489	2204	Special Industry Machinery, Nec	3494	2204
Screws, Washers	3489	2204	Speed Changers	3489	2206
Security & Commodity Brokers	0347	1108	Sporting & Athletic Goods	0348	4319
Semiconductors	1333	1012	Sporting Goods (Export Promo)	5478	4327
Semiconductors (Export Promo)	5014	1015	Steel Industry Products	0608	4025
Semiconductor Prod Eqmt & Materials	3360	1012	Steel Industry	0606	4023
Semiconductor Prod Eqmt & Materials (Export Promo)	5014	1015	Steel Markets	0608	4025
Services, DAS	5261	1128	Storage Batteries	0575	4053
Shingles (Wood)	0375	4020	Sugar Products	5124	4027
Silicon	5158	4059	Supercomputers	0572	1104
Silverware	1178	4325	Superconductors	0402	1209
Sisal Products	5124	4029	Superconductors, Electronics	1330	1016
Small Business Policy Development	4806	1128	Switchgear & Switchboard Apparatus	0682	2213
Snackfood	2250	4318	System Integration	4781	1114
Soaps, Detergents, Cleaners	0128	4033	Tantalum	5158	4059
			Tea	2250	4318
Soft Drink	2428	4320	Technology Affairs	4694	4043
Software	0571	1104	Telecommunications	4466	1001A
	0571	1104			
	2053	1004	Telecommunications (CPE)	4466	1001A
Software (Export Promo)	4936	1008	Telecommunications (Cellular)	4466	1001A
Solar Cells/ Photovoltaic Devices/Small Hydro	0556	2209	Telecommunications (Fiber Optics)	4466	1001A
Solar Eqmt Ocean/Biomass/ Geoth	0556	2209	Telecommunications (Major Projects)	4466	1001A

Industry Sector	Telephone Number 202–482–	Room	Industry Sector	Telephone Number 202–482–	Room
Telecommunications (Network Equip)	4466	1001A	Uranium	1466	4411
Telecommunications (Radio)	4466	1001A	Value Added Telecommunications Serv	4781	1114
Telecommunications (Satellites)	4466	1001A	Valves, Pipe Fittings Ex Brass	3489	2206
Telecommunications (Services)	4466	1001A	Vanadium	5158	4059
Telecommunications (Trade Promo)	4466	1001A	Vegetables	3346	4320
			Video Services	5820	1114
Telecommunications (TVBroadcast)	4466	1001A	Videotex Services	5820	1114
Teletext Services	5820	1114	Wallets, Billfolds, Flatgoods	4034	4318
Textile Machinery	0679	2107	Warm Air Heating Eqmt	3509	2213
Textiles	4058	3117	Wastepaper	0375	4018
Textiles (Trade Promotion)	2043	3109	Watches	1178	4325
Timber Products (Tropical)	5124	4027	Water and Sewage Treatment Plants (Major Proj)	4643	2013
Tin Products	5158	4059	Water Resource Eqmt	3509	2213
Tires	0128	4033	Welding/Cutting Apparatus	5956	2014A
Tobacco Products	2428	4320	Wholesale Trade	5086	1120
Tools/Dies/Jigs/ Fixtures	0314	2204	Windmill Components	0556	2209
Tourism (Major Proj)	4160	2007	Wire & Wire Products	0606	4023
Tourism Services	4582	1120	Wire Cloth, Industrial	3489	2206
Toys	0338	4312	Wire Cloth	0132	4024
Toys & Games (Export Promo)	5478	4327	Wood Containers	0375	4022
Trade Related Employment	8056	2223	Wood Preserving	0375	4022
Transformers	0682	2213	Wood Products	0375	4018
Transportation Industries	4581	1120	Wood Products, Misc	0375	4018
Travel & Tourism	4582	1120	Wood Working Machinery	0680	2122
Tropical Commodities	5124	4027	Workstations	2990	1104
Trucking Services	4581	1120	Yeast	2250	4318
Tungsten Products	5124	4033			

Source: ITA.

Note: This list was current in October 1992. However, all offices, personnel, and telephone numbers were being changed. To obtain current information on industry specialists, telephone numbers, or room numbers, telephone one of the following:

Assistant Secretary for Trade Development	(202) 482-1461
Deputy Assistant Secretary for Trade Development	(202) 482-1112
Director, Office of Planning, Coordination, and Resource Management	(202) 482-4921
Deputy Assistant Secretary, Technology and Aerospace Industries	(202) 482-1872
Deputy Assistant Secretary, Basic Industries	(202) 482-5023
Deputy Assistant Secretary, Service Industries and Finance	(202) 482-5261
Deputy Assistant Secretary, Textiles, Apparel, and Consumer Goods	(202) 482-3737

Appendix D
Country Specialists: U.S. Department of Commerce, International Trade Administration

Country desk officers are found within the International Economic Policy Division of the International Trade Administration. The Assistant Secretary for International Economic Policy reports to the Undersecretary for International Trade within the ITA.

Country desk officers support the information needs of individuals, companies, associations, and others regarding international trade events and issues relative to their assigned country. Each country officer should be aware of current trends in the export and import trade; economic environment; and political, social, and cultural climate regarding their assigned country and the United States. They can assist exporters and investors with economic, political, and trade information.

Organizationally, country officers function within "offices." These are:

1. Office of Africa
2. Office of the Near East
3. Office of South Asia
4. Office of Western Europe
5. Office of European Community Affairs
6. Office of Eastern Europe, Russia, and Independent States

7. Office of Latin America
8. Office of Mexico
9. Office of Canada
10. Office of PRC and Hong Kong
11. Office of the Pacific Basin
12. Office of Japan Trade Policy
13. Office of Japan Commercial Programs

The following lists the countries to which personnel have been assigned, along with their telephone numbers. Your closest US&FCS district office can give you current desk officer names. Mail to individual desk officers should be addressed to the appropriate room at the U.S. Department of Commerce, 14th Street & Constitution Avenue, NW, Washington, DC 20230.

Country	Telephone Number 202–482–	Room	Country	Telephone Number 202–482–	Room
Afghanistan	2954	2029B	Cambodia	3875	2308
Albania	2645	6043	Cameroon	4228	3317
Algeria	4652	2039	Canada	3101	3033
Angola	5148	3317	Cape Verde	4388	3317
Anguilla	2527	3021	Caribbean		
Argentina	1548	3021	Basin	0841	1235
Aruba	2527	3017	Caymans	2527	3020
ASEAN	3875	2308	Central African		
Antigua/Barbuda	2527	3021	Rep	4228	3317
Australia	3647	2308	Chad	4228	3317
Austria	2920	3029	Chile	1495	3017
Bahamas	2527	3021	Colombia	1659	2036
Bahrain	5545	2039	Comoros	4564	3317
Bangladesh	2954	2029B	Congo	4228	3317
Barbados	2527	3021	Costa Rica	2527	3021
Belgium	5041	3046	Croatia &		
Belize	2527	3021	Slovenia	4915	3413
Benin	4288	3317	Cuba	2527	3021
Bermuda	2527	3021	Cyprus	3945	3044
Bhutan	2954	2029B	Czechoslovakia	2645	6043
Bolivia	2521	2038	Denmark	3254	3413
Botswana	5148	3317	D'Jibouti	4564	3317
Brazil	3871	3017	Dominica	2527	3021
Brunei	3875	2308	Dominican		
Bulgaria	2645	6043	Republic	2527	3021
Burkina Faso	4388	3317	East Caribbean	2527	3021
Burma			Ecuador	1659	3025
(Myanmar)	3875	2308	Egypt	4441	2039
Burundi	4228	3317	El Salvador	2527	3020

Country	Telephone Number 202–482–	Room	Country	Telephone Number 202–482–	Room
Equatorial			Malawi	5148	3317
Guinea	4228	3317	Malaysia	3875	2308
Estonia	4915	3413	Maldives	2954	2029B
Ethiopia	4564	3317	Mali	4388	3317
European			Malta	3748	3049
Community	5276	3036	Martinique	2527	3021
Finland	3254	3413	Mauritania	4564	3317
France	8008	3042	Mauritius	4564	3317
Gabon	4228	3317	Mexico	4464	3028
Gambia	4388	3317	Mongolia	2642	2323
Germany	2841	3409	Montserrat	2527	3314
Ghana	4228	3317	Morocco	5545	2039
Greece	3945	3042	Mozambique	5148	3317
Grenada	2527	3021	Namibia	5148	3317
Guadeloupe	2527	3021	Nepal	2954	2029B
Guatemala	2527	3021	Netherlands	5401	3039
Guinea	4388	3317	Netherlands		
Guinea-Bissau	4388	3317	Antilles	2527	3021
Guyana	2527	3021	New Zealand	3647	2308
Haiti	2527	3021	Nicaragua	2527	3021
Honduras	2527	3020	Niger	4388	3317
Hong Kong	3583	2317	Nigeria	4228	3317
Hungary	2645	6043	Norway	4414	3037
Iceland	3254	3037	Oman	4652	2039
India	2954	2029B	Pacific Islands	3647	2308
Indonesia	3875	2308	Pakistan	2954	2029B
Iran	4652	2039	Panama	2527	3020
Iraq	4441	2039	Paraguay	1548	3021
Ireland	2177	3039	People's		
Israel	4652	2039	Republic of		
Italy	2177	3045	China	3583	2317
Ivory Coast	4388	3317	Peru	2521	3029
Jamaica	2527	3021	Philippines	3875	2308
Japan	2425	2324	Poland	2645	6043
Jordan	2515	2039	Portugal	4508	3044
Kenya	4564	3317	Puerto Rico	2527	3021
Korea	4957	2327	Qatar	4562	2039
Kuwait	2515	2039	Romania	2645	6043
Laos	3875	2308	Russia	4655	3318
Latvia	4915	3413	Rwanda	4228	3317
Lebanon	2515	2039	Sao Tome &		
Lesotho	5148	3317	Principe	4228	3317
Liberia	4388	3317	Saudi Arabia	4652	2039
Libya	5545	2039	Senegal	4388	3317
Lithuania	4915	3413	Seychelles	4564	3317
Luxembourg	5401	3046	Sierra Leone	4388	3317
Macao	2462	2323	Singapore	3875	2308
Madagascar	4564	3317	Somalia	4564	3317

Country	Telephone Number 202–482–	Room	Country	Telephone Number 202–482–	Room
South Africa	5148	3317	Turkey	5373	3045
Spain	4508	3045	Turks & Caicos		
Sri Lanka	2954	2029B	Islands	2527	3021
St. Bartholemey	2527	3031	Uganda	4564	3317
St. Kitts-Nevis	2527	3021	United Arab		
St. Lucia	2527	3021	Emirates	5545	2039
St. Martin	2527	3021	United Kingdom	3748	3045
St. Vincent-			Uruguay	1495	3021
Grenadines	2527	3021	Venezuela	4303	3029
Sudan	4564	3317	Vietnam	3875	2308
Suriname	2527	3021	Virgin Islands		
Swaziland	5148	3317	(UK)	2527	3020
Sweden	4414	3037	Virgin Islands		
Switzerland	2920	3039	(US)	2527	3021
Syria	2515	2039	Yemen, Republic		
Taiwan	4957	2308	of	4652	2039
Tanzania	5148	3317	Yugoslavia	2645	6043
Thailand	3875	2308	Zaire	4228	3317
Togo	4228	3021	Zambia	5148	3317
Trinidad &			Zimbabwe	5148	3317
Tobago	2537	3021			
Tunisia	2515	2039	Source: ITA.		

Note: In September 1992, the U.S. Department of Commerce telephone prefix 377 was changed to 482. As a result, some of the telephone numbers listed above may not reach the intended party. If this occurs, contact one of the following offices to obtain a current telephone number:

Assistant Secretary for International Economic Policy (202) 482-3022

Deputy Assistant Secretary for International
Economic Policy (202) 482-2993

Deputy Assistant Secretary, Europe (202) 482-5638

Deputy Assistant Secretary, Western Hemisphere (202) 482-5324

Deputy Assistant Secretary, East Asia and the Pacific (202) 482-5251

Deputy Assistant Secretary, Japan (202) 482-4527

Deputy Assistant Secretary, Africa, the Near East,
and South Asia (202) 482-4925

Appendix E
Schedule of Weights and Measures

APPROXIMATE CONVERSIONS: CUSTOMARY AND METRIC

Customary and Metric Length and Area

inches (in) = 2.54 centimeters (cm)
feet (ft)   = .305 meter (m)
yard (yd)   = .914 m
miles (mi) = 1.609 kilometers (km)
square in   = 6.452 square centimeters (cm)
square ft   = .093 square m
square yd   = .836 square m

Metric and Customary Length and Area

mm (millimeter) = .039 in
cm   = .394 in
m   = 3.281 ft
km   = .621 mi
Square cm   = .155 square in
Square m   = 10.765 square ft
cm   = .394 in

CUSTOMARY U.S. MEASURES
Cubic

1,728 cu inches = 1 cu ft
27 cu ft   = 1 cu yd

Linear

12 in	= 1 ft	
3 ft	= 1 yd	
5,280 ft	= 1 land mile	
6,076.12 ft	= 1 nautical mile	

Area

144 sq in	= 1 sq yd	
9 sq ft	= 1 sq yd	= 1,296 sq in
43,560 sq ft	= 1 sq acre	
640 sq acre	= 1 sq mile	= 1 section

METRIC WEIGHTS AND MEASURES

Linear

10 millimeters (mm)	= 1 centimeter (cm)	
10 centimeters	= 1 decimeter (dm)	= 100 millimeters
10 decimeters	= 1 meter (m)	= 1,000 millimeters
10 meters	= 1 dekameter (dam)	
10 dekameters	= 1 hectometer (hm)	= 100 meters
10 hectometers	= 1 kilometer (km)	= 1,000 meters

Cubic

1,000 cubic mm (mm^3)	= 1 cu centimeter (cm^3)
1,000 cubic cm	= 1 cu decimeter (dm^3)
1,000 cubic dm	= 1 cu meter (m^3)
1 cu m	= 1 stere

CUSTOMARY AND METRIC (AVOIRDUPOIS) WEIGHTS

Grain	= .065 gram	
15.385 grains	= .035 oz	= 1 gram
Ounce	= 437.5 Grains	= 28,350 grams
Pound	= 7000 grain	= .454 kg
100 lbs	= 45.359 kg	
Ton, short	= 2,000 lbs	= .907 metric ton
Ton, long	= 2,240 lbs	= 1.016 metric ton
	2,204 lbs	= 1 metric ton
1.102 short ton		= 1 metric ton
0.984 long ton		= 1 metric ton

Glossary

This is a glossary of terms commonly used in international trade. Exercise care in your interpretation and application of these terms; some of them have a somewhat different meaning outside of the international trade environment.

Acceptance A time draft on the face of which the drawee has written the word "accepted," the date it is payable, and his or her signature. An acceptance is a negotiable bill or negotiable paper money. As such, within the United States it is governed by the Uniform Commercial Code.

A/DS Agent/Distributor Service, US&FCS.

AfDB African Development Bank.

Á Forfait Similar to factoring, á forfait, or forfait, is the sale without recourse of a long-term receivable, usually with the guarantee of a major national bank of the buyer's country. The receivable usually represents the sale of capital goods.

Air Waybill A Bill of Lading issued by an airline.

APEC Asian-Pacific Economic Cooperation.

AR Insurance term for All Risk policy. A misnomer as several risks are not covered.

Appreciation A rise in the value of a currency in relationship to the market or another currency.

Arbitrage The process of buying foreign exchange, commodities, or securities in one market and immediately selling them in another market at higher prices.

ATA Carnet An international customs document used for the temporary duty-free importation of certain goods into a country in lieu of the usual required customs documents and import duties. The Carnet serves as a guarantee of payment of customs duties that may become due on goods that are temporarily imported and not re-exported. ATA stands for the combined French and English words "Admission Temporaire—Temporary Admission."

Back to Back Letter of Credit A letter of credit supported by (backed by) a separate letter of credit with nearly identical documentary requirements. There are four normal differences: the name of the beneficiary, the account party, the amount, and the shipping date.

Band of Intervention In multinational foreign exchange rate management agreements among governments, one or more governments have, at various times, agreed to either buy or sell their currency or others when their currency, or others, moved out of the "bands of intervention," which were artificial and agreed foreign exchange rate relationships. The objective is generally to control the relationship of one currency to another.

Banker's Acceptance A time draft on the face of which the drawee bank has written the word "Accepted," the date, and the signature of an authorized officer. Like the

Acceptance above, the Uniform Commercial Code governs the operation of this instrument within the United States.

Barratry Negligence or fraud on the part of a ship's officers or crew resulting in injury or loss to the ship's owners.

Barter The precursor to today's countertrade. It is the direct exchange of goods between two trading parties. No cash changes hands.

Bill of Exchange (draft) An unconditional order in writing addressed by one person to another, signed by the person giving it, requiring the other party to pay at a fixed or determinable future date a specified sum to the order of a specified party.

Bill of Lading (B/L or Blading) A document from a transportation company acknowledging receipt of a shipment and a contract to move the shipment from the place named to the destination named.

Bonded Warehouse A warehouse authorized by customs authorities (here or abroad) for storage of goods on which payment of duties is deferred until the goods are removed.

BOP Balance of Payments.

Bureau of Export Administration (BXA) The agency of the U.S. Department of Commerce that handles export licensing and controls. It is also responsible for technology analysis and policy, foreign availability analysis, export enforcement, intelligence review, and antiboycott compliance.

Buying Rate The rate at which a foreign exchange dealer will buy a foreign currency.

Cable A means of international telecommunications arranged for through Western Union. Messages are transmitted via underwater transoceanic cables.

CACM Central American Common Market.

Carnet See ATA Carnet.

Carnet de Passage See ATA Carnet.

CBI Caribbean Basin Initiative.

CCCN Customs Cooperation Council Nomenclature.

CCL The Commerce Control List. This is the listing of products that require export licenses. Products are classified by ECCN.

CFR A term of sale meaning Cost and Freight. All costs except insurance are paid by the exporter from his or her warehouse to a port in the importer's country.

CH-18 Consultative Groupings of Eighteen (GATT).

CIF A term of sale meaning Cost, Insurance, and Freight are all paid by the exporter.

C/L Carload lots in railroad usage.

Clean Bill of Lading A blading that indicates the goods were received in apparent good order and condition, without damage or other irregularities.

Clean Document A document without any notation thereon of shortage or damage.

Clean Draft A draft to which no documents have been attached.

Clearing Agreement Countertrade agreement(s) between exporters, importers, and central banks that require that all transactions "clear" at the central bank to the credit or debit of the parties to the transactions. No monies change hands, and central bank accounts are settled at predetermined dates.

CNUSA   Commercial News USA (Department of Commerce).

COCOM   Coordination Committee on Multilateral Export Controls.

Collection   In international trade, the formal process of transmitting documents from the exporter's bank to a bank in the buyer's country for presentation to the buyer for payment. The documents are not released to the buyer unless and until the buyer (1) pays the sight draft or (2) accepts the time or usance draft.

Collection Documents   All documents submitted, as in Collection above.

Combination Export Manager (CEM)   A term equivalent in meaning to Export Management Company. The CEM takes on the duties of the export department for a manufacturer or for manufacturers in similar and noncompeting product lines.

Commercial Transaction   For a foreign exchange dealing bank, this is a transaction with a nonbanking (commercial) party.

Commerce Control List (CCL)   Section 799.1 of the Export Administration Regulations, it lists all commodities that are subject to export control by the Export Administration Regulations of the United States.

Commodity Credit Corporation (CCC)   An agency of the U.S. Department of Agriculture that provides short-term and medium-term export financing of U.S. agricultural commodities, enabling U.S. exporters to sell on a deferred payment basis.

Compensation   Countertrade arrangement whereby the value of the supplier's capital goods export are partially or fully repaid by delivery of the subsequent output from the client country.

Concessional Financing   Obtaining, usually from a government agency, financing at a far lower rate of interest than that charged on a similar project by traditional lenders. A countervail may be applied for under these circumstances.

Confirmation   The written communication to the counterparty in the transaction that recites all the relevant details that were agreed by phone or telex.

Confirmed Letter of Credit   Confirmation is the addition of the obligation of a second bank to the obligation of the bank that issued the letter of credit, to honor drafts and documents presented in accordance with the terms of the letter of credit.

Container Freight Station (CFS)   A U.S.-Customs-approved facility for the receipt, unloading, consolidation, loading, and forwarding of freight.

Convertibility   The fact that one currency may be obtained in exchange for another and move freely in international commerce. The U.S. dollar is a convertible currency. The Russian ruble is not. Do not accept payment in a currency that is not convertible.

Correspondent Bank   A bank in another city, state, or country with which the first bank maintains a deposit account and a service agreement.

Countertrade   A term that describes various methods of linking of the purchase of foreign goods and services to exports of domestic goods and services.

Counterpurchase   Also known as *indirect compensation*. In order to export to some countries, the exporter is required to purchase the output of the country, which may not result from the initiating export.

Countervailing Duty If a subsidy from any level of government has been paid to a foreign manufacturer that would reduce the price of the goods manufactured, then any country to which these goods are exported may launch action with their government agency to impose a "countervail." If the action is successful, the countervail would offset the subsidy.

Country Risk These are business risks associated with the environment of a particular country. Country risk includes political risk, laws, ethics, business practices, and factors relating to the level of asset exposure to that country.

Credit Risk In foreign exchange, the possibility that the buyer or seller of foreign exchange may be unable to meet his or her obligation on maturity.

CTA Committee on Trade in Agriculture (GATT).

Currency Adjustment Factor A percentage of the freight rate quoted in international commerce to compensate the carrier for the risk of providing a fixed rate for the transport of goods. A CAF of 20 percent for Japan would not be uncommon.

D/A (Documents against Acceptance) The buyer/importer must "accept" the draft in order to obtain control of the documents. Payment of the draft is at a later predetermined date. Also denoted as DOA in some countries.

Daily Settlement Used in connection with foreign exchange credit lines; the maximum net amount of foreign exchange that may fall due on any single day.

Demurrage The cost of excess time for loading or unloading a vessel, truck, or rail car. Demurrage is the fault of the shipper or his or her agent.

Dealers, or Foreign Exchange Traders Bank employees in foreign exchange departments engaged in operations in the market with other banks or with foreign exchange brokers.

DEC District Export Council. Business leaders experienced in international trade that are appointed by the U.S. Secretary of Commerce to promote exports from their district.

Depreciation A drop in the value of a currency in relationship to the market or another currency.

Destination Control Statement Any statement the U.S. government requires the exporter (1) to provide to it or (2) to display on export shipments, and that specifies the destination for which the export has been licensed. Validated export licenses require a destination control statement procedure.

Devaluation A downward change in the official parity of an exchange or of an exchange rate at which it had been pegged for some time.

DDP Delivered, duty paid to named destination in the country of import.

Discount In foreign exchange, the adjustment to a spot price that is made in arriving at a quote for future delivery. If a dealer quotes $1.60–$1.65 (bid and asked) for British pounds and the discounts for six months forward are .0300–.0275, the forward quotes would be adjusted to $1.5700–$1.6225. The discount usually represents differences in interest rates for comparable instruments in the two countries. In times of crisis for a currency, the discount can represent the market's anticipation of a lower price.

Dock Receipt A receipt issued by the foreman at the ocean dock for merchandise received at a dock or shipping point for onward shipment.

DP (Documents against Payment) The buyer/importer must pay the draft in order to obtain the documents. The draft and documents are sent by the seller through his or her bank to the buyer's bank for presentation and payment. Also used in some countries is DOP, documents on payment.

Draft A signed order by one party (the drawer) to another (the drawee) directing the drawee to pay a specified sum to the order of a third party (the payee).

Drawback A refund paid by U.S. Customs Service under the following circumstances. Goods imported into the United States and duties paid, and the goods are subsequently re-exported whether further processed or not. Refund is up to 99 percent of the total of fees paid. Available only on application by the importer against proof of the subsequent export.

Dumping When goods are sold for export at a far lower price than offered in the country of manufacture, or sold below cost. Any firm injured in the buyer's country by such dumping may apply to its government to impose an antidumping duty to offset the low price.

EC (European Community) Twelve nations of western Europe. See Chapter 20.

ECCN (Export Control Classification Number) The number that identifies each entry in the Commerce Control List of the Bureau of Export Administration. This is the correct and acceptable nomenclature.

EFTA (European Free Trade Association) Seven nations of Western Europe that have applied for associate membership in the EC.

EIN (Export Identification Number) Assigned by the Bureau of Export Administration if you have been required to obtain an Individual Validated License. If not, your Federal Tax ID number or your SSN if a sole proprietor.

ELAIN Export License Application and Information Network, in the Bureau of Export Administration.

EPROM Electronically Programmable Read Only Memory.

Eurocurrency The currency of one country on deposit in another, e.g., a Deutsche mark claim owned by a U.K. exporter and on deposit in the United Kingdom.

Eurodollar A U.S. dollar claim on deposit outside the United States.

Exchange Contracts Documents issued by foreign exchange brokers to both parties, confirming a foreign exchange transaction.

Exchange Control or Exchange Restrictions Limitation of free dealings in exchanges or of free transfers of funds into other currencies and other countries.

Exchange Rates The middle rates for telegraphic transfers quoted for spot exchanges in interbank dealings. The rates quoted in *The Wall Street Journal* or other newspapers are obtained from leading banks on the basis of telegraphic transfers of transactions equal to or in excess of US$1,000,000 or its equivalent.

Exchange Risk The risk of market fluctuation of an asset or liability denominated in a foreign currency, such as the ownership of a currency (spot or forward) or trade accounts receivable or payable in a foreign currency.

Eximbank (The Export-Import Bank of the United States) A government corporation that exists to promote U.S. exports by the provision of guarantees of export finance and by the provision of export financing when circumstances warrant. From 1991, Eximbank now issues export credit insurance.

Exotic Currencies Currencies of the less developed countries that are traded infrequently.

Export Administration Regulations (EAR) Regulations governing the export of U.S. goods and services.

Export Agent A sales agent for a line of products. The term loosely defines many different types of export intermediaries.

Export Commodity Classification Number See ECCN.

Export Declaration Also known as the Shipper's Export Declaration (SED) or ExDec, this document must be filed with U.S. Customs on any export from the U.S. of a value of over $2,500, or over $500 if by mail, or for any value if an IVL or other type of validated export license is required.

Export License The U.S. government believes that the ability to export is a privilege and not a right and, therefore, exercises control over export by the license process. A license is required as set out in the Export Administration Regulations of the United States.

Export Management Company (EMC) A company that acts at the export department for a U.S. company, providing services that may include market research, overseas representation and distribution, exhibition of goods, advertising, shipping, financing, documentation, and other functions as necessary.

Export Merchant A company that may or may not act as an EMC. A company that buys and sells for its own account, in response to its own market development efforts, which may not relate to a domestic manufacturer.

Export Trading Company (ETC) The scope of this organization is generally broader than that of an EMC. The ETC acquires goods for its own account and distribution, whereas the EMC generally serves the requirements of the manufacturer.

FAK (Freight All Kinds) A basis for freight rate quotes for ocean and inland cartage.

FAS A term of sale. Free Alongside the vessel at named port ready for loading aboard. *Free* means no charges to that point are separately assessed against the foreign importer.

FAS Foreign Agricultural Service of the U.S. Department of Agriculture.

Fax Short for facsimile transmission. The transmission of information by a telecopy process. Fax is in standard usage in international trade.

FCIA FCIA Management, Inc., is a management company that administers private sector export credit insurance programs.

FCL Full Container Load.

FI (Free In) A pricing term for chartered vessels placing the cost of loading the goods onto the vessel on the charterer.

FIO (Free In and Out) The charterer of a chartered vessel is responsible for the cost of loading and unloading the goods from the vessel.

Fixed Rate of Exchange A rigid rate of exchange set by a foreign government vis the dollar, gold, another currency or other basis. It remains in effect as long as that government is willing or is able to buy and sell at the predetermined rates. Taiwan, South Korea, Hong Kong, and some other nations dependent on export trade with the U.S. have tied their currency to the U.S. dollar.

FMC (Federal Maritime Commission) A U.S. government organization that, among other things, licenses foreign freight forwarders and administers the rate-setting and scheduling activities of ocean liner conferences.

FO (Free Out) The charterer of a chartered vessel is responsible for the cost of unloading the goods from the vessel.

FOA A term of sale used in domestic trade only. Not an approved INCOTERM. It means free on board at named airport of departure. The importer pays all costs from that point.

FOR A term of sale used in domestic trade only. Not an approved INCOTERM. It means the exporter delivers the goods to a railway at a named place, for onward transport by rail.

Force Majeure A standard clause in marine contracts exempting the parties of their obligations as a result of conditions beyond their control, such as earthquake, war, or flood. This clause is also customary in negotiated contracts.

Foreign Exchange or Foreign Currency The currency of a country other than the dealer's home currency. While the funds may be in actual cash, they are usually on deposit in a foreign bank account.

Foreign Exchange Rate The cost of a foreign currency in terms of the buyer's currency, as quoted by foreign exchange dealers.

Foreign Sales Corp. See FSC.

Forfait See á forfait.

Foreign Exchange Trader See Dealers.

Forward Contract (or Future Contract) An exchange contract due farther in the future than SPOT, which is settled in two business days for major European currencies and one day for Canadian dollars.

Free In marine insurance, this means the insurer is not liable for whatever follows that word.

Free of Capture and Seizure The insurer is not liable for loss by war. Coverage is given by adding an endorsement. Many perils can be avoided by the addition of a policy endorsement.

Free of Particular Average (FPA) Particular Average means Partial Loss. Thus, with an FPA policy, an insurer is not liable for partial loss. *Note:* In a few unique circumstances, an insurer may pay a partial loss, but not generally.

Free Trade Zone (FTZ) A security zone under U.S. Customs Service supervision where goods may be imported from a foreign country and placed in a warehouse without any duty or customs taxes paid. Goods may either be stored or may be further processed within the zone. If the goods are then exported from the United States, no import duties are assessed or paid (avoids the drawback situation). If the goods leave the zone and enter into the commerce of the United States, applicable taxes and duties are payable. If goods have been processed, the rates of duty often are lower than would have been paid on the original shipment. There are over 150 Free Trade Zones in the United States.

FSC (Foreign Sales Corporation) A U.S. government incentive for exporters. A corporation that is formed by one or more companies, headquartered outside the United States in an acceptable jurisdiction, which by its nature can avoid U.S. income tax on a portion of its revenues generated from export sales. See Chapter 8.

Full Set B/L At least two negotiable copies and three nonnegotiable copies of the B/L. More copies are issued by the carrier if requested by the shipper.

GATT (General Agreement on Tariffs and Trade) Initiated by 23 developed and developing countries in Geneva in 1947, the organization was formed to have wide powers to police and regulate international competition in such areas as business practices, investments, commodities, and employment. Rounds of negotiation take place at somewhat irregular intervals to expand the scope of international cooperation and the reduction of barriers to trade.

General Average Claim An assessment in proportion to the value of the shipment and value of the vessel is made against every party to a marine adventure to pay for losses by some parties to the adventure.

Hard Currencies The currencies of major industrial countries that can be easily and readily traded, i.e., US$, DM, SF.

Hedging Foreign exchange contract or foreign borrowing operations to safeguard against indefinite and indirect exchange risk arising from assets or liabilities the value of which are apt to be affected by changes in exchange rates. The hedge contract may be for a period that approximates the expected liquidation of the asset, or for another period or series of periods to offset the exchange risk for an asset that is expected to be held for a very long term. Cost of hedge contracts is a consideration in this latter instance.

HS The Harmonized System of classification of goods for customs duty purposes. Agreed to by all major trading nations at the International Customs Union, Brussels. The HS system operates through a six-digit identifier allotted to each type of good regardless of country of origin. This gives the customs officials of all signatory countries a standard for the classification of goods for duty purposes. Though rates may vary from country to country, the classification upon which rates are based is standard. The U.S. HS export classification system (Schedule B) classifies over 5,000 products. The U.S. HS import classification system (HTS) classifies over 12,000 items for U.S. customs purposes.

IDA International Development Association.

IDB Inter-American Development Bank.

IFC International Finance Corporation.

Import License Import licenses are utilized to control the outflow of foreign exchange, control the inflow of certain types of goods, foster or control industries, and for other national goals.

INCOTERMS Terms of trade adopted by the International Chamber of Commerce for the international movement of goods. INCOTERMS explain how responsibilities for the goods and their carriage are allocated among parties. The version currently in effect was adopted July 1, 1990.

ITA (International Trade Administration) A unit of the U.S. Department of Commerce. The five branches of the International Trade Administration are

1. The Trade Development Division (industry officers).
2. The International Economic Policy Division (country officers).
3. The US&FCS, with field offices in the United States and abroad. See Appendixes A and B.
4. The Import Administration Division.
5. The Administration Division (staff departments)

JETRO Japan External Trade Organization.

LASH Lighter aboard ship. See Lighter.

L/C See Letter of Credit.

LCL Less than Carload lot. A basis for the quotation of freight rates.

Letter of Credit A formal letter issued by a bank that authorizes a certain party to draw drafts against the bank up to a fixed money limit, by a specific time, accompanied by certain documents, and under specific terms. The liability for payment of the draft(s) is that of the bank and not of its customers. The obligor bank may be the issuing bank or the confirming bank.

License A license is a contract for the use of an intellectual property, such as a patent, trademark, trade name, or trade style. The licensee receives the legal right to use the licensed property, and the licensor receives a contracted income stream usually called a *royalty.* Also see Export License.

Lighter A barge, motored or otherwise, used to move goods from a ship or floating dock to a dock or shore facility, or the reverse. Many ports use lighters to expand capacity or to serve areas with insufficient draft for ocean carriers.

Managed Float When a floating currency is not allowed to float freely and is managed in a desired direction by central bank intervention. The term "dirty" float is often used by those who feel abused by this practice.

Marine Adventure The ship owners and every shipper of goods on that vessel are part of the adventure—a term of art in the marine insurance business.

Maturity Date The settlement date or delivery date agreed upon for the forward contract.

NIC Newly industrialized country.

NES Not elsewhere specified.

NME Nonmarket Economy. Generally used to refer to the economies of the former Soviet Bloc, the PRC, and other socialist states.

NOS Not otherwise specified.

NTDB National Trade Data Bank. See Chapter 3.

NTIS National Technical Information Service (USDOC).

NVOCC (Non-Vessel Operating Common Carrier) Also known as NVO. This form of transportation service company purchases "space" on a common carrier at a bulk rate discount and resells this "space" at a mark-up to others who, due to their volume, may not be able to negotiate discounts on standard conference rates.

OECD (Organization for Economic Cooperation and Development) A group of the leading industrialized countries in the western world, which tend to act in concert on broad issues of international economics and politics. The Group of Seven and the Group of Ten, which meet and act for financial and economic reasons, are subsets of the OECD.

OPIC (Overseas Private Investment Corporation) This U.S. government corporation encourages private-sector investment in lesser developed countries, by programs of political risk insurance and investment guarantees. It may take a minority investment position in some projects.

Option Contract A form of foreign exchange contract wherein the buyer [of a buy (call) or sell (put) option] has the right to settle all or part of the contract at an agreed time prior to maturity at the price shown in the contract. There is a nonrefundable payment required to enter the option.

PEC (President's Export Council) A national version of the DEC.

PEFCO (Private Export Funding Corporation) A private corporation formed to provide intermediate term finance for U.S. exports, under guarantee of the Eximbank.

Phytosanitary Certificate Issued by the U.S. Department of Agriculture to satisfy the import regulations of foreign countries. It states that the U.S. shipment has been inspected and is free from harmful pests or plant diseases or from other items specified on the certificate.

P.L.-480 (Public Law 480) The Food for Peace program provides foreign buyers with concessional financing for the purchase of U.S. agricultural commodities.

Political Risk Commonly defined to include war, cancellation of an existing import or export license, insurrection, political unrest, expropriation, confiscation, and currency inconvertibility.

Premium The adjustment to a spot price made in arriving at a quote for future delivery. If a foreign exchange dealer quotes $1.60–$1.65 (bid and asked) for British Pounds and the premium for six months forward is .0275–.0300, the forward quote will be adjusted to $1.6275–$1.6800. The premium usually represents differences in interest rates for comparable instruments in the two countries. In a volatile situation, the premium can represent the market anticipation of a higher price.

Protest The formal presentation of documents evidencing the shipment of goods or services and the demand for payment. This service is normally performed by a notary or other official at the request of the seller in the event the buyer fails to perform in accordance with the terms of collection documents.

Quota A numerical constraint on the import or export of a good or service. The United States has quotas on the import of cotton clothing, by country, by year, for example.

Rail Pig A modified over-the-road trailer on a flat car. The trailer has been manufactured to rail-car dimensions.

Revised American Foreign Trade Definitions (1941) These definitions of terms of trade were agreed to by members of the National Foreign Trade Council, the Chamber of Commerce of the United States, and the National Association of Manufacturers in 1941. The purpose was to standardize usage and understanding in the terms of movement of goods in international trade. These terms are not accepted in international trade.

Revocable Letter of Credit A letter of credit, the terms of which can be changed or cancelled by the account party at any time without the consent of the beneficiary.

RoRo (Roll on-Roll off) A form of ocean transport of containerized freight. The over-the-road container is driven into the vessel, and the container with its trailer is left for movement to its destination.

Shipper's Export Declaration (SED) See Export Declaration.

SIC (Standard Industrial Classification) A U.S.-only system of classification of farmers, manufacturers, distributors, and retailers by the product they produce.

Sight Draft A draft that on its face is payable at sight. *Sight* means first presentation to the drawee. In practice, the drawee tends to pay at the time of arrival of the shipment, at which time the collecting bank, as agent for the exporter's bank, will release the documents of title.

SITC (Standard International Trade Classification) A UN-based product classification system used by UN members to report export and import trade figures to the United Nations.

Single Internal Market The European Community Single Market '92 initiative.

Snake An artificial band of intervention established in the 1970s by the members of the European Community to maintain a predetermined interrelationship between the currencies of the principal economies of the Community. The "skin" of the "snake" was a sleeve that varied in size from 1 percent to 2 1/2 percent of the midpoint of the currency exchange rate objectives. When exchange rates "pushed" at the skin, the parties to the snake were required to intervene.

Space The term for the space taken up by any one shipment on an ocean vessel. Space must be reserved.

Spot The foreign exchange rate for immediate delivery and settlement, which means two days.

STELA (System for Tracking Export License Applications) A BXA touch-tone access system. Telephone 202-482-3856 to work with STELA.

Swap Purchase of spot exchange against sale of forward exchange or sale of spot exchange against purchase of forward exchange. Simultaneous transactions.

Tariff (1) A freight or service rate. A tariff schedule is the schedule of rates for a particular service. (2) A fee on imports imposed by the government of the importing country. The U.S. tariff on polyester running suits, for example, is a dollar amount equal to a percentage of the CIF cost of the goods plus $.XX per pound.

TDP (The Trade and Development Program) A U.S. government program to encourage infrastructure development in less developed countries.

Terminals The total of three charges made against each "ton" of outgoing and incoming cargo to cover wharfage (to maintain the wharf), harbor dues (to maintain the harbor), and loading and unloading charges. Terminals are only a few dollars per ton. Ocean vessels are also charged terminals.

Time Draft A draft that, by its terms, matures at a certain determinable time after presentation or acceptance. A draft with the terms "90 days from on board bill of lading date" is due and payable 90 days from the "on board" date of the bill of lading. The drawee on the draft must accept the draft to obtain the documents evidencing title to the goods.

TOF (Trailer on Flatcar) An over-the-road trailer moved by rail.

Transferrable Letter of Credit A letter of credit that, by its terms, may be transferred to another party.

Transfer Risk The risk that remittance of the currency of your receivable by the debtor will not be permitted by the debtor's government, and conversion of that currency to your functional currency will not be permitted; imposition or reinforcement of exchange controls.

Unconfirmed Letter of Credit A letter of credit that is not confirmed. See Confirmed Letter of Credit.

UNCTAD The United Nations Conference on Trade and Development.

UNCTC The United Nations Center on Transnational Corporations.

Unit of Account The currency in which an export/import transaction or foreign borrowing is denominated.

Usance Bankerspeak for "time" or "tenor." A 90-day usance draft is a 90-day sight draft.

USDOC The United States Department of Commerce.

USITC The United States International Trade Commission.

US&FCS The U.S. and Foreign Commercial Service of the USDOC.

USTR The United States Trade Representative.

Value Compensated The payment or collection of the settlement cost on an open forward contract to cancel the contract rather than enter an offsetting contract for the same maturity date.

VER (Voluntary Export Restraint) Usually imposed by the United States on others.

VRA (Voluntary Restraint Agreement) Usually imposed by the United States on others.

WA (With Average) An insurance term. WA means the insurer does pay a partial loss claim provided it is over the amount of a "franchise" listed in the insurance policy. This is usually 3 percent. If the loss is less than 3 percent, no payment is made. If it is in excess of 3 percent, the whole loss is paid. The "franchise" thus is not a deductible.

W/M (Weight or Measure) Ocean and air freight are assessed on one of these bases, which results in the greatest revenue to the transportation company. Ocean freight is based on either *American measurements,* a 2,000 pound ton and a 40 cubic foot ton, or on a *metric measurement* of a 2,204 pound ton and a 35.3 cubic foot ton. Light cargo is charged on measure, heavy cargo on weight.

Window Contracts A commercial foreign exchange transaction wherein the buyer, uncertain about the date of receipt of the funds to be delivered, contracts for a window period for settlement. A forward rate can be assured, although it is not as fine as a fixed date forward.

Index

AID, *See* U.S. Agency for International
    Development
ABN-AMRO Bank, 180
Acceptance
    finance, 177
    of offer, 129
Accounting, 74
ADM, 85
ADS, *See* Agent/Distributor Service
Advertising, 15, 79
Africa, country specialists, 364
African Development Bank, 103
Agent, 56, 57
    as employee, 71
    selection, 59
Agent/Distributor Service (ADS), 27, 59
Agent/Distributor survey, 61
Agreement, written, 67
Agreement checklist, 71
Agriculture, finance 169
Air express, 220
Air freight, 218
Air waybill, 219
Airborne Freight Corp., 258
Aldus Corp., 328
AmCham, 28
American Arbitration Association, 68
American Chamber of Commerce Abroad,
    28, 59
American Countertrade Association, 206
Antiboycott, 150
Antitrust, 88, 89
APEC, *See* Asia-Pacific Economic
    Cooperation Forum
Apparel, industry specialists, 352
Applied Microsystems Corp., 117
Arbitration, 68, 75, 81
ASEAN, 302
Asia-Pacific Economic Cooperation Forum
    (APEC), 303
Asiadollar, 195
Asian Bloc, 301
Asian Development Bank, 103

Asian Intelligence, 301
Assignment of proceeds, 164
ATA Carnet, 41
Automotive, industry specialists, 351
Aval, 177, 181
Average
    general, 238
    particular, 237

Back-to-back letter of credit, 163
Banks, 16, 158
    correspondent, 161
    foreign, 161
Barovick, Richard, vii, 166
Barter, 197
Beneficiaries Certificate, 247
Bill of lading, 215, 246
    straight, 225
Boeing, iii, 1, 17
Branch office, sales and marketing, 55
Broadfoot, Robert C., vii, 280, 301
Budgeting, 338
Bunge Corp., 85
Bureau of Export Administration (BXA),
    91, 93
Bureau of National Affairs, 32
Burlington Northern Railroad, 209
Business equipment, industry specialists, 351
Business plan, 16, 331
Buyback, 200
Buyer finance, 16
Buying Agent, 91
BXA, *See* Bureau of Export Administration

Canada, country specialists, 365
Cargill, 85
Caribbean Development Bank, 103
Carnet de Passage, 38, 41
Caterpillar Corp., 17
CCC, *See* Commodity Credit Corporation
CCL, *See* Commerce Control List
CD-ROM, 23
Census Bureau, 16

Certificate
  of insurance, 229
  of Origin, 320
  of Review, 88
CFR, *See* Cost and freight
CFTA, *See* United States/Canada Free Trade
  Agreement
Chambers of Commerce, 28
Checklist, travel, 43
Chemicals, industry specialists, 352
Chinese States, 304
CIF, *See* Cost, insurance, and freight
CISG, *See* Contracts for the International
  Sale of Goods
Civil law, 70
Claim, insurance, 234
Clearing agreement, 199
COCOM, *See* Coordinating Committee for
  Multilateral Export Controls
Collections, 151, 162, 177
Combination Export Manager, 89
Commerce Control List (CCL), 264
Commercial Invoice, 244
Commitment, 10, 11, 18
Commodity Credit Corporation (CCC), 169
Common law, 70
Communications, 118, 124
Communications, EC, 291
Compensation, 199
Complaints, 133
Compliance, 14
Compliance Office, Antiboycott 150
Computers, industry specialists, 351
Conferences, steamship, 210
Confirmed letter of credit, 144
Confirming house, 169, 178
Consignment, 130
Consular Invoice, 248
Consumer goods, industry specialists, 351
Container Freight Station, 218
Continental Grain, 85
Contracts for the International Sale of
  Goods (CISG), United Nations
  Convention for, 76
Control Data Corp., 85
Control, management, 53
Control of foreign exchange, 188
Coordinating Committee for Multilateral
  Export Controls (COCOM), 263
Copyrights, 68
Correspondent bank, 161
Cost and freight (CFR), 223
Cost, insurance, and freight (CIF), 222, 223
Costing, 111
  worksheet, 111
Counteroffers, 129
Counterpurchase, 200

Countertrade, 197
  barter, 197
  buyback, 200
  clearing agreement, 199
  compensation, 199
  counterpurchase, 200
  Office of, 197
  offset, 201
  project finance, 199
  switch trade, 203
Countervailing duty, 204
Country specialists, 364
Credit risk, 141
Critical success factors, 12
Crowell & Moring Ltd., 285
Culture, 38

David-Valentine, Leann, vii, 261
Delay, 233
Delivery, 73
Denial Orders, export, 266
Direct collections, 152
Direct exports, 83
Direct foreign investment, 95
Direct market entry, 53
Disputes, 68, 75
Distributor, 14, 18, 57
  selection, 59
  survey, 61
District Export Council, 93
Dock Receipt, 215, 249
Documentary Collections, 151
Documentation, 241
  Beneficiary's Certificate, 247
  bill of lading, 246, 248
  commercial invoice, 244
  consular invoice, 247, 248
  dock receipt, 249
  draft, 246
  Inspection Certificate, 247
  packing list, 245
  Shipper's Export Declaration, 242, 243
  warehouse receipt, 249
Drafts, 139, 151, 163, 176, 177, 246
Drawback, 110, 116, 315
Duties, 273
  of exporter, 72
  of representative, 72

East Asia, 306
East Asia Common Market, 302
Eastern Europe, country specialists, 364
EC, *See* European Community
ECCN, *See* Export Control Classification
  Number
ECU, *See* European Currency Unit
EDI, *See* Electronic Data Interchange

Electronic Data Interchange (EDI), 126, 221
EMC, *See* Export Management Company
Emerald Technology, 1
Employee, agent, 71
End user, 55
Energy, industry specialists, 352
Environment, industry specialists, 352
ETC, *See* Export Trading Company
Ethnocentrism, 45
Eurocurrency, 195
Eurodollars, 195
European Bloc, 285
European Community (EC), 3, 97, 285
  communications, 291
  currency, 297
  public procurement, 291
  single market, 286
  standards, 289
  taxation, 293
  transportation, 292
European Community Affairs
  country specialists, 364
  Office of, 82
European Currency Unit (ECU), 297
European Economic Area, 286
Exchange risk, 141
Exclusive agreements 68, 81
ExDec, *See* Shipper's Export Declaration
Eximbank, *See* Export-Import Bank of the
  United States
Export Administration Act, 150
Export Administration Regulations, 91, 98,
  103
Export business plan, 16
Export Certificate of Review, 88
Export Control Classification Number
  (ECCN), 265
Export controls, 91
Export costs, 110
Export Declaration, 242
Export finance, 137, 162, 172
  Agriculture, 169
  SBA, 169
Export Hotline, 33
Export-Import Bank of the United States
  (Eximbank), 7
  finance, 182
  guarantees, 167
  insurance, 164, 178
  Letter, 166
Export Information Service, 33
Export Information System (XIS), 29, 33
Export insurance, 178
Export license 14, 74, 242, 261, 264
Export License Management System, 258
Export Management Company (EMC), 19,
  89, 93

Export merchant, 90
Export mindset, 11
Export packing, 14
Export plan, 331, 336
Export Qualifier Program, 8, 340
Export regulations, 257
Export Trading Company (ETC), 19, 85
  Act of 1982, 87, 93, 170
  Affairs, Office of, 88, 93
  industry specialists, 352
  service strategies, 121
Exporter Magazine, 3, 9
Exporter's Encyclopedia, 32
Exports
  direct, 83
  indirect, 83

Factor, 178
FAS, *See* Free alongside ship
FASB, *See* Financial Accounting Standards
  Board
FCIA Management Company, Inc. 164
Female businessperson, 46, 49
Finance, 15
  acceptance, 177
  long-term, 182
  medium-term, 179
  short-term, 175
Financial Accounting Standards Board
  (FASB), 194
Financing, 58, 173
  for investment, 101
  strategies, 175
  techniques, 139
Fluoroware Systems, 1
FOB, *See* Free on board
Foreign Agricultural Service, 8
Foreign banks, 161
Foreign Corrupt Practices Act, 75
Foreign currency, 40
Foreign economic trends, 40
Foreign Exchange (FX), 40, 48, 70, 185
  control, 188
  forward, 190
  for marketing, 189
  hedging, 194
  markets, 185, 193
  options, 191
  risk, 70
  risk insurance, 194
  spot, 188
Foreign investment, 94
Foreign Sales Corporation (FSC), 88, 107
Foreign sales representative, 53
Foreign Trade Zone (FTZ), 13, 18, 20, 160,
  315
Foreign Traders Index (FTI), 25, 59

Foreign Travel, 34
á forfait, 181
Franchise, 95
  insurance, 232
Franchising, 53
Free alongside ship (FAS), 222, 223
Free on board (FOB), 222 223
Freight, 14
Freight forwarder, 114, 210
FSC, *See* Foreign Sales Corporation
FTI, *See* Foreign Traders Index
FTZ, *See* Foreign Trade Zone
FX, *See* Foreign exchange

GATT, *See* General Agreement on Tariffs
  and Trade
General Agreement on Tariffs and Trade
  (GATT), 107, 258, 270, 272, 276
General Average, 238
General Electric Corp., 17, 85
Giambattista, Michael, vii, 51
Gifts, 39
Gold Key Service, 27, 37
Government
  approvals, 74
  regulations, 257
Graham & Dunn, 272
GSM 102 and 103, 169

Harmonized Tariff Schedule (HS, HTS), 22,
  277
Hatch, R. Steve, vii, 35
Hedging, 194
Honeywell, 17
Hong Kong, country specialists, 365
HS, *See* Harmonized Tariff Schedule
HTS, *See* Harmonized Tariff Schedule

IATA, *See* International Air Transport
  Association
IBRD, *See* International Bank for
  Reconstruction and Development
ICC Publishing Corp., 170
IDA, *See* International Development
  Association
IEP, *See* International Economic Policy
  Division
IFC, *See* International Finance Corporation
IMF, *See* International Monetary Fund
Import barriers, 94
INCOTERMS, 115, 134, 136, 221, 228
Independent States, country specialists, 364
Indirect exports, 83
Industrial materials, industry specialists, 352
Industry specialists, 351
Infrastructure, industry specialists, 352
Inspection, 73, 115

Inspection Certificate, 247
Insurable interest, 227, 235
Insurance, 114, 133, 151, 156
  management, 207
  type, 230
Intellectual property rights, 68, 74
Intermodal shipping, 221
International Air Transport Association
  (IATA), 220
International Bank for Reconstruction and
  Development (IBRD), 102
International Development Association
  (IDA), 102
International Economic Policy Division
  (IEP), of ITA, 364
International Finance Corporation (IFC),
  102
International Mail Manual, 220
International Monetary Fund (IMF), 48,
  142, 186, 195
International pricing, 52
International Trade Administration (ITA), 8
International trade consultant, 56, 59
International Trade Reporter, 32
Inventory control, 13
Investment, 4
Investment, pre-, *See* Pre-investment
Invoice, pro forma, 245
ITA, *See* International Trade Association
  offices, 342
  services, 341

Japan, 303
  country specialists, 365
Japan/East Asia Market, 305
Japanese trading companies, 84
Joint venture, 5, 19, 53, 94
Jones, Fred, vii, 117
Journal of Commerce, 20
Junker, Joel, vii, 272
Jurisdiction, 69, 71

Kapp, Robert, vii, 279
Keiretsu, 310
Kiser, Larry, vii, 209

Labor, 16
Language, 124
Latin America, country specialists, 365
Letter of credit
  back-to-back, 163
  confirmed, 144
  revocable, 145
  standby, 176
  transferrable, 163
Letterhead, 125
Letters of credit, 139, 143

License, 19, 53, 95, 98
  export, 261
Line of credit, 160, 162
Logistics, 207, 209

Machinery, industry specialists, 352
Mail, 220
Mail Manual, International, See
  International Mail Manual
Management
  commitment, 10
  competence, 1
  decision factors, 54
  financial strategy, 183
  issues, 8
Management, Export License, 258
Managing the representative, 77
Manufacturing and product development,
  11, 12
Maquiladora, 315
MARCO, 1
Marginal costs, 105
Marine insurance, 207, 227
Market entry
  control, 53
  decision factors, 54
  factors, 336
  research, 21, 80
  risk management, 53
  strategies, 53, 54
Marketing, 14
  active, 51
  issues, 8
  mix, 14
  passive, 51
  strategy, 337
Marking, 223
Measurement, 368
Metric, 12, 368
Mexico, country specialists, 365
Microsoft, 1, 17
Modification, product, 12
MTB Banking Corp., 158
Multilateral Trade Organization (MTO),
  258
Multimodal shipping, 221

NACM/FCIB, *See* National Association of
  Credit Management
NAFTA, *See* North American Free Trade
  Agreement
National Association of Credit
  Management/Finance Credit and
  International Business (NACM/FCIB),
  170
National Council on International Trade
  Documentation (NCITD), 254

National Trade Data Bank (NTDB), 22, 23,
  32
NCITD, *See* National Council on
  International Trade Documentation
Near East, country specialists, 364
Negotiation, 129
Neville, Peterson & Williams, 325
Newly Independent States, 284
Nonexclusive agreements, 68, 91
Nonmarket Economies, 198
Nontariff barriers, 272, 275
Non-vessel operating common carrier
  (NVOCC, NVO), 22, 212
North America Bloc, 314
North America Export Strategy, 322
NTC International, 49
NTDB, *See* National Trade Data Bank
NVOCC, *See* Non-vessel operating common
  carrier
NVO, *See* Non-vessel operating common
  carrier
The New York Journal of Commerce, 20

OBRs, See *Overseas Business Reports*
Ocean freight, 14, 210
OECD, *See* Organization for Economic
  Cooperation and Development
Offers, 127
Office of Export Trading Company Affairs,
  88, 93
Office of European Community Affairs, 82
Offset, 201
OPIC, *See* Overseas Private Investment
  Corporation
Organization for Economic Cooperation
  and Development (OECD), members,
  174
Overseas Business Reports, 40
Overseas Private Investment Corporation
  (OPIC), 101, 103
  finance, 182

Pacific Basin, country specialists, 365
Packing, 14, 223
Packing list, 245
Parcel post, 220
Particular average, 237
Passive marketing, 51
Passport, 42
Patents, 68
Payment, 70
  risk, 156
Peoples Republic of China, country
  specialists, 365
Performance
  bond, 182
  evaluation, 338

Personnel, 16
Peterson, John, vii, 314
Piggyback, 91
Plan
    budgeting, 338
    business, 331
    export, 331, 336
    market factors, 336
    marketing strategy, 337
    performance evaluation, 338
Political risk, 142
Powlesland, Jaime, viii, 46
PRC, 365
Pre-investment, 95
Price maintenance, 69
Pricing, 15, 52, 60, 73, 104
Pro forma invoice, 130, 245
Product
    liability, 68
    modification, 12
Project management, 5
Public Law 480, 169
Public procurement, EC, 291

Questionnaire, 60, 61

Rail shipments, 215
Rail-pigs, 215
Railway bill of lading, 216
Raima Corp., 51
Rate
    advantage, 178
    agreements, 210
Rates, ocean freight, 213
Readiness, 5
Recreational Equipment, Inc., 328
Relationships, 6
Resale price maintenance, 69
Research, 21
Resolution of disputes, 68
Resources, 7
Restraint of trade, 121
Revocable letter of credit, 145
Ribicoff Amendment, 150
Risk
    management, 53
    payment, 156
Risks, 141
Road-rail, 214
Roll-on, l-off, 214
Russia, country specialists, 364
SWIFT, See Society for Worldwide
    Interbank Financial Transactions
Sales finance, 176
Sales territory, 66, 69
SBA, See Small Business Administration
Schedule B, 22, 242

Schulman, Darren, vii, 158
SED, See Shipper's Export Declaration
Selection of distributor, 59
Self-reference criterion, 45
Service, 117
    contracts, 126
    strategies, 119, 121
Shipper's Export Declaration (SED, Ex
    Dec), 22, 242
Shipping containers, 213
SIC Code, See Standard Industrial
    Classification Code
Simburg, Ketter, Sheppard & Purdy, 57, 76
Simburg, Melvyn Jay, viii, 57, 76, 98
Single market, 286
SITC, See Standard International Trade
    Classification
Small Business Administration (SBA), 29,
    32, 169, 176, 340
Society for Worldwide Interbank Financial
    Transactions (SWIFT), 145
South Asia, country specialists, 364
Standard costs, 104
Standard Industrial Classification Code
    (SIC), 22
Standard International Trade Classification
    (SITC), 22
Standards, 289
Standby letter of credit, 176
State buying company, 55
Straight bill of lading, 225
Strategies
    financing, 175
    market entry, 54
Stroh, L., viii, 3
Subsidiary, 53
Sun Microsystems, 1
Survey, 60, 61
Switch trade, 203
Systems approach, 109

Table of Denial Orders, 266
Target pricing, 106
Tariff, 213, 273
Taxation, EC, 293
TDP, See Trade and Development Program
Teare, Peter A.D., viii, 285
Telecommunications, industry specialists,
    351
Terminals, 215
Termination, 66, 68, 70, 75
Territory, 66, 72
Testing, product, 290
Textiles, industry specialists, 352
Thomas Cook Foreign Exchange, 40
3M, 1, 17, 136
Toro Corp., 1, 17, 179

Trade
barriers, 272
blocs, 97, 137, 279
fairs, 35, 49, 59
Trade and Development Program (TDP),
102, 103
Trade Promotion Coordinating Committee,
32
Trade Show Bureau, 49
Trade specialists, *See* U.S. Foreign and
Commercial Service
Trademarks, 68
Trading companies, 84
Traffic, 14
Training, 79
Transfer risk, 142
Transferrable letter of credit, 163
Translation, 80
Transportation, 14, 209, 210
EC, 292
Travel, 34
checklist, 43
Treaty of Rome, 69
Trips, 34
Truck bill of lading, 217
Trucks, 217
Trust, 6
Turnkey projects, 5
UCP 322, 170
UCP 400, 143, 170
U.N. Convention, CISG, *See* Contracts for
International Sale of Goods
UNCTAD/GATT, *See* United Nations
Center for Trade and Development
UNDP, *See* United Nations Development
Fund
Uniform Commercial Code, 136
United Nations, 29
United Nations Development Program
(UNDP), 103
United States/Canada Free Trade Agreement
(CFTA), 315
United Nations Center for Trade and
Development (UNCTAD/GATT), 277

U.S. Agency for International Development
(USAID), 167
U.S. Council on International Business, 42,
49
U.S. Department of Agriculture, 169
U.S. Department of Commerce, 7, 27
U.S. Food & Drug Administration, 133
U.S. Foreign and Commercial Service
(US&FCS), 7, 10, 17, 27
district offices, 342
overseas offices, 345
USAID, *See* U.S. Agency for International
Development

Validated Export License, 91
Valuation, 277
Value added tax (VAT), 293
VAT, *See* Value added tax

Waldmann, Raymond J., iv
Warehouse receipt, 249
Warehousing, 13
Warranty, 73
Washington Council on International Trade,
279
Washington State International Trade Fair,
35, 49
Weights and measures, 368
Western Europe, country specialists, 364
Westinghouse, 85, 163
Wharfage, 215
Wholly owned investment, 5
Wholly owned subsidiary, 53
World Bank, 21, 102, 103
finance, 182
World Health Organization, 29
World Trade Associations, 28
World Trade Center Association, 28, 32
World Trade Clubs, 28
World Traders Data Report (WTDR), 170
Written agreement, 67
WTDR, *See* World Traders Data Report

XIS, *See* Export Information System